BAKER & TAYLOR

JACK LONDON

JACK LONDON

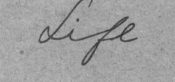

EARLE LABOR

FARRAR, STRAUS AND GIROUX
New York

Farrar, Straus and Giroux
18 West 18th Street, New York 10011

Grateful acknowledgment is made for permission to reprint the following material:
Excerpts from previously unpublished letters from Jack London to Charmian Kittredge;
permission granted by Joy S. Shaffer, Trustee, Trust of Irving Shepard. Excerpts from The
Letters of Jack London, edited by Earle Labor; Robert C. Leitz, III; and I. Milo Shepard,
3 vols, copyright © 1988 by the Board of Trustees of the Leland Stanford Jr. University
for compilation and editorial matter. All rights reserved. Used with the permission of
Stanford University Press.

Library of Congress Cataloging-in-Publication Data

Labor, Earle, 1928–
    Jack London : an American life / Earle Labor. — First edition.
        pages   cm
    Includes bibliographical references and index.
    ISBN 978-0-374-17848-2 (hardback)
        1. London, Jack, 1876–1916.   2. Authors, American—19th century—Biography.
    3. Authors, American—20th century—Biography.   I. Title.

PS3523.O46 Z6825 2013
813'.52—dc23
[B]
                                                                2012050948

Designed by Abby Kagan

Farrar, Straus and Giroux books may be purchased for educational, business, or
promotional use. For information on bulk purchases, please contact the Macmillan
Corporate and Premium Sales Department at 1-800-221-7945, extension 5442, or write
to specialmarkets@macmillan.com.

www.fsgbooks.com
www.twitter.com/fsgbooks • www.facebook.com/fsgbooks

3 5 7 9 10 8 6 4

Frontispiece: Photograph by Arnold Genthe (Earle Labor Collection, gift of Milo Shepard)

The preparation of this work was made possible in part by a
grant from the National Endowment for the Humanities,
an independent federal agency.

DEDICATED WITH GRATEFUL AFFECTION

TO THE LABOR FAMILY

AND

TO THE MEMORY OF

IRVING, MILDRED, AND MILO SHEPARD

The truth about its men of genius is something which the world has a right to and will ultimately get.

—UPTON SINCLAIR TO JOAN LONDON

CONTENTS

PREFACE

> It is easy to criticize him, of course, because his faults are large
> and obvious, but it is much more profitable to get on the inside
> of him and sympathize with his outlook on life.
>
> —ANNA STRUNSKY WALLING

More than a score of books about Jack London have appeared since his death, and while several have been notably insightful, many others have been closer to caricature than reality. No American writer has been subjected to more misleading commentaries. The canards about London's alleged drug addiction and suicide, to name only two examples, have persisted in the face of clear evidence to the contrary, as have half-truths about his drinking problems and womanizing. At worst, he has been portrayed as a rowdy hack who produced some popular adventure stories for "boy-men," a two-fisted "he-man" who "vowed to have one thousand women before he died" and who drugged and drank himself into desperate oblivion at the age of forty.

London's vigorous self-promotion was responsible for many of these distortions, and his sensational exploits made him a magnet for the tabloid newsmongers. Yet even dedicated scholars have been challenged to deal with the complexity of his character. His wife Charmian, who knew him best, may have come closer than any other biographer to explaining this challenge when she said that "an attempt to set down his kaleidoscopic personality can result only in seeming paradox. He is so many, infinitely many, things." He is indeed so many things. Most prominent is the popular image of "Jack London, Tough Guy." "Ask people who know me today, what I am," he wrote to Charmian shortly after their romantic affair had begun in 1903:

> A rough, savage fellow, they will say, who likes prizefights and brutalities, who has a clever turn of the pen, a charlatan's smattering of art, and the inevitable deficiencies of the untrained, unrefined, self-made man which he strives with a fair measure of success to hide beneath an attitude of roughness and unconventionality. Do I endeavor to unconvince them? It's so much easier to leave their convictions alone.

It was also more profitable to leave their convictions alone, and he worked overtime to promote his image as the premier icon of the Strenuous Age. Beneath this persona, however, was a different Jack London: hypersensitive, contentious, moody (possibly bipolar), and medically frail despite his vigorous muscularity. Famous for his ever-ready public smile and generosity of spirit, he was subject to spells of mordant invective and emotional cruelty, especially as his health deteriorated. While he rejected all forms of the supernatural and maintained that he was a thoroughgoing materialist, he regarded Jesus Christ as a great hero and infused his finest work with mythic power. Though devoted to the manly art of boxing and quick with his fists when challenged, he could weep unashamedly over the death of an animal or over a tragic episode in a novel. As he depicted the hero in one of his earliest stories, "though the attributes of the lion were there, was there wanting a certain softness, the hint of womanliness, which bespoke the emotional nature." Perhaps the famous portrait artist Arnold Genthe described him most accurately: "Jack London had a poignantly sensitive face. His were the eyes of a dreamer, and there was an almost feminine wistfulness about him. And yet at the same time he gave the feeling of a terrible and unconquerable physical force."

Granting the "large and obvious" personal faults to which Anna Strunsky Walling alluded, the unembellished facts of London's career are the stuff that dreams and legends are made of, more fabulous than anything Horatio Alger ever imagined. Here was an infant born out of wedlock into near poverty, one whose paternity has never been definitely established. Here was the child who spent his precious boyhood years delivering newspapers, hauling ice, and setting up pins in bowling alleys to augment the family's meager income. Here was the mere youth forced to become a factory "work-beast," apparently condemned, like thousands of other poor unfortunates in his social class, either to die an early death from overwork, malnutrition, and disease or, if he deserted his post at the machines, to spend what miserable life that was left in him wandering the underworld among the social degenerates and misfits known as the "submerged tenth."

Yet by means of luck, pluck, and sheer determination—undergirded by a rare genius—he succeeded in escaping "the pit," transforming himself into "Prince of the Oyster Pirates" and a "man among men" at the age of fifteen, able-bodied seaman and prize-winning author at seventeen, recruit in General Kelly's Industrial Army (also hobo and convict) at eighteen, notorious Boy Socialist of Oakland at twenty, Klondike argonaut at twenty-one, the "American Kipling" at twenty-four, internationally acclaimed author of *The Call of the Wild* at twenty-seven, Hearst war correspondent at twenty-eight, celebrated lecturer and first president of the Intercollegiate Socialist Society at twenty-nine, world traveler on his famous *Snark* at thirty-one, model farmer at thirty-four, blue-ribbon stock breeder and rancher at thirty-eight, and the producer of more than fifty books (several of which have achieved the status of world classics) before his death at forty. The sum total of these achievements underscores Alfred Kazin's comment that the "greatest story Jack London ever wrote was the story he lived."

London's story is quintessentially American. It is difficult to imagine his meteoric rise from rags to riches in a different setting or in a different time in American history. E. L. Doctorow remarks that London "leapt on the history of his times like a man on the back of a horse." He rode this horse from his childhood to his death. Even while he was outraged by the inequities and injustices in the American socioeconomic system—and even though his apparent indictment of the myth might seem to be the major theme in his quasi-autobiographical novel *Martin Eden*—as a boy he had already bought wholeheartedly into the Dream of Success. His idiosyncratic political attitude, a peculiar amalgamation of socialism and individualism, was a spin-off of this mythology. The literary historian Kenneth S. Lynn has suggested that London's conversion to socialism "had more to do with rising in the world than with world revolution."

I will elaborate London's rise in the world in the chapters that follow. Before that, however, I'd like to rehearse a few details of my personal connection with Jack London, whose call I first heard more than seventy years ago as a boy in a one-story redbrick schoolhouse nestled amid clean-smelling clusters of pines and oaks in the heart of the Kiamichi Mountains of southeastern Oklahoma. Ours was a consolidated school, meaning that kids, except for the few lucky ones living in the town of Tuskahoma, were bussed in from the surrounding farms on unpaved roads that were dusty in late summer and fall, frost-covered in winter, muddy in spring, and deep-rutted the year around. Six teachers accommodated twelve grades: two grades in each classroom.

This was my last year in elementary school, and while our teacher, Mr. Theo Smith, was instructing the seventh-graders, we were expected to be studying our lessons. Having completed my assignment one afternoon, I decided to look through the modest collection in our closet-size library. A thick maroon book with a bright gilt spine titled *Jack London's Stories for Boys* caught my attention. Pulling it down from the shelf, I opened it and was immediately fascinated by the frontispiece: the dramatic picture of an Eskimo holding a slender spear in front of a gigantic polar bear—and below the picture: AND THEN DID THE BEAR GROW ANGRY, AND RISE UP ON HIS HIND LEGS, AND GROWL. My curiosity aroused, I checked the table of contents: "The Story of Keesh" (the one with the angry polar bear), "To Build a Fire," "Lost Face," "The Shadow and the Flash," and "Love of Life"—these and more, enough to fill many an afternoon while waiting to be released from that stuffy old building.

Here was a new kind of liberation for a twelve-year-old boy, in some magical way more exciting than fishing the Kiamichi River for bass and perch with crawdads and grub worms or hunting the piney woods for rabbits and squirrels (and occasional copperheads and rattlesnakes) with my new .22 rifle. Unforgettable to this day are the vivid images the author had created with mere words in that book: the sharp crackle of tobacco juice that freezes to solid amber before it hits the snow in "To Build a Fire"; the quick-witted stratagem devised by the Russian fur trader to escape unspeakable torture by his Indian captors in "Lost Face"; the spectacular fight to the death by two young men who discover the secret, and curse, of invisibility in "The Shadow and the Flash"; and the flat-bitter taste of muskeg berries on the tongue of the starving Klondiker in "Love of Life." Reading these wonderful stories constituted the first rites of an initiation into a special culture, rites that promised a literary bonanza.

Except for a couple of movies—*The Call of the Wild*, starring Clark Gable, Jack Oakie, and Loretta Young; and *The Sea Wolf*, with Edward G. Robinson, John Garfield, and Ida Lupino—I encountered no more of Jack London until I was a senior at Southern Methodist University in 1948. It was then that my best friend, a World War II veteran named P. B. Lindsey, urged me to read *Martin Eden*. Lindsey was trying his hand at writing fiction and, like many other aspiring novelists, had been captivated by London's intense story about a young author's creative passions and frustrations.

I had more interesting stuff on my mind at the time—mostly nonliterary. Four years later, however, as I was browsing at a Manhattan newsstand on a weekend pass from the U.S. Navy Training Center in Bainbridge, Maryland, I spotted a twenty-five-cent Penguin edition of *Martin Eden* and thought I would check to see why Lindsey had recommended it so highly. Once I started reading the book on the bus back to the base, I couldn't put it down. I finished it with a flashlight in my bunk that night and decided that when I returned to graduate school, Jack London would be the project for my dissertation. Six years after that, under the direction of Professor Harry Hayden Clark at the University of Wisconsin, I began writing the first extensive study of London's craftsmanship ever published in this country. This subsequently became the basis for my critical biography as part of Twayne's United States Authors Series in 1974. Prior to that publication, several career-shaping events occurred:

My first visit to the Jack London Ranch, in 1963, marked the beginning of both a productive scholarly relationship and a lasting friendship with the Shepard family. Irving Shepard, who had known the Londons personally, was an invaluable source of firsthand information about Jack and Charmian. He was also responsible for my meeting his friend and coeditor King Hendricks, chair of the English Department at Utah State University. It was Professor Hendricks who invited me to teach the first American course on Jack London, in the summer of

1966, and to research with him the immense collection of London materials Shepard had donated to Utah State University. King had never met Jack, but he and his wife, Barbara, had been friends and travel companions with Charmian. Although my work with King ended with his death in 1970, our friendship established my important continued relationship with the Special Collections staff at Utah State's Merrill-Cazier Library.

I also had the good fortune to become acquainted with two individuals who were quite closely related to Jack London: his daughters, Joan and Becky. In December 1969, I received a letter from Joan thanking me for my recently published "An Open Letter to Irving Stone." This initiated a correspondence as warmhearted as it was revelatory, but sadly cut short by Joan's death from cancer thirteen months later.

"An Open Letter to Irving Stone" also won the attention of Russ Kingman, publicity director for the Jack London Square in Oakland. Thanks to his invitation, I met London's other daughter in 1972. Thus began a twenty-year friendship that lasted until Becky's death in 1992. Her comments about her father both complemented and counterbalanced Joan's bittersweet memories. "When he was with us he was always happy," she said. "So in a way it was a shock to me as I grew older and learned more about him, to find that other people thought of him differently . . . Specifically—what do I remember as his outstanding characteristic? He was a happy, generous, friendly, gregarious person. He liked people, all kinds of people. He was as interested in talking with a shoeshine boy or a deckhand on the ferryboat as with the captain of the ferry or with my aunts (Mother's sisters) who were 'Victorian Ladies.'"

I experienced a major epiphany in 1973 when, at his father's suggestion, Milo Shepard opened the massive safe in the Londons' "Cottage," revealing Charmian London's personal diaries. Because of their intimate frankness, Charmian called them her "one disloyalty" to her "Mate"; they serve as one of the most reliable sources of information I have used for this biography. Three other diaries have also provided reasonably dependable information: the diaries London kept during tramp experiences in 1894 and his trip down the Yukon River in 1898, plus his partner Fred Thompson's 1897 Klondike diary. Other accounts of London's life, including his own, may be approached only with open-minded discretion and corroboration by alternate sources.

At least one other personal contact is worth mentioning: Andrew Furer's 1995 invitation to his family's summer home on Cape Cod resulted in our two-hour visit and interview with Anna Walling Hamburger. Then in her eighties, Anna (as she asked us to call her) was the vivacious, petite mirror-image of her famous mother, Anna Strunsky Walling. The daughter's gracious and open responses to our questions made it clear that her mother had never fallen out of love with Jack: "She thought that he was the most beautiful young man—an Adonis, godlike. You know my mother's hyperbole. She carried a miniature portrait of him in her purse throughout her life."

The following near-personal contact also plays a very important role in the making of this biography: During the past decade I have managed to acquire at auction a number of London's hitherto unpublished letters to Charmian. Although the typescript copies Bob Leitz, Milo Shepard, and I worked with when we were preparing the Stanford edition are generally accurate, they occasionally differ from the originals. More notably, there are no copies of some of the most interesting letters, which I quote in my account of London's life. Most interesting of all are the intensely passionate letters he wrote to Charmian in 1903, which reveal him to be not merely lovesick but at moments love-mad.

Returning to 1963, I'd like to recount one of my favorite anecdotes: When the Michigan College English Association held its annual conference that fall on the Adrian College campus, MCEA president Sam Baskett introduced me to the participants as "the other Jack London scholar." Not quite accurate, this nonetheless represented the state of London scholarship at the time. London was generally branded a popular hack and treated as an untouchable by most members of the academic and critical establishment. However, except perhaps among those whom Eric Miles Williamson calls the "Ivy Mafia," the five decades since then have witnessed an astonishing increase in scholarly activities focused on Jack London's works. Even so, the world of Jack London is still calling for a reliable account of his life story. The present volume is a response to that call.

It is impossible, of course, to compress London's complete story into one volume. London himself had planned before his death to write a series of what he called "one-phase autobiographies" to cover his varied careers. For those readers who wish to pursue his life further, I have included in my bibliography and notes numerous supplementary studies on what London called the different "phases" of his career. For example, check Carolyn Johnston on London's socialism; Jeanne Reesman on his racial attitudes and short stories; Reesman and Hodson on his photography; Milo Shepard on London's agrarian vision; Clarice Stasz and Jacqueline Tavernier-Courbin on the London women; Charles Watson on the novels; Franklin Walker and Mike Wilson on the Klondike; Tony Williams on the movies; and Mark Zamen on London's lectures. The several collections of critical essays I've listed provide eloquent testimony to the burgeoning of scholarly work on London during the past half century. Readers may also find a wealth of informative material in *The Call: The Magazine* [formerly *The Newsletter*] *of the Jack London Society* and *Jack London Foundation, Inc., Quarterly Newsletter*, and in past issues of *Jack London Echoes, The Jack London Journal*, and *The Jack London Newsletter*.

This biography is as accurate, fair, and balanced as I can make it, based upon more than a half century of serious study. I have attempted neither to maximize nor to minimize London's faults. At the same time, I agree with Anna Strunsky Walling that it is "more profitable to get on the inside of him and sympathize with his outlook on life." The reader should discover here a natural-born "seeker": an extraordinarily gifted artist with exceptional intelligence, sensitivity, and personal charisma driven by immense willpower to succeed not only in his authorial career but in all his manifold callings, regardless of obstacles both internal and external.

Now, welcome to the wide world of Jack London, which ranges from the industrial wasteland of late-nineteenth-century America to the summer heat of California's Big Valley; from the bountiful farmlands of midwestern America to the soulless Erie County Pen and slums of London's East End; from the sordid saloons of the Oakland waterfront and Barbary Coast to the fashionable salons of Nob Hill and the golden poppy fields of Piedmont; from the congenial teahouses of Japan across the icy waters of Korean seas to the battlefields of Manchuria; from the frozen-hearted Northland wilderness to the flower-swept paradise of Polynesia and the fever-ridden jungles of Melanesia; from the blood-soaked bullrings of South America and boxing rings of North America to the green pastures of the Sonoma Valley and Beauty Ranch.

Here is truly God's plenty and a biographer's plenitude.

JACK LONDON

1

MOTHERS AND FATHERS

I was impotent at that time, the result of hardship, privation &
too much brain-work. Therefore I cannot be your father, nor
am I sure who your father is.

— W. H. CHANEY TO JACK LONDON

The future was anything but promising for the child who entered the
world on January 12, 1876. His mother was scarcely strong enough to
nurse him, and his putative father had abandoned them both. During
the first few weeks following his birth, the infant destined to win international fame as Jack London appeared to have no future at all.

His mother was Flora Wellman, a fascinating woman worthy of
being a character in one of London's stories. Jack quite likely had her in
mind as model for Mrs. Grantly, the spiritualist in his story "Planchette":

"A weird little thing . . . Bundle of nerves and black eyes. I'll wager she
doesn't weigh ninety pounds, and most of that's magnetism."
"Positively uncanny."

Uncanny is one of several words that might fit the character of Flora
Wellman. To her own granddaughters she was an enigma. Joan London
provides this illuminating vignette:

It is her face which commands attention. Spectacled, large-nosed,
square-jawed, it could be the face of a man. Beneath well-defined brows

her gaze is disconcerting, faintly hostile, even a little contemptuous; above the determined chin, her mouth is a firm straight line. Humorless, stubborn, opinionated, intelligent—it is an extraordinary face.

Flora was an extraordinary woman. She was born on August 17, 1843, the daughter of Marshall Daniel Wellman, the "Wheat King" of Massillon, Ohio. Two events particularly would shape Flora's character: the death of her mother when she was three years old and a severe case of typhoid fever she came down with at thirteen. The first stunted her emotional growth and left her with permanent psychological scars. (Although pampered by her father, she passionately hated the woman he married in 1847 and never fully recovered from her mother's untimely death.) The second stunted her physical growth, impaired her eyesight, and cost her the loss of much of her hair. She reached her maturity standing barely four and a half feet tall.

At sixteen she ran away from Massillon to Alliance, Ohio, where she lived for a while with her sister Mary Everhard. She returned home a few years later to help care for another sister, but the prodigal daughter was never again quite welcome in the Wellman family. After the Civil War she left Massillon for good, with no regrets on her part or on the part of the townspeople—local whispers insinuated a covertly scandalous affair with a married man. Little is known about her wanderings until 1873, when she stopped off in Seattle. There she boarded for several months in the home of "Mayor" Henry Yesler and his wife. Yesler, former mayor of Springfield, Ohio, knew that the Wellmans were a family of considerable prestige, but he may not have known of Flora's apostasy. It was in the Yesler home that she first met the man destined to play the most dramatic role in her life: William Henry Chaney.

While Flora has been treated unkindly by many of London's biographers, Chaney has fared even worse. Usually disparaged as a kind of footloose astrological huckster, "Professor" Chaney was in fact a celebrity of considerable distinction. He made for good newspaper copy: a dynamic figure who drew serious audiences to his popular public lectures. His friendship with the Yeslers attests to his respectability. In Flora Wellman he would find a soul mate. Although their backgrounds were vastly different, their personalities were weirdly similar—perhaps too similar.

Born on January 13, 1821, in the backwoods of Maine, the son of a yeoman farmer who died when the boy was nine years old, Chaney was bound out to several farmers, all of whom he detested. At the age of sixteen he ran off and worked for a while as a carpenter before going to sea. He served for a short time in the U.S. Navy, but in 1840 he jumped ship in Boston. He then headed west for the Mississippi River with a dream that he would travel downriver to the Gulf Coast and join a gang of pirates. The dream faded into reality when, stricken with an attack of fever, he was sidetracked in the Ohio country and compelled to settle for less romantic ventures, such as school teaching and store clerking. At the age of twenty-five he read for the law in Virginia and, during the next two decades, worked as an itinerant attorney, editor, and sometime preacher. In October 1866, now in New York City, he reached a major turning point in his checkered career: he met Dr. Luke Broughton, the famous English lecturer and editor of *Broughton's Monthly Planet Reader and Astrological Journal*.

Broughton had settled in America a decade earlier and had launched his journal on April 1, 1860, explaining that "it would serve as a handbook on such various subjects as Astrology, Astronomy, Astro-Phrenology, Zodiacal Physiognomy, Hygiene, Medical Botany, Astro-Meteorology, and the useful branches of Mathematics [for the] farmer, traveler, merchant, and the youthful inquirer after truth."

In his October 1864 issue, Broughton managed to erase a bit of the April Fool's Day stigma that some skeptics had attached to his work when he warned that, during the coming months, President Lincoln would have "a number of evil aspects afflicting his Nativity" and that he should be "especially on his guard against attempts to take his life; by such as fire arms." When Chaney met him, Broughton, while planning to establish an institution to be called the Eclectic Medical University, had set up headquarters in a spectacular Broadway suite. One reporter described Broughton's sanctum as "luxuriously furnished, with winged mythological beings, Cupids, Venuses, and Dianas, presided over by Mercury, [and enhanced by] mystical configurations and puzzles cabalistic hanging against the wall in mysterious and uninterpreted grandeur."

Chaney was captivated when he met Broughton in these exotic surroundings, and his conversion to astrology was immediate. Broughton himself was impressed by this intense young Jack-of-many-trades and took him at once under his astrological wing. To this newfound religion Chaney remained faithful to the end. Appearances to the contrary, he was at heart a humanitarian idealist who envisioned astrology as a panacea for the spiritual malaise of modern civilization.

Chaney's marital fidelity was less constant than his devotion to Broughton's creed. In 1867 he married the third in a series of six wives. In 1869, leaving this wife behind, he headed west to spread the word about astrology. He spent a couple of years in Salem, Oregon, then moved to San Francisco, where he began delivering lectures on "Astro-Theology." On June 11, 1874, according to his autobiography, he "took another wife," with whom he lived until June 3, 1875.

This new wife was Flora Wellman. By 1874, Flora had come a long way from Massillon, Ohio. After her stay in Seattle, she headed south for San Francisco, accompanying "a lady as a traveling companion," she vaguely explained to her curious granddaughter years afterward. Arriving in "The City," she found a locale far more congenial to a free-thinking individualist than her home town had been.

By 1874, San Francisco had also come a long way from the rough-and-tumble frontier fishing port it had been a couple of generations earlier. The American Dream to "Go West for Wealth and Success" had metamorphosed into the California Dream, climaxing in the 1849 gold rush. By the end of the Civil War, San Francisco had become transformed. It was now the Mecca of the Great American West: a cosmopolitan metropolis of some quarter million people worthy of competing with anything the East could offer. It could boast of a booming economy; paved thoroughfares; fancy Victorian architecture; theaters; modern sanitation, gas, water, and educational systems. It could match Boston's Beacon Hill with Nob Hill and Boston's *Atlantic Monthly* with the *Overland Monthly*. And the City had even more than Boston, with its own "public characters": Joshua, promoting himself as "Norton I, Emperor of the United States," dressed out in imperial regalia, issuing proclamations and scrip, which the newspapers published and the merchants honored; Krause, self-proclaimed City laureate, chanting and hawking his ballads on the street to all passersby; Father Elphick, preaching the gospel of "air, water, and sun," along with socialism; Li Po Tai, promoting Chinese herbs as the cure of every human ailment.

In short, the City of the Golden Gate had become a natural magnet for fortune-seekers of all kinds, including fortune-tellers, astrologists, and spiritualists.

Nowhere could Flora Wellman and William Chaney have found an environment more congenial to their idiosyncratic needs. When the two met again, Flora was making a modest living by teaching piano lessons while becoming increasingly committed to the emotional raptures of spiritualism. She had become friends with Amanda and William Slocum, publishers of a new weekly called *Common Sense*, a "Journal of Live Ideas," devoted to multifarious reforms and freethinking, including spiritualism. While Chaney's own idealistic penchant stopped short of spiritualism, he found in *Common Sense* a handy forum for his political and philosophical essays, and in Flora Wellman, a willing partner for his personal and social career.

The two apparently lived happily together for nearly a year—Flora keeping up with her tutoring and her spiritual exercises while assisting Chaney with his lectures and various reformist diatribes—until one evening in early June the next year, when she told him she was carrying his child. Chaney was indignant and furious in his denial. After a hotly contested verbal war that lasted for hours with apparently no winner, he pulled out—to what would be a timeless misfortune for both of them but a timely fortune for the local tabloids. The incident made headlines in the *San Francisco Chronicle* on June 4, 1875:

A DISCARDED WIFE
WHY MRS. CHANEY TWICE ATTEMPTED SUICIDE

The newspaper reported that, after attempting to take her life with laudanum, Flora had borrowed a neighbor's pistol and shot herself in the forehead: "The ball glanced off, inflicting only a flesh wound, and friends interfered before she could accomplish her suicidal purpose." If Flora's alleged suicide attempt was a failure, her attempt to gain the sympathies of the community was an unqualified success:

> The married life of the couple is said to have been full of self-denial and devoted affection on the part of the wife, and of harsh words and unkind treatment on the part of the husband . . . The wife assisted him

in the details of business, darned his hose, drudged at the wash-tub, took care of other people's children for hire, and generously gave him whatever money she earned and could spare beyond her actual expenses . . . She says that about three weeks ago she discovered, with a natural feeling of maternal pleasure, that she was *enceinte* . . . Then he told her she had better destroy her unborn babe. This she indignantly declined to do, and on last Thursday he said to her, "Flora, I want you to pack up and leave this house." She replied, "I have no money and nowhere to go." He said, "Neither have I any to give you." A woman in the house offered her $25, but she flung it from her with a burst of anguish, saying, "What do I care for this? It will be of no use to me without my husband's love."

Chaney gave a different account of the affair. Twenty-two years later, London wrote two letters searching for the truth of his paternity. Chaney replied to both, fervently denying that he was Jack's father. He insisted that he had been impotent at the time of the child's conception and attested that Flora had been sexually involved with two other men. In his first letter, postmarked in Chicago and dated June 4, 1897, he explained that neighbors had gossiped about an affair in the spring of 1875 between Flora and a young man she had known in Springfield, Ohio, but added he knew nothing himself of the liaison. He also mentioned a married businessman for whom he had written a "nativity" and with whom Flora was rumored to have had an affair.

"There was a time when I had a very tender affection for Flora," Chaney continued, "but there came a time when I hated her with all the intensity of my intense nature, & even thought of killing her and myself . . . Time, however, has healed the wounds & I feel no unkindness towards her, while for you I feel a warm sympathy, for I can imagine my emotions were I in your place."

The tone of Chaney's letter hardly resembles his attitude as a younger man—it is the voice of a broken old man: "I am past 76 & quite poor," he laments after recounting the disgrace and misery wrought by Flora's public accusations. Even his family, except for one sister, had disowned him as a disgrace, he confesses. Oddly enough, he kept the door open, offering to send further information about himself to the address given in Jack's letter: 402 Plymouth Avenue, Oakland, California.

Four hundred and two Plymouth Avenue was the address of Edward "Ted" Applegarth, the close friend with whom London had discussed the discovery that Chaney might be his biological father. To avoid any embarrassment to his family, particularly to Flora, Jack had asked Chaney to reply in care of Applegarth. Still unsatisfied after reading the June 4 letter, he wrote again, and received a second, twelve-page handwritten apologia dated June 14. Here, Chaney detailed more specifically the circumstances that caused his rupture with Flora:

> Flora was known as my wife, in the same lodging house, Mrs. Upstone's, where she had passed as the wife of Lee Smith & we stayed there a month. It was a very respectable place, & one day when I came home I found all the lodgers moving away & great excitement throughout the house. As soon as I entered our room Flora locked the door, fell on her knees before me & between sobs begged me to forgive her. I said I had nothing to forgive. Finally, after much delay & pleading she confessed about Lee Smith & said the lodgers were leaving on account of her being known as "Miss Wellman," "Mrs. Smith" & "Mrs. Chaney," all at nearly the same time.

Chaney explains that "a very loose connection of society was fashionable" at that time in the City, and "it was not thought disgraceful for two to live together without marriage," but San Franciscans drew the line at promiscuousness. Members of the boarding house were scandalized that "Mrs. Chaney" was also having sexual relations with a fellow lodger named Lee Smith. Because of his own atypical romantic history and his self-confessed impotence, Chaney says he was willing to make allowances for Flora's adultery. What had finally roused his ire, however, was her claiming he was the father of her unborn child. "This brought up a wrangle that lasted all day & all night," he wrote, adding that "her temper was a great trial & I had often thought before that time that I must leave her on account of it." The battle reached its dramatic climax the next morning, when she rushed out to the backyard of a neighbor's house and returned with blood streaming down her face, a double-barreled pistol in one hand and a box of cartridges in the other.

"This little woman has been trying to kill herself & made a bad job of it," she cried to her startled neighbor.

Her outcry sounded an alarm to the entire neighborhood, as Chaney describes the scene, "A great excitement followed [and a] mob of 150 gathered, swearing to hang me from the nearest lamp-post . . . believing her story of my cruelty & that I had turned her out of doors, penniless, because she would not submit to an abortion."

According to Chaney, a detective assigned to the case reported that no one in the neighborhood had heard a pistol shot and that his examination of the alleged suicide weapon revealed the smell of oil but not of gunpowder. The major injury caused by the gun was not Flora's superficial cut but the damage to Chaney's reputation, a wound from which he would never fully recover.

"My own life had been a very sad one, more so than I think yours will be," he prophetically concluded.

This was the last letter London received from Chaney, and presumably the last he wanted.

Regardless of Chaney's denials, Flora entered the name "John Griffith Chaney" on the birth certificate when her child was delivered—and "Chaney" remained the infant's surname for the first eight months of his life.

That Flora had been serious in her alleged suicide attempt is questionable, but the hearts of San Franciscans went out to this helpless mother-to-be, especially the hearts of her spiritualist friends. She was taken in by the Slocums for the next year. An accomplished seamstress, she was able to earn some money for herself by sewing and by giving piano lessons, but she was not vigorous enough to nurse her newborn child. On her doctor's advice she entrusted the infant into the care of a wet nurse, Daphne Virginia Prentiss, known as Jennie.

Mrs. Prentiss, destined to become one of the most important individuals in London's life, had been born a slave on a Tennessee plantation in 1832 and named Daphne Virginia Parker by her owners, John Parker and his associates, James West and T. M. Isbell. As a worker in the "Big House" on the plantation, she had learned to read and write. Free at the age of thirty-three, she left the Parker plantation and, two years later, married Alonzo Prentiss, a former Union officer in the Civil War. They moved from Tennessee to Chicago and, then, to San Francisco, where Alonzo worked as a carpenter.

The Prentisses prospered in San Francisco, living in a handsome redwood house with a garden in the Nob Hill area. Their happiness was shattered when Jennie's third child was stillborn, but what was a tragedy for them proved to be a godsend for Flora and her newborn son. The same physician had delivered both infants, and in consideration of Virginia's painful condition and Flora's inability to provide enough milk to keep her son alive, he arranged for the baby to live with the Prentiss family, with Jennie serving as his wet nurse—and, for all practical purposes, his mother—until he could be weaned.

The arrangement gave the infant the physical nourishment he needed to survive. Beyond this, it provided the emotional nurturing so essential during his first year. A vital connection was established during those early months between this loving caregiver and her "Jackie," as she named her little "Jack-in-a-box." The Prentiss home provided a wholesome environment for the baby. The two older Prentiss children, Will and Priscilla, welcomed their new "brother." Jennie read the Bible daily to the children, sang, and told them stories. Many years later, Jack nostalgically recollected the lullabies with which she soothed him to sleep each night. Although he left the Prentiss home when he was weaned (probably between the ages of two and three), he visited the family frequently during his younger years, and his bond with Jennie lasted a lifetime. Jack's daughters fondly remembered her as "Aunt Jennie," and snapshots from the London albums include a number of pictures of her with the two London girls. "I loved her deeply, with the same quality of devotion I had for Mother," exclaimed Joan. It was Joan who gave Jennie the courtesy title of "Aunt" in place of the less dignified "Mammy."

The Prentiss family may also have provided more than a surrogate mother for the child: possibly a foster father as well. One of Alonzo Prentiss's acquaintances was a fellow carpenter named John London. John London had been born January 11, 1831, on a farm in Clearfield County, Pennsylvania. His father, Manley London—the grandson of Sir William London, who had renounced his wealth and British citizenship to fight with General Washington for American independence—was a farmer and lumberman. One of John's two older brothers, Joseph, was a carpenter. From his father, John acquired his agricultural expertise; from Joseph, his carpentry skills.

At the age of nineteen John London left the farm to become boss of a construction gang for the Pennsylvania Railroad. While working on this job he met and married Anna Jane Cavett, daughter of one of the railroad's officials. The young couple initially set up housekeeping in the Cavett mansion but moved out a few months after the delivery of the first of the eleven children Anna Jane would bear before dying of consumption on December 19, 1873. After leaving the Cavetts, the Londons moved to Wisconsin, then down to Illinois, where John farmed until enlisting in the Union Army at Quincy on November 9, 1864.

Army records reveal John London to have been average in height and weight: five foot eight and 155 pounds. A few weeks following his enlistment, he was stricken with pneumonia after standing guard duty at night in cold weather. This was "followed by measles, resulting in a second attack of pneumonia in April 1865." Eight months after his enlistment, he was discharged from the army, having spent more than half his tour of duty in the hospital. His lungs were so badly damaged that he was never again capable of performing sustained strenuous manual labor.

John London's brief army career was less than spectacular; however, his subsequent history was more impressive. Frank Atherton, Jack's closest boyhood chum, recalled how the elder London loved to regale the boys with stories of his adventures as a scout and Indian fighter: "Surely, he must be the bravest man in the world, I thought. And in my boyish fancy I again viewed the great battle fields literally strewn with the vanquished savages." John had stretched the truth in entertaining the boys, but in view of his physical condition, his post-army career was courageous.

Following his discharge from the army, he moved his family to Moscow, Iowa. Here he superintended the building of a bridge across the Cedar River. From some accounts he also served as sheriff and deacon of the local Methodist church. Here were born Anna's two youngest daughters: Eliza on October 13, 1867, and Ida on February 28, 1870. Shortly after Ida's birth, the family moved onto a section of government land outside Moscow. However, when it was discovered that Anna had contracted consumption, they decided to fulfill "their mutual dreams to play at gipsying," so that John could devote himself full-time to her care.

For the next two years they adventured across the western plains in a prairie schooner. Instead of fighting the Indians, John befriended them. "Play fair with an Indian," he insisted, "and you can trust him with anything, anywhere. It's wrong treatment that's made sly devils of 'em." He shared his hunting, trapping, and bee-hunting skills with the Plains Indians—and, unlike his neighbors, he never lost a single head of stock to marauding Pawnee. One of his favorite Indian stories was recorded by Charmian London in *The Book of Jack London*:

> John had loaned to an old brave fifty cents and a musket, but forgot to mention the little transaction to his wife. It happened that she was alone when the chief came to redeem his obligations, and being very ill, she was badly frightened when his gaunt frame filled the doorway. In round terms she ordered him away; but the Indian, when she refused to touch the fifty cents, strode furiously in, grandly threw the coins into the middle of the floor, and stood the well-cleaned gun carefully in the corner. Stalking as furiously forth, he met his benefactor coming home, to whom he clipped out that the white-face squaw was no good—too foolish even to take money or guns offered her.

Despite the rigors of bearing eleven children and the hardships of frontier living, Anna was, from all reports, happy in her marriage. "No one ever saw [her] angry or disagreeable," Charmian records, "nor John London cross or harsh. He was always protecting some one." He was devastated by his wife's death from consumption the week before Christmas in 1873, and his suffering was compounded a few months later when Charles, their youngest son, was hit hard in the chest by a ball while playing baseball. The blow was a serious one, causing severe internal injuries. On their doctor's advice that ocean air might be therapeutic, John left for California, taking Charles as well as the young girls Eliza and Ida with him. The boy died eleven days after arriving in San Francisco. The girls were placed in the Protestant Orphan Asylum. John was able to pay for their room and board from the money he was earning as a carpenter, but he wanted a home and a mother for them. Eliza later recalled that period in the orphanage as one of the happiest of her life and hoped that her father would propose to a teacher she adored. He proposed, instead, to Flora Wellman Chaney.

Biographers differ concerning the exact circumstances of the first meeting between John and Flora. Charmian suggests that John was invited by one of his friends to attend a spiritualist meeting at which he became entranced by Flora. Joan London reports something more mundane: John admired one of Alonzo Prentiss's beautifully sewn shirts, asked him who made it so that he could order one for himself, thereby being introduced to Flora. It is possible that they had already become acquainted, as their marriage license, dated September 4, 1876, lists them both living at the same address (946 Harrison Street, San Francisco). Recalling the neighbors' gossip about the scandalous relationship between Flora and the "young man from Springfield" alleged in Chaney's first letter to Jack, one scholar has speculated that the man might have been John London from Springfield, Illinois, rather than Springfield, Ohio.

There is no question about the marriage between Flora and London. The official wedding document certifies "That on the Seventh day of September In the Year of Our Lord 1876 John London and Flora Cheney [sic] were by me united in Marriage at San Francisco according to the laws of the State of California," signed by James C. Perrine, Justice of the Peace.

Theirs was a marriage of convenience. John London needed a wife and a mother for his daughters; Flora needed a husband and a father for her son. Their mutual needs seemed to be ideally met—except for two major problems: Flora was obsessed with the idea of regaining her lost social status, and John possessed neither the physical stamina nor the psychological toughness to achieve this kind of success.

When a diphtheria epidemic broke out in 1879, little "Johnny" and twelve-year-old Eliza were seriously stricken, and lapsed into comas. Eliza later remembered rousing long enough to hear Flora ask the attending physician, "Can the two of them be buried in the same coffin, doctor, to save expenses?" Many years afterward, Eliza asserted that Flora had saved her life with this question by shocking her into recovery, but major credit is due John London, who refused to accept the attendant physician's dire prognosis. Having heard of an Oakland doctor who had cured several diphtheria victims, he ferried over and persuaded the man to treat Jack and Eliza. The doctor managed to remove the choking cankers from the children's throats and thus save their lives. He also advised John to move his family out of San Francisco, to a more healthful location.

As soon as the two children recovered, the Londons moved across the Bay, to Oakland, where John started a business in truck farming. Using his savings to lease and cultivate a parcel of land near Emeryville, a suburb of Oakland, he grew corn, tomatoes, and other vegetables. Because he sold only the finest produce, giving the culls to poor neighbors, he gained a reputation as the best farmer in the Bay Area. One of Eliza's childhood memories was the musical sound of peddlers hawking their vegetables with "J. L. Corn! J. L. Corn!"

This new venture was succeeding until Flora persuaded her husband to set up his own grocery store in partnership with a man named G. H. Stowell. A few months afterward, in 1881, John London found himself back on the farm. He had made the mistake of leaving the job of running the store in Stowell's hands while he went to outlying districts contracting and taking orders. One weekend, arriving back from a trip, he discovered he had been sold out and cleaned out. As Charmian observes, "Stowell must have been a clever crook and known his man well, for John was quite unequal to the tangle in which he found himself when he appealed to the law. Fight he did, and manfully; only a pitiful few dollars remained to him at the end of a legal battle." Many years afterward, Jack remarked, "My father was the best man I have ever known—too intrinsically good to get ahead in the soulless scramble for a living that a man must cope with if he would survive in our anarchical capitalist system."

With what few financial resources he had left, John London moved his family to Alameda, where he worked a twenty-acre tract for a man named Matthew Davenport. The family history becomes somewhat clearer at this time, for the 1881 records show "Johnny London," along with Eliza and Ida, enrolled in the West End School in Alameda. Once again John London seemed to prosper, and once again Flora could not stand modest prosperity. She felt they could do better on a bigger farm. On Jack's seventh birthday, in 1883, the family moved to a ranch in San Mateo County. As Jack later described their move, "We had horses and a farm wagon, and onto that we piled all our household belongings, all hands climbing up on the top of the load, and with the cow tied behind, we moved 'bag and baggage' to the coast in San Mateo County, six miles beyond Colma."

Jack remembered this place along the coast as "bleak, barren and foggy." He also recollected that it was here that he had experienced his first traumatic encounter with alcohol: "It was a wild, primitive countryside in those days, and often I heard my mother pride herself that we were old American stock and not immigrant Irish and Italians like our neighbors." Flora was especially hard on the Italian immigrants. "My mother had theories," he recalled:

> First, she steadfastly maintained that brunettes and all the tribe of dark-eyed humans were deceitful. Next, she was convinced that the dark-eyed Latin races were profoundly sensitive, profoundly treacherous, and profoundly murderous . . . I had heard her state that if one offended an Italian, no matter how slightly and unintentionally, he was certain to retaliate by stabbing one in the back. That was her particular phrase—"stab you in the back."

Young Jack's fears almost cost him his life at the age of seven. The episode occurred when a group of Irish youths, promising to take him to a dance, lured him to a neighboring Italian ranch—"a bachelor establishment." Here, fearful but fascinated, the boy watched while the high-spirited young men and women drank and danced. One mischievous Italian youth named Peter approached, proffering a half tumbler of new wine. "My faith was implicit in my mother's exposition of the Italian character. Besides, I had some glimmering inkling of the sacredness of hospitality. Here was a treacherous, sensitive, murdering Italian, offering me hospitality . . . What could I do?"

Fearing "a stab in the back" at any moment, he gulped down the wine. Peter, impressed, poured another half tumbler to see the feat repeated, then invited others to watch as the frightened youngster downed several more tumblerfuls. By the time the ordeal was over and the crowd had lost interest, the boy had consumed enough wine to knock out a full-grown man—more than enough to suffocate a child. As the crowd left the party, little Jack, thoroughly inebriated, staggered out and fell into a ditch. He was rescued by a group of the young women who pulled him out and became alarmed when they noticed his half-paralyzed, glassy-eyed condition. Without realizing how close to death he was, they managed to drag and carry him four miles back home and put him to bed. Here he writhed in delirium, envisioning himself in the evil dens of San Francisco's Chinatown:

> I wandered deep beneath the ground through a thousand of these dens, and behind locked doors of iron I suffered and died a thousand deaths. And when I would come upon my father, seated at table in these subterranean crypts, gambling with Chinese for great stakes of gold, all my outrage gave vent to the vilest cursing . . . All the inconceivable filth a child running at large in a primitive countryside may hear men utter, was mine; and though I had never dared utter such oaths, they now poured from me, at the top of my lungs.

"The child will lose his reason," cried Flora, thinking his brain permanently seared. "My mother had been dreadfully shocked. She held that I had done wrong . . . that I had gone contrary to all her teaching. And how was I, who was never allowed to talk back . . . to tell my mother that it was her teaching that was directly responsible for my drunkenness?"

Jack attributed other childhood traumas to his mother. One episode involved John London, whom Flora forced to spank the youngster when neither the man nor the boy thought he deserved it. Another involved a less corporeal kind of punishment. The culprit was "Plume," the alleged Indian chief who occasionally seized control over Flora during her séances. Jack never forgave her making him stand on a levitating table in what his schoolmates called the London "spook-house" while she whooped loudly in Plume's guttural voice.

London's memories of his boyhood in the country were a far cry from the pastoral dream he would realize twenty-five years later in the Valley of the Moon. "Everything was squalid and sordid . . . I took a violent prejudice—nay, it was almost a hatred—to country life at this time." Yet in *John Barleycorn* he says that in the near-fatal drinking episode he saw "a bright and gorgeous episode in the monotony of life and labor on that bleak, fog-girt coast . . . The Irish ranchers twitted me good-naturedly on my exploit, and patted me on the back until I felt that I had done something heroic."

Except for this episode, he remembered nothing heroic in his boyhood on the farm. "My body and soul were starved when I was a child," he wrote to Mabel Applegarth in 1898:

> When I was seven years old, at the country school of San Pedro, this happened. Meat, I was that hungry for it I once opened a girl's basket and stole a piece of meat—a little piece the size of my two fingers . . . In those days, like Esau, I would have literally sold my birthright for a mess of pottage, a piece of meat. Great God! when those youngsters threw chunks of meat on the ground because of surfeit, I could have dragged it from the dirt and eaten it; but I did not. Just imagine the development of my mind, my soul, under such material conditions.

That he was emotionally deprived is believable. However, most of his physical deprivations were more likely imagined than real. His mother was especially quick to react when she read about his version of boyhood hunger: "Here Jack has written that he didn't have enough to eat," she exclaimed to Eliza. "Do you remember any time when we did not set a good table? I can't. He didn't go hungry in our house! . . . Why, you know, his father always had vegetables, and if meat was ever scarce, there were plenty of chickens."

Still, chickens were not the good red meat Jack hungered for. "I was a dreamer, on a farm, but early, at only nine, the hard hand of the world was laid upon me," he later confessed to Anna Strunsky. "It has left me sentiment, but destroyed sentimentalism. It has made me practical, so that I am known as harsh, stern, uncompromising. It has taught me that reason is mightier than imagination; that the scientific man is superior to the emotional man."

What was "the hard hand of the world" that changed the young dreamer into the tough, practical realist at the age of nine? It might have been chickens. If so, Flora served as catalytic agent. She decided that John's modest but real prosperity with his produce business was not enough. They would get rich and rise more quickly in the world if they added chicken raising to their farm ventures.

"One unversed in such matters can have no notion of the many and tragic things that can happen to a chicken," Sherwood Anderson explains in "The Egg," his poignant story of broken American dreams:

It is born out of an egg, lives for a few weeks as a tiny fluffy thing such as you will see pictured on Easter cards, then becomes hideously naked, eats quantities of corn and meal bought by the sweat of your father's brow, gets diseases called pip, cholera, and other names, stands looking with stupid eyes at the sun, becomes sick and dies . . . Most philosophers must have been raised on chicken farms. One hopes for so much from a chicken and is so dreadfully disillusioned.

Neither Flora nor John had an inkling of such "tragic things." Within months, their flock had been wiped out by an epidemic. Unable to make mortgage payments, the family was forced to move back into the city, leaving farm life behind. It would be two decades before Jack realized the bountiful agrarian legacy John London had left him.

2

---·---

CHILDHOOD'S END

Somewhere around my ninth year we removed to Oakland . . .
Here most precious to me was a free library . . . However, from
my ninth year, with the exception of hours spent at school (and
I earned them by hard labor), my life has been one of toil.

—LONDON TO HOUGHTON MIFFLIN AND CO., 1900

Oakland in the late 1880s was a raw young city in the making, just beginning to enjoy the mixed blessings of industrialization. The population, having more than doubled during the preceding generation, was
now approaching sixty-five thousand. Though destined never to rival
its romantic urban sibling across the bay, it would develop a distinctive
character of its own. If San Francisco was the boston of the West Coast,
Oakland could be its Chicago.

The stately residential section west of Broadway was gradually being
abandoned to factories, warehouses, and livery stables, and its wealth-
ier residents were being replaced by lower-middle-class working people.
While the city leaders were celebrating the newly macadamized, gaslit
downtown area, the West Oakland population was enduring the summer dust and winter mud of unpaved, deeply rutted streets. It was an
uncouth environment, noisier and more exciting than the world of sick
chickens and dying agricultural dreams. Here was a place to test the
mettle of a boy who would shortly be forced into adulthood with few of
the transitional privileges of adolescence.

In his 1900 letter to Houghton Mifflin, the publisher of his first book, Jack said that his life had been "one of toil" but declined to explain why, merely noting that it was "worthless to give the long list of sordid occupations, none of them trades, all heavy manual labor." He was more explicit in an 1898 letter to his former sweetheart Mabel Applegarth, who had told him it was his "duty" to get a steady job and give up his futile efforts to become a professional writer. This letter, written during one of the darkest nights of his soul, reveals the bitterness with which he remembered his childhood deprivations:

> Duty—at ten years I was on the street selling newspapers. Every cent was turned over to my people, and I went to school in constant shame of the hats, shoes, clothes I wore . . . From then on, I had no childhood. Up at three o'clock in the morning to carry papers. When that was finished I did not go home but continued on to school. School out, my evening papers. Saturday I worked on an ice wagon. Sunday I went to a bowling alley and set up pins for drunken Dutchmen. Duty—I turned over every cent and went dressed like a scarecrow.

While he spoke from his heart, Jack dramatized his "life of toil." In fact, he improvised ways to relieve the drudgery. His earliest means of escape was through the magic portals of literature. "[I was] an omnivorous reader, principally because reading matter was scarce and I had to be grateful for whatever fell into my hands," he told Houghton Mifflin:

> [I remember] reading some of Trowbridge's works for boys at six years of age. At seven I was reading Paul du Chaillu's *Travels*, Captain Cook's *Voyages*, and *Life of Garfield*. And all through this Period I devoured what Seaside Library novels I could borrow from womenfolk, and dime novels from farm hands. At eight I was deep in Ouida and Washington Irving.

Of paramount importance among these early readings were the books by Washington Irving and Ouida. Jack's teacher had lent him a copy of Irving's *The Alhambra*, "which he proceeded to bolt whole, and reread and digest for the period spent on the Livermore farm," wrote Charmian. Thus inspired, he built his own miniature version of the splendid Moorish castle: "From the mellow-red bricks of a fallen chimney he reared its towers and laid out terraces and arcades, labeling with his school chalk its various sections."

Most significant on his childhood reading list was the work by "Ouida," née Maria Louise de la Ramée, the famous English children's author. In 1914, responding to a letter from a teacher of children's literature at the University of Wisconsin Library School, he said that "two wonderful things" had directed the course of his life: The first was finding a tattered copy of Ouida's novel *Signa*. "The end of the book was missing, but I read and reread countless times the story of Signa and it put in me the ambition to get beyond the sky lines of my narrow California valley and opened up to me the possibilities of the world of art. In fact it became my star to which I hitched my child's wagon." *Signa* is the tale of a poor Italian foundling who fights to overcome tremendous odds on his way to becoming a world-famous composer and violin virtuoso. Fortunately the last pages were missing in Jack's copy: he might have hitched his wagon to a different star had he known that in the end the hero kills himself over the love of a heartless tart.

The second "wonderful thing" was his discovery of the Oakland Public Library: "It was this world of books, now accessible, that practically gave me the basis of my education. Not until I began fighting for a living and making my first successes so that I was able to buy books for myself did I ever discontinue drawing many books on many library cards from out of the Oakland free public library."

Presiding over this new world was Ina Coolbrith, one of California's best-known authors, who would become the state's first poet laureate in 1915. During her eighteen years as librarian, she was an inspirational figure for countless young people, including the novelist Mary Austin, the dancer Isadora Duncan, and Jack London. "Do you know, you were the first one who ever complimented me on my choice of reading matter," he wrote to her at the height of his career. "I was an eager, thirsty, hungry little kid—and one day, at the library, I drew out a volume on Pizarro of Peru . . . You got the book & stamped it for me. And as you handed it to me you praised me for reading books of that nature. Proud! if you only knew how proud your words made me . . . You were a goddess to me."

So thoroughly enchanted was the hungry child with his discovery of a seemingly unlimited supply of books that could be his for the taking, he persuaded all the members of his family to fill out applications for library cards so that he could check out books under all their names. And so desperately did he crave the riches he had discovered in this literary treasure trove that he haunted the library for weeks, spending every spare hour with his bounties. Years afterward he recalled with some humor that he had very nearly developed a case of St. Vitus dance in his hollow-eyed nervous exhaustion. "I read mornings, afternoons, and nights. I read in bed, I read at table, I read as I walked to and from school, and I read at recess while the other boys were playing," he recalled. "I began to get the 'jerks.' To everybody I replied: 'Go away. You make me nervous.'"

In stark contrast to the gregarious man of action he later became, the young Jack was regarded by his grade-school classmates as a book-loving "loner." His closest boyhood friend, Frank Atherton, recounted the event that first brought Jack to his attention: "It was recess at Cole School, and the pupils marched out into the school yard to the rhythmic beats of a snare drum. Upon reaching the yard they broke ranks, running helterskelter about the grounds, shouting boisterously as they began their various games. In spite of the confusion, however, one boy hurried across the school yard to a wooden bench, where he sat down and began to read a book."

The solitary reader was ignored by everyone except Mike Panella, leader of a school gang, who decided on that particular day to bully him:

"Hey, kid, w'y don'cha ever play wid us guys? Don'cha git 'nough books in d' school room, widout readin' at recess like a sissy?"

When Jack glanced up and then resumed reading, ignoring the challenge, Panella rushed over, grabbed his book, and threw it across the playground, this time calling him "a dam' sissy."

Although Jack was smaller than Panella, he jumped to his feet, bloodied the bully's nose, and knocked him down in front of the crowd of youngsters who had gathered around yelling, "Fight! Fight!" Furious that he had been humiliated, Mike pulled out his knife, but before he could use it, he was disarmed by several other boys. At that point one of the teachers intervened and took the two combatants to the principal's office.

John P. Garlick, Cole Grammar School principal, was a strict disciplinarian who had to use a firm hand in controlling the pupils, a number of whom were from the Oakland slums. Aware of Panella's bullying ways, he realized that Jack had been the victim, not the assailant. In this case he told the boys that if they agreed to "hug each other and make up," he would suspend punishment. Jack refused.

"Mr. Garlick, I know I was in the right, and I'd do it again if I have to defend myself," he said as he held out his hand to be whipped by the principal's big oaken ruler. The principal, impressed by Jack's integrity, allowed him to return to class without punishment. Panella, on the other hand, "was not let off so easily," Atherton recalls: "As the heavy ruler came down on his hand, his screams could be heard far down the long corridor."

The incident made a school hero out of the quiet "loner" who preferred the company of books to that of his classmates. "Gosh, Johnny, I didn't know you could fight like that," said one as they crowded admiringly around him after school. "I'll bet Mike won't tackle you again." This prediction held true. The incident also broke the social ice for Jack at Cole School. Though he continued his reading habits, now he would occasionally stop to join in games with his classmates. "Then he would play with great zealousness, apparently determined to excel in any chosen game," Atherton remembered. "No game was ever too rough; no feat too difficult in which he would willingly permit another to defeat him. If it were boxing or wrestling, he always strove to be the conqueror."

That compulsion "to be the conqueror"—fueled by his "seeking" drive—would prove to be his greatest asset and his greatest liability. It was a primary factor in his astonishing rise to success, and it would become a factor in his failing health at the zenith of that success. "Jack London was an extremist" was Frank Atherton's simple explanation: "In everything he did or endeavored to do, he went the limit. There could be no half way mark; it was the goal or nothing."

Atherton's memoir serves to modify if not totally dispel some of the self-created myths of London's boyhood. On the one hand, Frank corroborates Jack's claim that his life had been "one of toil." As an eleven-year-old boy, he had not one but two paper routes, morning and evening, for three dollars a month, after Flora told him to take both routes because he needed the exercise on account of spending too much time reading. (He boasted to Frank that he often stayed up reading till 1:00 and 2:00 a.m. to keep up with his quota of "two good-sized books a week.") It was also true that he had worked on weekends carrying ice and setting up pins in a bowling alley. Finally, Atherton confirms Jack's statement that all the money he earned was turned over to his mother, who managed the family's finances.

On the other hand, Frank makes it clear that Jack's regimen was far from being all work and no play. The two boys regularly found time for fun and games after Jack finished his evening route. They had first been drawn together by their mutual interest in collecting cigarette coupons. Attached to packs of cigarettes and other tobacco products, these coupons could be exchanged for picture cards of bright-colored birds, racehorses, flags of all nations, famous actors, and prizefighters—a popular hobby much like baseball-card collecting. Atherton writes that as he was going to the corner store after school a few days following the schoolyard fight, he was spotted by Jack, who was on his afternoon paper route. Noticing that Frank had some cigarette coupons in his hand, Jack announced that he had the biggest collection in West Oakland, and that he was willing to trade some of his duplicates.

Thus began a friendship that would last a lifetime. It was both timely and therapeutic. Where Jennie's loving care and the congeniality of the Prentiss home had counterbalanced Flora's social aloofness, Frank Atherton's friendship counteracted the effects of alienation, saving young Jack from that sense of isolation wrought by too many books and too few playmates.

A genuine friend was especially important at this time in Jack's life. His only other close childhood friend—and the one other person besides Jennie from whom he had received maternal love as a child—had moved out. In 1884, Eliza London had escaped the drudgery of farm life by marrying widower and Civil War veteran Captain James H. Shepard. She was sixteen years old; he was forty-one. He had three children by his first marriage—such was Eliza's maternal reputation that neighbors joked she had actually fallen in love with and married the children, not their father.

Charmian London says that Eliza's departure was emotionally devastating for eight-year-old Jack, who had dreamed of a different future for the two of them. He pledged that he would not marry until he was forty because marriage and children would interfere with his reading schedule. In the meantime, he would build a big house for Eliza, himself, and his thousands of books. She would take care of their home and shield him from annoying interruptions of his study. With her sudden wedding, his "dream was smashed and he left desolate." The Shepards moved only as far as Oakland, but a married Eliza with three stepchildren could not provide Jack with the companionship he had received before.

Nor could his mother fill the emotional vacuum. Jack was obviously remembering Flora and his early days in Oakland when he gave the following speech to one of his characters in *The Star Rover*:

> "My mother believed in spirits. When I was a kid she was always seeing them and talking with them and getting advice from them. But she never came across with any goods from them. The spirits couldn't tell her where the old man could nail a job or find a gold mine or mark an eight-spot in a Chinese lottery. Not on your life. The bunk they told her was that the old man's uncle had had a goitre, or that the old man's grandfather had died of galloping consumption, or that we were going to move house inside four months, which last was dead easy, seeing as we moved on an average of six times a year."

The "average of six times a year" is an exaggeration, but the Londons did move a half-dozen times during Jack's grade-school years. They had started off well enough when they moved from the Alameda farm but again were undone by Flora's ambitious scheming. They would make good money, she figured, by boarding the young women who had been imported from Scotland to work in the nearby cotton mills—and, for a while, they did, but then she decided they could make money faster by expanding their enterprise: they mortgaged the lot next door so they could build a second rooming house. "Her idea was Utopian, for was it not a fine thing for these factory women each to have her own private apartment?" says Charmian London about Flora's plan. "But her altruism did not go hand in hand with ability to see it through, and scheme as she and her good husband might, in the end both properties were forfeited to the mortgage."

The result was a series of moves into poorer quarters. John London returned to railroad work for a while, but an accident broke several of his ribs, after which he was never again able to hold a regular job. For the last decade of his life he brought home only modest wages from a sequence of jobs as night watchman, deputy constable, and special officer on the Oakland police force.

When Frank Atherton first visited Jack at home, the Londons were living in what he described as "a dingy little cottage" on Pine Street, near the estuary and waterfront in West Oakland. Inside the house the "furnishings were plain, but serviceable," he recalled. "A wood and coal stove, portable cupboard, bare wooden chairs and a drop leaf table at which we sat. The floor was bare, but clean from frequent scrubbing."

Atherton's recollection belies London's claim that he never had enough meat as a boy: "Our meal consisted of beefsteak, fried potatoes, bread and butter and coffee, and there was plenty for all." On the other hand, "There was no dessert, neither were there any pretenses of style, newspapers being used in lieu of a table cloth." Atherton remembers that Flora was frying beefsteak and potatoes in a broken skillet on his first visit. He thought at first they were too poor to buy a new skillet. Jack confided that Flora actually had another skillet, but took special pride in the broken one, insisting that it did a better job of cooking.

By this time, while still a boy, Jack had already learned to treat his mother's eccentricities with good-natured humor. "I hope you'll excuse our humble circumstances," he said to Atherton. "We've always been too poor to buy a tablecloth, so we have to use newspapers."

"Why, my goodness, Johnny, you know better!" Flora exclaimed, taking the bait. "You know we have tablecloths, and I use newspapers to save laundering."

"I shouldn't have told tales out of school, Frank, but now the cat is out of the bag, I may as well explain," Jack persisted. "You see, Mama don't like to let anyone know how extremely poor we really are, so she pretends to have all kinds of nice things; but the funny part of it is she's the only one who ever sees them. So we always use newspapers for a tablecloth. When one side gets dirty we turn them over, and then of course sometimes they have to be replaced with new ones."

Her pride wounded, Flora jumped up, went to her linen closet, and brought back several fine linen tablecloths, displaying them proudly. "Now, Frank, you see I have plenty of tablecloths!"

"Why, Mama, those are bed sheets," Jack said, laughing. "Don't you remember how you used to wake me up early in the morning so you could use my sheet for a tablecloth? But then it was so hard to get me up, you began using newspapers instead."

Her sense of the absurd finally aroused, Flora was forced to join her husband and the boys in laughter. Coming to her defense, John London said, "We don't try to put on any style here, Frank; we don't have pies and cakes, but what we have is good, plain substantial food, and usually we have plenty."

Jack was also able, despite his disgust with Flora's séances, to treat them with wry humor. Atherton visited his chum one Saturday morning in the spring of 1888 and found him sitting on the front porch reading a book: "Hello, Frank, come and sit on the porch, but don't talk too loud" was his greeting.

Hearing muffled voices from inside the house, Atherton asked, "Is someone sick?"

"No," Jack replied. "My mother is having a séance." Unfamiliar with the word, Frank asked, "Is it anything serious or contagious?" Forgetting his warning to be quiet, Jack burst into laughter, then explained:

> "A séance is a meeting of spiritualists to evoke manifestations of de-parted persons. But I guess that's too deep for you to understand; I'll have to simplify my explanation . . . My mother is a spiritualist me-dium, and once in a while her followers meet here to communicate with the spirits. My mother believes she's guided by the spirit of an Indian chief named 'Plume.' When she holds a séance she goes into a trance; her eyes roll around and she mumbles something to the big Chief . . . And then the fun begins; her followers imagine they can see spirits, and they begin to moan and chant like so many ignorant savages gath-ered to start a war dance . . . Gosh, Frank, it's just like a comedy."

Atherton's memoir possibly provides additional insights into the true nature of London's youth, further modifying the self-created poor-boy myth of "all work and no play." On Sundays, when Jack wasn't working in the bowling alley, John London often took the two boys fishing. On other occasions, they went hunting mud hens on the Oak-land Estuary with their homemade slingshots. Once they even hiked up into the Piedmont Hills looking for wildcats, but encountered only a fearsome cow. They also strolled along the waterfront watching ships sail through the Golden Gate. Here it was that Jack visualized future adventures, some of which eventually materialized, furnishing the substance for his famous stories. Frank also recounts the evenings spent with Jack watching Shakespeare's plays at the McDonough Theatre, noting that even at this early age his friend had several Shakespeare books in his personal library.

Nor were these pleasures limited to evenings and weekends. In early 1889 the Athertons moved from Oakland to Auburn, a mountain town on the American River. Accepting their invitation, Jack visited the family in early July. Noticing that his friend was having some trouble with the burden of his luggage, Frank volunteered to help: "Let me carry your suit case, Johnny," he said, picking it up. "Gee, but it's awful heavy. What's in it, books or twenty-dollar gold pieces?"

"I wish it were twenties, but then we couldn't even lift them. I brought a few books, but I don't suppose I'll have much time to read; not if we visit all the places you wrote about."

Some years later, London would discover that books—particularly those he produced—would be worth a good many twenty-dollar gold pieces, but in 1889 he was just concerned with reading them, not writing them. Frank assured him that they would have plenty of time for exploring and reading, too: "We have kerosene lamps and you can read as late as you want at night."

That summer in the mountains was idyllic. "Now, every day was Sunday to us. It was a real vacation. There was no school, no paper route, no bowling alley, nor were there any mandatory duties except occasional errands and minor chores about the house, to interfere with our plans," Atherton reminisced. "We went and came as pleased us most, and always the song of the wood was in our hearts."

Some days they spent climbing the nearby mountain and exploring the deep canyon on its other side. It seemed to them that they were venturing into territory that no humans had ever seen or set foot in before them. On other days, they raced each other down the narrow, precipitous trails to the swimming holes on the American River. Here was a world far removed from the drudgery of the city. Here there were no saloons, no bowling alleys, no ice wagons, and no newspaper routes.

Our evenings were passed in the great dooryard, sprawled out on old blankets. Here we listened to the weird cries of owls and coyotes and other nocturnal creatures, while the brook rippled merrily on its course to the river, and the soft summer breeze sighed gently through the lofty pines.

In fancy, we saw many wonderful pictures: magnificent scenes of strange, distant lands, primitive and unexplored. And we became eager and restless with youthful ambition, to travel all over the world that we might see these things in reality.

One fine day Jack would run fast enough and far enough to see these wonderful sights in reality. However, that day would be a while in coming. The summer of 1890 would be as miserable as the preceding one had been pleasurable—but those miseries would impel young Jack toward a dramatic course of action.

3

THE APOSTATE

Now I wake me up to work;
I pray the Lord I may not shirk.
If I should die before the night,
I pray the Lord my work's all right.
Amen.

—EPIGRAPH TO "THE APOSTATE"

Jack's return to Oakland from his 1889 summer vacation in the mountains was a falling off or, more accurately, a falling back, back into the daily grind of work-school-work: up before dawn to throw his morning newspapers, off to class, back to his evening paper route, working in the bowling alley and sweeping out saloons on weekends. The only breaks in his monotonous cycle came in the brief intervals when he could find time to read his precious books and, on Sundays, sail around the estuary in the old boat he had bought for two dollars and painstakingly restored. He was elected class historian and given the honor of delivering an address at graduation, but declined because he was ashamed to appear at this special occasion in his shabby clothes.

There were no plans for high school. John London's physical condition had continued to deteriorate after his railroad accident. He was no longer able do any kind of strenuous work. The family needed more money. Jack's only apparent option now was full-time work, and the only available full-time work was in the factory. Child labor laws were in their infancy, and children were the cheapest labor force. At fourteen Jack started work in Hickmott's Cannery in West Oakland.

He was not the youngest employee at Hickmott's; six- and seven-year-old children were also there. The enormity of such ruthless exploitation left an indelible impression on him: "For months at a time, during that year, I was up and at work at six in the morning," he bitterly recalled. "I took half an hour for dinner. I took half an hour for supper. I worked every night till ten, eleven, and twelve o'clock. My wages were small, but I worked such long hours that I sometimes made as high as fifty dollars a month . . . I have worked in that hell hole for thirty-six straight hours, at a machine, and I was only a child." He dramatized this bitterness a decade later in one of his most poignant stories, "The Apostate." Johnny, the protagonist in this story, has worked in the jute mills for eleven years. Eighteen years old, thin-chested with a recurrent cough and weighing scarcely more than a normal youth half his age, he has "won mastership of the mills." He has never known the joys of boyhood, much less the excitements of adolescence: "Manhood, full-blown manhood, had come when he was eleven, at which time he had gone to work on the night shift for six months. No child works on the night shift and remains a child." Johnny's is the world of the factory: a world without regulated hours or minimum wages, without compensation for overloads or work-related injuries, without health care, without retirement plans—in short, without heart.

Finally, after recovering from a severe bout of influenza, an illness that has sent him to bed and given him time to calculate the millions of mechanical motions to which he has subjected his worn-out body, Johnny decides to abandon the machine: "Jes' ain' goin' to do nothin'," he mutters to himself as he leaves the decrepit shanty that has been his only home and limps out of the industrial city into the clean, sun-washed countryside beside a railroad track: "He did not look like a man. He was a travesty of the human. It was a twisted and stunted and nameless piece of life that shambled like a sickly ape, arms loose-hanging, stoop-shouldered, narrow-chested, grotesque and terrible."

Coming to a small railroad station in the late afternoon, he lies down under a tree to rest. There he spends the rest of daylight alternately dozing and watching through the leaves the birds as they soar freely in the blue sky above. That evening, seeing a freight train stop at the station to switch cars, he creeps up and laboriously pulls open the side door of an empty boxcar: "He closed the door. The engine whistled. Johnny was lying down, and in the darkness he smiled."

Unlike his fictional namesake, young "Johnny" London wore out neither body nor soul by toiling eleven years in the factories. Even so, this is one of his most autobiographical stories—emotionally if not literally. Like Johnny, Jack grew to abhor the lethal effects of factory labor, and like Johnny, he rejected the specious creed of the industrial work cult, switching roles from apostle to apostate. At the age of fifteen, he decided to become an outlaw and joined a gang of oyster pirates.

By 1891, oyster pirating had become a major black market industry in the Bay Area. Because the oyster beds were owned by the railroad "octopus," whose monopoly controlled the industry and raised prices to "all the traffic would bear," oyster pirating was a very profitable business. Underselling the monopoly to the saloons and stores along the waterfront, a pirate could earn the equivalent of a month's factory wages from one good night's haul.

It was also a very dangerous business. Jack later remarked that the great miracle of his life was that he lived to the age of twenty-one, because most of his friends wound up dead or in jail. Stealing oysters was not an easy game. The beds were protected by armed guards, and by members of the quasi-legal Fish Patrol, who were little more than officially sanctioned bounty hunters. Every dark night's raid was an invitation to get shot or arrested. A successful pirate had to be intrepid. He also had to be very skillful in handling sailboats that were frailer but faster than those of the patrolmen. London's boyhood experience with his own small boats had turned him into an expert sailor; in fact, he considered himself a natural-born sailor—"not the average efficient and hopeless creature who is found to-day in the forecastle of deepwater ships, but the man who will take a fabric compounded of wood and iron and rope and canvas and compel it to obey his will on the surface of the sea." In his essay "Small-Boat Sailing," he testifies that by the age of twelve he had already mastered the difficult art. But after his graduation from Cole Grammar School, factory work left him no leisure time for sailing.

He already knew something firsthand about the delinquents who roamed the Oakland waterfront, and the oyster pirates were the most highly glamorized of the seedy bunch. To their admirers, who hated the legally empowered robber barons, they were the Robin Hoods of the Bay. To fifteen-year-old Jack, their daring underworld exploits represented a wonderful escape from the drudgery of the industrial underworld. "I wanted to be where the winds of adventure blew," he recalled:

> And the winds of adventure blew the oyster pirate sloops up and down San Francisco Bay, from raided oyster-beds and fights at night on shoal and flat, to markets in the morning against city wharves . . . Every raid on an oyster-bed was a felony. The penalty was state imprisonment, the stripes and the lockstep. And what of that? The men in stripes worked a shorter day than I at my machine. And there was vastly more romance in being an oyster pirate or a convict than in being a machine slave. And behind it all, behind all of me with youth a-bubble, whispered Romance, Adventure.

So, when he learned that one of the most notorious oyster pirates of them all, "French Frank," was putting his boat the *Razzle Dazzle* up for sale, he went straight to Jennie Prentiss. Would she lend her "white child" the princely sum of three hundred dollars? *"Would she?"* he remembered her response: "What she had was mine."

Three hundred dollars—a year's wages in the factory! Never in his entire life had Jack seen that much money in one lump sum. The contract with French Frank was bound with a golden double eagle over a huge demijohn of red wine that afternoon. The full transaction could wait till the morrow, the day being Sunday and Frank hosting a party of friends. The half-dozen guests, according to London, included Frank's girlfriend Mamie, "Queen of the Oyster Pirates." The sale—with Jack "tapping" into the fraternity—was cause for celebration. Wine flowed freely. Social and moral inhibitions did likewise. While the others were singing bawdy songs, Mamie quietly lured Jack topside and put him through the final stage of his initiation: "The Queen began to make love to me," he says without detailing the affair, "the latest recruit to the oyster pirate fleet, and no mere hand, but a master and owner." At that moment, Jack London was crowned "Prince of the Oyster Pirates." His initiatory ritual was prophetic: it signified the pattern that would be played out for the rest of his life:

> There it was, the smack and slap of the spirit of revolt, of adventure, of romance, of the things forbidden and done defiantly and grandly. And I knew that on the morrow I would not go back to my machine . . . To-morrow I would be an oyster pirate, as free a freebooter as the century and the waters of San Francisco Bay would permit . . . And at last my dream would be realized: I would sleep upon the water. And next morning I would wake upon the water; and thereafter all my days and nights would be on the water.

His dream was realized—with interludes that were nightmarish. For the next year and a half, he managed to survive a series of escapades from which he was lucky to emerge relatively unscathed. Some of these adventures he would later fictionalize in *The Cruise of the Dazzler* (1902) and *Tales of the Fish Patrol* (1905), and in appropriately sanitized stories for the juvenile readers of *St. Nicholas for Young Folks* and *The Youth's Companion*.

The real story, however, was hardly fitting material for young readers. At the age of fifteen, Jack had, indeed, become "a man amongst men," and those men were some of the toughest and meanest on the Oakland waterfront. Their characters were hinted at in such names as Old Cole, Old Smoudge, Big Alec ("the King of the Greeks"), "Spider" Healey, "Clam," and "Whisky" Bob: "rough men, big and unafraid, and weazened wharf-rats, some of them ex-convicts, all of them enemies of the law and meriting jail, in sea-boots and sea-gear, talking in gruff, low voices, and 'Big' George with revolvers strapped about his waist to show that he meant business."

Toughest of the tough was "Young Scratch" Nelson (to distinguish him from his father, "Old Scratch"), who had earned his sobriquet from his ugly habit of tearing off the faces of his fighting opponents. "Clam," the elder Nelson's partner on the sloop *Reindeer*, "was a daredevil, but [the younger] Nelson was a reckless maniac, with the body of a Hercules. When he was shot in Benicia a couple of years later, the coroner said he was the greatest-shouldered man he had ever seen laid on a slab."

Nelson could neither read nor write, but "his strength was prodigious, and his reputation along the waterfront for violence was anything but savory. He had Berserker rages and did mad, terrible things."

Jack allied himself with this young madman a few months after his initiation when his crew "Scotty" accidentally set fire to the mainsail, disabling the *Razzle Dazzle*. Though he may have been best known for his notorious rages, Young Nelson was an expert boat handler. The two partners spent the next few months exploring the large Bay Area in between oyster raids, enabling London to hone his seamanship—and his boozing skills.

Like most men of their era, the oyster pirates celebrated their scruffy camaraderie in saloons. To become a full-fledged member of this gang required "rubbing shoulders with John Barleycorn." Jack stubbornly insisted that he neither cared for the taste of liquor nor was chemically dependent upon it. However, from the days of his boyhood, when he accompanied John London on his trips from farm to town, he had witnessed the bonhomie shared by workingmen who gathered in bars to relax their tired bodies and relieve their tiresome worries. He claimed he never got over his physical dislike of alcohol, while confessing that saloons provided the few truly happy moments of his childhood.

He reminisced about sitting on top of the wagonload sacks of potatoes as John London drove the plodding horses slowly through the heavy chilling fog into town to deliver his produce, recalling that "one bright vision" made the tedious journey worthwhile: the saloon in Colma, where his father stopped for a drink. Here the boy could warm his feet by the big woodstove while he savored the bartender's gift of a soda cracker: "Just one soda cracker, but a fabulous luxury," which he would spend an hour nibbling and savoring. He remembered also the more luxurious San Francisco saloons with all their mouthwatering free snacks: "strange breads and crackers, cheeses, sausages, sardines— wonderful foods I never saw on our meager home table." He remembered, too, a sweet, specially mixed drink of cherry syrup and soda water: "It was the barkeeper's treat, and he became my ideal of a good, kind man . . . He and my father talked long, and I sipped my sweet drink and worshiped him."

The stuff Jack drank with the oyster pirates was more lethal than the cherry nectar the San Francisco bartender gave him. Hot and raw, it was a drink to be guzzled, not sipped, and he quickly learned to order it like a true veteran: "'Whisky,' I said, with the careless air of one who had said it a thousand times. And such whisky!"

Not only did it taste rotten, but it was expensive: ten cents a glass, an hour's wages at the factory. But what did that matter to an industrial apostate? "Better to reign among booze-fighters, a prince, than to toil twelve hours a day at a machine for ten cents an hour." Besides, with the cast-iron constitution of youth and plenty of money to be made in pirating, why not continue to impress his elder comrades with his ability to hold his liquor? While undoubtedly stretching the truth, he boasted that he could drink the best of them under the table. Heinold's First and Last Chance Saloon—now a historic landmark on the Oakland waterfront—became his home away from home. London claims that on one spectacular night, he blew one hundred and eighty dollars (over a half year's factory wages) boozing with his buddies. To his credit, he managed to pay off his loan to Jennie Prentiss, and he continued to provide extra dollars for his family. Still, Flora later complained that he had become much too bossy and rowdy for her taste. For days, sometimes weeks, at a time, he was absent from home, returning occasionally to give money to Flora and to get clean clothes.

In the spring of 1891, Frank Atherton moved in with the Londons for a month while commuting to San Francisco, where he had started taking taxidermy lessons. Jack happened to return home one evening, and Frank noticed at once that he was not the same person who had romped through the mountains with him at Auburn two summers before. "In truth," recalled Atherton, "he was vastly different from the Johnny London I had formerly known; he had changed completely in many ways."

Although Jack was clearly making a good deal of money, the saloon keepers got more of it than his parents did. He "was drifting farther and farther away from the high ideals of his early boyhood" and had apparently abandoned books and his ambition to become a writer. "Adventure—wild adventure; strange, extravagant dreams of great conquests and impossible achievements seemed to have taken possession of his very soul, leading him on and on into the most reckless escapades his young imagination could portray," says Atherton. "He talked and acted like a far different lad; as one who had abandoned all the grand ideals of his boyhood dreams, and given himself up to the desperate life of an outlaw."

His apparently inevitable downfall was prevented by several fortunate turns of fate. First, after the mainsail on the *Razzle Dazzle* was destroyed by fire, and while he was off adventuring with Young Scratch Nelson, his boat was vandalized beyond repair. Then, during one of his sober days, he wandered back into the Oakland Public Library, where he discovered a story in *St. Nicholas* magazine about the leader of a juvenile gang who winds up in prison after stealing a yacht and trying his hand at pirating. This story, coming hard on the heels of a sequence of his own close brushes with catastrophe, brought him to the realization that he was on the wrong side of the law.

According to London, he was offered a job as deputy officer for the California Fish Patrol in early 1892. He took it, and moved his headquarters from the Oakland waterfront to Benicia, on the Carquinez Strait—far enough away so that he was in no danger of confronting his former pirating colleagues. He no longer ran the risk of imprisonment, yet he ran another risk equally dangerous and more sinister: "I had longer spells ashore, between fooling with salmon fishing and making raids up and down bay and rivers as a deputy fish patrolman, and I drank more and learned more about drinking. I held my own with any one, drink for drink; and often drank more than my share to show the strength of my manhood."

From this danger he nearly paid with his life, thanks to "a trick John Barleycorn played me—a monstrous, incredible trick that showed abysses of intoxication hitherto undreamed." Late one night after a prodigious drinking bout, he tried to stumble aboard a sloop anchored at the end of a wharf in Benecia, where he intended to "sleep it off." But in his drunken stupor he missed his step, fell overboard, and was swept into the treacherous tides of the Carquinez Strait. As he recounted the episode, he was so thoroughly under alcohol's sway that he decided the Fates had provided perfect romantic closure to his adventurous life and that he would go out with the tide. "Thoughts of suicide had never entered my head. And now that they entered, I thought it fine, a splendid culmination, a perfect rounding off of my short but exciting career . . . It was a hero's death, and by the hero's own hand and will."

After he had spent four hours of "dreaming long drunken dreams" while alternately floating and swimming, the effects of the liquor began to fade in the chilling cross tide off Mare Island. With the approach of daylight, it finally dawned on him that he was "very weary and very cold, and quite sober and didn't in the least want to be drowned." In fact, he now realized he had all kinds of reasons for living. Yet he had gone out too far, and all those hours in the cold water had sapped his strength. In short, he had exhausted his reserves and knew that he would never make it back to shore: "A stiff breeze had sprung up, and the crisp little waves were persistently lapping into my mouth, and I was beginning to swallow salt water. With my swimmer's knowledge, I knew the end was near."

Had it not been for the appearance of a Greek fisherman who was running his boat into Vallejo, Jack's heroic adventures would have ceased forever during those early morning hours between the Carquinez and Vallejo straits. This close call with death prompted him to leave the Fish Patrol at Benecia and head back to Oakland, where he renewed acquaintance with Young Scratch Nelson and the other hoodlums loafing around the waterfront. The near drowning had been a sobering experience, but not sobering enough to stop him from drinking. However, he had grown "respectfully suspicious of John Barleycorn," he attested. "I could not forget the trick he had played on me—on *me*, who did not want to die. So I continued to drink, and to keep a sharp eye on John Barleycorn, resolved to resist all future suggestions of self-destruction."

He was sixteen years old and apparently going nowhere. He worked at occasional odd jobs but spent most of his time loafing and drinking with other "wharf-rats." One significant event occurred during the summer of 1892. Offered a ten-dollar reward to retrieve a boat stolen from his friend Dinny McCrea and left at Port Costa on Suison Bay, Jack and Nickey the Greek got McCrea's boat, but only after a close scrape with the constable who had been holding it for an anticipated twenty-five-dollar reward. Figuring the law might be waiting for them if they immediately sailed back down the Carquinez Strait, they decided that it would be fun to go upriver to Sacramento before returning to Oakland.

Near Sacramento they encountered a gang of teenage boys swimming in the river. These were a different breed from the Oakland gang: younger and cleaner but, as Jack would discover, just as tough and sometimes—especially when they ran in packs—meaner. He found out that they were "road kids," a motley band of pariahs from poverty-stricken families and broken homes who survived by begging, stealing, mugging, and hoboing.

Jack was fascinated with their talk and decided to let Nickey take the boat back to Oakland while he lingered in Sacramento to learn more about the gang's adventures. It was then and there he was initiated into the fraternity of "the Road." Here was a brave world with such people in it as he had never met before:

> These wanderers made my oyster-piracy look like thirty cents. A new world was calling to me in every word that was spoken—a world of rods and gunnels, blind baggages and "side-door Pullman," "bulls," and "shacks," "floppings" and "chewin's," "pinches" and "get-aways," "strong arms" and "bindle-stiffs," "punks" and "profesh." And it spelled Adventure.

"The Road," which would become the title of another of his pioneering works fifteen years later, was not Route 66 or any modern highway—for, in 1892, there were no highways and no automobiles, only the vast network of iron rails that had brought traffic and civilization to the American West in the years following the Civil War. Anyone, even a penniless youth, with wit and grit, could now ride the rails coast to coast, from San Francisco to New York and Boston.

This new adventure excited Jack more than any since his early days as an oyster pirate. But for those who could not afford the price of a ticket, such travel often came at a heavier cost than mere dollars: mangled legs, arms, and, sometimes, lives. It took courage and agility to hop a freight train, and even more to get a free ride on a moving passenger car at night. "And let me say right here that only a young and vigorous tramp is able to deck [board and ride atop] a passenger train, and also, that the young and vigorous tramp must have his nerve with him as well":

> Registering the fervent hope that there are no tunnels in the next half mile, I rise to my feet and walk down the train half a dozen cars . . . The roofs of passenger cars are not made for midnight promenades. And if any one thinks they are, let me advise him to try it. Just let him walk along the roof of a jolting, lurching car, with nothing to hold on to but the black and empty air, and when he comes to the down-curving end of the roof, all wet and slippery with dew, let him accelerate his speed so as to step across to the next roof, down-curving and wet and slippery. Believe me, he will learn whether his heart is weak or his head is giddy.

To complete his initiatory rites (to become a full-fledged "road-kid"), the novice was required to go "over the hill" (over the Sierra Nevada). Encouraged by a gang of some forty initiates, Jack managed to "deck" a Central Pacific freight train out of Sacramento one night, arriving in Truckee at seven o'clock the next morning. Upon returning, he was awarded his moniker "Sailor Kid," subsequently to become " 'Frisco Kid," and, a couple of years later, when he had attained the status of "profesh" (the elite order of hobodom), "Sailor Jack." A fellow novice, "French Kid," was less fortunate: on that first attempt to deck the Central Pacific overland, he slipped and fell under the wheels, losing both legs.

That summer of hoboing, brief though it was, would have long-term effects for London. For one thing, the necessary begging for handouts would sharpen his skills as natural-born raconteur. "I have often thought that to this training of my tramp days is due much of my success as a story-teller," he says in *The Road*:

> In order to get the food whereby I lived, I was compelled to tell tales that rang true. At the back door, out of inexorable necessity, is developed the convincingness and sincerity laid down by all authorities on the art of the short-story. Also, I quite believe it was my tramp apprenticeship that made a realist out of me. Realism constitutes the only goods one can exchange at the kitchen door for grub.

His hobo apprenticeship would also prepare him for a major odyssey two years later. During each of those intervening years, he would experience another life-changing adventure: one, a harrowing brush with death aboard a train bound for hell, the other, initiation into life aboard a sealing ship bound for the Pacific and Japan.

4

A BOY AMONG MEN

A sailor is born, not made . . . And if a man is a born sailor, and has gone to the school of the sea, never in all his life can he get away from the sea again. The salt of it is in his bones as well as his nostrils, and the sea will call to him until he dies.

—*THE HUMAN DRIFT*

In the early fall of 1892, having his fill of hoboing for a while, Jack wandered back to the Oakland waterfront, where once again he took up company with the West Oakland gang and the waterfront saloons:

I drank every day, and whenever opportunity offered I drank to excess; for I still labored under the misconception that the secret of John Barleycorn lay in drinking to bestiality and unconsciousness. I became pretty thoroughly alcohol-soaked during this period. I practically lived in saloons; became a barroom loafer, and worse.

He does not elaborate what he means by "worse." However, he does describe another binge that nearly cost him his life. This happened during a torchlight parade sponsored by one of the political parties during the November elections, when he and Young Scratch Nelson were lounging in one of the saloons, broke, and waiting for someone to buy them a drink. Because it was election time, the politicians—well dressed and "exhaling an atmosphere of prosperity and fellowship"—were visiting the saloons, offering drinks for votes: And "when these politicians swing wide the doors and come in, with their broad shoulders, their deep chests, and their generous stomachs which cannot help making them optimists and masters of life, why, you perk right up . . . and you know you'll get a souse started at the very least." It was now, Jack admits, that he was "having illusions punctured—I, who had pored and thrilled over 'The Rail-Splitter,' and 'From Canal Boy to President' . . . I was learning how noble politics and politicians are."

The nobility of these politicians and their minions manifested itself generously that evening with the announcement of "Free booze—all you want of it!" All the recipients needed to do in payment was to don red shirts and helmets, carry torches, and board a train to Haywards as members of the "Hancock Fire Brigade." In preparation for the election, politicians had bought out the stocks in all the local saloons. The town would be "wide open," the whiskey "would run like water," and "all hell would break loose!"

That evening turned into one of the most hellish nights in London's memories. Jack and Scratch, accompanied by another bum named "Joe Goose," ran to get their red uniforms and torches, and were then herded along with several scores of volunteers onto the train to Haywards for their torchlight parade. Only after they had finished their marching were the saloon doors unlocked. Then all hell did indeed break loose as gangs of thirsty men crowded the bars. Frustrated in their attempts to get through the crowd to the whiskey, Jack and his two buddies did a quick end-around rush, knocking the bartenders aside and grabbing armloads of whiskey bottles. Back outside, they began guzzling. Unlike his buddies, Jack had not yet learned that the risks of consuming straight whiskey in quantity were greater than chugging beer. "I haven't the slightest idea of how much I drank—whether it was two quarts or five. I do know that I began the orgy with half-pint draughts and with no water afterward to wash the taste away and to dilute the whisky."

The politicians weren't about to leave all the drunks littering the streets of Haywards. At the scheduled time, they rounded up the gangs and paraded them back to the Oakland train. By now the surfeit of whiskey was beginning to register on Jack's system. Without comprehending the precariousness of his condition, he was feeling the first lethal symptoms of alcohol poisoning: He staggered along toward the train, legs tottering, head swimming, heart pounding, lungs desperately gasping for oxygen:

> My helplessness was coming on so rapidly that my reeling brain told me I would go down and out and never reach the train if I remained at the rear of the procession. I left the ranks and ran down a pathway beside the road under broad-spreading trees. Nelson pursued me, laughing. Certain things stand out, as in memories of nightmare. I remember those trees especially, and my desperate running along under them, and how, every time I fell, roars of laughter went up from other drunks. They thought I was merely antic drunk. They did not dream that John Barleycorn had me by the throat in a death-clutch.

With his nervous system shutting down, he finally passed out and collapsed. Although he could not remember what happened after that, he was told that Nelson managed to pick him up and get him aboard the train:

> I was scorching up, burning alive internally, in an agony of fire and suffocation, and I wanted air. I madly wanted air. My efforts to raise a window were vain, for all the windows in the car were screwed down. Nelson had seen drink-crazed men and thought I wanted to throw myself out. He tried to restrain me, but I fought on. I seized some man's torch and smashed the glass.

Breaking that window precipitated a battle between the drunken anti-Nelson and pro-Nelson factions from the Oakland waterfront. As soon as Jack broke the window, the free-for-all started. Virtually all the windows in the coach were broken, and both Jack and Scratch were knocked cold. This knockout—serving to slow down London's dangerously fibrillating heart—along with the rush of fresh air, may have been a life-saving accident.

He didn't remember what happened after he regained consciousness, but Nelson later told him he started desperately crying out "Air!

Air!" and struggling to get his head and torso out the open window. Scratch, also recovering from the knockout, cleared the jagged glass from the window frame and held on to Jack to keep him from falling out—though he fought "like a maniac" whenever his buddy tried to pull him back into the coach.

Jack said all he remembered from the moment he fell down under the trees was desperately hanging his head out that window despite the cinders that were burning his face and eyelids:

> All my will was concentrated on breathing—on breathing the air in the hugest lung-full gulps I could, pumping the greatest amount of air into my lungs in the shortest possible time. It was that or death, and I was a swimmer and diver and knew it; and in the most intolerable agony of prolonged suffocation, during those moments I was conscious, I faced the wind and the cinders and breathed for life.

The harrowing experience taught him to drink more wisely, and though he continued boozing with his waterfront pals for a while, it gradually dawned on him that he was headed toward an inglorious end. Fortunately he found a way out of his downward spiral, an escape propelled by his "seeking drive" into the vast world beyond the Golden Gate that he had dreamed of since boyhood. Toward the end of 1892 he began to meet members from the sealing fleet that was wintering in Oakland. Among them was a seal hunter named Pete Holt. Despite Jack's obvious youth, Holt could discern in his character an exceptional maturity, toughness, and capacity for camaraderie. He therefore agreed to take him on as his own boat puller on his next cruise. Eight days after his seventeenth birthday, Jack signed on as an able-bodied seaman aboard the *Sophia Sutherland*, a 157-ton, three-topmast schooner bound for the Bering Sea to hunt seals.

While he possessed a wealth of small-boat sailing experience, London had never sailed before the mast on a larger vessel. Moreover, his shipmates on the *Sophia Sutherland* were veteran mariners and resented a seventeen-year-old who had the audacity to claim membership in their able-bodied fraternity. The ten "hard-bit Scandinavians" Jack joined in the forecastle had spent years enduring the rigors of initiation. As youths, they had started out as apprentice cooks or cabin boys and, according to the stern rules of the sea, suffered as virtual "slaves of the ordinary and able-bodied seamen." Even after having earned the status of "ordinary seaman," they still suffered as slaves of their superiors. "Thus, in the forecastle, with the watch below, an able seaman, lying in his bunk, will order an ordinary seaman to fetch him his shoes or bring him a drink of water," London explains. Even though the ordinary seaman may be lying in his own bunk as tired as the able-bodied seaman, he must nonetheless obey the order. "If he refuses, he will be beaten." If he puts up a good fight against a weaker member of the fraternity, this "luckless devil" will be given an even worse beating by the rest of the able-bodied seamen.

Though his was a man's body, Jack's muscular shoulders were betrayed by his boyish features—nearly cherubic until a quick smile revealed the loss of several front teeth. Moreover, it was obvious that this was his first ocean voyage. "I had never been to sea before . . . It was either a case of holding my own with them or going under. I had signed on as an equal, and as an equal I must maintain myself, or else endure seven months of hell under their hands."

His hard-won lessons as an oyster pirate had impressed upon him the attitude necessary for survival according to the strict unwritten maritime code. First of all, he was determined to do his share of the work, or more, regardless of danger or difficulty: "I made it a point to be among the first of the watch going on deck, among the last going below, never leaving a sheet or tackle for some one else to coil over a pin. I was always eager for the run aloft for the shifting of topsail sheets and tacks, or for the setting or taking in of topsails."

His grade-school encounter with Mike Panella, underscored by his experiences on the waterfront, had educated him in the psychology of the bully. He had learned that the typical bully would take advantage of the least sign of weakness in his prospective victim:

> I knew better than to accept any abuse or the slightest patronizing. At the first hint of such, I went off—I exploded. I might be beaten in the subsequent fight, but I left the impression that I was a wildcat and that I would just as willingly fight again . . . After a bit of strife, my attitude was accepted, and it was my pride that I was taken in as an equal in spirit as well as in fact.

The "bit of strife" occurred when one veteran shipmate, a burly Swede nicknamed "Big Red John," tried to cow him into subservience. The incident occurred on "Peggy day," the seamen's term for the day each hand was scheduled to take his turn at scullery work aboard ship: cleaning off the mess table, washing dishes, filling the slush lamps, and refilling jars of condiments, sugar, and the like. On this particular day, Red John, figuring he could force the undersize greenhorn to do his work, ordered Jack to fill the molasses jar. Instead of jumping to the command, Jack, sitting in his bunk and weaving a rope-yarn mat, calmly replied: "I never taste it. T'aint fit for a hog. It's your day to grub, so do it yourself."

Every shipmate within hearing distance, knowing Red John's bad temper, envisioned total annihilation for the reckless youth. None of the others had dared challenge Red John so openly. Jack said nothing more and continued his work. At this point, realizing he had a ready audience, the Swede swore a loud oath and "threatened bloodcurdling consequences if he were not obeyed." Regardless, Jack kept on silently weaving his mat.

Red John, realizing his bluff had been called in the presence of others, became genuinely angry. He dropped the coffee pot he was holding and backhanded the impudent upstart across the mouth. To the spectators' shock, instead of cowering, Jack struck back, hitting the Swede with a straight right squarely between the eyes. Amazed, Red John instantly became furious. No longer content with backhanding now, he struck out with his huge fist. Jack managed to dodge the blow and jumped onto the Swede's massive back, digging his fingers into his huge throat. Bellowing with rage, Red John began jumping up and down, trying to dislodge the rider by banging his head on the deck beams. Even though his scalp and face were streaming with blood, Jack hung on desperately, digging his fingers even deeper into his opponent's larynx. Luckily the Swede could not see the serious damage he was doing, but felt he was getting the worst of the fight as he began gasping for air. By now the slush lamp overhead had crashed down, broken crockery littered the floor, and the cabin had become a shambles as the crew members watched in astonishment.

Hanging on for dear life and afraid of losing consciousness, Jack yelled, "Will you promise to leave me alone? You gonna promise or not!" Afraid of losing consciousness as the choking fingers refused to relax, Red John, his face "tortured and purple," gurgled a breathless "Yeah." Only then did Jack loosen his grip and lower his body to the floor, and the Swede "reeled and stumbled to his knees like a felled bullock." The audience immediately crowded around the battered but unbowed victor, offering their congratulations and assistance. From that day forward, Jack got their respect as a true able-bodied seaman.

This first "run across" the Pacific from San Francisco to Japan was one of London's fondest memories. More than this, the voyage provided the inspiration for his first publication. His "Story of a Typhoon off the Coast of Japan," a prizewinning sketch that appeared in *The San Francisco Morning Call* a couple of months after his return home, was a firsthand account of a terrific storm the ship encountered. Materials from this voyage were also later used in several items he published in the Oakland High School *Aegis*. Most important, they were the basis for his bestselling classic *The Sea-Wolf*.

Although the *Sophie* (as London called the ship) sailed within sight of the Hawaiian Islands, it did not drop anchor for fifty-one days. "Ah! the very remembrance of the glories of such a voyage is intoxicating," he rhapsodized in one of his *Aegis* sketches. "Days, dreamy and bewitching in their sleepy beauty—days, in which the morn breaks with unrivalled tropic splendor, and the evening shades away almost imperceptibly into night . . . Nothing is harsh or discordant; everything harmonizes . . . and causes one to become dreamy and to sink into reverie."

He was roused from his sea dreams on March 12, 1893, when the *Sophie* dropped anchor at St. Johns in the Bonin (Ogasawara) Islands, owned by Japan, six hundred miles south-southeast of Tokyo. These sparsely inhabited volcanic islands appeared to Jack's youthful eyes a lush tropical paradise. His sense of nostalgic enchantment is still evident in an article he wrote for the *Aegis* two years afterward:

[The] manifest charm in the scenery of these islands is that of variety—the sharp and telling contrasts which abound on every hand and in such grand magnitude . . . Here high mountains rise perpendicularly from the sea, covered to their very summits by the luxuriant growth of tropical vegetation; there, a little coral beach of purest, dazzling white, reposes at the base of some mighty cliff, ever washed by the ceaseless surf . . . Far up among the cliffs at the head of the deep, cavern-like gorges, pure springs of ice-cold water send down sparkling streams and rivulets to meet the fierce surge of the surf far below.

So attractive was the picturesque vista that he determined to make the most of his opportunity. "I had won to the other side of the world," he recalled, "and I would see all I had read about in the books come true. I was wild to get ashore." He made a compact with two of his mates—a Swede named Victor and a Norwegian named Axel—that they would spend their ten-day sailor's leave climbing the mountain lava paths and exploring this flowery wilderness.

Unwisely, they decided to seal their compact with a drink. They got no farther inland than the village pubs, where they encountered crews from several other ships, including a number of sailors they had previously met in saloons back home. "Each meeting meant a drink, and there was much to talk about; and more drinks, and songs to be sung; and pranks and antics to be performed." All this seemed "great and wonderful" in the eyes of a seventeen-year-old youth on his first deep-sea adventure, and these scruffy barflies were magically transformed into "knights at table in the great banquet-halls . . . Vikings feasting fresh from sea and ripe for battle . . . and I knew that the old times were not dead and that we belonged to that self-same ancient breed."

Within less than a week, what had at first appeared to be a quiet paradisal retreat was transformed into an alcoholic debacle. If not quite ripe for battle, the invaders were ripe for rioting. Filled with crews from a dozen or so vessels, the main street of the village became "a madness." Hundreds of sailors rollicked up and down. Because the chief of police and his small force were helpless, the governor of the colony had issued orders to the captains to have all their men on board by sunset. His orders proved counterproductive:

It was hours after sunset, and the men wanted to see anybody try to put them on board . . . In front of the governor's house they were gathered thickest, bawling sea-songs, circulating square-faces, and dancing uproarious Virginia reels and old-country dances . . . And I thought the saturnalia was great . . . it was adventure. And I was part of it, a chesty sea-rover along with all these other chesty sea-rovers.

Because Jack spent much of the next few days hopping from bar to bar, his recollection of the experience was hazy. However, he did recall bonding with a group of English teenagers who had run away from secure middle-class homes, driven, as he had been, to seek adventure in the vast world. "They were healthy, smooth-skinned, clear-eyed, and they were young—youths like me, learning the way of the feet in the world of men." And they had already fully adapted themselves. "No mild *sake* for them, but square-faces illicitly refilled with corrosive fire that flamed through their veins and burst into conflagrations in their heads." Jack joined them in singing a nostalgic lyric with this refrain, which he could still recite from memory:

This but a little golden ring,
I give it to thee with pride,
Wear it for your mother's sake
When you are on the tide.

The youths shed tears as they sang, drunkenly wallowing in their guilty pathos:

We—the apprentices and I—are swaying and clinging to one another
under the stars. We are singing a rollicking sea-song, all save one who
sits on the ground and weeps; and we are marking the rhythm with
waving square-faces. From up and down the street come far choruses
of sea-voices similarly singing, and life is great, and beautiful, and
romantic and magnificently mad.

The magnificent madness faded with the stars. In the early dawn, Jack awakened "chilled and shivering," lying in the doorway of the Japanese port pilot's wife, who was bending over him, "solicitously anxious"—for good reason: Not only was he cold and sick from the debauch, but he was very scantily clothed. The runaway apprentices had absconded with his wallet and all his money, his watch, his coat, his belt, and even his shoes. He "caroused somewhat more discreetly" after that.

On March 22, the *Sophie* hoisted anchor and sailed north to pick up a seal herd off the Siberian coast. They spent the next hundred days in those cold, foggy waters engaged in a bloody orgy the likes of which Jack had never imagined. No more Vikings "ripe for battle": in the sober light of reality, these were filthy butchers ruthlessly decimating a helpless species in this maritime slaughterhouse. The ship's deck became a sodden, slippery mess of gore, and the naked carcasses of once-beautiful creatures were cast overboard as food for the sharks.

Their bloody exploit finished, the *Sophie* headed back south to Yokohama, encountering off the coast of northern Japan a typhoon that provided inspiration for the story to launch London's literary career a few months later. The crew spent two weeks in Yokohama, and though London says in *John Barleycorn* that he saw little there except the drinking places, he may in fact have wandered beyond the waterfront into the city itself. In another *Aegis* sketch, titled "Sakaicho, Hona Asi and Hakadaki," the narrator (named Jack) tells of being invited to lunch at the little home of a rickshaw driver. During the visit, "Jock," as his host calls him, learns that Sakaicho has managed to save enough money over the years to buy two rickshaws, one of which he rents. His wife, Hona Asi, "a true helpmate," also works, hem-stitching silk handkerchiefs at home. The two of them have one child, a ten-year-old boy, whom they hope to send to America someday to complete his education.

Following their meal of "bean soup, boiled fish, stewed leeks, pickles and soy, raw fish, thin sliced and eaten with radishes, *kurage*, a kind of jelly fish, and tea [with] bowls of steaming rice" and warm sake, Hona Asi brings in two glasses of ice cream she has bought at "the little shop round the corner." Appreciating how much this extra treat must have taken from their modest budget, the narrator tries to reimburse them—but they will have none of it. "They gave me to understand very emphatically that it was their treat, and I was forced to accept it, though I knew they could ill afford such extravagance." When the little son, Hakadaki, comes home from school, Jack does manage to slip "a Mexican dollar" into the boy's hand.

Following this pleasant experience, the story takes a tragic turn: Returning to Yokohama from a trip to Tokyo the next week, Jack fails to find Sakaicho at his usual stand and is forced to hire another rick-shaw driver. Since this is his last day ashore, he wants to do a bit more sightseeing in the city. Late that afternoon he spots a funeral procession. Overtaking it, he is shocked to see a group of natives bearing two plain, white wooden caskets on their shoulders, followed by a solitary mourner: Sakaicho. "But O! how changed! Aroused by my coming he slowly raised his listless head, and, with dull, apathetic glance, returned my greet-ing." Jack learns from his rickshaw driver that a fire had swept through Sakaicho's neighborhood, destroying his house and suffocating his wife and child. When they reach the grave, priests from a nearby Buddhist temple chant the requiem.

> With glassy eye, Sakaicho followed the movements of the priests, and, when the last clod had been thrown on, he erected a memorial stone to his loved ones. Then he turned away, to place among the mementos before his household God two little wooden tablets, marked with the name and date of birth and death of his wife and boy, while I returned in haste to my ship.

London's accurate description of the local setting, customs, and cuisine suggests firsthand experience. Furthermore, after missing his chance to enjoy the natural splendors of the Bonin Islands, he may have spent more of his two weeks ashore getting outside the saloons on the Yokohama waterfront. Worth noting, regardless, is the compassion for his fellow human beings in many different cultures, a quality that man-ifests itself time and again in his works, fiction as well as nonfiction.

When the *Sophia Sutherland* docked in San Francisco on August 26, 1893, Jack realized that his earnings from the voyage would be needed for his family. Instead of squandering those earnings as most of his shipmates would do, he took the ferry over to Oakland. Five years afterward, in a letter to Mabel Applegarth, he explained the sense of duty he felt:

> When I returned from seven months at sea, what did I do with my pay day? I bought a second-hand hat, some forty-cent shirts, two fifty-cent suits of underclothes, and a second-hand coat and vest. I spent exactly

seventy cents for drinks among the crowd I had known before I went to sea. The rest went to pay the debts of my father and to the family.

Even while his prospects were less dismal than those of the bereaved Japanese rickshaw driver, his present call to duty was a far cry from the voice of the sea.

5

THE DREAM AS NIGHTMARE

I still believed in the old myths which were the heritage of the American boy when I was a boy . . . Any boy who took employment with any firm, could, by thrift, energy, and sobriety, learn the business and rise from position to position until he was taken in as a junior partner. After that the senior partnership was only a matter of time.

—JOHN BARLEYCORN

Jack London could hardly have picked a less opportune year than 1893 to trade adventure for business. Eighteen ninety-three was the most crucial year of the 1890s. This was the year in which a young professor from the University of Wisconsin delivered a paper at the annual convention of the American Historical Society that established a new field of historiography. "American social development has been continually beginning over again on the frontier," he announced:

This perennial rebirth, this fluidity of American life, this expansion westward with its new opportunities, its continuous touch with the simplicity of primitive society, furnish the forces dominating American character. And now, four centuries from the discovery of America, at the end of a hundred years of life under the Constitution, the frontier has gone, and with its going has closed the first period of American history.

The speaker was Frederick Jackson Turner, and his declaration contains the essence of the famous "Turner Thesis." The frontier had vanished, according to Turner, and vanished with it was the dream of a new earthly paradise that had entranced a multitude of various adventurers and pilgrims from the Old World:

> Since the days when the fleet of Columbus sailed into the waters of the New World, America has been another name for opportunity, and the people of the United States have taken their tone from the incessant expansion which has not only been open but has even been forced upon them . . . But never again will such gifts of free land offer themselves.

If there was a touch of nostalgia in Turner's pronouncement, such was the only proper attitude for the late-nineteenth-century historian. Civilization had come to a crossroads, and America had already chosen its path. That path clearly departed from the Jeffersonian ideal of the yeoman farmer as mainstay of American democracy and led toward a more heavily industrialized civilization, with all its attendant economic and social problems. One such problem was the risk of severe economic recession. Eighteen ninety-three was consequently the year of the catastrophe that came to be known as the Great Panic, and it ushered in one of the darkest periods in American economic history. Without the protection of government or unions, workers' wages hit new lows while the number of individuals out of work reached new highs. In a quixotic scheme to rescue the nation, Jacob Coxey, a wealthy quarry owner from Flora Wellman's home town, determined that he would lead an army of unemployed workers in protest to the steps of the Capitol in Washington, D.C.

As "General" Coxey was formulating his grand strategy, Jack London would be learning the facts about the new American system at a much lower rank. He had already been disabused of any romantic illusions about the life he had been leading before he left for the sea, and what he discovered on the Oakland waterfront when he returned home from his Pacific adventures confirmed his disillusionment:

> Nelson was gone—shot to death while drunk and resisting officers. His partner in that affair was lying in prison. Whisky Bob was gone.

Old Cole, Old Smoudge and Bob Smith were gone . . . French Frank, they said, was lurking up river, afraid to come down because of something he had done. Others were wearing stripes in San Quentin or Folsom . . . Fitzsimmons, with whom I had sailed on the Fish Patrol, had been stabbed in the lung through the back and had died a lingering death from tuberculosis.

He also discovered that money was scarcer than ever in the London household. John London's frail health prevented his holding down any kind of regular job, and his veteran's pension was too small to cover living expenses. Jack's most depressing discovery was that he was worth no more on the labor market than he had been at the age of fourteen. He managed to find a job in the jute mills, but the pay was only ten cents an hour.

Despite this dreary labor, there were a few bright spots in his life during the fall of 1893. One was his rediscovery of the Oakland Public Library and the realization that he could now read "with greater understanding." Another was his friendship with Louis Shattuck, "a real innocently devilish young fellow who was quite convinced that he was a sophisticated town-boy." Unlike Louis, Jack had no experience with "nice" girls. "I had been too busy being a man," he confessed. "This was an entirely new phase of existence which had escaped me. And when I saw Louis say good-by to me, raise his hat to a girl of his acquaintance, and walk on by her side down the sidewalk, I was made excited and envious. I, too, wanted to play this game."

To play the game, however, the boy had to know a girl. Jack had already "known" a number of women, but he was woefully ignorant in the matter of nice girls. He had no clue how, and no convenient way, to meet them. That was the problem. He was no longer in school. He belonged to no church. Having no more than a dollar a week for personal spending, he lacked the money to attend public dances. Louis, who knew how to get a girl, was some help, but he always took the prettiest girls for himself, leaving the "weak sisters" for his pal. When left on his own, Jack was surprisingly inept:

The trouble was that in this Arcadian phase of my history, I, who had come through, case-hardened, from the other side of life, was timid and bashful. Again and again Louis nerved me up. But I didn't know girls. They were strange and wonderful to me after my precocious man's life. I failed of the bold front and the necessary forwardness when the crucial moment came.

His luck changed one evening when he and Louis decided to attend a Salvation Army meeting. There he found himself seated next to a lovely young woman who had dropped in "out of curiosity" with her visiting aunt from the country. "I shall call her Haydee," he explains:

> She was between fifteen and sixteen . . . We did not speak, but in that great half-hour we glanced shyly at each other, and shyly avoided or as shyly returned and met each other's glances more than several times. She had a slender oval face. Her brown eyes were beautiful. Her nose was a dream, as was her sweet-lipped, petulant-hinting mouth. She wore a tam o'shanter, and I thought her brown hair was the prettiest shade of brown I had ever seen.

Through Louis, "because Haydee was not his style of girl," Jack found out her address as well as a girlfriend who would be willing to convey a note to her. Jack wrote the note, and for the next few weeks he came to know "all the sweet madness of boy's love and girl's love." He was at first dumbstruck. The "tough guy" who had been called "the Prince" by his fellow Oyster Pirates and who had made love to French Frank's girlfriend, Mamie, and others like her; who had drunk many of the toughest under the table; who had ridden the rails with the prestigious hobo moniker of "Sailor Jack"; who had sailed halfway around the world as an able-bodied seaman; who had bloodied many a nose, including his own, as a barroom brawler—this manly, world-worn veteran was timidly tongue-tied in the presence of a nice young woman. "I didn't know the first thing I might say or do with this slender little chit of a girl-woman whose scant skirt just reached her shoe-tops and who was as abysmally ignorant of life as I was, or thought I was, profoundly wise."

One "starlight evening," as the two sat a foot apart on a park bench, Jack wondering what he was expected to do, Haydee tapped his lips with "a tiny flirt" of her gloves in "mock reproof" for something he had said. "I was like to swoon with delight," he recalled. "It was the most wonderful thing that had ever happened to me. And I remember yet the faint scent that clung to those gloves and that I breathed in the moment they touched my lips." The affair lasted only a few weeks and no more than "a dozen stolen meetings" and a dozen brief and innocent kisses. "We never went anywhere—not even to a matinee. We once shared together five cents' worth of red-hots. But I have always fondly believed that she loved me. I know I loved her; and I dreamed day dreams of her for a year or more, and the memory of her is very dear."

"Haydee" may have been Lucy Ann Cauldwell, the daughter of well-to-do citizens, Isaac and Marie Cauldwell. As a young man, Isaac Cohen had married Marie Craddock, his African American sweetheart, left his Jewish home in the East, changed his name to Cauldwell, and moved to California in 1855. Lucy's mixed racial heritage may explain why she was not Louis Shattuck's "style of girl." Because of his relationship with the Prentiss family, Jack's own connection with the black community in Oakland was more intimate and longer lived than has been generally recognized. According to the author Eugene Lasartemay, Lucy was Jack's first sweetheart, and "They were so close and such a beautiful couple together that some of us believed there would be a marriage." The probability of such a union was slim, considering not only the influence of Flora and other members of the white community but also the fact that, in terms of their economic situation, the Cauldwells' status was higher than the Londons'.

In addition to the brief love affair with "Haydee," there was another bright spot in Jack's life that fall. On October 27, 1893, *The San Francisco Call* announced a contest for young writers under the age of twenty-two with the prize of twenty-five dollars for the winner. The announcement caught the attention of Flora London. She was aware of her son's knack for telling a good story. She was also aware of the family's need for cash. Twenty-five dollars was nearly a month's factory wages. That evening when Jack arrived home, she showed him the newspaper and urged him to enter the contest. At first he hesitated:

"Only, what shall I write about?" he asked.

"Oh, why not tell about something you did or saw in Japan, or at sea," Flora suggested.

Suddenly brightening, he decided to go for the prize. With a surge of renewed energy, he ate a hasty supper, sat down at the kitchen table with pencil and an old school tablet, and began putting onto paper one of the most vivid memories from his voyage:

> It was four bells in the morning watch. We had just finished breakfast when the order came forward for the watch on deck to stand by to heave her to and all hands stand by the boats.
>
> "Port!—hard a port!" cried our sailing master. "Clew up the topsails! Let the flying jib run down! Back the jib over to windward and run down the foresail!" And so was our schooner *Sophie Sutherland* hove to off the Japan coast, near Cape Jerimo, on April 10, 1893.
>
> Then came moments of bustle and confusion. There were eighteen men to man the six boats. Some were hooking on the falls, others casting off the lashings, boat-steerers appeared with boat-compasses and water-breakers, and boat-pullers with lunch boxes. Hunters were staggering under two or three shotguns, a rifle and heavy ammunition box, all of which were soon stowed away with their oilskins and mittens in the boats . . .

Sustained by creative fervor and by the cups of steaming black coffee Flora kept bringing him, Jack wrote on through the night, stopping only for breakfast at five thirty the next morning before returning to work at the mill. This regimen was repeated the following night, and on the third night, "in a wakeful trance of exhaustion," he made his final revisions. That morning, the day of the deadline, Flora herself took the ferry over to San Francisco and hand-delivered the manuscript to *The Call*. She may have been the only person who consistently supported Jack's ambition to make writing his career, and his recognition of that support is apparent in the inscription he wrote when he presented her with a copy of *The God of His Fathers*:

> To my mother—
> —who has travailed sore with me in the making of men & women to breathe & move & do things in the printed pages of a book.
>   May 22, 1901   JACK

His "Story of a Typhoon off the Coast of Japan" was awarded first prize—winning over entries from students at Stanford and the University of California—and was printed in the Sunday, November 11, issue of *The Call*. John London was so proud of his son's achievement that he bought multiple copies of the paper to distribute among his friends.

Elated by his award, Jack jotted down another piece within the week and promptly sent it to *The Call*, which just as promptly rejected it. To put bread on the family table, he had to put his literary dreams on hold. Still, there was obviously no real future in unskilled labor. He would learn a trade. Electricity was a bright new industry; he would try that. There might be an opening for him at the power plant of the Oakland, San Leandro and Haywards Electric Railway. He went directly to the superintendent and explained that his ambition was to become a practical electrician. He also announced that he wasn't afraid of hard work. He was willing to begin at the bottom and work his way up to the top.

> The superintendent beamed as he listened. He told me that I was the right stuff for success, and that he believed in encouraging American youth that wanted to rise. Why, employers were always on the lookout for young fellows like me, and alas, they found them all too rarely. My ambition was fine and worthy, and he would see to it that I got my chance. (And as I listened with swelling heart, I wondered if it was his daughter I was to marry.)

The superintendent explained that to fully understand how the power plant supplied electricity, the young aspirant needed to work in the fire room, with the coal. "Now, are you prepared to begin?" he asked.

"The sooner the better," Jack eagerly replied.

Sooner it was: he began at seven o'clock the next morning. He would work ten hours a day, including Sundays, with one day off each month for thirty dollars a month. This was hardly what he had envisioned even at the bottom rung of the ladder—no better, in fact, than what he had earned working in the cannery and the jute mill—but this was different. He rationalized: "I was beginning to work for skill, for a trade, for career and fortune and the superintendent's daughter."

Unfortunately for him at the time, his work in the power plant led to neither career nor fortune—nor the superintendent's daughter. What he did not realize until later was that he was taking the place of two men—one for the day, another for the night shift—whom the superintendent had fired to save expenses.

> Work! I did more than the two men whom I had displaced. They had merely wheeled in the coal and dumped it on the plates. But while I did this for the day coal, the night coal I had to pile against the wall of the fire room. Now the fire room was small. It had been planned for a night coal-passer. So I had to pile the night coal higher and higher, buttressing up the heap with stout planks. Toward the top of the heap I had to handle the coal a second time, tossing it up with a shovel.

He struggled on until eight thirty that evening, then finally cleaned up, changed his dust-covered working outfit, and staggered to the streetcar that would take him home. He had received a pass allowing him to ride free—so long as all the paying passengers had seats. He collapsed into a seat, hoping no paying passenger would need it. The car was full, and when a woman got on, Jack felt compelled to let her have his seat, but when he struggled to get up, he discovered that he couldn't move: "With the chill wind blowing on me, my spent body had stiffened into the seat. It took me the rest of the run to unkink my complaining joints and muscles and get into a standing position on the lower step. And when the car stopped at my corner I nearly fell to the ground when I stepped off."

He managed to limp home the rest of the way, exhausted and famished. Flora had been waiting to cook his favorite pan-fried steak for supper, but before she could finish preparing the meal, he fell asleep at the table. She couldn't even rouse him enough to eat and needed John's help getting him undressed and into his bed. She managed to wake him and get him up the next morning despite his agony: "I was terribly sore, and worst of all my wrists were swelling. But I made up for my lost supper, eating an enormous breakfast, and when I hobbled to catch my car I carried a lunch twice as big as the one the day before."

His second day was more nightmarish than his first. The long hours of heavy work took a toll on his wrists:

There are few who do not know the pain of walking on a sprained ankle. Then imagine the pain of shoveling coal and trundling a loaded wheelbarrow with two sprained wrists . . . That second day was my hardest, and all that enabled me to survive it and get in the last of the night coal at the end of thirteen hours was the day fireman, who bound both my wrists with broad leather straps . . . They took the stresses and pressures which hitherto had been borne by my wrists, and they were so tight that there was no room for the inflammation to rise in the sprains.

So continued his initiation into the alleged trade of "practical electrician" for the next four weeks: struggling with Flora's help at daybreak to pull his pain-wracked body out of bed in time to wolf down his breakfast, carrying bigger and bigger lunches to work in his dinner pail, staggering back home at night too tired to finish his supper, helped into bed by his parents for a few precious hours of dreamless sleep. No time now for reading his library books, much less for dating girls. He had become, as he recalled, "a proper work-beast." There was only the mindless and meaningless cycle of working, eating, and sleeping.

The break came when the day fireman risked his own job by revealing the ruse: the two men whom Jack replaced had been paid forty dollars each, and Jack was doing all their work for a mere thirty dollars a month. In short, he had been "taken in." Instead of making an electrician out of him, the company was making fifty dollars a month out of him. As a matter of pride as well as financial necessity, he continued on the job until he got his month's pay.

The nightmare caused him no permanent physical damage; he quit the job in time to prevent that. However, the experience permanently altered his attitude toward manual labor. The very idea of physical work had become sickening. Never again would he voluntarily subject himself to that kind of ordeal: "The thought of work was repulsive. I didn't care if I never settled down. Learning a trade could go hang. It was a whole lot better to royster and frolic over the world in the way I had previously done. So I headed out on the adventure path again."

This time, the path would lead him to a frightful misadventure, one that would transform his view of the world and his rightful place in it.

6

THE OPEN ROAD

I became a tramp—well, because of the life that was in me, of the wanderlust in my blood that would not let me rest.

—FROM *THE ROAD*

"Seeking"—Jack calls it "wanderlust"—was in his blood and clearly would not let him rest. If the sea had served as his Harvard, "the Road"— and by this he meant the railroad—was his Yale. The "open road" was a distinctive American metaphor, representing adventure and freedom, with more than a hint of bravado and rebellion. Here was another major facet of the American Dream: the other side of the coin from the Myth of Success. James Fenimore Cooper and Walt Whitman as well as Mark Twain had romanticized the dream of "lightin' out for the territory." By the end of the nineteenth century, because of the rapid development of the American railroad system in the post–Civil War era, the dreamer could avail himself of a much faster means of travel. Also, by the end of the nineteenth century, because of the nation's economic crisis, "hitting the road" had become a necessity for many Americans. With no operative system of workman's compensation or welfare, the jobless man's options were limited: starve or become an outlaw—or take to the road. Hence, the hobo or tramp.

Although London's own joblessness was in this instance a matter of personal choice, his decision to hit the road in search of adventure again coincided with matters of greater historical significance. At the same time Jack was getting his fill of coal shoveling, a thirty-two-year-old

San Francisco printer and student of sociology named Charles T. Kelly was organizing an "Industrial Army." This was one of several western contingents of Coxey's Army of the Unemployed (or, as it came to be called, the Commonweal of Christ). Coxey's plan was a widely publicized cross-continent march designed to climax in a massive protest at the nation's capital at noon on May Day 1894.

Frank Leslie's Illustrated Weekly (May 3, 1894) described Kelly as a "mild-mannered young man" of few apparent vices: "He declined a drink of bourbon with a gesture when proffered by a wicked citizen. He said he used no tobacco when offered a cigar. He is evidently a man of considerable refinement and culture." The magazine noted further that Kelly's army was superior to Coxey's in both organization and discipline. Before acceptance, every member was required to register and to sign a pledge that he would "support the Constitution [and] never act in any manner to bring discredit upon the Industrial Army of the United States."

By the early morning hours of Friday, April 6, 1894, General Kelly and his duly appointed officers had convened with some seven hundred recruits at the Oakland depot. A score of different vocations and trades were represented in the group. Most members were day laborers and factory workers, along with out-of-work farmhands and miners. However, a census conducted by students at Drake University when the army reached Des Moines revealed more than eighty different trades, including barber, bookbinder, confectioner, comb maker, shoemaker, printer, stenographer, gunsmith, jockey, wood-carver, and ropewalker. Shortly after sunrise, the army pulled out from Oakland in twenty-four boxcars. Their destination: Washington, D.C.

Here was the opportunity Jack wanted. It provided the perfect alibi for the industrial work-beast's apostasy and at the same time promised exciting new worlds to conquer. He persuaded a pal, Frank Davis, to go along with him. Unaware that Kelly had been forced by the officials to leave before dawn, the two missed the army's departure. Determined to catch up with the group—and aided by the ten-dollar gold piece given Jack by Eliza—Jack and Frank bought tickets on the afternoon train to Sacramento. With the instinct of the born writer, Jack sensed that this new adventure would provide raw material to be transformed, someday, into print, and he decided to begin keeping a journal:

FRIDAY APR. 6.
Left Oakland Mole [Railway Station] at 4:30 p.m. & arrived at Sacra-
mento at 8 p.m. Went up to the Mississippi Kitchen & had supper.
Learning that the Industrial Army had arrived at noon & departed for
Ogden at 4. Went down & caught the 10 p.m. Overland bound East.

"Caught" means they "decked" the eastbound passenger train without
paying. This becomes clear in his next day's entry: "We held her down
all night till we arrived at Truckee at 7 a.m. As it was broad day light it
was impossible to proceed further." In other words, they could no longer hide from sight. He boasts that they succeeded in forcing the railroad officials to stop the train twice before they were finally "ditched."
He also notes that he and Frank decided at this juncture it would be
wise to send their suitcases back home by Wells Fargo before attempting any further exploits.

That evening they became separated when Frank managed to catch
the eight o'clock Overland while Jack was accidentally left behind. Shortly
before midnight Jack caught an eastbound freight train, hoping to
catch up with his buddy in Wadsworth. He was able to ride undis-
turbed in one of the boxcars but fell asleep and woke up only after the
car had been sidetracked in Reno.

His Sunday entry becomes more interesting:

Woke up at 3:30 a.m. half froze to death. I climbed out & walked
about till my circulation was restored when I sought shelter in the
Restaurant . . . Morning ablutions by the banks of the Truckee River.
Mourned the loss of the clothes brush & comb with Frank, but still
have the novel & soap. Went down the road & watched them loading
cattle & pigs . . . Watched the Indians gambling & listened to the salvation army & unemployed congregated on the corner. They are making
up an army & expect to start east tomorrow. All along the line from
Oakland on, we have met hundreds chasing the first detachment of the
industrial army.

On Monday he checked general delivery at the Reno Post Office,
where he received a card from Frank in Winnemucca. After a day's
delay in Wadsworth, he managed to hop a freight to Winnemucca,

arriving at 4:00 a.m. on Tuesday, April 10—without coat or overcoat, both of which had caught fire from a burning cinder. Later that morning, walking back from mailing a card home at the post office, he met Frank with "Great rejoicing & congratulations."

Their rejoicing was short-lived. Frank had decided he'd had more than enough of hoboing. "The road has no more charm for him," Jack jotted in his diary:

> The romance & adventure is gone & nothing remains but the stern reality of the hardships to be endured. Though he has decided to turn West again I am sure the experience has done him good, broadened his thoughts, given a better understanding of the low strata of society & surely will have made him more charitable to the tramps he will meet hereafter when he is in better circumstances.

For Jack, the road still promised "romance and adventure." It would be a few months before "the stern reality of the hardships to be endured" would deepen and broaden his own "understanding of the low strata of society." In the meantime, he pushed on to catch up with General Kelly's army in Omaha.

He caught up with the "after-push" of the army, the Reno detachment of some eighty strong, during a snowstorm at the Ames Monument, the summit of the Rockies, near Laramie, on the night of April 17. He found the men crowded together, most of them asleep or trying to sleep, on the straw in a sidetracked refrigerator car. "I climbed aboard & made myself at home," he simply recorded at the time. Fourteen years afterward, he wrote more dramatically about his initiation into the army:

> Up I climbed and in. I stepped on a man's leg, next on some other man's arm. The light was dim, and all I could make out was arms and legs and bodies inextricably confused . . . The men I stepped on were resentful. Their bodies heaved under me like the waves of the sea, and imparted an involuntary forward movement to me. I could not find any straw to step upon, so I stepped upon some men. The resentment increased, so did my forward movement . . . It was like going through a threshing-machine. I was bandied about from one end of the car to

the other. Those eighty-four hoboes winnowed me out till what little was left of me, by some miracle, found a bit of straw to rest upon.

Next morning, as the car pulled out, he was more formally inducted into the army. He told the group's leader, "Lieutenant" H. R. Lytle, that his real name was Jack London but that he was called Sailor Jack. Lytle remembered him as "a young man of about twenty, with round features and dark curly hair. He wore a chinchilla coat, a novel in each pocket, and a cap pulled well down over his head. His flannel shirt, shoes, and trousers had seen better days."

At 1:00 a.m. on April 19, the Reno Regiment arrived in Omaha, where they were met by a platoon of local police and herded across the Missouri River to Council Bluffs, Iowa. The weather was miserable (cold, driving rain mixed with sleet) and Kelly's army was camped at the Chautauqua park five miles outside town. The group started to march there on foot, but Jack and a fellow hobo called "the Swede" decided to stay behind, seeking shelter for the night in a derelict saloon. It was locked up, but impelled by the freezing wind and rain, they smashed through the door and stumbled into what they hoped was sanctuary. Jack's diary entry is once again succinct: "We went to sleep in a bar room which was being moved . . . I arose at five, said good bye to the Swede, & catching a freight train was eating breakfast in Omaha at 6." His later account is livelier:

I have made some tough camps in my time . . . bedded in pools of water, slept in the snow under two blankets when the spirit thermometer registered seventy-four degrees below zero . . . but I want to say right here that never did I make a tougher camp, pass a more miserable night, than that night I passed in Council Bluffs. In the first place, the building perched up as it was in the air, had exposed a multitude of openings in the floor through which the wind whistled. In the second place, the bar was empty; there was no bottled fire-water with which we could warm ourselves and forget our misery. We had no blankets, and in our wet clothes, wet to the skin, we tried to sleep [but the] holes and crevices in the floor made it impossible . . . And there we shivered and prayed for daylight . . . The Swede moaned and groaned, and every little while, through chattering teeth, he muttered, "Never again; never again." He muttered the phrase repeatedly, ceaselessly, a thousand times; and when he dozed, he went on muttering it in his sleep.

They survived the night, leaving what Jack called their "house of pain" as day broke. Half frozen and stiff-jointed, they hobbled back down to the railroad track. Their moment for parting had come:

> Our palsied hands went out to each other. We were both shivering. When we tried to speak, our teeth chattered us back into silence ... We stared dumbly at each other, our clasped hands shaking sympathetically. The Swede's face was blue with the cold ...
> "Never again what?" I managed to articulate ...
> "Never again a hobo. I'm going to get a job. You'd better do the same. Nights like this make rheumatism."

Yet Jack wasn't ready to abandon hoboing for a job; adventure still beckoned. After parting with the Swede, he hopped a freight car back across the river and was eating breakfast in Omaha by 6:00 a.m. After breakfast, he spent a couple of hours strolling about town, then—thanks to a sympathetic farmer who gave him a wagon ride across the toll bridge and to Camp Chautauqua—he joined Company L of the Industrial Army at ten thirty that morning. He had arrived just in time, for the army began marching out at 11:00 a.m. "The Army made quite an imposing array, with flags & banners & Gen. Kelly at their head on a fine black horse presented by an enthusiastic Council Bluffs citizen," he noted.

By the time the army reached the town of Weston that evening, the cold rain had turned into sleet and hail that was "coming down in torrents." Despite the weather, they managed to build fires and "made quite a meal in stew, bread & coffee." After supper, as the north wind became "bitter cold," the troops "scattered in search of lodgings." Three hundred were given permission to sleep in a grain elevator. Another hundred or so found shelter in a barn, where Jack climbed up into the hay loft. "Just as I was settled comfortably, the muffled crys [sic] of a cat aroused me & on digging, in the hay beneath my head, found a cat with a litter of kittens. A big Irishman & I pretty near had a fight. He wanted to throw them out in the storm, but I told him when he threw them out he threw me. The cat & kittens stayed."

The men—aside from General Kelly, astride his fine black charger—were now moving on foot because the railroads had decided it was against their own best interests to provide free transportation for a gang of unemployed protesters whose numbers had by this time grown to nearly two thousand. Having covered nearly two-thirds of their planned itinerary, Kelly and his men were in no mood to give up. In response to Kelly's widely broadcast appeals, the citizens of Iowa donated enough horses and wagons to carry supplies so that the army could march on toward the nation's capital and toward the planned rendezvous with Coxey's Commonweal of Christ.

The citizens were more sympathetic than the railroad operators, who not only denied access to their trains but also hired Pinkerton's private detectives to infiltrate and make trouble within the ranks of the army. Because of the railroads' reputation for shady dealings, the great majority of Iowans welcomed the opportunity to come to Kelly's aid. One group, including some of the railroad's own men, stole a Union Pacific train for the army. When Kelly refused the "gift" on principle, he was warmly praised by the Iowa press.

By April 22 the weather had warmed and the army had marched twenty miles from Weston, as far as Neola. But Jack was no longer able to march. His shoes were worn out, and he had walked a whole day barefoot when the commissary could not provide replacements. When he was finally given a new pair, they raised such blisters that he was worse off than before. "I walked 6 miles to the town of Walnut enduring the severest torture & arrived in a most horrible condition," he wrote on April 24. "I resolved to go no further on foot." Because his feet were so badly blistered, he was allowed to ride on one of the commissary wagons for several miles. However, his diary entry of April 30 records that he managed to walk the last fifteen miles into Des Moines.

The army spent the next week and a half in Des Moines, which gave Jack's battered feet time to heal. It was also a time of fun and games. On May 1, 1894, while General Coxey and his troops were being arrested for trespassing on the Capitol lawn, Kelly's army was celebrating May Day in proper American style. Jack records that the soldiers got up a football team and beat "the Des Moines boys" 27–19. His company "spent the evening around the fire singing and joking" until they went to bed at eleven.

Years afterward London had only the fondest memories of "the fat Iowa country" and "the hospitable Iowa farmer-folk":

> They turned out with their wagons and carried our baggage; gave us hot lunches by noon by the wayside; mayors of comfortable little towns made speeches of welcome and hastened us on our way; deputations of little girls and maidens came out to meet us, and the good citizens turned out by the hundreds, locked arms, and marched with us down their main streets. It was circus day when we came to town, and every day was circus day, for there were many towns.

But practical concerns would ultimately overcome hospitality in Des Moines. Tired of marching, the army vowed to go no farther on foot. During these warm spring days, they loafed, made political speeches, and played cards or baseball; in the evenings, they danced, sang, and told stories. During the entire time, they were living off the fat of the town and the surrounding land: two thousand men consuming three free meals a day. After a week, their hosts' patience as well as their resources began to run thin. Des Moines officials asked the railroads for help, but their pleas were rejected. The city was growing desperate, until some bright citizen provided a solution:

> We wouldn't walk. Very good. We should ride. From Des Moines to Keokuk on the Mississippi flowed the Des Moines River. This particular stretch of river was three hundred miles long. We could ride on it, said the local genius; and, once equipped with floating stock, we could ride on down the Mississippi to the Ohio, thence up the Ohio, winding up with a short portage over the mountains to Washington.

The city rallied to the idea, contributing money for lumber and nails to build enough flatboats to float the army on its way. There ensued "a tremendous era of shipbuilding" on the banks of the Des Moines River—and on May 9, the army was under way.

"Sailor Jack" was once again in his element: "I knew boats and boating." He also knew hustling. He was a virtuoso in "throwing his feet" for handouts. Because of these skills, he and the nine fellow boatmen—who christened their boat the *Pirate*—lived high on the hog for the next two weeks. Jack's diary reads simply, "Living fine." The full story, as told later, was that "the invincibles," as these ten rugged individualists called themselves, were managing to race a half day to a day ahead of the rest of the army. They decorated the boat with several American flags and, on reaching each town or gathering of farmers, announced that they were the advance guard of the army, sent ahead to gather food and supplies. As a result, they benefited from the initial bounty of provisions.

General Kelly discovered the scam soon enough and took measures to put a stop to it. First he sent out a couple of scouts in a light boat to "arrest" the miscreants, but, being outnumbered five to one, the scouts backed down and, instead, raced on to the next town to call on the police for help. The "invincibles," alerted to the danger, tied up until nightfall and slipped past the town in the dark. Next, Kelly sent two men ahead on horseback, one on each bank of the river, to warn farmers and townspeople. This worked. As Jack was returning to the boat a couple of days later, he found himself suddenly pursued by lawmen with a pack of dogs: "Two of the latter caught me with a barbed-wire fence between me and the river. I was carrying two buckets of milk for the pale Vienna [coffee brewed with milk]. I didn't damage the fence any; but we drank plebeian coffee boiled with vulgar water, and it was up to me to throw my feet for another pair of trousers."

On Saturday, May 19, the army reached the Mississippi River, and all the boats were lashed together to form one gigantic raft. Bad weather delayed them a day, but on Monday they headed downriver and, with the help of a steamboat that towed them partway, made the forty miles to Quincy, Illinois. Once again, Jack proved to be exceptionally talented not only as a boat handler but also as a panhandler. H. R. Lytle recalled that although "opposed to violent exercise" and such practical work as hauling wood and water, London was useful when it came to begging for handouts. While the rest of the soldiers were busy at more common work, Lytle appointed him to find replacements for the company's badly worn clothing. Jack quickly accepted the assignment when told that Quincy, Illinois, was the richest town of its size in the United States: "When I heard this, I was immediately overcome by an irresistible impulse to throw my feet. No 'blowed-in-the-glass profesh' could possibly pass up such a promising burg. I crossed the river to Quincy in a small dug-out; but I came back in a large river-boat, down to the gunwales with the results of my thrown feet." He kept for himself the cash and the best of all the clothes he had collected, and gave his crew their pick of the rest before turning over "a respectable heap" to Company L. He was "young and prodigal in those days," he confesses: "I told a thousand 'stories' to the good people of Quincy, and every story was 'good'; but since I have come to write for the magazines I have often regretted the wealth of story, the fecundity of fiction, I lavished that day in Quincy, Illinois."

However, even with his Quincy windfall, the week had been unpleasant. The full import of Coxey's anticlimactic May Day arrest for trespassing on the Capitol grounds, news of which had reached them in Des Moines, was now soaking in. Discipline had begun to deteriorate along with morale. No longer were there the adrenaline boosts of outmaneuvering General Kelly. Bad weather, with driving rains and chilling winds, had returned. The commissary was running short of food. Jack's diary entries become increasingly dispirited. May 21: "We had nothing to eat from six the day before till five to day." And three days later, after arriving at Hannibal, Missouri: "We went supperless to bed. Am going to pull out in the morning. I can't stand starvation."

On Saturday, May 25, he left camp with his pal the "Boiler Maker," rowed across the river to Illinois, and rode a handcar to Hulls, where they encountered four other deserters. During the weekend the six went separate ways, and on Monday, Jack caught a cattle train, which he rode all night into Chicago. On Tuesday, May 29, he jotted in his diary: "Arrived in Chicago at 7 a.m. Strolled down to the Post Office & found 9 letters, one registered awaiting me. Received $4 in Greenbacks."

Among the letters awaiting him were several from Flora, including the following:

Dear Son—
I sent you a few lines this afternoon as soon as I received your postal of the 16th and mailed it immediately that you should know immediately that there were some 8 or 10 letters at Chicago waiting for you each one of which contains stamps, paper and envelopes, two of which contains money in greenbacks . . . which you must stand very much in

need of . . . John take good care of yourself, and do not under any circumstances fight, if it should come to that. Remember you are all I have and both papa and I are growing old and you are all we have to look to in our old age . . . When we did not get a letter for three weeks I worried so that I could neither eat or sleep, but Papa would always say "never mind Jack, he knows how to take care of himself, and he will make his mark yet." John, Papa builds great expectations of your future success . . . John under no circumstances place yourself in a position to be imprisoned, you have gone to see the country and not to spend your time behind bars. Be careful of fever and ague that is the bane of the East . . . Now my dear son take good care of yourself and remember our thoughts and best wishes for your success, happiness and safe return are always with you.

WITH LOTS OF LOVE, PAPA, MAMA AND SISTER.

This letter provides a sympathetic insight into Flora's character. There is a genuine concern for the well-being of her son as the future family breadwinner, and she knows his love of danger and his penchant for fighting. Furthermore, the stamps and greenbacks could not have come easily to Flora and John. (The money may have come from Eliza.) Her closing sentiments reveal a tender affection rarely attributed to his mother by either London or his biographers. Finally, her letter contains a couple of noteworthy hints, one favorable, the other ominous: "Papa builds great expectations of your future success"; "you have gone to see the country and not to spend your time behind the bars." Both were prophetic.

Also included in Jack's diary entry for May 29 is the information that he used some of his money to refit himself with "shoes, overcoat, hat, pants & shirt. Then with a shave & a good dinner I started out to see the sights. Went to the theater in the evening, & then to bed. The first bed I had lain in since leaving home."

On May 31 he wrote the last entry in his tramp diary: "Went out in the morning to Lincoln Park & at 12 took the steamer City of Chicago for St. Joseph, Mich. It is a 60 mile & a half run across Lake Michigan. I found Aunt Mary lived a mile & a half from town, but I was soon there receiving a hearty welcome."

Mary Everhard took an immediate liking to her nephew. "Mother was greatly pleased at his coming," her son Harry wrote to Charmian after Jack's death. "Took him down town and rigged him out in a suit of store clothes, and gave little parties for him, inviting those of his age or a little older." Harry Everhard said that in his mother's eye Jack was "a 'hero,' and she just worshipped him." The affection was evidently mutual, for Jack stayed with the Everhards nearly a month before resuming his tramping. While there, he regaled Aunt Mary with tales of his adventures and with his plans for becoming a writer. Delighted that her little sister's son had turned out to be so talented, she listened with enthusiasm, assuring him that writing was his true calling.

Eager after he had rested and fattened up to resume his tramping version of the Grand Tour, he left St. Joseph near the end of June, heading east. First on his list of sights to see was Niagara Falls. He rode into the city in a "side-door Pullman" (boxcar) on the afternoon of June 28 and went directly to the great falls. So entranced was he that he lingered to watch the running water by moonlight until nearly midnight. After "flopping" in a hayfield outside town, he arose at five the next morning to see the falls in the dawn light—a sight he would never enjoy: On his way there he was arrested, without warning or due cause, for vagrancy and sentenced without trial to thirty days in the Erie County Penitentiary.

The official prison records give no clue to the horrors he witnessed during his incarceration or to the profound and lasting impression they made upon him: "On June 29, 1894, one John Lundon [sic], age 18; Single: Father & Mother Living, occupation—Sailor; Religion—Atheist—was received at the Erie County Penitentiary, for a term of 30 Days, charge of Tramp, sentenced by Police Justice Charles Piper—Niagara Falls, New York; and was released on July 29, 1894."

Those thirty days were one of the most critical single months of his life. "It would take a deep plummet to reach the bottom of the Erie County Pen," he wrote afterward. "It was a living hell, that prison." The things he saw were worse than unprintable: "They were unthinkable to me until I saw them, and I was no spring chicken in the ways of the world and the awful abysses of human degradation." He describes in detail the graft, the lesser perversions—for example, the "stupidly carnivorous beast" who trapped live sparrows and ate them raw—and the beatings, or "manhandlings," but leaves to our imaginations some of the worst horrors. However, he does describe one instance of man-handling in unforgettable detail:

> I remember a handsome young mulatto of about twenty who got the insane idea into his head that he should stand up for his rights . . . He lived on the topmost gallery. Eight hall-men took the conceit out of him in just about a minute and a half—for that was the length of time required to travel along his gallery to the end and down five flights of steel stairs. He travelled the whole distance on every portion of his anatomy except his feet, and the eight hall-men were not idle. The mulatto struck the pavement where I was standing watching it all. He regained his feet and stood upright for a moment. In that moment he threw his arms wide apart and emitted an awful scream of terror and pain and heartbreak. At the same instant, as in a transformation scene, the shreds of his stout prison clothes fell from him, leaving him wholly naked and streaming blood from every portion of the surface of his body. Then he collapsed in a heap, unconscious. He had learned his lesson, and every convict within those walls who heard him scream had learned a lesson . . . It is not a nice thing to see a man's heart broken in a minute and a half.

The Erie County Pen did not succeed in breaking Jack's heart, but it taught him more than one lesson. Adaptability, he quickly learned, was the key to survival; Charles Darwin and Herbert Spencer were right about that. Rugged individualism could be fatal; Marx and Engels were right about that. Prison was no place for the American youth bound for success; his mother was right about that.

Fortune had spared him from the worst that the Erie County Pen might have inflicted. On the train ride from Niagara Falls he had made pals by sharing his tobacco with a veteran "con," who took him under his wing and instructed him in the ways of avoiding trouble, mainly to "go along" with the system if he expected to "get along." His new pal also managed to get him appointed to the gang of hall men who dominated the prisoners, thereby saving Jack from abuse and from work, while enabling him to participate in the highly organized system of graft that had evolved within the prison walls. "Oh, we were wolves, believe me," he confesses, "—just like the fellows who do business on Wall Street."

He even went so far as to help his buddy plan "jobs" they would pull together when they got out. On the day of their release, the two walked down into the town of Buffalo to celebrate with "shupers" of beer while they made final plans for their first job together. Between beers, telling his pal he was going to the toilet, Jack made a much longer trip, going out the back of the saloon and jumping a fence: "It was a swift sneak, and a few minutes later I was on board a freight and heading south on the Western New York and Pennsylvania Railroad."

Traumatic as the prison experience had been, it did not deter him from his plans to see the East Coast. He toured the capital, working for a while in a livery stable for his lodging; spent a few days in Baltimore, listening to the soapbox orators in Druid Hill Park; then went on up to New York, where he was more deeply impressed by the poverty and slums than by the skyscrapers; and from there traveled to Boston. As autumn approached and the winds grew chill, he decided it was time to think about heading back home. He made his way up to Montreal and Ottawa, outfitted himself with heavier clothing, and rode the rails across southern Canada to Vancouver, where he negotiated to stoke coal for his passage down the coast aboard the *Umatilla* (the same ship he would take to the Klondike two and a half years later). He arrived back in Oakland in early December.

Joan London asserts that 1894 was the most important year in her father's life. Probably no other year in his life was packed with experiences so transformational in their influence on his view of the world, especially on his view of his country. What had started out as a lark had turned into an odyssey. Ten years afterward, in his essay "How I Became a Socialist," he recollected how that journey had transformed him:

> On rods and blind baggages I fought my way from the open West, where men bucked big and the job hunted the man, to the congested labor centers of the East, where men were small potatoes and hunted the job for all they were worth. And on this new *blond-beast* adventure I found myself looking upon life from a new and totally different angle. I had dropped down from the proletariat into what sociologists love to

call the "submerged tenth," and I was startled to discover the way in which that submerged tenth was recruited.

These victims of a ruthless, unregulated economic system had been recruited just as he had been recruited as a "work-beast," and when worn out and broken by the relentless grind, they had been tossed into the pit of human destitution. Listening to their life stories, Jack experienced a dreadful vision of his own future:

> I saw the picture of the Social Pit as vividly as though it were a concrete thing, and at the bottom of the Pit I saw [myself] hanging on to the slippery wall by main strength and sweat. And I confess a terror seized me . . . there and then I swore a great oath . . . All my days I have worked hard with my body, and according to the number of days I have worked, by just that much am I nearer the bottom of the Pit. I shall climb out of the pit, but not by the muscles of my body shall I climb out . . . and may God strike me dead if I do another day's hard work with my body more than I absolutely have to do.

London realized that education would lead him out of the Pit. He also saw that his odyssey had wrought a philosophical transformation. He was no longer a "rampant individualist" but had become a "Socialist" without realizing it: "I had been reborn, but not renamed, and I was running around to find out what manner of thing I was. I ran back to California and opened the books." In January 1895 he stopped running long enough to enroll in Oakland High School. Within the next two years he would indeed "find out what manner of thing [he] was."

7

A MAN AMONG BOYS

The other students were not impressed or attracted by him; as
a classmate he was unsociable and discourteous. At times he
was even gruff to some of the pupils who wished to have him
join in the general conversations in the assembly hall before
the lesson . . . He wanted deep down in his being to be one with
the class, but he just couldn't.

—GEORGIA LORING BAMFORD

Jack had been "a boy among men" during his oyster-pirating days.
He found himself a man among boys when he entered Oakland High
School in January 1895. Though only slightly older in chronological
years, he was light-years older in experience. He had sailed across the
Pacific Ocean and tramped all the way across the North American con-
tinent. Furthermore, he had traveled in an underworld undreamt of by
his adolescent schoolmates, most of whom had spent their formative
years in the safe bourgeois sanctuaries of Victorian America. Georgia
Loring, one of those classmates, was fascinated by this uncouth stranger.
Thirty-five years later (as the widow of London's friend Frederick Irons
Bamford), she still remembered her vivid first impressions of Jack at the
noisy beginning of Mme. Grand-Pre's French class:

The teacher rapped vigorously on her desk and pleaded with the pupils
to get ready for roll call . . . I was intently watching the strange boy
who, slouched forward, his arms sprawled on his desk, seemed highly

amused. He looked about the room, turning half way around in his seat in order to get a better view, smiling superciliously . . . He wore a dark blue suit, much worn, mussed, wrinkled and ill-fitting and a woolen shirt without a tie. His face was ruddy and sunburned, and his tawny, disheveled hair looked as though he constantly ran his fingers through it. His general appearance was unbelievably shabby, careless and uncleanly, unlike anything I had ever seen in a school room.

This strange boy's supercilious smile masked a deeply rooted sense of alienation and insecurity. Here were youngsters from another world, a world he had read about but scarcely glimpsed. Even so, because this was America, he might aspire to gain passage into this strange other world, and education was the ticket. If Horatio Alger's newsboys and bootblacks could do it with a little luck and plenty of pluck, a hobo and ex-con might do as well. Jack had pluck to spare, and in 1895 he also had a bit of luck. Because John London's health had sufficiently improved to enable him to work part-time as a special officer for the Oakland Police Department, and Flora was earning a few dollars with her piano lessons and needlework, Jack was not forced to take a full-time job. Instead, he could manage financially with odd jobs while devoting his time and energy to his studies.

One of his odd jobs was that of school janitor, a job Eliza had helped him get. "Are you going to the old Oakland High School on Twelfth Street?" he wrote to his daughter Joan twenty years later:

If you are, please remember that I have swept every room in that old High School from garret to basement. Also, that I have hoisted the American flag every high school day for two terms on top of the old High School Building. Also, just for the fun of it, walk around the entire block occupied by the High School Building and look up at all the windows from the ground floor to the top floor and just get the idea into your head that every one of those windows I have washed in the past. I washed them inside and out.

Flora, always ambitious for her son, supported his Dream of Success. Aware that to make the dream come true his studying was essential, she turned one of the bedrooms in their house on Twenty-Second

Avenue into Jack's den, with a big, comfortable bed according to his special request:

> Opposite the big bed, squarely against the window-sill, he set a plain table large enough for study books and writing materials . . . and by the bed a small stand to carry a reading-lamp, one of the "student" variety, with books, scribble-pads, and pencils. In one corner a dresser, of the style with a long mirror, two large drawers, and several small ones rising on the right of the glass, took care of his meager wardrobe and shaving outfit.

The furnishings were completed by a chair at the table, which at night supplemented the small bedside lamp stand to hold a dish of fruit and his cigarettes and matches.

Like his hero in *Martin Eden*, he experimented with his sleeping hours, trying to find his absolute minimum: two, three, four, and finally five, which would be the regimen for the rest of his life. He also needed exercise, and a neighbor provided the means with a bicycle: a quaint old model with the huge front wheel and tiny rear wheel. Determined as always, he sweated morning after morning to master it. "At first," his sister Eliza recalled, "he was most of the time sprawled about the ground; and he'd come over to my house for breakfast—bruised, dripping wet and red in the face, his curls all tousled, fighting mad, and explaining carefully what slow work it was getting the best of the 'infernal machine!' Then he'd burst out laughing at the idea of how he must look when he tangled up and went down in a heap with it." She came to his rescue, buying a "safety wheel" so that he could ride with confidence and make the forty-block trip to high school in record time.

She was dismayed, when he laughed, by the large gap where his upper front teeth should have been; she was appalled, when she examined his open mouth, to discover that his remaining teeth were riddled with cavities; and she was disgusted to observe that when he didn't have a cigarette in his mouth, he had a "chaw."

"You ought to be ashamed of yourself," she scolded, "you needn't have a mouth like that if you'd taken half-decent care of it . . . And no brother of mine is going to take any chewing tobacco into High School in my town." After he explained that he chewed tobacco to deaden the pain in his aching teeth, she made a bargain: if he abandoned his "plug," she would pay to have his cavities filled and buy him a set of "upper-fronts." Accepting her offer, he got his new "uppers" and his first toothbrush.

"Well," he boasted to her after his upper plate had been adjusted, "here I am with my first store teeth and my first toothbrush I ever bought—I got them both at the same time, at nineteen years of age."

"Well," she retorted, "it's nothing to be proud of. It's your own fault because you knew better. I didn't bring you up that way! And I wouldn't brag about it before anybody."

Had he foreseen the ultimate consequences of his dental neglect, he would have had even less to brag about. His early failure to take proper care of his teeth initiated a lifelong series of excruciating visits to the dentist. Worse, his rotten teeth and infected gums with their systemic poisoning would later become a factor in his poor health.

Eliza also bought him a fine woolen suit, and although he could never be fully at ease with his high school classmates, his new teeth and carefully brushed new blue suit enabled him to mingle without undue embarrassment. Some thought him "awful conceited," while others remained intimidated by his reputation as "a tough," but he managed to find friends among members of the Aegis Publishing Company, the school's most popular student organization, and the Henry Clay Debating Society. Both groups would play important roles in his later success.

The Call had raised false literary hopes by publishing his prizewinning sketch in 1893. *The Aegis*, though nonpaying, gave him the kind of encouragement that comes only from seeing one's work in print on a regular basis. This biweekly literary journal, operated by and for Oakland High School students, published ten of his contributions in 1895, beginning with the January 18 issue. Even though the work of an amateur, these articles offer an accurate preview of the different kinds of writing that would make him famous a few years later: vivid firsthand descriptive sketches, semiautobiographical fiction based upon personal experience, dramatic narratives drawn from stories he had heard or read, self-created fantasies, and sociopolitical diatribes. "Bonin Islands" (I and II) and "The Run Across" are first-person sketches describing his Pacific experiences aboard the *Sophia Sutherland*. "Sakaicho, Hona Asi and Hakadaki," as previously mentioned, is based upon his brief stay in

Yokohama. "Frisco Kid's Story" and "Frisco Kid Came Back" are fictionalized episodes based upon his tramping experiences, patterned in dialect after Twain's *Huckleberry Finn.* "One More Unfortunate" is also a piece of fiction, based upon an evening Jack and Frank Atherton visited a "vile place" called the Bella Union Theatre on the Barbary Coast. "A Night's Swim in Yeddo Bay" may have been a recounting of one of Jack's own adventures.

By current standards, these sketches seem relatively mild, but by the standards of the Genteel Age, they were shocking. "The little middle-class boys and girls had never seen anything like them," Joan London observes, "—hunks of raw life hammered into words, inexpertly, but with undeniable effectiveness." Less shocking, and less effective, "Who Believes in Ghosts!" is a bit of pure juvenilia reflecting, aside from his spoof of supernaturalism, Jack's newfound interest in the game of chess. Of special note is "Pessimism, Optimism and Patriotism," which appeared in the March 1 issue, alarming the school's principal, faculty, and students alike. This brief essay is the first published evidence of London's conversion to socialism: "Arise, ye Americans, patriots and optimists!" he exhorts his bourgeois readers: "Awake! Seize the reins of a corrupted government and educate your masses!"

Jack did not officially join the Socialist Labor Party of Oakland until April 1896, but he had evidently come in contact with *The Communist Manifesto.* More dramatic than the publication of his essay was the later public debate described by Bamford:

> The Christmas week exercises, held in the Assembly Hall at the end of the High School term, were surely a climax. Pupils, parents, relatives and friends filled the place to capacity . . . One feature was a debate with Jack London as a chief participant . . . before people knew it their ears were being assailed by the most truculent Socialist diatribe that I have ever heard. He was ready to destroy society and civilization; to break down all resistance with any force and commit the most scientific atrocities . . . I do not remember all he said, but the terrible impression of his words will never leave me.

Jack had always been a good talker—indeed, he loved a good argument—and the Henry Clay Debating Society helped sharpen his argumentative skills as a public speaker. More than that, the club provided him access into the respectable social world through which he would have to travel on his road to success. One of the charter members of the society was Edward Applegarth, who would serve as Jack's major tour guide of this new social realm.

Edward M. "Ted" Applegarth Jr. (1876–1964) was a member of a distinguished upper-middle-class family. His father was a mining engineer, and his mother was a paragon of Victorian propriety. Canadian born of British parents, Edward Applegarth Sr., after earning his mining degree, moved to England, where he married Marie Louise Hoppen in 1872. Ten years later, aware of the better mining opportunities in California, he moved his family to America and settled in Oakland. According to Joan London, the Applegarths were "very long on British culture, refinement and tradition." Mrs. Applegarth, while "delicately built, with finely chiseled features, concealed beneath a yielding femininity many of the traits of an astute commander in chief" and proudly instilled the values of that culture into her two children, encouraging their appreciation of music, art, and literature.

The Applegarth children were important facilitators in Jack's upward move from the working-class world into that of the middle class. Ted became a confidant, pen pal, and lifelong friend, bringing Jack into his home and introducing him to his parents and, most important, his sister. Mabel Maude Applegarth was the first great love of London's life, and she would later serve as a model for Ruth Morse in *Martin Eden*. His description of Ruth, and Martin's reaction to her, is a mirror image of Mabel, and Jack's initial reaction to her: "She was a pale, ethereal creature, with wide, spiritual blue eyes and a wealth of golden hair . . . He likened her to a pale gold flower upon a slender stem. No, she was a spirit, a divinity, a goddess; such sublimated beauty was not of the earth."

Just as Ruth inspires Martin to read poets such as Browning and Swinburne, so Mabel served to animate Jack's finer aesthetic sensibilities. Like Martin, "He was extraordinarily receptive and responsive, while his imagination, pitched high, was ever at work establishing relations of likeness and difference." And while helping to widen his literary vision, Mabel, like Ruth, also opened his eyes to a deeper emotional need: "He had starved for love all his life. His nature craved love. It was an organic demand of his being. Yet he had gone without, and hardened himself in the process."

In the long run, like Martin, Jack would come to understand that the object of this love was just that, an object. As Martin realizes at the end of their affair, "He knew, now, that he had not really loved her. It was an idealized Ruth he had loved, an ethereal creature of his own creating, the bright and luminous spirit of his love-poems."

At the same time Jack was discovering a new world in the Applegarth home, he was also exploring another very different world. City Hall Park, near the high school, was Oakland's version of the famous Hyde Park in London, England. On his way from school or to the library, Jack fell into the habit of stopping to hear the orators harangue each other and the crowds, which usually gathered more in hopes of seeing fistfights between the speakers than of learning anything about their political ideologies.

The most brilliant among these street-corner orators was Frank Strawn-Hamilton, the eminent "tramp genius" who had been born to a family of the East Coast aristocracy but who had forsaken his social birthright for a unique brand of socialism. He was, in London's eyes, "a remarkable man, college-bred, qualified to practice law in all the courts, spilling over with the minutest details of every world-philosophy from Zeno to Nietzsche, deeply versed in political economy and sociology—in short, a genius of extraordinary caliber." Captivated by Strawn-Hamilton's encyclopedic knowledge and his eloquence, Jack eagerly sought him out as mentor and was introduced to Herbert Spencer, whose *First Principles* London would uncritically embrace as the Holy Scriptures.

Another socialist mentor, less scintillating than Strawn-Hamilton but no less important to Jack's intellectual growth, was Frederick Irons Bamford, associate librarian of the Oakland Free Public Library from 1895 to 1918. Joan London's portrait provides a clear sense of Bamford's character and of his contribution to her father's development, and to the enlightenment of other young aspirants:

A Canadian gentleman by birth and education, a Christian-Socialist by conviction, he brought to the provincial little library all that he could of the gentler cultural tradition of the late nineteenth century . . . He was greatly interested in young students, placing himself wholly at their disposal and searching always for a spark which he might fan into a blaze of devotion to knowledge for its own sake.

Under Bamford's tutelage, Jack found the library a congenial haven, roomier and more comfortable than his den at home. As often as his busy schedule would allow, he went there to read and study, and Bamford provided a steady hand in guiding him through the maze of new books he was discovering—not only Marx and Darwin but also cultural critics such as Arnold, Carlyle, and Ruskin. Their bond of friendship would last a lifetime.

A third important socialist friend was Herman "Jim" Whitaker. Whitaker had been a sports instructor in the British army before emigrating to western Canada in 1884. In 1895, after failing as a pioneer farmer (an experience he would fictionalize ten years afterward in *The Settler*), he moved with his wife and six small children to Oakland. There he found substantial support from members of the Socialist Labor Party, who hired him to run their cooperative grocery store. One afternoon, taking special note of the bright-eyed young man who stood at the edge of the crowd listening to the debaters in City Hall Park, Whitaker invited him to attend one of the socialists' Sunday evening meetings. This was Jack's first personal contact with the party, and, though he would not officially join until the next spring, he managed to win considerable socialist notoriety by the end of the year.

News of the audience's shocked reaction to the "truculent Socialist diatribe" Jack had delivered during the end-of-term exercises at Oakland High reached the Bay Area journalists, and one, A. Walter Tate, decided he had a "story." On Christmas morning of 1895, *The San Francisco Examiner* devoted nearly a full page to Tate's article and London's diatribe. Jack explained that, contrary to popular misconceptions, socialism does not advocate anarchy; it seeks to improve, not abolish, the laws—that "Any man is a socialist who strives for a better form of government than the one he is living under"—and that socialism's aim, ultimately, is "pure democracy."

This *Examiner* piece was reminiscent of Henry David Thoreau's famous essay "Civil Disobedience." Like Thoreau, London considered himself a true democrat: not demanding at once a radically different government, much less no government, but at once a better government. In this sense his political ideology was clearly more American than European and stemmed from a characteristic revulsion against social inequality and political injustice. His experience with the prison system demonstrated that something was rotten not just in the state of New York but in other states as well. He had discovered from personal experience that it was impossible to work effectively against such injustices while floundering in the "submerged tenth" of society. In America, upward mobility could be achieved through proper education. Here, if he studied hard enough, he might finally become "one with the class."

It was time for Jack London to move up to higher education.

8

HIGHER EDUCATION

HURRY! Faster, faster! This was the dominant characteristic
of Jack London's activity until the end of his life.

—JOAN LONDON

Jack's original plan, when he had returned from his tramping excursion, was to spend the next seven years getting a formal education, but
after a year at Oakland High, even with the incentives of *The Aegis* and
the Henry Clay Debating Society, he was impatient to move along in his
climb toward success. He stayed in high school awhile longer, supplementing the family income with his janitorial job at the school. He also
became more actively involved with the Socialist Labor Party, which
he joined officially in April. At the same time he discovered an educational shortcut.

Ted Applegarth and Fred Jacobs (another friend from the Oakland
Public Library) were preparing themselves for admission to college by
attending Professor W. W. Anderson's University Academy in Alameda. Seeing Jack's restiveness, they suggested he join them there.
The academy was a "cramming joint" that catered to students from
bourgeois families, and the tuition was accordingly high. The London
family had no such financial means, but Eliza again came to Jack's aid,
paying his fees for the spring semester. He was admitted, and crammed
night and day, apparently managing to condense the two-year standard
prep school regimen into four months. It was seen as too much too soon

and an embarrassment to the regular students as well as to the head-master of the academy, who dismissed the ambitious pupil and refunded his tuition.

Jack was stunned. Here was still another instance of society's injus-tice: even in America the individual who aspired to rise in the world could be penalized not merely because he came from the lower class but, ironically, because he was more highly motivated than his class-mates. Yet it was still possible for the exceptionally driven individual to overcome these obstacles. He therefore decided to do his cramming without help from Anderson's academy. As he boasts in *John Barley-corn*: "There were three months yet before the university entrance examinations. Without laboratories, without coaching, sitting in my bedroom, I proceeded to compress that two years' work into three months." He spent nineteen hours a day studying the books and kept up this strenuous schedule for three months: "My body grew weary, my mind grew weary, but I stayed with it. My eyes grew weary and began to twitch, but they did not break down." He was not entirely without coaching for the examinations. While preparing on his own for the exams in English and history, he had help in physics from Fred Jacobs and in mathematics from Fred's girlfriend, Bess Maddern.

Only the occasional socialist activities disturbed his study schedule. On July 29, for instance, the *Oakland Times* printed a letter of his that defended the Socialist Labor Party while indicting the newspaper for not giving the party fair representation. The letter also criticized the Populists for their "sell-out" to the Democrats on the issue of free sil-ver: "The Populists have fallen—in as much, that their fundamental reform principles have been forgotten, and silver, a minor consider-ation, a side issue, has been made the main issue of their campaign. As they would have swallowed the Socialists, so have they been swallowed by the Democrats, who have stolen their thunder." During the next month, the *Oakland Times* published two more of his socialist letters, but most of his energy was devoted to readying himself for the univer-sity examinations, which began on August 10 and lasted for a week—at the end of which, he recalled, "I was in full possession of a splendid case of brain-fag."

By this time, his lifelong pattern of "work-and-run" was firmly set.

"I didn't want to see a book. I didn't want to think nor to lay eyes on anybody who was liable to think," he says. "There was but one prescription for such a condition, and I gave it to myself—the adventure-path." Without waiting to learn the results of his exams, he borrowed a small boat and set sail out of the Oakland Estuary, provisioned with blankets and enough food to last a day or so. All the weeks of intense study and stress were left behind as he raced along with the wind and tide. As he neared Benecia and "the clustering fishermen's arks where in the old days I had lived and drunk deep," another urge suddenly manifested itself: "And right here something happened to me, the gravity of which I had never dreamed for many a year to come. On the instant, out of the profound of my brain-fag, I knew what I wanted . . . For the first time in my life I consciously, deliberately desired to get drunk."

Get drunk he did. Docking his boat at the nearby wharf, he proceeded to renew old acquaintances. There was a reunion with Charley Le Grant, who had been his Fish Patrol sponsor, and Charley's warmhearted wife, Lizzie, along with Billy Murphy, Joe Lloyd, and "all the survivors of the old guard," who welcomed him back with open arms and fraternal hugs.

Because no reunion could be properly celebrated without drinks, Charley took his beer pail and started to the nearby saloon across the railroad tracks. But Jack craved stronger stuff than beer and called after him to bring a whiskey flask. That flask made repeated trips across the tracks, he recalled, and many more "old friends of the old free and easy times dropped in, fishermen, Greeks, and Russians, and French." As they continued drinking, they reminisced about the good old days and their lost comrades, including Young Scratch Nelson, who "had stretched out his great shoulders for the long sleep in this very town of Benecia," and they wept, remembering only the good things about him. "And Clam came in, Nelson's partner before me, handsome as ever, but more reckless, half insane, burning himself out with whisky."

Jack resisted the old gang's invitation to spend the night in further revelry. More compelling to him than whiskey's siren song was the call of the sea. Through the open door of their ark, he could see "the brave wind on the water, and my ears were filled with the roar of it." On this day, unlike the night four years earlier when he fell off the dock drunk and came near to drowning, he was helped down the rickety wharf by his friends, who switched his gear into a salmon boat, larger and more seaworthy than his skiff. Charley also supplied him with a charcoal brazier, frying pan, coffee pot, olive oil, and fresh sea bass. Waving goodbye to his old comrades, he set off against a "fierce tide and fiercer wind," chanting his "disdain for all the books and schools" and singing all "the old songs" he had learned during his days and nights of oyster pirating.

At sundown, nearing Antioch, he spotted a familiar-looking "potato sloop" and pulled in alongside it—"somewhat sobered and magnificently hungry." Once again, he found himself among old pals and was welcomed with open arms. They took his black bass, still fresh from the morning haul in Benecia, and fried it in olive oil. In addition to this mouthwatering repast, he was served "a meaty fisherman's stew, delicious with garlic, and crusty Italian bread without butter, and all washed down with pint mugs of thick and heady claret." That evening after dinner, they gathered in the snug cabin of his boat, where they "smoked and yarned of the old days, while overhead the wind screamed through the riggings and taut halyards drummed against the mast."

For a long time he reminisced about that day as a wonderful time of camaraderie, but eight years afterward, sinking into "the slough of brain-fag and intellectual weariness," during the period he called his "Long Sickness," he recognized "the craving for the anodyne that resides in alcohol." Another eight years after that, he would be moved to write a book-length treatise on the insidious effects of that anodyne— but there were other subjects on his mind during the summer of 1896.

After a week of sailing he returned home and found that he had passed the entrance examinations. He was admitted to the university as a special student in late August, taking courses in algebra, English, geometry, U.S. history, and physics. His official transcript reveals that he managed to pass the mathematics and science courses without distinction but fared better in English and history.

James Hopper, who would a few years hence become a member of George Sterling's bohemian colony at Carmel, recollected his initial impressions of London when they met again on the Berkeley campus.

Hopper says there was an aura around him as a man who had done "wild things and romantic things. His latest exploit—that of passing the University entrance examinations after three months vigorous cramming . . . was in many mouths." But Hopper was an entitled upperclassman. Editor of *Occident*, UC's literary magazine, and star lineman on UC's football team, he was "Big Man on Campus"—and "a bit of a bourgeois prig," he confessed. He had no intention of being impressed by a freshman, no matter how colorful his reputation: "Coming down the steps, I moved up and 'braced' him," Hopper recalled, "thinking consciously how nice and democratic this was of me!" If Jack sensed the condescension, he didn't show it. Instead, he responded to the gesture "with an open frankness that was like a flood of sunshine":

> He had a curly mop of hair which seemed spun of its gold . . . the forecastle had left a suspicion of a roll in his broad shoulders . . . He was a strange combination of Scandinavian sailor and Greek god . . . He was full of gigantic plans . . . He was going to take all the courses in English, all of them, nothing less. Also, of course, he meant to take most of the courses in the natural sciences, many in history, and bite a respectable chunk out of the philosophies.

Georgia Bamford's recollections of London's university days provide a counterbalance to Hopper's glowing portrait. She had been Jack's classmate during his brief tenure as student, janitor, and general tough guy at Oakland High School. Even though she later married his friend Fred Bamford, the cultural gap between her and Jack was never fully bridged. She was surprised when she met him one day on the UC campus and learned that he was enrolled as a student there. She was equally surprised to find that he had become friends with several fellow students. His attitude toward her, however, had not changed:

> Another time when we met on the campus, he asked me very abruptly: "Miss Loring, are your folks the owners of that 'Loring Hall' down on Eleventh and Clay Streets?" I answered "Yes," and at the moment had no thought of his idea. He gave me one searching look and without answering rushed off with a long stride, swinging his arms violently . . . I belonged to the hated "Capitalist Class" who robbed the

working people by charging them rent for the use of Loring Hall whenever they used it for their meetings.

She recounts still another incident that further reveals a less attractive side to Jack: "During this term there was a great bit of 'talk' on the campus. The cause? Jack London, of course . . . When the incident occurred even the Professors talked of it. I heard the tale many times." Jack evidently enjoyed going to the campus gym and playing his role as tough guy by challenging other students to box. Most of them were afraid to accept his challenges because of his reputation as a brawler, but one day he managed to persuade a young freshman to put on the gloves for a bit of friendly sparring—but the sparring was hardly friendly: "Jack sailed in with his old 'windmill' tactics so powerful on the water front; and in a very few minutes beat the poor, surprised freshman unmercifully and, in fact, knocked him out."

At that point an upperclassman who had witnessed the incident told Jack he should be ashamed of himself for beating up an unsuspecting boy smaller than he. "To be 'called down' in anything relating to sports, especially by one of the hated 'Capitalist' class, infuriated London," said Bamford:

> He was elated over his inglorious victory and told the junior to "go to _____ or you will get some of the same stuff yourself."
>
> "Oh, I don't think so," replied the junior. Jack London, without warning, then struck at him. He had not taken off his gloves and the other had no gloves on, but made a quick duck and escaped a powerful blow. "As you wish," said the junior as he put on the gloves.

Unknown to Jack, the upperclassman was a member of the varsity football team and an expert boxer. Jack's furious attack failed to dent his opponent's skilled defense. A crowd of students watched silently while he wore himself out with his undisciplined street-fighting tactics. At that point, "two blows were struck like lightning. One 'landed' on Jack's nose and the other 'got his jugular,' so that he was content to lie on the floor and, as the saying is, 'listen to church bells and the singing of birds.'" Although some of the students helped Jack to his feet and tried to lead him over to the locker room to wash the blood off his face, "he threw down the gloves, grabbed his coat and rushed away un-washed, just as he was." Bamford adds that the next time she saw Jack on campus, he snubbed her: "He would not pass me but turned aside into another path . . . Life from my point of view, he never could understand."

In January 1897, Jack registered for three English courses, two history courses, along with courses in military science and physical culture, but because the family needed his help with finances, he withdrew with "Honorable Dismissal" on February 4. The very next week, Oakland's "Boy Socialist" was arrested for violating Ordinance No. 1676, which forbade public speaking on any street within the Oakland fire limits without the mayor's written permission. The Socialist Party local had decided to challenge the constitutionality of the ordinance, and Jack had volunteered. He already had a reputation as a sharp debater and a passionate arguer, and though he was no great public orator, he had enough youthful good looks and notoriety to attract a crowd. Feeling shy and insecure, Jack asked Herman Whitaker to come with him to the platform. When the crowd of onlookers gathered to hear him, he "found himself tongue-tied," according to Joan London:

> Summoning all his courage, he jerked out a few inadequate sentences. The crowd cheered, faintly and ironically, then began to move away. Jack glanced despairingly at Whitaker . . . They exchanged places, and Jim managed to hold the crowd until he heard the hoped-for cry, "Hi, the cops!" Jack pushed him aside, remounted the box and was haranguing away in the best manner when he was hauled off the box and marched to jail.

He was acquitted and released shortly thereafter. Although the ordinance remained in effect, Joan remarks that Jack "had earned his first socialist laurels. Thus did he celebrate his rejection of the bourgeois academic life with a gesture whose sincerity outweighed its futility."

Another gesture whose sincerity outweighed its futility was a brief but intense flurry of creative writing during the spring of 1897. Remembering the handsome sum he had earned for his prizewinning sketch after the sealing voyage and emboldened by seeing his name in print in the local newspapers as well as in *The Aegis*, he decided to embark on a full-time writing career:

> Heavens, how I wrote! Never was there a creative fever such as mine from which the patient escaped fatal results . . . I wrote everything— ponderous essays, scientific and sociological, short stories, humorous verse, verse of all sorts from triolets and sonnets to blank verse tragedy and elephantine epics in Spenserian stanzas. On occasion I composed steadily, day after day, for fifteen hours a day. At times I forgot to eat, or refused to tear myself away from my passionate outpouring in order to eat.

He was turning out thousands of words every day, determined to make his big-time literary debut and not doubting for a minute that all the editors were just waiting to enjoy his masterpieces. Instead the editors were just waiting to return his manuscripts. He borrowed money from his family and sold his schoolbooks to used-book dealers for pennies to buy stamps—and still his progeny kept coming back home.

His frenzy lasted only a few weeks before he had to postpone his writing career. Setting aside his dreams of glory, he shifted his focus to more mundane matters. John London was growing still weaker and less able to work, and Jack needed a paying job. Herbert Shepard, Eliza's stepson, needed a helper in the laundry at Belmont Academy, an upper-class boarding school located down on the peninsula south of San Francisco. Jack would fictionalize it a dozen years later as one of Martin Eden's educational experiences. The job paid only thirty dollars a month—no more than he had earned working in the factory six years earlier—but even that small salary would benefit his family, especially since he would not be spending any of it, except for tobacco, while at the academy. He would get free room and board, and with Sundays off, he would still be able to do some serious reading—or so he thought.

What he did not know was that the owners of the institution had bought new equipment for the laundry with the assurance from the manufacturers that these machines would enable four men to do the work of twice that many. With this information in hand, the owners reasoned that two very sturdy men working at top speed and, if necessary, extra shifts without extra pay might do the work of four: "We sweated our way through long sizzling weeks at a task that was never done; and many a night, while the students snored in bed, my partner and I toiled on under the electric light at steam mangle or ironing board." Although he had brought along a trunkload of books to read during his leisure hours, he was too exhausted to finish reading any of them. Try as he might, he would fall asleep after reading the first few pages, and even those few pages he was too tired to remember.

In early June the academy closed for the summer, and Jack closed his book as a "work-beast" for the last time. If his coal-shoveling experience at the power plant had not been quite enough to convince him that he could never expect to rise in the world through the use of brawn, the Belmont Academy was the clincher. He renewed his vow to become a "brain merchant."

Even with his passion for socialism, he was seriously depressed at this time. Most disturbing was his recent discovery of the clouds hanging over his paternity and birth, which were darkened further by the two letters he had received from Chaney. How exactly he made this discovery is uncertain. It has been suggested that one of Jack's stepbrothers, envious of his drive to become more highly educated and therefore higher socially, taunted him with the revelation.

In any case, "What is significant is that Jack was deeply hurt by the affair at a time when his self-confidence needed bolstering, not shattering," says Joan London. "He lived at a time when illegitimacy was regarded with horror except by the enlightened few. It also seems probable that this knowledge determined his attitude toward his mother for the rest of his life. He was gentler to her thereafter, but he never quite forgave her."

As if the physical exhaustion of the laundry ordeal and the emotional devastation of his illegitimacy were not depressing enough, Jack was getting nothing but further negative reinforcement from the magazine editors. "I hardly know what to write—stamps are ephemeral—last week I had half-a-dollar's worth. Next week I shall receive numerous letters all graced on the outside by that same halfdollar's worth of stamps," he complained in a letter to Ted Applegarth in late June. "As for news, I am completely stagnated. I have none. I have isolated myself in almost claustral seclusion in my sanctum sanctorum, and am grinding out article after article."

That spell of depression was broken the next month when he "let career go hang, and went on the adventure-path again in quest of fortune."

9

THE GOLDEN DREAM

It was in the Klondike that I found myself. There you get your
perspective.

—*JACK LONDON BY HIMSELF*

When the steamship *Excelsior* docked in Seattle on July 14, 1897, it triggered the most spectacular gold rush in American history. The forty
miners who lugged a ton of gold down the gangplank were living proof
of the bonanza in the Far North. Seemingly overnight, the entire nation went mad. According to the historian Pierre Berton, "There had
been nothing like the Klondike before, there has been nothing like it
since, and there can never be anything like it again." The public frenzy
"reached a fever pitch at once, and remained at fever pitch until the following spring, when, with the coming of the Spanish-American War,
the only died almost as swiftly as it arose." Unlike the gold that only
one in twenty found, the reasons for the stampede are readily discovered: escape, adventure, freedom, wealth, a "second chance" for success and happiness.

The mood of unquiet desperation in America's response may also
be understood if one understands the time in which it took place. The
United States was still recovering from its worst depression. The swelling of American cities after the Civil War; the spreading stain of slums
and poverty; the suffocating railroad tariffs imposed on the western
farmers; the squeezing out of the small businessman by the giant mo-
nopolies; the dehumanizing effects of big business and industry; the

political corruption of what the historian V. L. Parrington called "the Great Barbecue"; the moral hypocrisies and social affectations of the genteel mode—in short, revulsion against all the decadence of the Gilded Age galvanized the nation's yearning to recapture the illusory promise of its Golden Age.

Now, unexpectedly, the vast mysterious Northland held forth one final opportunity for a return to the unsullied wilderness—for regeneration as well as for riches. "I believed that I was about to see and take part in a most picturesque and impressive movement across the wilderness," the novelist and short-story writer Hamlin Garland reminisced. "I wished to forget books and theories of art and social problems, and come again face to face with the great free spaces of woods and skies and streams." His confession is a fair representation of the mythic vision that characterized the rush. It is small wonder, then, that before the turn of the century, disregarding the warnings of the cynics who branded them "a horde of fools suffering from acute Klondicitis," one hundred thousand argonauts had struck out under the mass illusion that the end of the great American rainbow was located somewhere near the junction of the Klondike and Yukon rivers.

Jack London was among the first of the stampeders. Two years of schooling and drudgery had passed since he had returned home from the adventure path, and he had little to show for his efforts except a drawerful of rejection slips. Time for him to escape from editors and publishers—but how? He needed money if he was to get to the Klondike gold fields. Even if he could somehow get ship fare to Alaska, he couldn't get past the Canadian border without a year's worth of food and supplies: the Mounties were turning back anyone short of these. He checked with the local newspapers to see if they would hire him to go as their reporter. No luck.

Suddenly his sixty-year-old brother-in-law, Captain James Shepard, was stricken with gold fever. Announcing "Klondike or bust!" he made a proposition: he would finance an expedition for the two of them in exchange for Jack's youthful stamina and "road" experience. The proposed capital for their trip came not only from the firm of Shepard and Company but also from the mortgaging of his wife's home. Eliza told them they were both "crazy as loons" but agreed to help them get the best outfit money could buy. She said her money "flowed like water" during their shopping spree, as Jack and her husband loaded up with all the stuff needed for gold hunting in the frozen Northland: "fur-lined coats, fur caps, heavy high boots, thick mittens; and red-flannel shirts and underdrawers of the warmest quality." Clothing was only part of it. They needed mining gear along with axes, tents, blankets, and "Klondike stoves"—everything, in short, for building cabins and boats as well as for survival in the wilderness.

At dawn on Sunday, July 25, the two arrived with their new outfit at the Broadway Wharf in San Francisco. The *Umatilla*, licensed to carry 290 passengers, was scheduled to sail for Victoria, Port Townsend, and Seattle at 9:00 a.m.; however, 471 passengers were crowded aboard. Overburdened nearly to the gunwales, it was 10:30 before the *Umatilla* slowly lumbered out through the Golden Gate.

When they reached Port Townsend, forty nautical miles north-northwest of Seattle, Jack, his brother-in-law, and fifty-nine other passengers switched ships to the *City of Topeka*, which was bound for Juneau. Among those other passengers were three with whom London and Shepard had bonded to make a "Klondike Party": James Goodman, Ira Merritt Sloper, and Fred C. Thompson. Except for Shepard, whose frail health would work against his gold fever, the new partners were well suited for their quest. Most important, they shared such essential qualities as adaptability and camaraderie. They also possessed complementary talents. "Big Jim" was a powerful physical specimen, experienced in both mining and hunting. Thompson, a former clerk, was good at organizing and recording; he kept a diary that became a valuable source of information about their odyssey. Sloper was the grittiest of the four: a California carpenter-mechanic, he was also a veteran adventurer, later distinguished in one of London's stories: "His weight was probably ninety pounds, with the heavy hunting-knife thrown in, and his grizzled hair told of a prime which had ceased to be. But he could walk [many younger men] into the earth in a day's journey."

Jack rounded out his partners' various capabilities with his own expertise from the road and the sea, as well as his youthful exuberance. Four decades later, interviewed on his ranch near St. Helena, eighty-two-year-old Sloper remembered London as a "strong, vital man, full of the joy of living and getting the most from life [who] soon had found every book in camp and eagerly devoured every bit of reading matter he could secure." None of the group would strike it rich in the Klondike, but all would return home infinitely richer in experiences. Those experiences were often far from pleasant.

Simply getting to the Klondike gold fields—not to mention surviving the ferocious Arctic winter—was an ordeal in 1897. There were no roads. There were few trails, commercial propaganda notwithstanding. The most notorious case in point was the Edmonton Trail, advertised by the merchants of Edmonton, Alberta, as "the back door to the Yukon." The Edmonton Board of Trade claimed that "the trail was good all winter [and that] the Klondike could be reached with horses in ninety days." But the alleged "trail" was two thousand miles of impenetrable virgin forests, muskeg marshes, rapids, whirlpools, canyons, mountains, and "Dog-Eating Prairie"—a vast wasteland that got its unsavory name from Indians who staved off starvation on this lifeless expanse by killing and eating their dogs. For dogs and horses alike, the Edmonton Trail was deadly. The horses died from drowning or starvation, or had to be shot because of broken legs. The route from Edmonton was permeated with the stench of rotting horseflesh, "the telltale perfume of the Klondike stampede."

Men fared scarcely better. Scores of them died from exposure, scurvy, and starvation. Some went insane, and more than a few committed suicide. "Hell can't be worse than this trail. I'll chance it," one disenchanted argonaut scribbled on a scrap of paper and posted on a tree before putting a gun to his head. Two other men had wandered futilely over four thousand miles—hiking across barren prairies, crossing wild rivers, struggling over mountains, hacking and chopping their paths through dense underbrush and forest—before they finally happened upon a deserted cabin on the Porcupine River. Near dead from their ordeal, they decided to spend the winter here. When discovered, "they were frozen rock-solid beside a stew kettle hanging above a long-dead fire. The pot contained a pair of partly cooked moccasins embedded in a cake of ice. The rest was ashes." Of more than two thousand men, women, and children who took the Edmonton Trail in 1897/98, fewer than one hundred made it to Dawson, and virtually none found any gold to compensate for their experience.

There were other routes. The easiest was the "Rich Man's Route," which took one from Seattle to St. Michael in a cruise ship, then upstream to Dawson in a shallow-bottom steamer. It was a long trip (nearly four thousand miles), but the passengers were assured they would have to walk no more than a few feet aboard ship and could therefore conserve their energies for the gold they planned to find after reaching their destination. En route, they would be spared the hardships faced by the those traveling on land. Food would be plentiful and, in most cases, well prepared. Snug cabins would protect them from the bad weather.

One critical element was overlooked in the Rich Man's Route: the subarctic weather. Most failed to reckon how early winter arrives in that region: sometimes even before the end of summer. None of the affluent passengers who sailed after the end of July in 1897 got to Dawson City before the following summer. It had begun to snow in August, and within a month the Yukon River was turning to ice. During the winter of 1897/98, more than two thousand frustrated would-be gold hunters were left stranded along the seventeen hundred miles of river between Norton Sound and Dawson City. The scene at St. Michael, where hundreds were dumped to await passage upstream, was typical. Instead of cozy cabins aboard ship, they were crowded into tents. Instead of haute cuisine, they were fed the beans-and-bacon diet of the mining camps. When the river was again navigable, many would return home, their resources exhausted and their gold fever permanently cured. By that time, Jack was also on his way home.

He and his partners had taken the "Poor Man's Route," from the port of Dyea over the Chilkoot Pass and down the Yukon River to the Klondike—more arduous but also quicker. They arrived in Juneau on August 2 and left three days later "with Indians and canoes," according to Thompson. On August 7 they "Arrived at Dyea at 3:30 p.m."

Thompson's succinct entry provides no vision of the "Dyea Drama." Here was the end of the ocean voyage and the start of the infamous Chilkoot Trail. Today Dyea is virtually deserted except for a few log cabins and, during the brief summer, an abundance of wildflowers. Before 1897 it was a lonely trading post, but by the time Jack's party arrived, it had become a busy town packed with jerry-built hotels, saloons, stores, and casinos.

Although a point of disembarkation, Dyea was scarcely a harbor. There were no wharves for unloading the stampeders' supplies. Worse, there were no shelters for protecting the supplies after they reached the poor excuse for a beach, which was little more than a mudflat located between a thirty-foot tide from the ocean on one side and a rushing stream from mountain glaciers on the other. Worse still, impatient skippers usually dumped their passengers along with their cumbersome gear offshore regardless of worth and safety. Consequently, many lost their entire outfits, and some were drowned in the cold, murky waters.

Because they were wise enough to make the trip from Juneau in Indian canoes instead of ships, Jack's party landed its goods without mishap. On August 8, while waiting to hit the trail, London wrote to Mabel Applegarth from Dyea, with no mention of the chaos others less fortunate were suffering:

> I am laying on the grass in sight of a score of glaciers, yet the slight exertion of writing causes me to sweat prodigiously.
>
> We lay several days in Juneau, then hired canoes & paddled 100 miles to our present quarters. The Indians with us brought along their squaws, papooses & dogs. Had a pleasant time. The 100 miles lay between mountains which formed a Yosemite Valley the whole length, & in many places the heights were stupendous . . .
>
> Am certain we will reach the lake in 30 days . . .
>
> Pleas [sic] forward to Teddy—have little time to write now—but next winter will be able to write good, long, & real letters. This is not a letter—but am rushed for anything better.

He wrote no "good, long, & real letters" during the coming winter. Instead of writing, he spent much of his time listening. He was right, however, in his prediction that in thirty days they would get to Lake Lindeman, the starting place for the water journey to Dawson City. Before reaching that point, however, they had to traverse the "meanest thirty-three miles in history": the Chilkoot Trail. A bare outline of their traverse, with a hint of the ordeal, may be found in Thompson's diary:

> August 14.
> This morning very hot, and the road was rough. We are now nine

miles from Dyea . . . Mr. Shepard left us today for his home . . . his rheumatism got very bad.

August 15.

Met Tarwater of Santa Rosa—took him as a passenger, exchanging board and passage for his work.

Nineteen years later, Martin Tarwater would be fictionalized as "John Tarwater," the hero of London's story "Like Argus of the Ancient Times." Thompson's comment that "the road was rough" is an understatement, considering the obstacles facing the hikers on the Chilkoot Trail. Foremost among these were the physical demands and the climatic vagaries. The trail itself was a formidable challenge: it zigzagged uphill over rocky terrain and through a virgin forest of thick brush and evergreens; it led them over mossy rocks and across a turbulent mountain river. Now the autumn rains had started, turning the rocky trail into slippery muck. "Crossed the Dyea River three times on logs, one tied across the other," Thompson wrote on August 20. "They are very hard to walk on, with water rushing underneath and one hundred pounds on your back." Curses of frustration and cries of despair were a common refrain. Injuries were frequent, often severe, and sometimes fatal. While some of the bodies were buried in a makeshift cemetery outside Dyea, others were dumped into shallow trailside graves.

On August 21, Jack and his partners reached Sheep Camp, described by Thompson in laconic understatement as "a tough hold." He says they decided to pitch their own tent a good three hundred yards away from the main camp, but he does not elaborate the reason for this decision. A detailed description reveals why: Named "Sheep Camp" because it had once served as headquarters for adventurers hunting mountain sheep, this was the last fairly level stopping place before the steep ascent that climaxed up at the tiny notch in the surrounding mountains called "Chilkoot Pass." By the time London's party got there, the camp was occupied by more than a thousand men who had pitched their tents so close together that it was nearly impossible to squeeze in among them. At the center of camp were a dozen shanties generously described as "hotels." In one shack, named the "Palmer House," the owner was getting rich by feeding five hundred customers a day and sleeping forty a night packed together wall to wall on the plank floor.

One significant event is omitted from Thompson's August 21 entry. On that day his party (possibly including Jack), along with a dozen or so other miners, posed long enough to get their picture taken by Frank La Roche, a photographer commissioned by the U.S. Geological Survey to record the gold rush. The Yukon historian Dick North, who discovered this rare photograph among others in the La Roche collection at the University of Washington Library, says that it was "the most important" photo La Roche ever took because it is possibly the only picture of Jack London in Alaska. Although other London scholars have questioned whether the figure of the young man in the photograph is Jack, North states that the authenticity has been verified by an identification expert in the Toronto Police Department. Also, the date of the photograph coincides with the date in Thompson's diary.

Ten days later Thompson made the following quick entry in his journal: "Got our goods all over the summit." Again, this hardly does justice to their heroic achievement in trudging four miles uphill from Sheep Camp to the near-vertical climb to the 3,739-foot Chilkoot Pass, where the Canadian authorities were waiting to make sure each climber had a year's supply of provisions. In view of the difficulty of the ascent, some were hiring Indian packers to carry their goods, and the Indians were charging up to a dollar per pound of supplies. Jack was determined to carry his own goods and save those precious dollars. Experimenting with various ways to ease the burden—readjusting and padding the straps where they had rubbed his shoulders raw, and stripping down to his red flannel underwear to prevent heat exhaustion—he managed to haul all his supplies over the pass and on to Lake Linderman. He later boasted that he "was packing up with the Indians and outpacking many an Indian. The last pack into Linderman was three miles. I back-tripped it four times a day, and on each forward trip carried one hundred and fifty pounds." A vivid image of the ordeal appears in his first novel, *A Daughter of the Snows*:

> The midday sun beat down upon the stone "Scales." The forest had given up the struggle, and dizzying heat recoiled from the unclothed rock. On either hand rose the ice-marred ribs of earth, naked and strenuous in their nakedness. Above towered the storm-beaten Chilkoot. Up its gaunt and ragged front crawled a slender string of

men . . . It came out of the last fringe of dwarfed shrub below, drew a black line across a dazzling stretch of ice [and] went on, up the pitch of the steep, growing fainter and smaller, till it squirmed and twisted like a column of ants and vanished over the crest of the pass.

Once they had arrived at Lindeman, Jack and his partners knew time was running out: winter was coming on fast, and within days the six hundred miles of waterways to the Klondike would be impassable. They needed a boat, so they built their own. On September 10, Thompson recorded, "This morning, took pack on my back to the woods up river five miles, where the boys were getting out logs and sawing lumber to build our boats." Sloper knew how to build boats, while the others had the muscles needed to follow his directions, and Jack knew how to handle the boats. Thompson wrote one of his most detailed entries on September 21:

Sailed from Lake Lindeman at 12:00 noon, and got to portage at Lake Bennett at 1:00 p.m. Had our dinner, got one boat over portage and our goods packed to Bennett. Weather very cold. At the point where the Skagway trail comes in, and all along the hillside up from Bennett, there are hundreds of dead horses that have been used on the Skagway trail and here have played out—died for want of food, bad usage, or shot after no more use could be got from them. Parties coming off the Skagway trail tell me there are enough dead horses and mules along the trail to lay them side by side, so that one can walk on horse flesh the entire length (fifty miles).

Jack later delineated this horror in his story "Which Make Men Remember," concluding, "Their hearts turned to stone—those which did not break—and they became beasts, the men on Dead Horse Trail."

During the next four days, the *Yukon Belle*, the name they had given their boat, sailed smoothly down Lakes Bennett, Tagish, and Marsh, but they stopped at Box Canyon on September 25 to make another critical decision. Lewis River flowed out of Marsh Lake at a width of one-eighth to one-quarter of a mile before squeezing into this narrow canyon so that the river squirted out like water out of a giant fire hydrant into the Whitehorse Rapids. Records reveal that after the spring thaw of 1898, one hundred and fifty boats were wrecked and at least ten men drowned in this section of the river. It was much safer to pack around, but that took four days, and their time was running out. Cold weather with snow and ice was close at hand; Dawson City was still several hundred miles away. The river would become impassable before long. They voted unanimously to shoot the rapids.

Hundreds of fascinated spectators watched from the cliffs above the canyon, expecting to see the disastrous end of the *Yukon Belle* and her foolhardy sailors as they set loose into the foaming river. As if shot from a launching pad, the heavily laden craft—more raft than proper boat— was propelled down the rapids. Jack steered at the helm and shouted orders to his crew as they frantically rowed and fought to keep the *Yukon Belle* from capsizing or crashing against the rocks as she careened crazily down the swirling torrent. At one point they came so close to being swamped that Sloper leaped off the boat and onto the top of a rock—then as quickly jumped back on "like a man boarding a comet." Thanks as much to luck as to Jack's expert boatmanship, the crew survived the escapade with no broken bones and only two broken paddles.

The party now moved on down to the shore of Lake Laberge, where they encountered an unexpected hurdle. Laberge was a sizable lake, thirty miles long and noted for its bad weather. Near the end of September it had become another bottleneck on the water route to Dawson because of bitter winds and blinding snowstorms. Again they were facing a dilemma: wait for better weather and risk being stranded for six months or move on. They voted again to move on. Though less hazardous than the rapids, moving down Laberge was more arduous. Their sail rendered useless by the strong north wind, they were reduced to rowing.

At the end of the month they were stalled by blizzards and heavy seas. The weather cleared on October 2, and they broke camp early to get across the lake during the brief calm. Because there was no wind, they rowed hard all day, reaching the upper tributary of the Yukon River named the Thirty Mile by late afternoon. Pushing on downriver through the ever-thickening slush, they arrived at the Stewart River, eighty miles south of Dawson City, on October 9. They spotted a deserted cabin on Split-Up Island at the juncture of the Stewart River and Henderson Creek. "This is a good place, and we think we shall make it our headquarters," Thompson wrote.

It was a wise decision. They would avoid food-and-fuel shortages as well as the crowded and unsanitary housing conditions facing Dawson during the coming winter. They would find game and wood aplenty in the surrounding forest, and their snug little cabin would provide adequate shelter from the icy Northland winds. As soon as the river froze, they could easily sled into the city.

During the next week, they unpacked, worked to get properly settled into their winter quarters, and did some prospecting up Henderson Creek. On Saturday, October 16, the Yukon remaining navigable, London and Thompson headed downriver for Dawson to get news and file their claims. Arriving the following Monday morning, they pitched their camp near a cabin owned by Louis and Marshall Bond.

Of all London's Klondike experiences, his camping near the Bond cabin was perhaps the most fortuitous. The two Bond brothers, Louis and Marshall, were the Yale-educated sons of Judge Hiram Gilbert Bond, one of California's wealthiest men, who owned a large ranch in Santa Clara. Wealthy enough to hire packers and boats, the Bonds had arrived at Dawson City a week or so before London and Thompson. Despite the difference in social status, Jack and the two brothers immediately found a common bond. Many years afterward, Marshall remembered their first meeting. He recalled that the two men, after setting up their tent, had asked if they might put their provisions inside the Bonds' cache, to save them from the stray dogs that wandered around the city looking for food:

> One of these men was of medium height with very square broad shoulders. His face was masked by a thick stubbly beard . . . On a box, out of the circle of light from the lamp, he sat in silence one night [until our discussion] turned to the subject of socialism. Some of those present confused it with anarchism . . . Then from out of the shadow of the lamp, from the blur of beard and cap, came a quick-speaking, sympathetic voice. He took up the subject from its earliest history [and] carried it on through a rapid survey of its most important points . . . This was my first introduction to Jack London.

Marshall Bond was less impressed with Jack's mining talents: "Outside of the rare piece of luck which occasionally leads a man to set his stakes on a bonanza piece of ground, mining success calls for a knowledge of the subject and a certain, if not a decided, business faculty. London lacked both."

What London did not lack was something more valuable: imagination. While he was a good talker, he was an even better listener. His mining ventures were a failure—he would bring home less than five dollars' worth of gold—but he mined an infinitely richer lode during the long Arctic nights, listening to the tales swapped between the "sourdoughs" and newly arrived *chechaquos*. Many of the stories that passed for fact were undoubtedly fictions and glamorized truths. As Jack said later, "The Alaskan gold hunter is proverbial, not so much for his unveracity, as for his inability to tell the precise truth. In a country of exaggerations, he likewise is prone to hyperbolic descriptions of things actual. But when it came to [the] Klondike, he could not stretch the truth as fast as the truth itself stretched." During the long Arctic winter, he was collecting the raw material he would later shape into fictional character and narrative. More than this, he was absorbing the very atmosphere of the Northland itself. This distinctive quality accounts for the fact that of the numerous contemporary books written about the Klondike gold rush, London's works are some of the few to have remained continually in print for more than a century.

Another quality that Jack possessed was his rapport with animals, especially with dogs. Beyond rapport, it was a rare psychological empathy, demonstrated nowhere more impressively than in *The Call of the Wild*. The model for his hero, Buck, was a St. Bernard/Scotch shepherd owned by the Bond brothers and also named Jack. London's "manner of dealing with dogs was different from anyone I ever knew," said Marshall Bond. "Most people, including myself, pat, caress, and talk in more or less affectionate terms to a dog. London did none of this. He always spoke and acted toward the dog as if he recognized his noble qualities, respected them, but took them as a matter of course . . . He had an appreciative and instant eye for fine traits and honored them in a dog as he would in a man."

London and Thompson spent over six weeks in Dawson City before returning to their cabin on Split-Up Island. The "City" was anything but an ideal tourist attraction. It was an unsightly, overcrowded shantytown only slightly less noxious than the tainted "Louse Town," across the river. Both were often shrouded in chilling fog, and the weather was not yet icy enough to stifle the spreading stench of human and animal filth. To make matters worse, food was already scarce, and the prospects for bringing in new supplies were growing slimmer every day. As early as August, Inspector Charles Constantine had written to the Ottawa headquarters of the Mounted Police that "the outlook for grub is not assuring for the number of people here—about four thousand crazy or lazy men, chiefly American miners and toughs from the coast towns."

As winter approached, many tried to escape the impending disaster, but it was too late. Among them was the "Singer of the Sierras," the poet Joaquin Miller, who attempted retreat down the frozen river but was turned in his tracks by the merciless winds after no more than a hundred miles. Forced to retrace his frozen steps to Dawson, he was in pitiful shape by the time he got back. His cheeks and ears were badly frostbitten, part of his big toe and all of one finger had to be amputated, and he was suffering from snow blindness. Writing to a friend a week before Christmas, he described the Arctic cold as a "vast white silence, as if all the earth lay still and stark dead in her white shroud waiting the judgment day."

By Christmas Eve, supplies had run so low that all the restaurants had closed. The novelist Rex Beach, compelled by the weather to spend the winter several hundred miles downriver, recorded the following sentiments of one of the newspapermen he met: "There's no drama up here, no comedy, no warmth. Life is as pale and cold as the snow . . . we'll never read any great stories about Alaska and the Klondike. This country is too drab and dreary."

Jack London would prove that comment wrong, producing nearly eighty Klondike stories rich in drama, comedy, and warmth as well as in brutality, violence, and death. Furthermore, the icy stillness that had so oppressed Joaquin Miller would be rendered by London into one of the most powerful descriptions in his early Northland tales:

The afternoon wore on, and with the awe, born of the White Silence, the voiceless travelers bent to their work. Nature has many tricks wherewith she convinces man of his finity,—the easeless flow of the tides, the fury of the storm, the shock of the earthquake, the long roll of heaven's artillery,—but the most tremendous, the most stupefying of all, is the passive phase of the White Silence. All movement ceases, the sky clears, the heavens are as brass; the slightest whisper seems sacrilege, and man becomes timid, affrighted at the sound of his own voice. Sole speck of life journeying across the ghostly wastes of a dead world, he trembles at his audacity, realizes that his is a maggot's life, nothing more. Strange thoughts arise unsummoned, and the mystery of all things strives for utterance. And the fear of death, of God, of the universe, comes over him—the hope of the Resurrection and the Life, the yearning for immortality, the vain striving of the imprisoned essence—it is then, if ever, man walks alone with God.

In sharp contrast to the cold heartlessness of the landscape was the warm camaraderie London witnessed in the saloons: "Business appointments and deals were made and consummated in the saloons, enterprises projected, shop talked, the latest news discussed, and a general good fellowship maintained. There all life rubbed shoulders, and kings and dog-drivers, oldtimers and chechaquos, met on a common level."

His glowing description of the saloons may have been due in some measure to the fact that he and Thompson had left Dawson before the worst effects of the famine and sickness were apparent. They returned upriver to their cabin the first week in December, shortly after the temperature had dipped to sixty-seven degrees below zero. Jack would later describe this awesome cold in numerous Northland stories, but most notably in his classic "To Build a Fire," where his lone protagonist, spitting tobacco juice, is shocked to hear it crackle and freeze before it hits the ground. The man succumbs to this awesome cold not only because he lacks the capacity for comradeship but also because he is "without imagination. He was quick and alert in the things of life, but only in the things, and not in the significances." London lacked neither of these qualities. Even so, his Klondike winter was not without discontent. Regardless of the camaraderie he may have felt for his friends, cabin fever was common. He dramatizes the typical cabin's interior as its ice-bound inhabitants are trying to relieve their boredom with a game of cards in "The End of the Story":

The table was of hand-hewn spruce boards, and the men who played whist had frequent difficulties in drawing home their tricks across the uneven surface. Though they sat in their undershirts, the sweat noduled and oozed on their faces; yet their feet, heavily moccasined and woolen-socked, tingled with the bite of the frost . . . The sheet-iron Yukon stove roared redhot, yet, eight feet away, on the meat-shelf, placed low and beside the door, lay chunks of solidly frozen moose and bacon.

Cooped up in such quarters, men often found themselves getting on each other's nerves, their tempers growing shorter as the seemingly endless Arctic night grew longer. Jack's years on the sea and on the road had taught him that bad tempers inevitably led to fights—and sometimes to even worse consequences. Those who knew him in the Klondike praised his amiability. One of the finest tributes was given by W. B. "Bert" Hargrave, who first met Jack in October of 1897:

> I remember well the first time I entered [his cabin]. London was seated on the edge of a bunk, rolling a cigarette. One of his partners, Goodman, was preparing a meal, and the other, Sloper, was doing some carpentry work. [Jack's] hospitality was so cordial, his smile so genial, his goodfellowship so real, that it instantly dispelled all reserve . . . He was intrinsically kind and irrationally generous.

Jack's irrational generosity extended itself to all comers, and he regularly offered invitations to visitors at mealtime. While this endeared him to others, it was a source of increasing tension between him and Merritt Sloper. Matters came to a head when Jack accidentally broke Sloper's favorite ax while chopping ice from their water hole. Although Jack tried to make a joke about the accident, Sloper, whose patience with Jack's easygoing attitude had already worn thin, started cursing him. Instead of responding in kind, Jack took the abuse silently while calmly lighting a cigarette. Yet Hargrave, who was visiting the cabin with his two partners that night, noted a glint in Jack's eye. After a quick consultation with his partners, Hargrave invited him to move into their cabin for the rest of the winter.

Hargrave's partners were Judge E. H. Sullivan and Dr. B. F. Harvey. In *John Barleycorn*, London alludes to Harvey, without naming him:

"In my personal medicine chest was a quart of whisky. I never drew the cork till six months afterward, in a lonely camp, where, without anaesthetics, a doctor was compelled to operate on a man. The doctor and the patient emptied my bottle between them and then proceeded to the operation." His fellow argonaut Emil Jensen, the model for London's hero Malemute Kid in *The Son of the Wolf*, later revealed that "Doc" Harvey was in fact the surgeon, that Jensen's partner, Charlie Borg, was the patient, and that the operation involved the amputation of Borg's gangrenous foot: "One quarter of the bottle, or jug, went down [Harvey's] throat to steady his nerves, and the remainder of the whisky saved the life of his patient . . . Thanks to the benumbing effect of that whisky, my partner survived the butchering, for butchering it was, as cruel as it was necessary."

Jack was lucky enough to avoid such butchering but was not lucky enough to avoid the most dreaded Klondike ailment: "Arctic leprosy," or scurvy, the common result of a diet of flour, sugar, beans, and salt pork without fresh vegetables. The spring thaw opened up the Yukon in time so that Jack would be able to get help before being afflicted with the symptoms suffered by the "Two Incapables" in his story "In a Far Country":

> In the absence of fresh vegetables and exercise, their blood became impoverished, and a loathsome purple rash crept over their bodies. Yet they refused to heed the warning. Next, their muscles and joints began to swell, the flesh turning black, while their mouths, gums, and lips took on the color of rich cream. Instead of being drawn together by their misery, each gloated over the other's symptoms as the scurvy took its course.

Near the first of June, he and Doc Harvey tore down their cabin and rafted the logs down to Dawson, where they sold the wood for six hundred dollars. Jack had originally planned to spend a second year prospecting, but the scurvy changed his mind. On June 8 he teamed up with with two men, Charley Taylor and John Thorson, and the three began a three-week trip down to the Bering Sea at St. Michael on a jerry-built houseboat.

Although his scurvy was causing considerable discomfort in walking,

Jack mentioned it only once in the diary he kept on the trip. On June 18, the day their boat reached Anvik, he wrote, "Given some fresh potatoes & a can of tomatoes for my scurvy, which has now almost entirely crippled me from the waist down . . . These few raw potatoes & tomatoes are worth more to me at the present stage of the game than an Eldorado claim." Causing him more discomfort were the aggressive hordes of mosquitoes, which, he complained, had been biting not only "under netting" but even "through overalls and heavy underwear."

His final diary entry was June 28: "Leave St. Michaels [*sic*]— unregrettable moment."

A month later, after working his way as a coal passer aboard a steamer headed for San Francisco, he was back home. Although he complained he'd brought nothing from the Klondike but scurvy, he was already beginning to refine the raw materials that would bring him fame greater than that of any bonanza king.

10

BREAKTHROUGH:
OVERLAND AND *THE BLACK CAT*

And here is the funny thing. Some are born to fortune, and
some have fortune thrust upon them. But in my case I was
clubbed into fortune, and bitter necessity wielded the club.

—*JOHN BARLEYCORN*

When Jack arrived back home in late July 1898, he discovered that the
man he had known for years as his father was dead and had been buried in Oakland's Mountain View Cemetery. John London had succumbed to multiple debilitating ailments on October 17, 1897.

With little gold to show for his year in the Klondike, Jack had to
go to work. He later claimed that circumstances forced him to become
"the head and the sole bread-winner" of the household, which now included Ida London Miller's six-year-old son, Johnny, but he may have
been stretching the truth. According to Joan London, John's death
"shocked Flora out of her long apathy. The brisk, businesslike woman of
twenty years earlier had returned. By the time Jack reached Oakland,
she had increased the number of her music pupils, and on the income
from this teaching and her small pension, was managing her affairs
very capably." Such seems to have been the case, for shortly after getting home, her son headed out for the Nevada goldfields to try his hand
at prospecting one more time. Discovering no gold, he returned to Oakland in late August and looked for a steady job—with little success.

In desperation, he pawned everything of value he owned: his watch, his bicycle, and even his "sole legacy in this world," John London's beautiful mackintosh worth a half month's salary, sacrificed to the pawnbroker for two dollars. He managed to get another five dollars by pawning a secondhand dress suit he'd acquired in a trade with one of his old "waterfront" buddies. Though still in prime condition and "a bargain in the labor market," he could find no steady job. He even applied for a job as "studio model, but there were too many fine-bodied young fellows out of jobs." He considered selling sewing machines, but the pay was commission-based, and "poor people don't buy sewing machines in hard times."

He resorted to every kind of odd job he could find: mowing lawns, trimming hedges, taking up and beating carpets. Thinking he might have a chance to become a government employee, he took the civil service exam for mail carrier, passing with the top score, but there were no openings at the time, and he was told he would have to wait for one. "And while I waited, and in between the odd-jobs I managed to procure, I started to earn ten dollars by writing a newspaper account of a voyage I had made, in an open boat down the Yukon . . . I had long since abandoned all thought of writing as a career. My honest intention in writing that article was to earn ten dollars."

The first newspaper to which he sent his Klondike article, *The San Francisco Examiner*, neither acknowledged receipt nor returned his manuscript. Consequently, he wrote the following letter to *The San Francisco Bulletin* on September 17:

> I have returned from a year's residence in the Clondyke, entering the country by way of Dyea and Chilkoot Pass. I left by way of St. Michaels, thus making altogether a journey of 2,500 miles on the Yukon in a small boat. I have sailed and traveled quite extensively in other parts of the world and have learned to seize upon that which is interesting, to grasp the true romance of things, and to understand the people I may be thrown amongst.
>
> I have just completed an article of 4,000 words, describing the trip from Dawson to St. Michaels in a rowboat. Kindly let me know if there would be any demand in your columns for it—of course, thoroughly understanding that the acceptance of the manuscript is to depend upon its literary and intrinsic value.

The editor returned Jack's letter with this reply scribbled on the bottom of the page: "Interest in Alaska has subsided in an amazing degree. Then, again, so much has been written, that I do not think it would pay us to buy your story." It was true that the media had been flooded with Klondike items, and the major wave of enthusiasm had already crested if not altogether subsided. But what that editor failed to appreciate were those three essential factors that would distinguish London's contribution from that of most of the others: human interest, romantic imagination, and sympathetic understanding. Fueled by creative genius, these qualities would make him one of the most popular writers in the world.

During the fall of 1898, prospects for fame and fortune seemed remote. London's immediate concern was putting food on the family table. Between odd jobs, working on a rented typewriter, he kept pounding out stuff he thought might sell. He also began keeping a record of his manuscript submissions, rejections, and acceptances. The acceptances were slow in coming. Spurred on by desperation, he was now writing furiously, spraying the marketplace indiscriminately with essays, stories, poems, jokes—anything he thought might sell. By the end of November, the strain was taking its toll: "Forgive me for not writing, for I have been miserable and half sick. So nervous this morning that I could hardly shave myself," he wrote to Mabel Applegarth. "Everything seems to have gone wrong—why, I haven't received my twenty dollars for those essays yet. Not a word as to how I stood in my Civil Service Exs. Not a word from the *Youth's Companion*, and it means to me what no one can possibly realize."

He had submitted essays in the Oakland Fifth Ward Republican contest for campaign essays and been awarded two prizes, worth ten dollars each. He had taken the civil service examination for mail carrier on October 14. His twenty-one-thousand-word, seven-chapter serial "Where Boys Are Men" would be rejected by *Youth's Companion*. "I made ambitious efforts once," he continued:

It makes me laugh to look back on them, though sometimes I am nearer to weeping. I was the greenest of tyros, dipping my brush into whitewash and coal-tar, and without the slightest knowledge of perspective, proportion or color, attempted masterpieces—without a soul to say you are all wrong; herein you err; there is your mistake . . . So you see, to-day, I am unlearning and learning anew.

In his learning program, he gave special attention to vocabulary, scribbling the definitions of new words on scraps of paper, carrying these in his pockets or fastening them to a clothesline in his bedroom, using and repeating each word until confident he had mastered it, then replacing that scrap of paper with still another unfamiliar word until it, in turn, was mastered. He spent most of the daylight hours writing, taking time off only for meals, eaten with a book in his left hand. Evenings he spent in the Oakland Public Library, where his friend Fred Bamford introduced him to significant works on history, literature, politics, and science. Nights he spent reading, limiting himself to a maximum of five hours' sleep. Only occasionally did he interrupt this schedule by taking on an odd job to get money for writing paper, stamps, and tobacco.

In the back pages of his notebook "NO. 1 MAGAZINE SALES FROM 1898 TO MAY 1900," he jotted down the names and addresses of more than fifty magazines, newspapers, and publishing syndicates, ranging from *The Atlantic* and *Frank Leslie's Boys' and Girls' Weekly* newspaper to *The Saturday Evening Post* and *Youth's Companion*. Baffled by the incessant stream of rejection slips, he studied the popular newspaper and magazine stories, trying to find the magic formula for success. Like Martin Eden, he "reasoned out the perfect formula" for the newspaper storiette: it "should never be tragic, should never end unhappily, and should never contain beauty of language, subtlety of thought, nor real delicacy of sentiment. Sentiment it must contain, plenty of it, pure and noble [but it must be the] 'I-may-be-poor-but-I-am-honest' brand of sentiment." And like Martin, Jack resorted to this kind of hackwork. Because the models he was using were at best second-rate, his imitations were third-rate, and he was revulsed by this kind of sentimental claptrap even as he tried to produce it. What he envisioned was "an impassioned realism, shot through with human aspiration and faith . . . life as it was, with all its spirit-groping and soul-reaching left in."

His visions could not be communicated through sentimental formulas. In "unlearning and learning anew," he reread the old masters—

not only modern fictionists such as Poe and Melville but also Homer, Shakespeare, and Milton—along with contemporary virtuosos such as Kipling and Stevenson. He was particularly impressed by Kipling's "plain style," and practiced copying page after page of Kipling's work in order to get the hang of it for himself. At the same time, he read Herbert Spencer's "The Philosophy of Style," which he said taught him "the subtle and manifold operations necessary to transmute thought, beauty, sensation and emotion into black symbols on white paper [and] to select the symbols that would compel [the reader's] brain to realize my thought, or vision, or emotion." He also learned that "the right symbols were the ones that would require the expenditure of the minimum of my reader's brain energy, leaving the maximum of his brain energy to realize and enjoy the content of my mind, as conveyed to his mind."

Jack was now finding his own style, but the winter of 1898 was darker than his previous winter in the frozen-hearted Northland. Physically and emotionally drained from trying to become a successful writer, he was sinking into depression, feeling he had been deserted by his friends and betrayed by his family. Even his beloved Eliza was urging him to give up his quest for literary success and get steady work. And Mabel Applegarth, whom he had so passionately idealized earlier, seemed insensitive to his vision. "I do appreciate your interest in my affairs, but we have no common ground," he snapped bitterly on November 30 in a seven-page letter, the gist of which is evident in the following excerpt:

In a general, vaguely general, way, you know my aspirations; but of the real Jack, his thoughts, feelings, etc., you are positively ignorant . . .

From the hunger of my childhood, cold eyes have looked upon me, or questioned, or snickered and sneered. What hurt above all was that they were some of my friends—not professed but real friends. I have calloused my exterior and receive the strokes as though they were not; as to how they hurt, no one knows but my own soul and me.

So be it. The end is not yet. If I die I shall die hard, fighting to the last, and hell shall receive no fitter inmate than myself. But for good or ill, it shall be as it has been—alone.

Mabel, remember this . . . I don't care if the whole present, if all I possess, were swept away from me—I will build a new present; If I am left naked and hungry to-morrow—before I give in I will go naked and hungry; if I were a woman I would prostitute myself to all men but that I would succeed—in short, I will.

His letter to Mabel one week later had a different tone as he mentioned his first magazine acceptance: "Received a letter from the *Overland Monthly*. This is the substance of it: We have read your MS. Are so greatly pleased with it, that, though we have an enormous quantity of accepted and paid-for material on hand, we will at once publish it in the January number, if—aye, if you can content yourself with five dollars."

The manuscript that had "so greatly pleased" the editors was London's "To the Man on Trail." The editor, James Howard Bridge, wanted to publish the story because it was a Yuletide tale that would fit nicely into the *Overland*'s special holiday number. But five dollars was not the kind of reward Jack had been looking for; he had received five times that amount for an amateurish sketch written five years earlier. "What do you think of that for a first class magazine like the *Overland*?" he complained to Mabel. "Every magazine has its clique of writers, on whom it depends, and whom it patronizes in preference to all other writers . . . Well, a newcomer must excel them in their own fields before he is accepted, or else he must create a new field." He didn't realize that the *Overland* was short of funds and, since its revival in 1883, had been gradually slipping down from its pinnacle as the "Gold Coast *Atlantic*." Short of funds himself, Jack agreed to the offer.

The *Overland* acceptance did little to alleviate either his economic or his emotional depression. Furthermore, he had received recent news that his close friend Fred Jacobs, who had enlisted in the army to fight in the "Yanko-Spanko War," had died—not heroically in battle, but from food poisoning aboard a troopship en route to the Philippines. "About the loneliest Christmas I ever faced," he wrote to Mabel on December 25:

Nobody to talk to, no friend to visit—nay, if there were, and if I so desired, I would not be in position to. Hereafter and for some time to come, you'll have to content yourself with my beastly scrawl, for this is, most probably, the last machine-made letter I shall send you . . . The typewriter goes back on the thirty-first of December . . . Then the New Year, and an entire change of front.

On New Year's Eve he confessed in a letter to Ted Applegarth, "I have never been so hard up in my life." With the letter to Ted, in order to save postage, he enclosed another addressed to Mabel. What is most remarkable about these letters is not Jack's depression so much as his persistence in the face of discouragement. "I have reached a conclusion," he said to Mabel: "there is no such thing as inspiration. I thought so once, and made an ass of myself accordingly. Dig is the arcana of literature, as it is of all things save being born with a silver spoon and going to the Klondike."

Though broke, he was not broken. His morale had been boosted by the appearance of the magazine's holiday number on the newsstand, and he was sending a copy to Mabel:

It's the only one I possess, and I had to borrow a dime to buy it. Then I had no stamps, not one . . . But the unkindness of the Eastern Editors served your purpose. I often receive my MSS. back, with their stamps on the envelope; mine being still in the fold of the MS. [Today] I received four two cent stamps in this way, also two ones. Behold the letters and magazine.

In this same letter he mentioned that he was meeting with other prizewinners the next week to sue the Fifth Ward Republican Club for failure to give out their promised rewards. But most significant was the following comment:

The Black Cat writes me concerning a MS. submitted to them. They want references, as I am unknown. Then they wish to know if I wrote it myself, if the idea is mine, if it has ever been in print in part or whole, if it has ever been submitted elsewhere, and if others have or will have a copy of it. I complied. I wonder what they'll pay?

The Black Cat was a five-cent monthly magazine "devoted exclusively to original, unusual, fascinating stories," according to

H. D. Umbstaetter's editorial epigraph. "It pays nothing for the name or reputation of a writer, but the highest price on record for *Stories that are Stories*, and it pays not according to length, but according to strength." On November 13, Jack had submitted his manuscript "A Thousand Deaths," which he had disinterred from the box of stuff written and rejected during his writing spree in the spring of 1897: a pseudoscientific tale about a mad scientist who uses his son as a subject in a gruesome series of experiments to test a formula he has devised for bringing the dead back to life.

In terms of his career this was one of the most valuable stories London ever wrote. He didn't hesitate to explain its importance when he wrote the introduction to Umbstaetter's edition of *The Red-Hot Dollar and Other Stories from The Black Cat* in 1911. "He saved my literary life, if he did not save my literal life," Jack testified. "And I think he was guilty of the second crime, too . . .

> The end was in sight . . . I was finished . . . I was too miserable to plan anything save that I would never write again. And then . . . the mail brought a short, thin letter from Mr. Umbstaetter of the "Black Cat." He told me that the four-thousand-word story submitted to him was more lengthy than strengthy, but that if I would give permission to cut it in half, he would immediately send me a check for forty dollars.
>
> Give permission! It was equivalent to twenty dollars per thousand, or double the minimum rate. Give permission! I told Mr. Umbstaetter he could cut down two-halves if he'd only send the money along. He did, by return mail. And that is just precisely how and why I stayed by the writing game.

Jack's memory was playing tricks on him when he wrote Umbstaetter's introduction. He didn't receive the forty dollars from *The Black Cat* until February 23, 1899. He recorded this date in "No. 1 MAGAZINE SALES" with the note: "First money I ever received." While not factually accurate, London's later account conveyed his true feelings about the importance of Umbstaetter's acceptance.

One other notable event occurred at this time: the Oakland postmaster phoned to say there was a vacancy for mail carrier and that Jack could have the job. The starting pay would be sixty-five dollars a month, twice what he had made as a common laborer, with opportunities for regular increases, as well as security and retirement benefits. One month of delivering mail would pay more than he had made from two years of writing. On the other hand, *The Black Cat* was paying top dollar for the kind of fiction he could write with his eyes shut; the *Overland* had now accepted "The White Silence," and Bridge had offered to take the rest of his Malemute Kid stories at $7.50 apiece, with the promise of giving them prime space in the magazine. Even though the *Overland* had lost some of its former luster, it was still a big-name magazine and might serve as a springboard for an unknown young writer.

The prospects for literary success were now more promising than ever. Jack suddenly found himself caught on the horns of a dilemma:

> I'll never be able to forgive the postmaster of Oakland. I answered the call, and I talked to him like a man. I frankly told him the situation. It looked as if I might win out at writing. The chance was good, but not certain. Now, if he would pass me by and select the next man on the eligible list, and give me a call at the next vacancy—
>
> But he shut me off with: "Then you don't want the position?"
>
> "But I do," I protested. "Don't you see, if you will pass me over this time—"
>
> "If you want it you will take it," he said coldly.
>
> Happily for me, the cursed brutality of the man made me angry.
>
> "Very well," I said. "I won't take it."

Had there been an open position just a few weeks earlier, or a more sympathetic postmaster, America might have gained a dutiful public servant, one who would merely deliver other people's mail while relegating the name Jack London to the office of dead letters.

11

BEST IN CLASS: *THE ATLANTIC*

> You look back and see how hard you worked, and how poor
> you were, and how desperately anxious you were to succeed,
> and all you can remember is how happy you were. You were
> young, and you were working at something you believed in
> with all your heart, and you knew you were going to succeed.
>
> —JACK TO JOAN LONDON

"I am afraid I always was an extremist," London admitted; and the statement could have served as a fitting epitaph on his tombstone. Having rejected his opportunity with the post office, he threw himself anew into a routine more rigorous than ever. He was now working nearly nineteen hours a day, trying his hand at different literary genres and studying the works of other successful authors: "My light burned till two and three in the morning, which led a good neighbor woman into a bit of sentimental Sherlock Holmes deduction. Never seeing me in the daytime, she concluded that I was a gambler, and that the light in my window was placed there by my mother to guide her erring son home."

He said that part of his new routine was unlearning what his English teachers had taught him: "They knew all about 'Snow Bound' and 'Sartor Resartus'; but the American editors of 1899 did not want such truck. They wanted the 1899 truck." The "Mauve Decade," with its genteel manners and sentimental matters, was passing. This was the new Progressive Era, the Strenuous Age in American culture as well as in American politics. It was also the Golden Age of the Magazine. Magazines were *the* cultural medium, and magazine editors wielded enormous power to mold cultural values as well as political opinions—a power rarely possessed since that era before cinema, radio, television, and the Internet. The new editorial breed—men such as S. S. McClure, George Horace Lorimer, and Frank Munsey—were sending out their call for "Good easy reading for the people—no frills, no fine finishes, no hair-splitting niceties, but action, action, always action."

The short story was the ideal genre for this kind of action-packed reading. It was also ideally suited to a culture whose readers were often too busy for longer narratives. It was, for all practical purposes, an American invention, starting respectably with Irving's *Sketch Book*, taking on distinct form and psychological impact with Poe's *Tales of the Grotesque and Arabesque*, assuming moral and philosophical depth with the shorter fictions of Hawthorne and Melville, and gaining mass approval with Twain's tall tales and Harte's stories of a romanticized frontier. But mass approval depended upon mass circulation, and mass circulation depended upon affordable prices. The Golden Age of the Magazine resulted from technological advances in paper production, printing, and photoengraving—enhanced by cheaper mailing costs through the Postal Act of 1879 and, further, by the post–Civil War boom in business, specifically in advertising, as a source of increased revenue. Instead of a quarter or more, magazines could now be sold profitably for a dime or even a nickel.

By the end of the century, magazine publishing had become a major American industry, and the market was putting out its call for a correspondingly large new workforce. The old masters were now out of touch. William Dean Howells had moved into his "Editor's Easy Chair" at *Harper's*. Mark Twain had retired into his uneasy rocking chair at Nook Farm. Henry James had taken up permanent residence at Lamb House in Rye. Also gone to England was Bret Harte, sliding on thin financial ice and thinning literary acclaim, and Stephen Crane, the brightest of the new literary lights, dying from tuberculosis at Brede Place. Two New England local colorists, a feminist reformer, a shocking southerner, and a sophisticated New Yorker—Sarah Orne Jewett, Mary E. Wilkins Freeman, Charlotte Perkins Gilman, Kate Chopin, and Edith Wharton—had been producing first-rate fiction, but it wasn't the "virile" stuff the editor Frank Munsey wanted. Among male authors, the best stories were now being written by the Polish-born Joseph Conrad and three Britishers: H. G. Wells, Robert Louis Stevenson, and Rudyard Kipling. Jack acknowledged all four as masters, but it was Kipling, with his action-packed *Plain Tales from the Hills*, who made the greatest impact upon him. "I would never [have] written anywhere near the way I did had Kipling never been," he said; "there is no end of Kipling in my work." Reacting against a critic's attack on Kipling, London wrote a passionate testimonial that he might also have delivered in defense of his own work: "*That man of us is imperishable who makes his century imperishable. That man of us who seizes upon the salient facts of our life, who tells us what we thought, what we were, and for what we stood—that man shall be the mouthpiece to the centuries, and so long as they listen he shall endure.*"

London was still "groping for [his] own particular style" when he wrote to Cloudesley Johns in June 1899, but a letter he received in late July put an end to the groping: "Did you ever write a yarn of, say, twelve thousand words, every word essential to atmosphere, and then get an order to cut out three thousand of those words, somewhere, somehow?" he asked. "That's what the *Atlantic* has just done to me. Hardly know whether I shall do it or not. It's like the pound of flesh."

Of course he would do it. *The Atlantic* was America's premier magazine. The *Overland* had provided literary recognition, and *The Black Cat* had given financial reassurance: publication in *The Atlantic* guaranteed prestige. Henceforth there would be no further groping for his own particular style. What was good enough for *The Atlantic* would suffice for the rest. Within less than three days he had reduced his story to ten thousand words and mailed off his revised manuscript. Three months later he received a check for the sum of $120, plus a year's subscription to *The Atlantic*.

His story, "An Odyssey of the North," appeared in the January issue, and signaled a noteworthy change in Jack's literary fortunes. His entry for this item appears halfway through "NO. 1 MAGAZINE SALES FROM 1898 TO MAY 1900": the fifty-third of 103 entries. Of the fifty-eight items that were published during these two years, exactly twice as many were accepted after "An Odyssey" as those entered before. No longer working nineteen hours a day, he settled into a more professional routine, one he would follow the rest of his career: a minimum one thousand words a day, six days a week. As he explained to Cloudesley Johns, "I am sure a man can turn out more, and much better in the long run, working this way, than if he works by fits and starts."

Johns, postmaster at the desert village of Harold, California, was a young aspiring writer and socialist, a year older than London. Like Jack, Cloudesley was gifted with an exceptionally strong seeking drive. He had hit the adventure path as cowboy, longshoreman, hobo, and tracklayer. Burned out on the last job (laying rails for the Southern Pacific in 120-degree desert heat), he retreated to the family ranch outside Harold and took up writing as his career. In 1896, having successfully petitioned for a new Harold post office, he was appointed acting postmaster. He sold less than a dollar's worth of stamps a week, but the position allowed him free postage for mailing his manuscripts and plenty of spare time for writing. When he read "The White Silence" in the February 1899 *Overland Monthly*, he thought the magazine had made an even greater literary discovery than its discovery of Bret Harte. He wrote an enthusiastic letter to the editors, predicting the author's greatness and asking if "Jack London" was a pen name. The letter was forwarded to Jack, whose response was immediate:

> Dear sir:
>
> What an encouragement your short note was! From the same I judge you can appreciate one's groping in the dark on strange trails. It's the first word of cheer I have received (a cheer, far more potent than publisher's checks) . . .
>
> Yes, my name is Jack London—rather an un-American heritage from a Yankee ancestry, dating beyond the French and Indian Wars.
>
> Thanking you for your kindness,
>
> > I am,
> > very truly yours,
> > JACK LONDON.

This was the first of more than three hundred letters London would write to Johns during his lifetime, the most extensive of all his personal correspondence. Many of their letters, especially those written during the first year of their friendship, were more than two thousand words long, covering a range of topics from literature and editors to politics and science.

In response to Cloudesley's suggestion that they exchange photographs of each other, on February 22, Jack replied that he had only one picture of himself, taken in Yokohama wearing his sailor uniform, but he would describe himself: "Stand five foot seven or eight . . . weigh 168 lbs . . . Greenish-grey eyes . . . brown hair . . . Several scars—hiatus of eight front upper teeth, usually disguised with false plate . . . Now, reciprocate."

Cloudelsey did reciprocate, by sending a portrait of himself drawn by his mother, and Jack responded with his usual frankness. He liked what he saw except for Cloudesley's chin, which looked too "artistic": "It almost has the touch of effemicacy [sic] about it which I so detest to see in men. And yet, from your letters I have always derived the opposite conclusion—that you were strongly masculine. It had seemed there was so much in you, of rudeness, roughness, wildness, hurrah-for-hell sort of stuff, such as I possess—a certain affinity you see. I can't reconcile the two."

London's difficulty in reconciling these two natures—the roughly masculine and the softly feminine—was typical of his era. "Virility in a man, first and always," he exclaimed in another letter to Johns. "As for cowardice in man: I can forgive the errors of a generation of women far more easily than one poltroon of the opposite gender . . . A man without courage is to me the most dispicable [sic] thing under the sun, a travesty on the whole scheme of creation." When Cloudesley recounted a life-threatening encounter with two Mexican tracklayers armed with knife and gun, Jack replied, "How I envy the thrill of life [you must have felt] . . . one cannot really come to appreciate one's life, save by playing with it and hazarding it a little."

His letters to Cloudesley over the next several months revealed an increasing self-confidence along with the increasing number of acceptances over rejections from the magazines. By the end of summer, he was no longer complaining of rejections but talking of unexpected acceptances. His recent successes had also given him enough confidence to begin counseling other aspiring writers. On August 22, three days after sending "The Economics of the Klondike" to *The Review of Reviews*, he mailed off the first of a half-dozen essays on the writing profession he would publish during the early years of his career. "On the Writer's Philosophy of Life" defined the professional attitude that would characterize his entire career: "The literary hack, the one who is satisfied to turn out 'pot boilers' for the rest of his or her life, will save time and vexation by passing this article by. This is for the writer—no matter how much hack-work he is turning out just now—who cherishes ambitions and ideals." How may this serious young writer win success? By "*being original*," he advises. And how did such successful writers as Poe, Kipling, and Stevenson master the marketplace?

> They, with the countless failures, started even in the race . . . But in one thing they differed from the failures; they drew straight from the source, rejecting the material which filtered through other hands . . . So, from the world and its traditions—which is another term for knowledge and culture—they drew at first hand, certain materials, which they builded into an individual philosophy of life . . . you must know the spirit that moves to action individuals and peoples, which gives birth and momentum to great ideas, which hangs a John Brown or crucifies a Savior . . . And the sum of all this will be your working philosophy.

By the time he wrote to Cloudesley on September 6, Jack was receiving enough money not only to pay his bills but also to buy a brand-new Cleveland bicycle, which would take him around Oakland and as far south as San Jose, where the Applegarths were now living. Though he was no longer in love with Mabel, he had remained a close friend to her and to Ted.

Two other women who would play prominent roles in his life became close friends in 1899. The first was Elizabeth May ("Bess") Maddern. Jack had met her three years earlier, through his friend Fred Jacobs, to whom she was engaged before Jacobs's death in 1898. He had liked her from the beginning, and especially valued the help she had given him with his math and grammar in preparation for the entrance exams to Berkeley. Their daughter Joan noted her weakness along with her strength:

> Bess was several months younger than Jack, slender and athletic, with vigorous blue-black hair and hazel eyes. For several years she had been

earning her living by tutoring, but her manner of sturdy independence, which Jack admired even while in thrall to Mabel's helpless-
ness, was deceptive. Few knew that it was a gallant mask for unsureness
and a lack of self-confidence which assailed her whenever she stepped
outside the limits of her knowledge. Calmly and efficiently she would
have explained an algebra problem to the President of the United States
himself . . . but confronted by a discussion on literature, which she
dearly loved but felt she did not properly understand, she was struck
dumb.

During the summer of 1899, still trying to recover emotionally from
the loss of her fiancé, Bess found in Jack a cheerful companion. For
him, she filled an emotional void with her wholesome femininity, offering a nice balance between the effete gentility of Mabel's world and the
profligacies of the Barbary Coast. In July they began bicycling together
on the weekends, and Bess helped him develop his growing interest in
photography. By that fall they were "going steady"—not as sweethearts
but as good friends.

Late that fall, Jack met another young woman who promised a kind
of excitement missing from his previous relationships. Their first meeting took place toward the middle of December in San Francisco's Turk
Street Temple at a gathering of the Socialist Labor Party, commemorat-
ing the Paris Commune of 1871. She was Anna Strunsky, a nineteen-
year-old Stanford student who later married the "millionaire Socialist"
William English Walling. Anna recalled that as she was walking up
afterward to congratulate the speaker, Austin Lewis, she could not help
glancing at a very handsome young stranger. Frank Strawn-Hamilton
whispered, "Do you want to meet him? [He] is Jack London, a Comrade
who has been speaking in the streets of Oakland. He has been to the
Klondike and writes short stories for a living."

She did want to meet him. Their attraction was immediate and
mutual. By all accounts, Anna was exceptionally charming, a woman
whose photographs scarcely convey the full impact of her petite, exotic
beauty. Joseph Noel remembered her as "a pretty little ingenue who
played the part of a Stanford University intellectual to perfection,
[who] had soft brown eyes, a kindly smile and a throaty little voice that
did things to your spine." She was unlike any woman Jack had ever

met: vivacious, articulate, and exceptionally intelligent. Born in Russia on March 21, 1879, she had immigrated to America with her parents and five siblings in 1893. After a short time in New York City, the family settled in San Francisco, where her father, Elias Strunsky, operated a profitable liquor business. The Strunsky family was conservative in its moral standards—Anna's mother was the daughter of a rabbi—but liberal in intellectual and political attitudes. They welcomed into their home the Bay Area's leading bohemian artists, writers, and socialists. Anna herself had already achieved some notoriety because of a rumor that she had been temporarily suspended from Stanford for entertaining a male visitor in her room rather than in the dormitory parlor.

Jack was quick to recognize her as a fellow socialist and equally quick to sense that she might be a more personal fellow traveler as well. "My dear Miss Strunsky:—Seems as if I have known you for an age," he wrote on December 19. "[As] I sat there listening to you, I seemed to sum you up somewhat in this way: A woman to whom it is given to feel the deeps and the heights of emotion in an extraordinary degree; who can grasp the intensity of transcendental feeling, the dramatic force of a situation, as few women, or men either, can."

Anna's memoirs make it clear that she was no less infatuated than Jack. He was unlike any man she had ever met. Extraordinarily handsome and charismatic, intellectually as well as physically impressive, he "seemed the incarnation of the Platonic ideal of man," she recorded. As she told Jack's widow, Charmian, in 1919, "It was as if I were meeting in their youth Lasalle, Karl Marx or Byron, so instantly did I feel that I was in the presence of a historical character."

Jack London was not yet a literary celebrity in 1899, but he was a published author, which Anna aspired to become. While not on her social level, he could compensate by being her literary mentor. "Through much travail" he had learned how to deal with the "silent sullen peoples who run the magazines," he told her. He could also explain such practical matters as suitability of subject matter and rates of payment. "Should you stand in need of anything in this line (economic man), believe me sincerely at your service," he volunteered.

She accepted his offer, and they began corresponding regularly. Although her letters are not extant, his replies indicate that he was sensitive to his rough edges and eager to bridge the personal as well as social gap between them. He wanted her to understand that if he seemed too materialistic and lacking in "deftness of touch," it was due to his encounters with the "hard hand of the world," which had been laid upon him early in life. "Take me this way," he said, "a stray guest, a bird of passage, splashing with salt-rimed wings through a brief moment of your life—a rude and blundering bird, used to large airs and great spaces, unaccustomed to the amenities of confined existence."

Anna would gladly take him that way, for she later confessed that she had fallen in love with Jack at first sight. By the end of the year, the feeling was evidently mutual: "I came to you like a parched soul out of the wilderness, thirsting for I knew not what [and] from the little I have seen of you my lips have been moistened, my head lifted," he confided. "I do hope we shall be friends." They would be much more than friends. His professional affairs had already taken a turn, and with the new century, his personal affairs would take an even more dramatic turn.

12

MARRIAGE AND SUCCESS

As a brain merchant I was a success. Society opened its portals
to me. I entered right in on the parlor floor . . .

—"WHAT LIFE MEANS TO ME"

Nineteen hundred: a new century, the culmination of a millennium. At
the beginning of the century, the United States had emerged as a young
giant among nations; by the end, the country would be the greatest
power in human history.

Nineteen hundred: a new life for Jack London, the culmination of a
rigorous initiation. During that year, he was acclaimed the "American
Kipling," brightest of the new lights on the literary horizon; by the end
of the century, his works would be translated into nearly a hundred
languages and he would be widely recognized as America's greatest
"World Author." The lives of few writers have synchronized so precisely
with the life of their nation. And the careers of few writers mirror so
clearly the American Dream of Success and the corollary ideal of the
Self-Made Man.

Resolutely committed to the Dream through his chosen career, Jack
was determined to succeed on his own. He had learned by bitter experience that there was no financial future in selling his brawn. He had also
learned that he could count on no one else to help him along the less-
traveled road he had taken. But with "pluck and pertinacity" exceeding
the most ambitious of Horatio Alger's self-made heroes, he had at last
found a profitable market for his brain. He was quite candid about his

reasons for writing: "I am writing for money," he announced to Cloudesley; "if I can procure fame, that means more money." On March 1,
after *McClure's* had sent him a check equivalent to ten months' factory
work, he exclaimed, "Why certes, if they wish to buy me, body and
soul, they are welcome—if they pay the price."

Only superficially, however, was his obsession to get money materialistic: fundamentally, it was ideal. Money was the means to an end,
never an end in itself. The concept was essential to the American
Dream, inherited from the Puritan ethic and popularized by Ben
Franklin: material gain was a sign of spiritual grace. Money was the
coin of the New Realm, for it promised to buy happiness, security, es-
teem—in sum, the better life. "More money means more life to me,"
he declared. "I shall always hate the task of getting money; every time
I sit down to write it is with great disgust. I'd sooner be out in the open
wandering around most any old place. So the habit of money-getting
will never become one of my vices. But the habit of money spending, ah
God! I shall always be its victim."

His confession has provided his critics with an excuse for labeling
him a "popular hack" while overlooking Dr. Samuel Johnson's famous
quip that "No man but a blockhead ever wrote except for money." The
truth is that London's attitude toward his writing career was thoroughly professional: he deliberately chose writing as his principal
means of making his livelihood; he underwent rigorous training to acquire the special expertise of his chosen field; he wrote with the full
expectation of being paid well for his investment; he maintained the
discipline of steady application of his time and energies to his vocation;
and, having mastered his craft, he regarded it with a confidence border-
ing on contempt.

The formula for success as a "brain merchant" required the writer
to be a businessman. London reinforced this self-image by meticulous
bookkeeping, maintaining an exact record of all his literary submissions and sales. Based on this record, the first year of the new century
was a very good year, his best yet financially. His recorded earnings
amounted to $2,534.13, more than six times the $388.75 his work had
earned in 1899.

His career was now in full swing. On Christmas Day 1899, he had
signed a contract with the distinguished Boston firm of Houghton,

Mifflin and Company to publish his first book: a collection titled *The Son of the Wolf,* which included "An Odyssey of the North" from *The Atlantic* along with the eight Northland tales that had appeared in the *Overland.* On the last day of January 1900, responding to his publisher's request for biographical data to be used in advertising his book, he wrote his first major self-promotional letter. Not only the Man but also the Legend would henceforth be Self-Made.

First, the Son of the Frontier: "My father was Pennsylvania-born, a soldier, scout, backwoodsman, trapper, and wanderer . . . My life, from my fourth to my ninth years, was spent upon California ranches." Next, like Abe Lincoln, the Boy as Reader: "Was an omnivorous reader, principally because reading matter was scarce and I had to be grateful for whatever fell into my hands." Then, the Boy as Worker: "[From] my ninth year, with the exception of the hours spent at school (and I earned them by hard labor), my life has been one of toil." Further yet, the Youth as Adventurer: "At fifteen left home and went upon a Bay life. San Francisco Bay is no mill pond by the way. I was a salmon fisher, an oyster pirate, a schooner sailor, a fish patrolman, a longshoreman, and a general sort of bay-faring adventurer . . . Have been all over Canada, Northwest Ty. Alaska, etc., etc., at different times, besides mining, prospecting, and wandering through the Sierra Nevadas." Finally, the Writer as Self-Reliant Individual: "In the main I am self-educated; have had no mentor but myself."

He concluded his letter with a prophetic admission: "Am healthy, love exercise, and take little. Shall pay the penalty some day." He would indeed "pay the penalty," but for the time being he was running strong, personally and socially as well as professionally.

Personally speaking, his relationship with Anna Strunsky was moving ahead rapidly, and he was eager to dispense with the customary social formalities. "Dear Miss Strunsky," he began a letter on January 21,

> O Pshaw!
> Dear Anna:
> There! Let's get our friendship down to a comfortable basis. The superscription, "Miss Strunsky," is as disagreeable as the putting on of a white collar, and both are equally detestable.

Socially speaking, he mentioned to her his "fatal faculty" for friendships: "My home is the Mecca for every returned Klondiker, sailor, or soldier of fortune I ever met . . . Some day I shall build an establishment, invite them all, and turn them loose upon each other. Such a mingling of castes and creeds and characters could not be duplicated."

One of those characters was Cloudesley Johns, who had found a substitute postmaster and hoboed across the desert to meet his pen pal. After taking a week off to serve as host and tour guide, Jack returned to work as efficient businessman when his visitor left.

"Have to get in a dig now," he wrote to Johns on January 22, "have jumped my stint to 1500 words per diem till I get out of the hole." Eight days later he boasted that even though he was sometimes managing to do as many as two thousand words a day while keeping up his studies and correcting proofsheets, he had broken none of his social engagements.

One special engagement he had no intention of breaking was the next day at Stanford with Anna Strunsky, whom he had promised to meet in the University Library. "Ah! the physical basis—you a lunch and I an appetite," he exclaimed. While intellectually precocious, she was quite properly naïve in sexual matters and evidently took no offense from Jack's suggestive metaphor. And since he had not yet discovered Freud, he may not have been fully aware of his implications. Aware or not, both were in love. Many years afterward, she reminisced:

> I see him, steering his bicycle with one hand and with the other clasping a great bunch of yellow roses which he had just gathered out of his own garden, a cap moved back on his thick brown hair, the large blue eyes with their long lashes looking out star-like upon the world—an indescribably virile and beautiful boy, the kindness and wisdom of his expression somehow belying his youth.

Here, for the first time in Jack's life, was a woman who possessed a mind and a spirit to match the beauty of her body and the charm of her voice. Impressed by her literary ambitions, he had encouraged her to seek publication. Understanding that he had already completed his initiation into the marketplace, she wanted him to be more than the "economic man" who gave her tips about rates and such. She told him she wanted him to be her literary "taskmaster."

"Good!" he responded on February 13: "I'll not be sparing, and I promise you I'll handle you without gloves. We'll get right down to the naked facts of life . . . I do not know you very well, so I may make mistakes and do you many injustices; so you must forgive all things in advance. It's safest, you know, to obtain indulgence before you sin."

Within the next few weeks, he would get to know her very well. He would also make more than one mistake and do her some injustices, at least one very grave one, for which she would forgive him. Anna herself, concerned that she might seem overly forward in their relationship, refrained from addressing him as "Jack" for several weeks. "Nobody ever 'Mr. London's' me, so every time I opened a letter of yours I felt a starched collar round my neck," he fussed on February 20. "Pray permit me softer neck-gear for the remainder of our correspondence."

By the end of the month he felt comfortable enough to send her a box of his early, unpublished literary efforts. He was careful to let her know that this gesture was an exceptional compliment as well as favor to her: "I am doing thus to you what I have done to no other person, and sheerly with the desire to encourage you," he confided. "Do you show them to no one. Like the leper, I have exposed my sores; be gentle with me, and merciful in your judgment."

Their romance blossomed in March. He was writing or seeing her almost every day—bringing her flowers and books; reading Browning, Swinburne, and Wordsworth with her; attending the theater with her and her brothers; hiking on the nearby hills; and enjoying her softly sensuous poetry recitations during their strolls. On March 24 he put his courtship on temporary hold, biking down to San Jose for a three-day visit with the Applegarths. He returned home on March 27 having decided to make his conclusive move during his rendezvous with Anna the next day: He would ask her to marry him. What actually occurred that next day would burn itself into her memory, leaving a permanent emotional scar: "On a certain Wednesday they had climbed the slopes, slippery with pine needles and sun-parched grass, still warm to the touch," she wrote later, evidently intending to publish her memoirs narrated in the third person:

There was a feeling of crisis between them—of something nearer, sweeter about to be born. [However,] his hands straying over her loosened hair, she threw a vista of distance and struggle between them [and] her soul followed the fashion . . . She had taken refuge in a remark about going to Russia, fearing that she had been overbold, fearing that he might feel she had made some demand upon him . . . She feared he might think that she was wooing him, that she was "invading his personality," a phrase she had learned from her Anarchist friends . . . If he had asked her to marry him, sitting there on that knoll, the book on her lap, she might have thrown her young arms around his neck, pressing her head against his shoulder which it hardly reached. He did not ask her.

Why didn't he ask her? It had evidently been his intention. Three months of knowing Anna and the Strunsky family—so attractive, so loving, so alive both socially and intellectually—had shown him that domesticity could be dynamic as well as respectable. Having sown his share of wild oats, he was finally ready to settle down and marry, if he could find the right woman. From all he had seen, Anna was the right one.

So why indeed had he not proposed to her at that critical moment? Anna herself has given the clues in her memoir. Just as Jack was ready to commit himself, "his hands straying over her loosened hair," she suppressed her own feelings. Despite her seeming independence and her liberal politics, Anna was still a child of her times, conditioned by the standards of Victorian gentility. Her natural instincts—to "have thrown her young arms around his neck, pressing her head against his shoulder" and telling how deeply his loving words and touch thrilled her—were therefore bound to fail.

And what about Jack's behavior at this critical moment? In such delicate sexual/cultural matters, he was no less than Anna a child of the times. Had this been a working-class girl, he would easily have asserted himself without inhibition. But because Anna was a member of that higher class to which he aspired but whose rules he did not yet fully comprehend, he felt compelled to play it safe. Unsure and hesitant, fearful at the crucial moment that the lady would respond to his proposal with a nonchalant rebuff, he had tried, as tactfully as he knew how, to force the moment to its crisis by gently stroking her hair and asking about her future plans. And she, compelled "to follow the fashion," had drawn away, coyly remarking that she was thinking of traveling back to Russia, to share the Revolution beginning there.

"Youth says one thing and means another," she reflected sadly.

Not recognizing the evasive intricacies of the genteel flirting game, Jack misinterpreted her coyness as disinterest or, more threatening to his male ego, rejection. Apprehensive that he himself had been too forward and exposed himself too openly, instead of gallantly persisting according to the rules of the game, he abruptly withdrew without further incriminating himself.

Youth feels one thing and does another. Four days after that, Jack reinforced his ego by ungallantly proposing marriage to Bessie Maddern. He did not love her, but he had genuine affection and respect for her as a friend. Furthermore, he thought she possessed all the right stuff to become a fine wife and mother, and he needed someone to help him settle down. He also thought he would be a faithful husband and good family provider.

Unaware of his true motive, Bessie hastily accepted his proposal. She did not love him, but she enjoyed his natural charm and friendship. She had lost her true love, Fred Jacobs, but she was ready for marriage and agreed that she could make Jack a good wife and mother to their children. Love would come later—or so she thought. The day Jack proposed was Sunday, the first day of April. He may have chosen that date deliberately. In any event, his choice would prove to be worse than foolhardy. "You must be amused, lest you die," he wrote to Cloudesley Johns two days later. "Here goes. You will observe that I have moved [from 962 East Sixteenth Street to a larger house at 1130 East Fifteenth Street in Oakland]. Good! Next Saturday I shall be married. Better? Eh? Will send announcement to the funeral later."

Cloudesley was not amused. His succinct reply was "Jesus H. Christ!" After receiving the engraved wedding invitation a few days later, he wrote, "May I defer my congratulations of you and Mrs. Jack for ten years? Then I shall tender them—Thursday, April 7, 1910 . . . I heartily wish you both permanent satisfaction."

"Why certainly you may defer congratulations till April 7th, 1910," Jack replied: "Permit me to felicitate you upon your last letter bar this one I am answering. We all had a good laugh over it and enjoyed it immensely. I was away on the little wedding trip when it arrived, and my sister (you met her), looked at it and said she'd give ten dollars to see what you had to say. And it was worth it."

He wanted Cloudesley to understand that marriage had not muddled his priorities, explaining that he'd already resumed his steady quota of one thousand words a day and boasting that he was even getting paid now for some of his hackwork.

Among others to whom Jack had written to announce his forthcoming marriage was Ninetta Eames. As the wife of Roscoe Eames, managing editor of the *Overland Monthly,* she was actively involved in the editorial affairs of the magazine. She had already interviewed London for an article she would publish in the May issue. She was also actively involved in the personal affairs of her niece Clara Charmian Kittredge. Seeing Jack as an eligible bachelor as well as a bright new star on the literary horizon, she had introduced the two, suggesting that Charmian review *The Son of the Wolf* when the *Overland* received its review copy. Advance copies were sent out in late March, and Mrs. Eames wrote to Jack to tell him how attractive the book looked—and to invite him to her home Saturday, April 7, for lunch with her and Miss Kittredge.

"Must confess you have the advantage of me. I have not yet seen my book, nor can I possibly imagine what it looks like," he answered on April 3:

Nor can you possibly imagine why I am going to beg off from going out to your place next Saturday. You know I do things quickly. Sunday morning, last, I had not the slightest intention of doing what I am going to do. I came down and looked over the house I was to move into—that fathered the thought. I made up my mind. Sunday evening I opened transactions for a wife; by Monday evening had the affair well under way; and next Saturday morning I shall marry—a Bessie Maddern, cousin to Minnie Maddern Fiske . . .

"The rash boy," I hear you say. Divers deep considerations have led me to do this thing; but I shall over-ride just one objection—that of being tied. I am already tied. Though single, I have had to support a

household just the same . . . As it is, I shall be steadied, and can be able
to devote more time to my work . . . I shall be a cleaner, wholesomer
man because of a restraint being laid upon me in place of being free to
drift wheresoever I listed.

He may have been lying, even to himself, when he told Eames that
he "had not the slightest intention" of marrying before looking over the
house on Fifteenth Street. He did need a larger place for Flora, Johnny
Miller, and himself—especially a house with a good working study for
his reading and writing. The spacious thirteen-by-fifteen-foot upstairs
room in the new two-story house would make him a perfect library
and study. It was also true that he was now "tied" to work to support
Flora and Johnny as well as himself. On the other hand, the intention to
marry was already in, if not on, his mind before he "looked over the
house." Now he was trying to convince others, and himself, that "this
thing," as he called it, was a good business transaction.

His dissimulation was transparent in a letter dated April 6, 1900, to
Anna, who had just replied to his April 3 announcement: "How glad
your letter has made me," he exclaimed. "It [the proposal] was rather sudden. I always do things that way. I have been so rushed that I have forgotten whether you were on the list of those I did write to, or did not," he
said, feigning disinterest even as he contradicted himself: "You see, I had
several hours to devote to letter writing, started in, and part way through
was called away. This is the first letter I have written since, and I do not
know whether I had got to you or not." She could hardly have congratu-
lated him so quickly if he had not notified her—in fact, she had just
written a response to his own letter. He continued to rationalize: "For a
thousand reasons I think myself justified in making this marriage." He
then committed a startling non sequitur: "It will not, however, interfere
much with my old life or my life as I had planned it for the future."

His vision was as murky as his logic.

On the next day—Saturday, April 7—the wedding was held privately in the Maddern home. On that same day, *The Son of the Wolf* was
officially released by Houghton Mifflin. The book was greeted with rave
reviews. "The Klondike has waited three years for its storyteller and
interpreter to set it in an imperishable mold," announced *The New York*

Times Saturday Review of Books and Art: "London catches the life and conflicts of the Far North with a sure touch, strong dramatic power, a keen eye for character drawing and a natural gift for storytelling . . . There is more than a trace of genius, together with much crude writing, refreshing frankness, and touches of poetic insight." Closer to home, in *The San Francisco Call*, B. G. Lathrop asserted that Rudyard Kipling and Hamlin Garland "have written no better." Reviewing the book for the *San Francisco Chronicle*, George Hamlin Fitch hailed London as "the Bret Harte of the Frozen North, with a touch of Kipling's savage realism, [worthy of] a foremost place among American short story writers."

Although receiving no rave reviews, Jack's hasty marriage seemed to be starting off well enough, except for one major problem: Bessie's mother-in-law. With her son's newly won success, Flora believed that for the first time since her girlhood as daughter of one of Massillon's most prominent citizens she would return to the manor to which she had been rightfully born. It was she who had urged the Bay Area's most celebrated young author to enter his first writing contest when he was an unknown common laborer. And she alone had stood by him, encouraging him to persist in his literary efforts when all the rest were pressuring him to give it up and get a steady job. Now, at last, with the Londons' move into their handsome new home, she should become Lady of the Manse, organizing the cultural calendar and presiding over the social activities for her famous son and his interesting and often influential friends. Such was Flora's own version of the Dream. For the first time in his life, Jack noted the hint of a smile on his mother's face.

That smile faded the moment Flora discovered her son was bringing another woman into the house. She was not pleased. Instead, she was angry and bitterly disappointed, and she made no effort to conceal her resentment. She reverted to the frequent temper tantrums that had characterized her spoiled childhood, and she refused to bite her tongue when she noted any slips in Bessie's housekeeping or cooking. Some civility was restored when Jack moved Flora and Johnny into their own cottage on the block behind. Eventually Flora and Bessie would become friends. "Grandma was loyal to me when it most counted, and ever since," Bessie told her daughter Joan.

London's political as well as his social activities were increasing along with his celebrity. He had been a charter member of the Ruskin Club (a group of Oakland intellectuals, mostly socialists, more Fabian than Marxian), founded by Frederick Bamford in 1898. The group was described by an area newspaper as a "high-up literary and philosophical society." With his rising stature, Jack now not only debated with his fellow members but also occasionally presided over their meetings and presented formal lectures that were reported in the local newspapers.

Other groups had begun inviting him to speak—for example, the Adelphian Club in Alameda, the Parlor Lecture Club in Fresno, and various socialist groups in the Bay Area. Sometimes he spoke on literary matters and read from his own works; on other occasions he lectured on socialism and the need for governmental reforms. Despite his claim that he was "a writing man primarily, and not a talker," he had become a popular speaker, more comfortable than that day he begged Jim Whitaker to help him mount the soapbox in City Hall Park. Unlike the typical platform orators of the nineteenth century, he lacked a powerful elocutionary voice, but his approach to public address, like his approach to writing, was quite modern: natural and unpretentious. As a result, he was a successful lecturer whose unaffected charm, youthful good looks, and enthusiasm, coupled with his genuine sincerity and his passion for ideas, seldom failed to elicit warm responses from his listeners. "Mr. London's smooth face is guiltless of lines, and his eyes twinkle with boyish enjoyment of life, excepting when a serious thought darkens the blue to grey, when they dim with womanish tenderness," wrote one San Francisco reporter: "With a gesture that is familiar to those who have seen him on the lecture platform, the author shakes his tawny hair from his brow as he speaks, and is a fluent talker, ready with his words, and uttering them in a voice as flexible as a child's."

Even with his busy schedule, 1900 was one of Jack's healthiest years. Marriage had proved a boon to both his work and his health. For the first time in his life, he began to get regular sleep and exercise: boxing and fencing with his tutor, Jim Whitaker, swimming and diving when he could get to the Oakland natatorium. His favorite was biking. "Ever bike?" he wrote to the author Ida Strobridge:

I take exercise every afternoon that way. O, just to grip your handle bars, and lay down to it (lie doesn't hit it at all), and go ripping and tearing through streets and roads, over railroad tracks and bridges, threading crowds, avoiding collisions, at twenty miles or more an hour, and wondering all the time when you're going to smash up—well, now, that's something.

Nineteen hundred was also a healthy year socially. Now that he had settled down, there were no more wild escapades on the Barbary Coast. Aside from meetings of the Ruskin Club and socialist gatherings, he was mainly limiting his camaraderie to Wednesday evenings with friends and fellow artists. His extraordinary vitality was now harnessed and, when he was not at work on manuscripts, devoted to fun and games. Card games of all sorts—blackjack, pedro, pinochle, poker, whist—were most popular. The guests chatted and entertained each other with jokes and stories; on some evenings, London read aloud his own latest literary creations.

Word about the Wednesday entertainments eventually attracted the attention of the Bay Area's most prominent artistic bons vivants. Principal among these was the bohemian group known as "the Crowd," which included such figures as Joaquin Miller (recovered from his Klondike trauma and more flamboyant than ever), James Hopper (graduated from UC Berkeley and a successful journalist and magazine writer), Jim Whitaker (who was now trying to make a literary name for himself with Jack's help), Xavier Martínez (long-haired and mustachioed Paris-trained painter who would shock the group by marrying Whitaker's daughter Elsie, a teenager half his age), Arnold Genthe (destined to become one of the century's renowned pioneers in portrait photography), the Partingtons (Blanche, drama critic for *The San Francisco Call*; Richard, celebrated portrait painter; and Phyllis, who would achieve operatic fame under the name Frances Peralta), and most notably, George Sterling, California's answer to Oscar Wilde and Wilde's fellow fin de siècle poets. Although the two would not meet for another year, Sterling was fated to play a major role in the complex drama of Jack London's life.

Within little more than a week after his wedding, Jack was reconnecting with another major player in his life: Anna Strunsky. "Well, I'm back and just going through the process of getting things in shape and settling down to work," he wrote on April 16. Ignoring the fact that he had already responded to her "kind letter" ten days before, he added, "Also, Mrs. Jack, as well as myself, wishes to thank you for your most kind letter of some time since, which same I do not remember whether I replied to or not."

Anna wanted him to continue as her literary mentor, and he seemed content to play this role. Later in May, when he sent one of her stories to *The Atlantic* accompanied by his personal letter of recommendation to the editor, Bliss Perry, he wrote to her, "O Anna, don't disappoint me. You have got everything; all you need is to work and work, and to work with the greatest care."

Jack was now confident that he had mastered his own tools of the trade. Proof that he had in fact done so is evident in the expert advice he gave Cloudesley on June 16: "You are handling stirring life, romance, things of human life and death, humor and pathos, etc. But God, man, handle them as they should be," he declared, commenting on a sketch Johns had drawn from his hoboing adventures:

> Don't you tell the reader the philosophy of the road (except where you are actually there as participant in the first person). Don't you tell the reader. Don't. Don't. Don't. But HAVE YOUR CHARACTERS TELL IT BY THEIR DEEDS, ACTIONS, TALK, ETC. Then, and not until then, are you writing fiction and not a sociological paper upon a certain sub-stratum of society.

Responding to another young writer, Elwyn Irving Hoffman, who had asked about London's method of composition, Jack explained, "In the first place I never begin a thing, but what I finish it before I begin anything else. Further; I type as fast as I write, so that each day sees the work all upon the final MS. which goes for editorial submission."

In answer to Hoffman's query about the origination of his plots, he confessed, "I'm damned if my stories just come to me. I had to work like the devil for the themes. Then, of course, it was easy to just write them down . . . To find some thought worthy of being clothed with enough verbiage to make it a story, there's the rub!"

Working with longer fictional structures was a more serious rub. By summer, Jack had won enough recognition to get the attention of S. S. McClure, who offered to advance $125 a month for the next five months on the agreement that Jack would produce a novel. "Did I tell you that McClure has bought me?" he wrote to Cloudesley. "Well, it is so, and I start in shortly, though filled with dismay in anticipation."

His apprehension was well founded, but the prospect of such additional money to offset his rising domestic expenses was too tempting to reject. On September 9 he told Cloudesley he had finished the first chapter of his novel: "Since it is my first attempt, I have chosen a simple subject and shall simply endeavor to make it true, artistic, and interesting." Five months later he would write that he was "on the home stretch of the novel" and admit that it was "a failure." He was right. *A Daughter of the Snows* was a clumsy Klondike romance overlaid by his pet ideas on social Darwinism, Anglo-Saxon supremacy, and environmental determinism. "Lord, Lord," he moaned, looking back on it years later, "how I squandered into it enough stuff for a dozen novels!" McClure declined to print it, and farmed out the manuscript to another publisher.

By midsummer Anna had become a regular visitor to the London home, welcomed by Bess as well as Jack. Perhaps none of the three was fully aware of what was beneath the friendly surface when Anna went sailing with the Londons in August. During the late afternoon, while the boat was becalmed, Jack initiated a discussion of eugenics. He argued that "love was a madness, a fever that passes, a trick. One should marry for qualities and not for love," Anna recalled. Jack therefore proposed that the two of them should collaborate on a book about eugenics versus romantic love: "Before we landed we had our plot, a novel in letter form in which Jack was to be an American, an economist, Herbert Wace, and I an Englishman, a poet, Dane Kempton, who stood in relation to him of father to son."

Anna, with an enthusiasm matching his own, accepted Jack's proposal. They would be not only respectably engaged in this common project but also properly wed to its fruition. Six weeks later he explained his latest project to Cloudesley: "A young Russian Jewess of 'Frisco and myself have often quarreled over our conceptions of love. She happens to be a genius. She is also a materialist by philosophy, and an idealist by innate preference, and is constantly being forced to twist all the facts of the universe in order to reconcile herself with herself. So, finally, we decided that the only way to argue the question would be by letter."

The question would be argued out, to be sure, but not in the way

Jack intended: the ultimate effect of the debate would be to purge him forever of his "scientific" conception of love. His confidence in his position had become badly shaken before the completion of their project. "For a week I have been suffering from the blues, during which time I have not done a stroke of work," he wrote to Anna on December 26. "I remember, now, when I was free. When there was no restraint, and I did what the heart willed. Yes, one restraint, the Law; but when one willed, one could fight the law, and break or be broken. But now, one's hands are tied, one may not fight, but only yield and bow the neck." Then, responding to her question about the complex nature of their relationship, he confessed:

> A happiness to me? . . . Why you have been a delight to me, dear, and a glory. Need I add, a trouble? . . . What you have been to me? I am not great enough or brave enough to say. This false thing, which the world would call my conscience, will not permit me. But it is not mine; it is a social conscience, the world's, which goes with the world's leg-bar and chain. A white beautiful friendship?—between a man and a woman?—the world cannot imagine such a thing.

Setting aside the world's social conscience, their "white beautiful friendship" would presently become a white-hot love affair.

13

IN KEY WITH THE WORLD

Every man, at the beginning of his career . . . has two choices.
He may choose immediate happiness, or ultimate happiness . . .
He who chooses ultimate happiness, and has the ability, and
works hard, will find that the reward for his efforts is cumulative, that the interest on his energy is compounded.

—LONDON TO CLOUDESLEY JOHNS

There is no question about Jack's ability or his dedication to hard
work. The reward for his efforts would be cumulative—but not in the
manner he suggested to Cloudesley, for he was too often compelled by
nature to choose immediate over ultimate happiness. He would learn
in the years following his literary debut that the success he had worked
so hard to achieve did not automatically bring financial security or
happiness.

He greeted the New Year with mixed emotions. He was working
hard if halfheartedly to finish *A Daughter of the Snows*, knowing all the
time it was less than his best. After his elation over the rave reviews on
his coming out with *The Son of the Wolf*, he was suffering a letdown.
"To tell you the truth," he complained to Cloudesley, "I haven't had any
decent work published recently." Although he was still getting his
monthly checks from McClure, his financial needs were now greater
than ever. "I am sorry that I cannot help you out just now," he responded
to a friend's request for a loan:

... a friend [Jim Whitaker] has taken up writing with seven children and an undeveloped ability, which said friend I have been helping to finance. Then my mother, to whose pension I add thirty dollars each month, got back in her debts and I have just finished straightening her out to the tune of thirty-six dollars . . . And my Mammie Jennie [needed a] December quarterly payment of interest on mortgage, and delinquent taxes.

On the other hand, he was neither halfhearted nor sorry about his relationship with Anna. "I should like to have you meet Miss Anna Strunsky some time," he wrote to Elwyn Hoffman on January 6. "She is deep, subtle, and psychological . . . a joy and a delight to her friends." On that same day, he wrote to Anna, inviting her to come see him on Saturday: "My birthday. A quarter of a century of breath. I feel very old." He and Bessie were expecting their first child—they hoped on Jack's own birthday. "I do pray for a boy," he confided to Anna. "No whining puny breed. It must be great and strong."

As Joan herself later admitted, her birth initially was a disappointment to her father. "I had failed him in three important ways: I was a girl, I arrived in bad shape, and I was not born on his birthday as scheduled."

She had indeed "arrived in bad shape." Bessie's labor had been dangerously protracted and painful. In a desperate measure to save the mother's life, if not the child's, the doctor resorted to the use of instruments, crushing the baby's temple with his forceps in the difficult delivery. Turning his immediate attention to the mother, he handed the infant to Melissa Maddern, Bessie's mother, who spent the next critical moments trying various methods to force the newborn to take her first breath: "spanking, chafing and rubbing the tiny body, immersing it alternately in hot and cold water, placing drops of brandy in the unresponsive mouth and, finally, for long minutes, forcing air from her own lungs into mine." Giving it up at length as a lost cause, Grandmother Maddern "laid me against her shoulder for the last time," Joan recounted the story as told to her, "patting me gently and murmuring words of pity and love." At that moment occurred the miracle of life: "My thin wail transfixed everyone."

"What have you done?" Jack cried at the sight of the baby's misshapen head, fearing he had fathered a monster. "You should have let it die!" Melissa rose to the moment again, this time rescuing the frantic father. "Dear Jack," she said, drawing him aside and likewise patting him gently, "you have a fine, healthy daughter. How else could she have survived what she has been through? And don't be concerned about her head. In a day or two, you'll see, it'll be rounded and sweet like the head of every girl-baby."

Grandmother Melissa had wrought a second miracle. The father's shock was transformed into exuberant joy. Before midafternoon he had jotted the announcement of his new daughter's birth on a postcard and bicycled down to the main post office to mail it off to Ted Applegarth. He then persuaded Bessie's nurse to dress the newborn girl in a lace-trimmed white frock and prop her up onto pillows while he arranged his camera, tripod, and flashpan for her photograph. This would be the first picture in an album titled *Joan, Her Book*. Over the next three years, the proud father regularly added photographs of Joan (named after his favorite heroine, Joan of Arc), with loving captions such as the following:

Joan meditateth on the Mystery of Things, Vieweth life Pessimistically, And striveth hard to be Reconciled—all at Three Weeks Old.

She Smileth at Three Months . . . And cryeth immediately after . . . at Three Months . . . at Three Months and Five Minutes. N.B.—And Weigheth Fifteen Pounds.

What maketh the Funny Noise? No, it is not the Camera that maketh the Funny Noise. It is the Squeaky Pig, which the Purple Cow Man giveth her at Five Months . . .

At Nine Months she Biketh with the Pater, Who is the Pater No longer, but Daddy. Behold Joan's House in the Distance.

Enhancing his joy in being a new father was Jack's pleasure in developing, with Bessie's help, the art of photography. This skill would prove invaluable professionally as well as personally during the next several years, particularly in that it allowed him to document his travelogues and war reports. He would become the first major American author to meld the media of literature and photography.

Another significant event occurred in January when he agreed to run for office of mayor on the Socialist ticket. "I understand that as soon as Jack London is elected Mayor of Oakland by the Social Democrats the name of the place will be changed," commented "Yorick" in *The San Francisco Evening Post*: "The Social Democrats, however, have not yet decided whether they will call it London or Jacktown." A reporter for *The San Francisco Examiner* was less facetious, noting that London "is still as eager a champion of the toilers and as strong a sympathizer with the unsuccessful as when he worked before the mast and tramped his hungry way to the East." Jack knew from the outset that he was in no danger of being elected—he would receive only 246 votes—but here was another opportunity to promote his own career along with the ideals of the party. In a letter to J. H. Eustice, secretary of the City Executive Committee of the Social Democratic Party, he explained that the local municipal platform was "part of a great world philosophy—an economic, political and social philosophy, reared on sound ethical, and humanely ethical, foundations. Its one great demand is justice, or, in other words, an equal chance for all men." Notwithstanding his later disenchantment with the party, he would remain true to this philosophy throughout his life.

By early spring of 1901, heavy rains had flooded the yard and basement of the Londons' house on East Fifteenth Street, forcing another move. Felix Peano, a local sculptor and fellow Ruskin Club member, came to their rescue: If Jack and Bessie provided free meals, he would provide rent-free housing at La Capricciosa, his rococo villa near Lake Merritt. "Am much more finely situated now," Jack wrote to Cloudesley on March 15, "nearer to Oakland, with a finer view, surroundings, air, etc., etc." He loved the place, with its "large, beautiful terrace high above the street, with pots of flowers and trailing vines, a pepper tree and a handsome pergola supported by neo-Corinthian columns," says Joan, "but Mother remembered it chiefly as chilly, badly planned, with small, dark rooms in which keeping house and caring for a baby were difficult."

Jack finished *A Daughter of the Snows* at the end of March. "The novel is off at last, and right glad am I that it is," he wrote to Cloudesley on April 1. He revealed in the same letter his penchant for urban living, advising Johns to resign from his postal job "off there on the edge of things . . . Get you a big city anywhere, and plunge into it and live and meet people and things." Cloudesley took the advice and moved to Los Angeles that same month.

Jack was practicing what he preached. Now he was meeting more people than ever. Besides his frequent lectures and socialist activities, his social activities, after months of domestication, were intensifying. A favorite rendezvous was Coppa's restaurant, located in San Francisco's famous Montgomery Block. Designed by Henry Wager Halleck to be erected upon a redwood raft foundation at the edge of the bay, this four-story "wonder of masonry" was the tallest (and most impressive) building west of the Mississippi when it was built in 1853. Initially dubbed by envious skeptics as "Halleck's Folly," it was one of the few structures to withstand the shock of the 1906 earthquake.

During the latter decades of the nineteenth century, the place became fondly called the "Monkey Block," as hundreds of various artists and bohemians not only met but also took rooms there. Among the notable tenants were Ambrose Bierce, Xavier Martínez, and Charles Warren Stoddard. The Norris novelists—Charles, Frank, and Kathleen—used it as a studio for painting and writing. Lawrence Ferlinghetti, the prominent Beat-era poet, notes that George Sterling, "resembling Pan or Peter Pan, kept a room for his many secret amours."

Although the historic moment of London's initial personal encounter with Sterling has been variously recorded, the consensus is that they first met through mutual friends in the spring of 1901, probably at Coppa's. They seemed at the beginning to have little in common. George Ansel Sterling III, the son of an eminent Sag Harbor physician, had been comfortably reared and educated in the East. He was ostensibly a businessman working toward executive advancement as a clerk for his uncle, the wealthy Oakland real estate agent Frank C. Havens. Coming under the tutelage of Ambrose Bierce, George decided at the age of twenty-six to become the last great fin de siècle poet. It was an unfortunate decision, because he possessed exceptional promise as a lyricist. Still, misguided by Bierce and artistically overvalued by the Crowd (who assured him that he had the ideal persona and profile), he felt compelled to adhere to the conventions of late-Victorian poetry while American poetry matured into the twentieth century through the "New Poetry" of writers such as Harriet Monroe, Ezra

Pound, and T. S. Eliot. Even so, he was a major figure among West Coast literati in the early twentieth century and the greatest of poets in the eyes of his new friend Jack London, who would subsequently valorize him as the brilliant tubercular cynic Russ Brissenden in *Martin Eden*.

As the two men became better acquainted, they found that their differences were superficial—that they were spiritual (and pagan) brothers beneath the skin. They shared a mutual interest in socialism and were intent upon drinking life to the lees. As a result, they also shared mutual interests in fun and games—and wild parties. Charmian described George as "a prince of extremists": "When he drank, he drank, anything and everything, without regard to the combination. When he went on the water-wagon, he did it thoroughly, perhaps a year or more at a time, and was very proud of himself and the ease of his experiment." She recounted, among other incidents, George's introduction of Jack to hashish at one of the Sterlings' parties. Heedless of caution, Jack apparently made himself a very thick "dream sandwich" that transported him not into dreamland but into a nightmare of nervous prostration and hysteria. "I told him to spread only a thin layer of the stuff and he would have a lovely time. Now look at him!" exclaimed Sterling in disgust. "Jack was afflicted with a plague of laughter" when the initial effects began to wear off several hours later, Charmian recalled, "and his giggles and gales were infectious. George was hugely entertained by this phase, which lasted over another day, and spent much time peering at the patient with an expression of wonderment and low exclamations that were as funny as Jack's pointless explosions."

Never one to be outdone, London introduced Sterling to some of the dens of sin he had frequented during his roistering days in the Bay underworld. According to their erstwhile friend Joseph Noel, George's penchant for sex stopped short of paying for female favors. Noel reported that Sterling, repulsed by the atmosphere of a high-class brothel to which London had led him, offended Jack by calling the buxom madam a "procuress." His use of this word, with its sanctimonious connotation, apparently hit a nerve. One of Jack's most remarkable traits, said Noel, "was a strange, fervid, almost prophetic eloquence, after deep drinking," as witnessed in his response to George:

"You think that woman is a pariah because she satisfies one of the great fundamental needs of man. Is the grocer a pariah? The manufacturer? Human needs are satisfied by them and for exactly the same reason. Profit. Look you, I'd rather be that stout provider of happiness in wholesale lots, whom you call a procuress, than a mill owner who exploits women and children. I'd rather be one of those girls of hers than a writer pandering to the mill owner."

During the dozen years following their initial meeting, the London-Sterling friendship grew steadily in mutual appreciation. Jack's inscriptions in the first editions he gave George reveal the depth of his affection, as witnessed by the following in *The Night-Born*:

Blessed, Beloved Greek:—The seasons change, but I change not toward you; the years pass, but I pass not for you, as you pass not for me. Ours is some friendship, and greater than that, it is love.

—Thine,

"THE WOLF" ALIAS JACK LONDON

Sadly, during the last few years of his life, Jack's behavior toward George would change, as reflected in the inscription in *The Acorn-Planter*, less than a month before his death: "Dearest Greek: Love me, forgive me . . . I'm all out of key with the world in which I live."

In 1901, Jack was very much "in key with the world." The highlight of his social life continued to be his playing master of ceremonies at the weekly Wednesday gatherings, which encompassed practical jokes, puzzles of all sorts, charades, card games, repartee, music—"piano and singing, ringing voices—and poetry . . . George Sterling's hushed recitation, or Jack's vibrant tone, or Anna's mellow, golden throat."

Anna was a regular visitor, not only on Wednesdays, but also on other days. As she and Jack worked together on *The Kempton-Wace Letters*, his personal letters revealed more than a purely professional collaboration. "[W]e are both large temperamentally," he wrote on April 3. "We have, flashed through us, you and I, each a bit of the universal, and so we draw together." "Dear, dear Anna," he addressed her on May 9, "My heart was full of you all evening. I hope no further strain was put upon you." He himself was feeling the strain of repressed desire when a few months later he declared, "I should like some time to be with you so long as to be sated; then I would not be hungry when you went away."

By late spring of 1901, London's monthly allowance from McClure was no longer meeting expenses, and his creditors were becoming increasingly restive as his bills mounted. In June, desperate for cash, he turned to newspaper work, writing special articles for *The San Francisco Examiner*. On June 16 appeared "Washoe Indians Resolve to Be White Men," a report on his interview with Captain Pete, chief of the Washoe Tribe in Nevada. The next month he was commissioned to do a series of ten articles on the Third National Bundes Shooting Festival (*Schuetzenfest*), sponsored by the National Shooting Bund at Shellmound Park in Oakland, for which the *Examiner* paid him two hundred dollars. Interspersed with these was a rush assignment to do what he called "a freak story," which the *Examiner* printed in the July 21 *American Magazine* Sunday supplement under the headline GIRL WHO CROSSED SWORDS WITH A BURGLAR TELLS HOW ATHLETIC TRAINING SAVED HER LIFE." Other 1901 *Examiner* pieces included an interview with Peter de Ville (ALASKA'S MOON COUNTRY EXPLORER), a review of Edwin Markham's *Lincoln and Other Poems*, and on November 16, a report of the prizefight between James J. Jeffries and Gus Ruhlin. It was hack stuff, he admitted, but it helped pay his mounting bills.

His second book, *The God of His Fathers*, a collection of eleven Klondike stories, was published by McClure, Phillips and Company in May. The volume was greeted with favorable if sometimes qualified praise. "Despite its crudeness and sensationalism, London shows the impulse of intense conviction and does even a better job for the Yukon than Bret Harte did for California," commented an anonymous critic in *The New York Times Saturday Review*. "London has little to fear from comparison to Kipling," claimed a reviewer for *The Nation*. "The tales in *The God of His Fathers* are vivid, concise, and dramatic. [Although] sometimes coarse, generally disagreeable, and always cynical and restless, [they nevertheless display] a wild, elemental savagery which is positively thrilling." A reviewer for *Public Opinion* was less enthusiastic, advising "people of fastidious tastes" to avoid the book. Anna could be counted on for a rave review: "He has caught the inner spirit and romance, the picturesqueness and poetry of the Klondike," she wrote for the October issue of *Impressions*. "He conveys the significance of the dramatic conflicts between man and nature, white and Indian by seeing them in broad perspective and keeping them strongly bound to the fact of life. There is greatness in this classic, written by a true artist."

Jack was faced with another financial crisis early that fall when McClure stopped sending his monthly check and said he was not writing the kind of stories that were marketable. He might take on occasional newspaper work as a stopgap measure, but he declined to write the popular formulaic stuff McClure wanted. At this same time, his rent-free agreement with Felix Peano also expired. Rather than move back down the social ladder into cheaper housing, he decided to move up into a more fashionable neighborhood, to 56 Bayo Vista Avenue. "Am all in the chaos of settling down in new quarters," he wrote to Cornelius ("Con") Gepfert, an old Klondike buddy, on September 22. "Have a great view, now, a clean sweep of the horizon—San Francisco across the bay, Goat, Angel, and Alcatraz islands, the Golden Gate and the Pacific, to say nothing of the Contra Costa and Berkely [sic] hills."

The upscale move may have raised his social status—he was listed for the first time in the Oakland city directory as "Jack London, author"—but it scarcely raised his spirits. Nor did the appearance of his name in the 1901 edition of *Who's Who in America*. By midwinter he had sunk into one of his cyclic depressions, and for the first time he confessed that city life was losing its appeal. "I am rotting here in town," he complained to Cloudesley on December 6. "Really, I can feel the bourgeois fear crawling up and up and twining round me. If I don't get out soon I shall be emasculated. The city folk are a poor folk anyway. To hell with them."

Within a year his professional situation would change dramatically. And within less than a year his personal situation would change even more dramatically as, once again, he confused immediate with ultimate happiness.

14

ANNA AND THE *ABYSS*

And how have I lived? Frankly and openly, though crudely. I have not been afraid of life. I have not shrunk from it. I have taken it for what it was at its own valuation. And I have not been ashamed of it. Just as it was, it was mine.

—LONDON TO ANNA STRUNSKY

For Jack the New Year, 1902, was beginning "full of worries, harassments, and disappointments"—so he wrote to Anna on January 5: "I dined yesterday on canvasback and terrapin, with champagne sparkling and all manner of wonderful drinks I had never before tasted warming my heart and brain, and I remembered the sordid orgies and carouses of my youth . . . then I dreamed dreams [and] thought of you . . ." He would be thinking considerably more of her during the following months. At the beginning of the New Year, however, he was suffering from acute depression. "But after all, what squirming, anywhere, damned or otherwise, means anything?" he wrote to Cloudesley on January 6: "What's this chemical ferment called life all about? Small wonder that small men down the ages have conjured gods in answer . . . But how about you and me, who have no god? . . . I am a materialistic monist, and there's dam [sic] little satisfaction in it . . . I shall be impelled to strong drink if something exciting doesn't happen along pretty soon."

Something exciting did happen—something that would prove to be a harbinger for his greater success. He signed a contract with the

Macmillan Company to publish a collection of his Northland Indian stories titled *Children of the Frost*. With this contract began the most important editorial relationship in his career. During the first week of the New Year, he had received a letter from George Platt Brett, president of the Macmillan Company, soliciting a manuscript and telling him that his stories seemed "to represent very much the best work of the kind that has been done on this side of the water." So impressed was Brett that he decided to publish all of London's future books. Except for *The Cruise of the Dazzler*, issued by the Century Company in October 1902, and Jack's brief apostasy in 1912–13, Macmillan was Jack's sole American publisher after then, releasing more than forty of his books.

It was Brett who managed the next year one of the most profitable deals ever made for the Macmillan Company. Recognizing when he read London's manuscript that the tale about a dog kidnapped and taken to the Klondike was much more than an ordinary animal story, he offered to pay the author two thousand dollars for full rights to the book, with the understanding that Macmillan would produce a deluxe edition and launch an extensive promotional campaign to ensure the book's success in the market. Brett's scheme worked even better than he had anticipated: *The Call of the Wild* was an immediate bestseller, enthusiastically received by reviewers and readers alike. It has remained in print since the first day of publication and has appeared in countless editions in the United States and abroad.

London never received a penny in royalties from the many millions of dollars earned for the Macmillan Company by *The Call of the Wild*. But he held no grudge. As he told Charmian, "Mr. Brett took a gamble, and a big chance to lose. It was the game, and I have no kick." He added further, "Mr. Brett stood almost certainly to lose on 'The Kempton-Wace Letters,' and I'm willing to lay a bet that the Company never much more than cleaned up expenses on that splendid but misunderstood and unpopular book." Jack's bet was well taken on *The Kempton-Wace Letters*, and on several other of his less popular books as well—notably on his socialistic and sociological writings and on the three plays Macmillan published out of courtesy.

During the first weeks of 1902, Jack didn't foresee the good fortune of Brett's letter. He hadn't yet emerged from the spell of morbidity that characterized his depression. He was fascinated with the phenomenon

of death. Therefore, when invited to witness the hanging of the convicted murderer Isaac Daily at San Quentin Prison on February 21, he
jumped at the chance. Here was another kind of experience. Here also
was a further opportunity to study human nature, and to test his own
nature in the process.

Anna disagreed with his decision, asking him not to go, saying the
incident would coarsen rather than enlighten him. Her plea elicited a
lengthy defensive response. "To live is to experience sensations. To see
living is to know living—so dying," he argued. "There is such wonder in
it all." He found particularly offensive her suggestion that he would be
"coarsened" by witnessing the event. "I do not purpose to live in the front
parlor with the blinds drawn. I want to see the kitchen and the scullery":

> By God! the man who is afraid to take the fish off the hook or the guts
> from the bird he expects to eat is no man at all . . . We are no cleaner
> because we have someone else to do our dirty work for us . . . And rest
> assured that the Law that protects you from insult and assault on the
> open street is stained with the blood of the man it hangs at San
> Quentin . . . And while you eat your fish and birds, and though you
> despise me, I shall unhook and gut. And it will taste good in your
> mouth and your hands will be as dirty as mine.

Reading over what he had typed, he realized that he had become far
more offensive than she. "I did not write the letter I intended to write. I
went astray somehow," he apologized. "I wished to meet your sweetness
with sweetness, and instead have called upon all that was harsh &
unlovable in my nature."

His mood improved when he moved to the Piedmont Hills above
Oakland. This rustic place, fondly called "the Bungalow," had been recommended by George Sterling, whose own home was nearby. They
were "beautifully located in new house," Jack wrote to Cloudesley on
February 23, explaining that their view overlooked "San Francisco Bay
for a sweep of thirty or forty miles, and all the opposing shores such as
San Francisco, Marin County & Mount Tamalpias [*sic*], (to say nothing of the Golden Gate & the Pacific Ocean)—and all for $35.00 per
month."

Neither Jack nor Bessie had ever lived in such spacious quarters. As he described it, the redwood-paneled living room itself was large enough to accommodate "almost four cottages." A "cute little cottage" was perfect for Flora and Ida London Miller's young son, Johnny, now under Flora's care. Among other details, Jack lists a huge barn, pigeon houses, and chicken coops, with "yards big enough for 500 chickens." There was also an orchard and a large field of California poppies.

"It's glorious here, more like a poppy dream than real living," he announced to Anna. The next several weeks in Piedmont were the happiest of his life with Bessie. His Wednesday parties expanded from parlor games to outdoor sports: quoits, kite flying, blackberry battles, fencing, boxing, and picnicking. Charmian recollected that "no one could surpass the joyous roar of Jack's fresh boyish lungs, nor out-invent him in bedevilment and sporting feats." She recounted one episode in which several young women, finding Jack asleep in a hammock, sewed him up and built a bonfire under him. He retaliated later by slinging a pan of very ripe tomatoes across the picnic table with a direct hit, after which he "took swift heels to the loftiest reaches of the landscape, pursued by a mad avenging mob." They were "children of a larger growth," Charmian said.

A central symbol of those Piedmont days was the California golden poppy itself. One of Jack's and Bessie's chief delights was their discovery that their new home was situated over an immense field of these flowers. When they first moved into the Bungalow, the field looked like the ordinary California hillside in winter. But the drab green began to turn golden as spring approached. "Every day we would walk down the path to see how much taller the poppies had grown since the day before and to look for the first buds. How impatient we were for the coming of the poppies!" Bessie later told her daughter Joan, "When the blooms reached their peak and the golden flood spread across the field, [our] happiness and confidence were boundless."

Unfortunately, the beautiful flowers were ultimately bound not merely to fade but to be violently uprooted. No sooner had the poppies burst forth in their full glory than the field was invaded by mobs of city dwellers, who proceeded to ravage the golden crop with consideration for neither propriety nor proprietor. They were insatiable and unstoppable. They were also inspirational, for they prompted Jack to write one of his most unusual sketches, "The Golden Poppy":

"We shall have great joy in our poppy field," said Bess.

"Yes," said I; "how the poor city folk will envy when they come to see us, and how we will make all well again when we send them off with great golden armfuls!"

"But those things will have to come down," I added, pointing to numerous obtrusive notices (relics of the last tenant) displayed conspicuously, along the boundaries, and bearing, each and all, this legend: "*Private Grounds. No Trespassing.*"

"Why should we refuse the poor city folk a ramble over our field, because, forsooth, they have not the advantage of our acquaintance?" . . .

"They shame the generous landscape," she said.

"Piggish!" quoth I, hotly. "Down with them!"

We looked forward to the coming of the poppies, did Bess and I, looked forward as only creatures of the city may look who have been long denied.

But the coming of the poppies was accompanied by a floral gold rush: hordes of urbanites invaded the field "with lustful hands ripping the poppies out by the roots" and leaving the once-golden landscape like "a pockmarked field of battle." Among the invading mobs, there were no distinctions of class or gender. Young hoodlums raided, taking cartloads of flowering gold to sell for a nickel a bunch. A "middle-aged gentleman, with white hands and shifty eyes," earned the title of the "Repeater" because he kept returning to the scene of his crimes, "each time getting away with an able-bodied man's share of plunder." Most shameless were the women, especially those well-dressed ladies who either turned a deaf ear or met the proprietor's pleas for moderation with haughty indignation.

"They are God's poppies," declared one young lady, her arms overladen with golden blossoms. "I have picked them, and my time is worth money. When you have paid me for my time you may have them."

The friends to whom Jack turned offered small consolation for his plight. Some looked at his case judgmentally. "It ill-befits your dignity to squabble over poppies," they admonished him. "It is unbecoming." Others feigned sympathy but patronized him with soothing insipidities. "I was consumed with anger, and there and then I renounced them all," he concludes. "So one pays for things."

On the other hand, editors were hardly ready to pay for things so offbeat as "The Golden Poppy." Mailed off to *Country Life* on April 15, it was rejected by eleven magazines prior to acceptance by *The Delineator* the following January. For this whimsical sketch Jack received fifty dollars, much less than he was getting for his "virile truck." During the same month, he was working overtime to pay off his mounting debts. He expanded *The Cruise of the Dazzler* from the fourteen-thousand-word juvenile narrative, written two years earlier and scheduled to appear in the July issue of *St. Nicholas for Young Folks*, to forty thousand words for book publication that fall by the Century Company. A week after finishing "The Golden Poppy," he mailed off to the *Youth's Companion* the first of his seven *Tales of the Fish Patrol*, each of which earned him seventy-five dollars. J.B. Lippincott had taken *A Daughter of the Snows* off McClure's hands, but London was forced to use their $750 advance to pay off his debts to McClure.

On April 28 he returned his signed contract for the *Children of the Frost*, promising Brett that he would have the completed manuscript in his hands for October publication. (In fact, the book would be published in September.) "I do not know whether *Children of the Frost* is an advance over previous work, but I do know there are big books in me and that when I find myself they will come out," he wrote prophetically. There were indeed big books in him, and three of them—*The Call of the Wild*, *The People of the Abyss*, and *The Sea-Wolf*—would come out during the next two years.

Meanwhile, as their collaboration on *The Kempton-Wace Letters* progressed, the affair between Anna and Jack also progressed. Near the end of April he persuaded her to come live in the bungalow while they were putting the finishing touches on the *Letters*. By this time, his attraction to her had ripened into a full-fledged obsession. On the evening of May 3, while Bessie and Joan were away from home visiting the Madderns, he could restrain himself no longer. He confessed to Anna that his marriage was a terrible mistake, that he had wed Bessie for all the wrong reasons.

"Marry me, Anna," he proposed. "Let us run away to New Zealand or Australia to start another more beautiful life together as man and wife. Will you marry me?"

"Yes, darling, with all my heart!" she responded.

Their happiness was immediate—but it could never be ultimate. Although it might be concealed awhile from the world, Jack's betrayal of his marital vows could not be concealed from his wife. Bessie said nothing, but she sensed something amiss, and Anna sensed her suspicion. "She said nothing of any importance to make me feel out of place," Anna acknowledged, "but, judging from several little occurrences, I decided it was best for me to leave the London home." Bessie later reported that the two would arise at four thirty in the morning, disappear into Jack's study until breakfast, after which they would "wander off into adjacent woods, to remain away all day," leaving her "to the pursuit of her household cares and duties." She said that on one occasion, she had seen Anna sitting on Jack's lap when they were supposed to be working on the *Letters*.

Anna's departure merely intensified Jack's passion. "I was out sailing Saturday, and you were with me. You are always with me," he wrote on June 2. "How I looked for you Tuesday afternoon. I felt sure you would come. Can you come Monday or Tuesday of next week?" he pleaded. "I shall be with you Friday afternoon the 13th, but do let us see each other before that." He signed the letter "Your very miserable Sahib." He addressed her as "Dear, Dear You" on June 10, feverish with unrequited desire: "I am doing 2000 words a day now, & every day, and my head is in such a whirl I can hardly think. But I feel. I am sick with love for you and need of you."

The next month, he found himself not in her arms but in a Pullman car en route to New York City. To alleviate his financial strain—he was then three thousand dollars in debt—he had accepted a commission from the American Press Association to report on post–Boer War conditions in South Africa. Upon arriving in New York, he learned that the APA was canceling his trip because the South African officials he was to have interviewed had left Cape Town for Europe. Determined to make the best of his situation, he met with George Brett and proposed that he go instead to England. There he would shed his celebrated identity and lose himself in the notorious East End of London, reputed to be the worst slums in the world. What Jacob Riis had done in exposing the horrors of New York's slums, he would do for the East End, with this difference: He would write from the viewpoint of an insider, not a reformer looking in. Because the times were ripe for sociological treatises, Brett approved the plan.

Jack arrived in London on August 6. Brushing aside warnings by well-wishers that he would never be seen alive again, he spent ten shillings at a secondhand clothing shop in Petticoat Lane for a change of wardrobe and, disguised as a stranded and penniless American sailor, disappeared into the black heart of the East End. On August 9 he emerged and stood in Trafalgar Square indistinguishable from the thousands of derelicts who threw their dirty caps into the air amid shouts of "God save the king!" as Edward VII rode past in his Coronation Day parade.

Although he had suffered hardships and poverty, nothing in his past experiences compared with what he now witnessed. He rented a room on Dempsey Street, Stepney, where he could write, and get an occasional bath, but he spent many days and nights with the East Enders, sometimes walking the streets all night long because sleeping on curbs and benches in public places was forbidden by law. "Am settled down and hard at work," he wrote to Anna on August 16. "The whole thing, all the conditions of life, the immensity of it, everything is overwhelming. I never conceived such a mass of misery in the world before." Five days later he wrote again, telling her that his book was one-fifth done: "Am rushing, for I am made sick by this human hellhole called London Town. I find it almost impossible to believe that some of the horrible things I have seen are really so." Years afterward, he said, "Of all my books on the long shelf, I love most 'The People of the Abyss.' No other book of mine took so much of my young heart and tears as that study of the economic degradation of the poor."

What affected him most deeply was the hopeless plight of the very old and the inevitable doom of the very young. There were "the Carter" and "the Carpenter," for example: decent, respectable tradesmen who were now too old and weak to compete with vigorous younger men in a ruthless industrial system. Their children were dead; and with no welfare system and no one to care for them, they had been cut loose without shelter or money, condemned to scavenge for bits of garbage along filthy sidewalks and to drift aimlessly toward death. At the other end of the abyss were the children: of every one hundred of these, seventy-five would die before the age of five—and perhaps they were the lucky ones.

Jack's memory of those ill-fated youngsters inspired one of his most poignant scenarios:

> There is one beautiful sight in the East End, and only one, and it is the children dancing in the street when the organ-grinder goes his round. It is fascinating to watch them, the new-born, the next generation, swaying and stepping, with pretty little mimicries and graceful inventions of their own, with muscles that move swiftly and easily, and bodies that leap airily, weaving rhythms never taught in dancing school . . . They delight in music, and motion, and color, and very often they betray a startling beauty of face and form under their filth and rags.
>
> But there is a Pied Piper of London Town who steals them away. They disappear. One never sees them again, or anything that suggests them. You may look for them in vain amongst the generation of grown-ups. Here you will find stunted forms, ugly faces, and blunt and stolid minds. Grace, beauty, imagination, all the resiliency of mind and muscle, are gone . . .
>
> If this is the best that civilization can do for the human, then give us howling and naked savagery. Far better to be a people of the wilderness and desert, of cave and the squatting-place, than to be a people of the machine and the Abyss.

This last paragraph was as close as he came to sermonizing, for this time his compassion overrode his compulsion to preach. When some critics called the book a "socialistic treatise," he responded, "I merely state the case as I saw it. I have not, within the pages of that book, stated the cure as I see it." In stating the case as he saw it—personally immersing himself in the ghetto with its ill-fated inhabitants—London produced a masterpiece in the genre now labeled New Journalism.

The series of shocks Jack received during his six weeks in London climaxed with a letter from Anna on August 25. He had received no word from her for more than a month, which should have raised his suspicions that all was not well. But he was totally unprepared for what he read. Although he destroyed the letter, Anna revealed its substance in her memoir when she wrote that her words had come "like a torrent of tears, stormy as her heart." She accused him of insulting their friendship and her love by lying to her about his relationship with his wife, telling her that he had never loved Bessie, that his marriage was a failure, and that they were no longer sleeping together. Now she had discovered that Bessie was expecting their second child. She concluded her "stormy" letter by telling him she pitied his children and would never speak of their impetuous love affair again.

Anna's letter roused all the latent male defensiveness that had prevented Jack's proposing to her in the spring of 1900, and he reacted at once: "You are one of the cruelest women I have ever know[n]," he wrote on August 25:

> I have insulted "our" friendship—let it go, it is a past issue. But I have insulted "your" love, and I have "lied" to you. Also, you have "pitied" me and my children. Please do not pity Joan. There you have me in my most vital spot. I would rather be called liar, even to you, a thousand times, than to have you pity Joan . . .
>
> To return . . . I expect a child to be born to me shortly. Work back nine months. Come ahead again to the time at the Bungalow when we held speech upon a very kindred subject. Bearing these two periods in mind, if you have a superficial knowledge of things sexual and physiological, you will fail to discover any lie . . . I promised that I would not tell you of any expected child . . . I promised, & I kept my word . . .
>
> And the Sahib is dead . . . Poor devil of a Sahib! He should have been all soft, or all hard; as it is he makes a mess of his life and of other lives.

Three days later, having managed to get some sleep in one of the local workhouses, he sent a calmer follow-up, apologizing that he was "very tired & blue" when he reacted so roughly to the shock of her letter and that he had posted his reply without taking time to reread it. "What rot this long-distance correspondence is! About the time you are receiving harsh letters from me, I am receiving the kindest letters from you," he wrote on September 28, having recovered his emotional balance. "You have never had the advantage of seeing a prizefighter knocked out . . . My arms flew out madly, blindly, that is all. And I am sorry," he apologized. "And now it is all over and done with . . . Henceforth I shall dream romances for other people and transmute them into bread and butter."

His romance with Anna was over and done with. Not so his friendship with her, which would endure till the end. But her love for Jack would never be over and done with. Though she married William English Walling four years later, she carried a miniature portrait of Jack in her wallet for the rest of her life. "Mother never stopped loving him," said her daughter and namesake, Anna Walling Hamburger. "Who that ever knew him can forget him, and how will life ever forget one who was so indissolubly a part of her?" Anna herself confessed in the spring before her death. "He loved greatly and was greatly loved."

On September 29, Jack wrote to George Brett that he had completed *The People of the Abyss* and was getting set for his "long-deferred vacation" on the Continent. He left England for France the next week. After a few days of sightseeing in Paris, he rode the train to Berlin and, from there, down to Italy. On October 15 he wrote a short letter to Anna, praising the socialists he had met in Europe and cursing the bourgeoisie for the world's miseries.

It was during this time, according to Joan London, that her father "wrote the first and only love letters" her mother would ever receive from him, "letters which left her incredulous, yet daring to hope that for them both the difficult years were over at last." Bessie's hopes would be dashed within a year, but for the next several months she felt more secure in their marriage. Their second child, Bess ("Becky"), was born on October 20. As soon as Jack got the cabled news, he cut short his vacation and headed back home, arriving in New York on November 4. Two days later he left for California.

Only after boarding the train west and reading through his stack of mail did Jack learn that Anna was at the same time bound east. "What an unlucky mischance!" he wrote to her from "Texas, Booming West" on November 9. "I have just written to Mr. Brett, president of Macmillan Company, telling him that you will come to get manuscript and revise same." (Anna wanted to do some general editing and to rewrite the last two letters in their manuscript.) "Now, dear you, do not be disheartened when you meet this Mr. Brett and hear him speak of the *Letters* just incidentally. Remember that he publishes more books each month than he has time to read, that he is saturated in books, books without end, and saturated from a business standpoint," he counseled her. "The thing for you to do when you see Mr. Brett, is to inspire him with confidence in the letters, as I know you to be well able to do. For I do believe that there is a big hit in our work if it is given only half a chance."

The Kempton-Wace Letters would hardly be a big hit even though Macmillan, spending two thousand dollars on advertisements, gave the book more than half a chance. On the other hand, Anna herself would enjoy favorable notice when the book appeared the following May— thanks to her prominent fellow socialist and Californian, the publisher Gaylord Wilshire, who arranged a special luncheon in her honor at the Astor House, attended by such eminent literary figures as William Dean Howells, R. W. Gilder (editor of *Century* magazine), Norman Hapgood (*Collier's*), and Leonard Abbott (*The Literary Digest*).

Arriving home on November 13, Jack went to work on the debts that had accumulated during his absence. Five days later he accepted an assignment as special correspondent for *The San Francisco Examiner* to report the laying of the cornerstone for the new Hearst Memorial Mining Building. Next day he expressed the revised manuscript of *The People of the Abyss* to Macmillan. Desperate for cash, he wrote to Brett on November 21, proposing that he would give Macmillan the exclusive American publishing rights for his next six books—promising three within the coming year—if Brett advanced him $150 per month for that year. "Without a certain sure income, it is impossible for me to sit down and write a book," he explained. "We live moderately. One hundred and fifty dollars per month runs us, though we are seven, and oft-times nine when my old nurse and her husband depend upon us. Now, if I am sure of this one hundred and fifty dollars per month, I can devote myself to larger and ambitious work." Brett accepted the proposition, extending the period of advances to two years rather than one. In the years to come, he would continue to meet Jack's financial requests with sympathetic generosity. London, on his own part, would be true to his word. During the next two years, he would provide Macmillan with the promised six books, two of which would become not just bestsellers but classics.

The Macmillan contract eased some of the financial stress, and Jack's return to his wife and daughters eased some of his emotional stress. But the ultimate happiness he had envisioned earlier that year still eluded him. "No, Dear Anna, I am neither in joy nor sorrow. I closed certain volumes in my life on a certain day in London. These volumes will remain closed. In them I shall read no more," he wrote to her on December 20. "The mystery of man & woman is behind me. I am deep in the mystery of father & daughter."

The mystery of man and woman was not behind him, as he would discover during the coming year. But in the last month of 1902 he found himself deeply immersed in another mystery—deeper even than the mysteries of "man & woman" and "father & daughter": the eternal mystery of the élan vital, the animating spirit of all creation, which he would celebrate in writing a masterpiece.

15

THE WONDERFUL YEAR

There is an ecstasy that marks the summit of life, and beyond which life cannot rise. And such is the paradox of living, this ecstasy comes when one is most alive, and it comes as a complete forgetfulness that one is alive. This ecstasy, this forgetfulness of living, comes to the artist, caught up and out of himself in a sheet of flame . . . He was sounding the deeps of his nature, and of the parts of his nature that were deeper than he . . .

—*THE CALL OF THE WILD*

If 1902 had ended "neither in joy nor sorrow," 1903 would be filled with enough of both. During 1903 he would witness the shattering of his dream of domestic felicity along with the ruin of his marriage. During that same year, he would discover a mate who could fulfill his dreams as no woman had ever done. And during those same twelve months, like the hero of his masterwork, he also would sound "the deeps of his nature, and of the parts of his nature that were deeper than he," creating his greatest novel.

How to account for such phenomenal creative achievements? While critics continue to ponder the mysteries of artistic genius, recent theories posit intensive practice and hard work as major keys. "Writers, like other makers of creative achievements, put enormous efforts into the task of acquiring exceptional expertise," according to Michael J. A. Howe in *Genius Explained*. Howe also notes that most great authors have been "lifelong readers."

Although Howe's comments fit Jack London, they do not fully account for the special genius that manifested itself in *The Call of the Wild*. In probing such creative mysteries, C. G. Jung discusses the difference between two fundamental approaches of the artist: the "psychological mode" and the "visionary mode." The former, rational and objective, always takes its materials from the vast realm of conscious human experience. The latter "is a strange something that derives its existence from the hinterland of man's mind . . . We are reminded of nothing of everyday, human life, but rather of dreams, night-time fears and the dark recesses of the mind." This "visionary mode" derives its materials from what Jung calls the "collective unconscious": the deep psychological reservoir of "racial memories" that transcend both the individual conscious and unconscious mind. Because the language of normal discourse is inadequate to express such materials, the artist must use the language of symbol and myth: "The primordial experience is the source of his creation; it cannot be fathomed, and therefore requires mythological imagery to give it form." Such imagery manifests itself through what Jung calls "archetypal images": tropes that elicit comparable responses in the myths of cultures throughout the world.

London thought of himself as a professional craftsman working rationally and objectively. When he sat down at the typewriter in late 1902, he intended to write a companion story to "Bâtard," a tale about a diabolical wolf dog that had appeared in *The Cosmopolitan* magazine six months earlier. He claimed he wanted to write a good dog story to redeem the species, but that story assumed a life of its own. The four-thousand-word narrative he had planned "got away from me," he confessed, growing to more than thirty thousand words "before I could call a halt." Joan London says that so far as her father was concerned, his masterpiece was "a purely fortuitous piece of work, a lucky shot in the dark that had unexpectedly found its mark," and that when reviewers enthusiastically interpreted the novel as a brilliant allegory, he seemed surprised: "I plead guilty," he admitted, "but I was unconscious of it at the time. I did not mean to do it."

Possessed by his artistic soul in a creative ecstasy, he had been "caught up and out of himself in a sheet of flame" during the short month it took him to write his masterpiece. Unconscious or not, he knew he had produced something unusual when he wrote *The Call of the Wild*. "It is an animal story, utterly different in subject and treatment from the rest of the animal stories which have been so successful; and yet it seems popular enough for the 'Saturday Evening Post,' for they snapped it up right away," he wrote to George Brett on February 12.

What inspired him to write such a book? His love of animals, especially of dogs, was a primary factor. One of his earliest photographs is of him and his ranch pet Rollo. He had been deeply moved by the dogs he had seen in the Klondike, not only the trail-hardened huskies but also the city-bred shorthair breeds that were doomed to perish in an alien land. Furthermore, he had just finished reading Egerton R. Young's *My Dogs in the Northland*, which brought back nostalgic memories of the Klondike sled dogs. Most important, perhaps, he had found in the canine species the selfless unconditional love celebrated in the Christian concept of agape. Joan London suggests further that a major factor that prompted her father to write the book was his revulsion at the sordid horrors he had discovered in the abyss of the East End: "In *The Call of the Wild* he fled from the unbearable reality of the struggle for existence in capitalist civilization as he had witnessed it in the London slums to a world of his own devising, a clean, beautiful, primitive world . . ."

There were obvious similarities between the histories of Buck and his creator. Like Buck, London had spent his early years on a ranch. Like Buck, he had known the agonies of hunger, drudgery, utter fatigue, and abuse. Like Buck, he had quickly learned that a major key to survival was adaptability. Like Buck, he had "won to mastery," often against considerable odds, through the successful amalgamation of courage, imagination, physical prowess, and willpower. And like Buck, he had answered more than once his own call of the wild.

At this time he was working to balance his financial budget: revising *The People of the Abyss* and *The Kempton-Wace Letters*, finishing his *Tales of the Fish Patrol* and Indian stories for *Children of the Frost*, and composing the essays "The Terrible and Tragic," "Stranger Than Fiction," and "How I Became a Socialist"—all during the first two months of 1903.

During these same months, he began mulling over the plot of another novel. "I am on the track of a sea story, [one that] shall have adventure, storm, struggle, tragedy, and love," he wrote to Brett on January 20:

The love-element will run throughout, as the man & woman will occupy the center of the stage pretty much all of the time . . . My idea is
to take a cultured, refined, super-civilized man and woman . . . and
throw them into a primitive sea-environment where all is stress &
struggle . . . and make this man & woman rise to the situation and
come out of it in flying colors . . . The motif, however, the human motif
underlying all, will be what I call mastery . . . The superficial reader
will get the love story & the adventure; while the deeper reader will get
all this, plus the bigger thing lying underneath.

Here was another novel destined to become a classic, one that would
inspire more film adaptations than any of his other works. This new
novel would dramatize the conflict between two fundamental philosophical attitudes: materialism and idealism. It would also reflect some
deeper tensions within Jack's own psyche. Those tensions would become evident in his behavior over the next several months as well as in
the developing narrative of his "sea story," which he decided to call *The
Sea-Wolf*.

A primary source of tension was his marital ambivalence. He had
returned from Europe apparently resigned to his proper domestic role.
The Strunsky affair was history; all affairs of the heart were now a thing
of the past, he declared. "Henceforth I shall dream romances for other
people and transmute them into bread and butter," he had written to
Anna. He had already seen much of the world and reveled in the escapades of more than a half-dozen normally adventurous lifetimes. It was
time, at last, to settle down into the saner, and safer, routines of conju-
gal and paternal maturity. He was now the father of two lovely daughters. He had a faithful wife who would, in due time, bear him the sons
he also wanted.

"By the way, I think your long-deferred congratulations upon my
marriage are about due," he chided Cloudesley in a January 27 letter. "I
have been married nearly three years, have a couple of kids, & think it's
great. So fire away. Or, come & take a look at us, and at the kids, & then
congratulate!"

Cloudesley accepted the invitation when he returned to California
from New York the next month. "Jack greeted me delightedly, Bessie
with kindly regard and a mild rebuke for the long deference of my

congratulations . . . and I was compelled to capitulate," Johns wrote in retrospect: "Yet even then I felt that all was not well with Jack and Bessie." Both Jack and Bessie had seemed to be trying too hard to convince him that they were happily married. Cloudesley discovered later that they had agreed for the sake of the children and Jack's career to play "a terrible and searing game of 'Let's pretend.'"

Their pretensions were short-lived. By early spring Jack was beginning to chafe under the regulations of their game, and Bessie herself was growing increasingly impatient with her husband's own fun and games—with what she viewed as the puerile follies of his Wednesday "entertainments" for the Crowd, his nights out with George Sterling, and the equally suspicious escapades with his coterie of female admirers.

He was struggling against not only Bessie's worrisome unhappiness but also his own chronic depression. In response he tried, as he had done in the past, to find escape on the water. On March 10 he bought a thirty-eight-foot sloop, the *Spray*, for sailing on the bay and neighboring waterways. He thought this would enable him to recapture some of the unlicensed pleasures he had enjoyed in his younger years. Once on board and away from Bessie, he could entertain any guests and play any games of his choice. "I was not in a very happy state," he admitted. "I was going out on the *Spray* to have a hell of a time, with any woman I could get hold of."

When not playing, he could also work on his sea story free from domestic interruptions. But while he might escape Bessie's restrictions, he could not so easily escape his own depression. No amount of sexual indulgence could remedy this malady. Out of this deep-seated melancholia was born one of the greatest characters he ever created. Even that master of mordant irony, Ambrose Bierce, while castigating what he considered the fatuous love element when he read *The Sea-Wolf*, was moved to sing the praises of London's "tremendous creation, Wolf Larsen. If that is not a permanent addition to literature, it is at least a permanent figure in the memory of the reader. You 'can't lose' Wolf Larsen . . . The hewing out and setting up of such a figure is enough for a man to do in a life-time."

Bierce was right: it is not easy to lose a character who, on the one hand, can readily quote at length passages from Shakespeare, Browning, and the Holy Bible and, on the other hand, can as readily kill a man with one blow of his fist. Wolf Larsen was superficially modeled after a notorious seal poacher named Alexander McLean, whose freebooting exploits had filled the newspapers during the 1890s. But London's rendering of that character is complex, comprising recognizable parts of Shakespeare's Hamlet, Milton's Satan, Nietzsche's Übermensch, and the author's own darker self. That dark side is dramatized in Larsen's pessimistic diatribes. "I believe that life is a mess," he declares. "It is like yeast, a ferment, a thing that moves and may move for a minute, an hour, a year, or a hundred years, but that in the end will cease to move." In a letter to George Sterling's wife, Carrie, two years later, London admitted that he had projected his own depression into such passages: "You will remember, yourself, the black moods that used to come upon me at that time, and the black philosophy that I worked out at the time, and put into Wolf Larsen's mouth."

During the spring of 1903, Jack's life was falling apart as his marriage collapsed. Neither Bessie nor he could keep up pretenses. She stopped making any efforts to play the loving wife and gracious hostess, opting instead for a lifetime role as "martyr and gossip," according to her younger daughter. "I don't know how Daddy stayed with my mother as long as he did," Becky said many years afterward, apparently not realizing the extent of her father's philandering.

Jack was now spending more nights out with George and more days and nights on the *Spray* with whomever he chose. He had alienated some of his socialist friends, because, while insisting on revolutionary tactics, he seemed to be luxuriating in the lap of capitalist success. His beloved Crowd had been infiltrated by bohemian hangers-on who came to his parties because of his celebrity. "Erstwhile worth-while fun and stunts seemed no longer worth while; and it was a torment to listen to the insipidities and stupidities of women, to the pompous, arrogant, sayings of little half-baked men," he complained. "For me the life, and light, and sparkle of human intercourse were dwindling." And though he could now get virtually any woman he wanted into bed, the sparkle of sexual conquest was likewise dwindling.

All his pessimism was impacting the romantic sea story he had originally described in his letter to Brett. Where now were the "super-civilized man and woman" who were supposed to "occupy the center of the stage pretty much all of the time"? And what had become of the love element that was to "run throughout"? Except for the "supercivilized" narrator, Humphrey Van Weyden, these other elements were nowhere to be seen in the narrative London was creating. Just as Larsen had overpowered his crew, so his character had overpowered London's plot.

The course of London's narrative changed along with the course of his personal life in the summer of 1903: Van Weyden falls in love with Maud Brewster as Jack fell in love with Charmian Kittredge. Charmian was no stranger to Jack. They had first met briefly three years earlier. She was also a member of the crowd who came to Jack's parties. In the spring of 1903 she had mentioned him in an article published in *Sunset* magazine: "Lusty yachtsmen skimming the familiar waters of San Francisco Bay may listen for the industrious click-clicking of a typewriter mingling with the singing of ropes and the swish of blown spray, as Jack London sails his boat and weaves romances."

Who was Clara Charmian Kittredge? She was born in Wilmington, California, on November 27, 1871, the daughter of Dayelle ("Daisy") Wiley and Willard ("Kitt") Kittredge. Daisy was a minor poet whose sentimental verses found welcome homes in *Godey's Lady's Book* and popular magazines of the day. In 1866 she had married Captain Willard Kittredge, a dashing cavalry officer eighteen years her senior. Her infatuation faded along with his romantic aura when, shortly after their marriage and his army discharge, "Kitt" exchanged his officer's uniform for the ordinary suit of an hotelier. Disenchanted, Daisy left him and went with her family to live on a ranch in Ventura County, California. Wearied of the rural tedium, she reunited with her husband in early 1871 and became pregnant shortly thereafter. She was a frail, indifferent mother, more interested in her romantic fantasies and maudlin verses than in her infant daughter. She had already turned Charmian over to her sister, Ninetta ("Netta"), long before her death from consumption in 1877. Kitt died nine years later, leaving his daughter solely under Netta's guidance.

Charmian's life with her aunt was a mixed blessing. Although Netta shared her older sister's porcelain beauty, she was anything but fragile. She possessed a will of iron and once confessed that she would have made a "good Inquisitionist." Ostensibly she was a good provider for her sister's little "Childie," as she called Charmian, supplying her with ample books and art supplies, teaching her to play the organ and piano, and making sure that she was dressed fashionably. But she made no attempt to provide the child with playmates. During the day, instead of sending her to school with other children, Netta taught her at home. "In the evenings, Netta would play music or invite friends over, perhaps for séances," as she was a fervent spiritualist, explains Clarice Stasz, but for her lonely niece there was "not one special friend."

As a consequence of her social isolation, Charmian invented a world of her own out of the books she read and her own imagination. Furthermore, as is often the case with children held hostage under the wills of those more powerful than they, "Charmian worshipped her enslaver, believing Netta could do no wrong. Netta's convictions became her own"—except for her aunt's spiritualistic ardors.

Her sexual ardors were another matter, for her aunt was a proponent of free love, a radical doctrine for women during the height of the Victorian age, and as Charmian matured, she demonstrated all the characteristics of a true believer. Because Netta instilled in her the need to acquiesce in the face of a greater authority, she also "learned to pose, and by early adulthood developed a captivating and gracious social manner that disguised the insecurities and rich fantasy life within her. She had the soul of an artist."

She also had the soul of a rebel. From her cavalry father she inherited a love of horses and started the wagging of many a gossip's tongue when she became the first woman in California to ride astride instead of sidesaddle as proper ladies were supposed to do. Most shockingly, by her mid-twenties she had engaged in a series of sexual relationships with married as well as unmarried men. At thirty (well past the proper marriageable age for Victorian maidens), she was attractive but remained unattached. She possessed a splendid figure and a fine complexion, and she was ahead of her time in knowing how best to maintain both.

By the time she had grown into womanhood, though never completely free from Netta's influence, she had managed to find a financial as well as a social life of her own. Exceptionally adroit, she learned to handle that latest boon to business correspondence, the typewriter, as expertly as she handled the keys of a piano. In an era when the vocation of secretary was considered the exclusive prerogative of males, her typing and shorthand skills were so impressive that she was hired in this capacity by a San Francisco shipping firm. She still had no special friends, but she had many amiable acquaintances. She was liked by most of the Crowd and participated regularly in their gatherings, including Jack's parties. She became a welcome guest at the London home, liked by Bessie as well as Jack. During Jack's 1902 marital apostasy in the Strunsky affair, Bessie had found in Charmian a reassuring confidante. Jack himself paid Kittredge no special attention until the early summer of 1903. It was chance rather than any deliberate plan of his, or hers, that brought them together.

By June, the tension between Bess and Jack had reached the breaking point. Suspicious for some time, she now confirmed any lingering doubts about his philandering by plundering his mail. To relieve some of the tension, he moved the family up to Glen Ellen for the summer. The town, scenically situated on a stream at the foot of Sonoma Mountain in the Valley of the Moon, was a popular summer resort. Charmian's aunt Netta had wed Roscoe Eames, now editor of the *Overland Monthly*. She and the magazine's business manager, Edward Biron Payne, had purchased a quaint Russian-style octagonal house they named Wake Robin Lodge, on a beautifully wooded thirteen-acre lot adjacent to Asbury Creek. As a means of supplementing their uncertain income from the *Overland*, they set up a profitable business of renting rooms, cabins, and tents to vacationers from the city. Jack decided to rent one of their cabins for his family. The pleasant surroundings, with the opportunity for swimming and playing in the clean, sunny air, would offer fun for the girls and some relief for their mother. The move would also offer some relief for their father, who would be relatively free to spend more time on the *Spray* with his work on *The Sea-Wolf* and other affairs.

Hoping this might be a step toward reconciliation, Bessie approved the idea. On June 11 she and the two daughters took the train up to Glen Ellen while Jack stayed behind in Oakland planning to take his boat out for a sail the next week. In the meantime he spent the weekend with the Sterlings at Dingee Place, their summer camp in Piedmont. Three days later, on his trip back to Oakland, the rig he was riding in threw a wheel and he was thrown out, severely spraining his knee and scraping skin off his arms and legs. The injury forced him to postpone his sailing venture and substitute a trip to Glen Ellen.

Charmian, having been commissioned by Bessie to do some shopping for her, brought the items over to Jack's place so that he could take them with him when he rode up to the Sonoma camp. She found him laid up in bed while his friend Frank Atherton packed for him. Gazing at her figure as she helped Frank pack, Jack was suddenly struck with the idea that she might be good for a fling. When she and Atherton were finished, he managed to drag himself out of bed long enough to see her off. As they were standing outside on the porch, just as she was leaving, he suddenly grabbed her and kissed her. That kiss changed the course of his life as well as the narrative course of *The Sea-Wolf.*

He went on up to Wake Robin the next day, but he couldn't get Charmian out of his mind. "I began to grow pretty desirous for her," he said afterward. It was an understatement. He wrote a note to her, saying he had to see her again, soon. Three days later he rode back down to Oakland, and on Saturday took her with him up to Dingee Place. He made no effort to conceal his intentions from the Sterlings—nor did she. "You will remember Charmian's and my conduct together at the camp-fire at your camp on that Saturday night," he wrote in a 1905 letter to Carrie Sterling. "We were just beginning to come together good and hard."

They were, to be sure. At the outset Jack had merely wanted her body. He had already made up his mind to go to pieces, as he admitted, and Charmian had struck him as an attractive pièce de résistance. He would make her his mistress. It was that simple, or so he thought at first. But it wasn't—and she surely wasn't—that simple. It took him less than a week to realize that she was no ordinary coquette. "Had you failed by a hair's breadth in anything, had you made but the one coy flutter of the average woman, or displayed the fear or shock of the average woman, we should have struggled, and somewhat sordidly," he wrote to her after their weekend at the Sterlings' camp. "But you were so frank, so honest, and, not least, so unafraid. Had you been less so, in one touch, one pressure, one action, one speech, I think I should have attempted to beat down your will to mine."

Charmian was wise enough not to try to make their relationship a contest of wills. Yet while she made no attempt to beat down Jack's will, she did manage to bend it to her own. If they were to engage in an affair, it would be on her terms. Because of her firm sense of self-worth, her fearlessness, and her frankness, his initial lust was transformed into the greatest love of his life. Within a week of their first sexual encounter, he committed himself to her, totally and irrevocably. "For you did so greaten, and my love for you did so greaten, that the struggle you felt was coming was no struggle at all. I was vanquished before the battle," he confessed. "It was inevitable that it should be no struggle, just as everything between us has been inevitable . . . We shall live life together, dear."

Years before, he had dreamed of his ideal friend as a "great Man-Comrade, an all-around man, who could weep over a strain of music, a bit of verse, and who could grapple with the fiercest life and fight good-naturedly or like a fiend as the case might be." Of all Jack's male friends, George Sterling would come closest to fulfilling his criteria for the great Man-Comrade. But by the end of July, he had already found his ideal companion. Charmian proved to be well suited to this demanding role. Here in the flesh as well as in the spirit was a real-life prototype of the New Woman: intelligent but not supercilious, athletic but nonetheless feminine, self-possessed but not arrogant, brave but not foolhardy, cultured but free-spirited, sexually discriminating but uninhibited. Beyond exemplifying all these qualities, she was gifted with an elusive charm that drew men to her. "And pray *who* are you that you should so disorder my life?—and the beautiful paradox is that you are really bringing order to the profound disorder of my life" was the ardent response of Charmian's newest lover in the long, hot summer of 1903.

Hers was more complex than a physical or sexual attractiveness, and Jack was madly in love—lovesick, in fact, as witnessed in his letters to her. The two were now corresponding daily. "If you could see me waiting for the postman these days. For the half hour preceding his arrival, I am unable to work. I wander restlessly up and down," he confessed on August 14:

I read over your letters. I sit down at my desk. I get up again and repeat the performance. And then, when I have quite decided that something has gone wrong with my watch or that the postman is dead, lo! his cart stops before the door. But the rascal always has mail for the side flat, and he goes there first.

But at last! at last! I am leaping up the stairs sorting your unmistakable yours from the heap as I move. Then, having read it three times through, I sit and wonder how long the day will be before to-morrow morning comes and I shall receive another from you . . .

But know, & know always that I am yours, that my last thought at night is of you, my first in the morning; and that I awake and look at your picture and am glad that it is all real, and that you are mine, my great, great love!

At the same time he was pouring out his heart, Netta was pouring water on the flames of this dangerous romance by telling her niece to consider the legal and social repercussions when Bessie retaliated. Jack countered by assuring Charmian that he was totally committed to her and that everything would "come out well": "You are my wife by the highest sanctions, and my wife you shall be by the sanction of petty man-made law as well . . . Remember I want all of you, and can never be content with less. And you are so made that all of you could not be mine unless the transfer be socially legal. We will make it socially legal . . ." This reassurance countered Netta's influence—at least for the time being. They managed to keep their affair secret from everyone except a handful of close friends and relatives: the Sterlings, Eameses, and Edward Payne. Bessie knew that Jack was having extramarital relations with someone, but she did not suspect Charmian. She had discovered fragments of a torn-up love letter in his wastebasket, but because it was typed and unsigned, she didn't realize it was from Charmian. She had also grabbed a telegram he was reading in which the correspondent asked Jack to accompany her on a trip to Stockton and Sacramento—but this was another woman, not Charmian, and there was no name on the telegram. He had intended to tell Bessie he was leaving her when they returned to Piedmont at the end of the summer, but their confrontation over the telegram prompted his announcement on July 14: "She asked me if I loved somebody else. I told her that I did, though I refused to tell her that person's name . . . So the separation was thus precipitated. The story is all told," he wrote to Carrie Sterling.

News of the breakup was told all over the Bay Area—and beyond. Because of London's celebrity, the newspapers and gossips' mouths were full of the story. Bessie expressed shock at Jack's announcement, but she had suspected for some time that separation was imminent. To protect Charmian from suspicion, Jack advised her to stay in touch with Bessie, adhering to her role as confidante. Uncomfortable though it was to betray the wife who had been so trusting, Charmian played her part successfully for the rest of the year.

Despite his ecstatic love notes, Jack was also uncomfortable with their enforced secrecy and his family breakup. He had invited Cloudesley to come up from Los Angeles so that they could go sailing on the *Spray*, but on July 24 he wrote, "Just a line to let you know I am suddenly back from camping, that my affairs are all in confusion, that I do not know yet what I shall do, that I need and can use no help other than my own strength may give me, and that you do not come North till you hear from me again." Five days later he wrote to Johns again, thanking him for his offer of help and remarking, "Am moving house & splitting up, just now. Poor, sad little Bungalow!"

By the following week he had moved into a six-room flat at 1216 Telegraph Avenue in Oakland, which he had rented to share with the Athertons. For his mother and Johnny Miller, he rented a house at 919 Jefferson Street; and for Bessie and the girls, a house at 330 Twenty-Fourth Street in Oakland. "I laugh when I think of what a hypocrite I was when, at the Bungalow, I demanded from you your long-deferred congratulations for my marriage—but, believe me, I was a hypocrite grinning on a grid," he wrote again to Cloudesley in August, adding that "it's all right for a man sometimes to marry philosophically, but remember, it's damned hard on the woman."

On August 10 he mailed his manuscript for the first half of *The Sea-Wolf* to Macmillan, along with a synopsis of the second half. Brett told Jack he was negotiating with R. W. Gilder, editor of the *Century* magazine, about the possibility of serializing the novel. Upon reading the manuscript, Gilder said he was interested but concerned over "the dead level of sickening brutality" in the first half and the impropriety of stranding the two lovers on a deserted island by themselves, as London summarized the second half. Jack gave Gilder permission to "blue pencil" the novel as much as he saw fit, reassuring him that he would not write anything "offensive." Humphrey and Maud would therefore behave with impeccable propriety during their several weeks stranded on "Endeavor Island"—even going so far as to build separate huts for sleeping. Only at the very end of the novel, as they see a rescue ship in the distance, are they permitted to kiss.

Gilder liked the finished product so much that he paid four thousand dollars for serial rights. The *Century* serial was hugely successful, and Macmillan's first printing of forty thousand copies sold out before publication in October 1904. *The Sea-Wolf* was London's second book to head the national bestseller list within a year—and, unlike *The Call of the Wild*, this one paid him handsome royalties.

Although Van Weyden and Brewster had been modeled to some extent on London and Kittredge, Jack and Charmian were anything but "sexless lovers": "That you should be the one woman to me of all women; that my hunger for you should be greater than any hunger for food I have ever felt; that my desire for you should bite harder than any other desire I have ever felt for fame and fortune and such thing;—all, all goes to show how big is this our love," he wrote to her on September 24. "My thoughts are upon you always, lingering over you always, caressing you always in myriad ways. I wonder if you feel those caresses sometimes!"

So impatient was he to be with her on a regular daily as well as nightly basis that he suggested they not wait until he could get a divorce but that they elope to Japan. "I was talking yesterday with a man from Japan. He has verified my plan of going to live, first, in Kobe. There is frost in the winter time in Kobe, but no snow," he wrote again on September 28. "We shall have two or three servants and a couple of ponies if they are at all ridable. And we shall have a second *Spray* on the bay, and make long cruises [and] dearest of all, will be you by my side."

Within little more than three months, Jack would be sailing to Japan—but not with Charmian by his side. Free-spirited and freethinking though she was, she was too wise to commit herself to a scheme that was as witless as it was lawless. Scandal she might endure, but not expatriation. If he loved her as deeply as his letters claimed, he could wait awhile longer.

Wait he did, but it wasn't easy. The ecstasies of his great new love and of the rave reviews *The Call of the Wild* was receiving scarcely diminished the agonies of the situation in which Jack found himself during the fall of 1903. Bessie, while distraught, still hoped for some kind of reconciliation. She took some comfort from Flora London, who had become her friend and ally. She also took some comfort from her counterfeit friend, Charmian, who continued to play her role as confidante. Charmian was at least honest enough with herself to acknowledge her betrayal; Jack was not. "At least believe this of me," he protested to Fannie K. Hamilton, a newspaper feature writer who had interviewed him earlier in the year, "that whatever I have done I have done with the sanction of my conscience."

With or without the sanction of his conscience, he felt compelled to escape by one means or another, hiding his deepest feelings under bravado. Now, after his separation, he had to pay rent on three places. Frank Atherton was shocked by London's extravagance, particularly by the exorbitant rent he agreed to pay for their six-room flat on Telegraph Avenue. But when Frank suggested the need to economize, Jack brushed aside the advice: "He smiled carelessly. 'We only live once, and we'll be dead a long time; so why not get the best out of life? This flat is just what I want at the present, and a few dollars more or less will neither make or break.'"

Driven to extraordinary excesses as well as to heroic extremes, London was compelled to outdo others, and himself, heedless of consequences and regardless of cost. Life itself was the biggest, most exciting game in town, and he was hell-bent on playing for the highest stakes. Toward the end he would try to conserve his diminishing vitality, but in the fall of 1903 he was running hard to escape from the mess of his excesses.

On October 9 he wrote to Cloudesley that he was planning to take the *Spray* out to cruise for a couple of months around the Bay and up the adjoining rivers and wanted him to come along. "We can both get our writing in each day and have a jolly time," he assured him. Jack needed the water and the *Spray*, as well as his good comrade, for healing. Cloudesley accepted, and during the next eight weeks they managed, at least for a while, to leave their worries onshore. Cloudesley recalled that they spent their days very pleasantly, "writing, playing chess, arguing, reading, sometimes aloud to each other, [and] swimming."

Their excursion was interrupted a few weeks after their departure when Jack received word from Bessie that Joan was critically ill with typhoid fever. Leaving Cloudesley to look after the *Spray* in Stockton, he rushed back to Oakland at once to be at his daughter's bedside. For several days it looked as if he might stay with Bessie and their daughters, and the newspapers were filled with stories of a reconciliation, but as soon as her fever had broken and Joan was out of danger, he left for the river.

Back on the *Spray*, he decided to visit Benecia after hearing a rumor that three surviving oyster pirates were still living there. Cloudesley records that they anchored the boat offshore near the ramshackle ark community south of town and rowed their skiff to the shaky old wharf. After several attempts to get information from the suspicious occupants, they were finally pointed toward one of the arks, and on they went, "over the maze of branching and crossing footingways." At last they saw three men approaching in single file along the shaky narrow boards:

Two were nearing middle age, lined and worn by hard living, the third being still youthful in appearance. The one in the lead, tall and rawboned, halted his shambling advance twenty feet from us, stared steadily for a few seconds with widening eyes and then uttered a joyous shout:

"Jack London! Why, you old _____" . . . The other older man echoed the cry, while the younger of the trio whooped in gladness:

"By God! The Prince!" . . .

"Well, Jack!" they babbled on delightedly, the younger one adding: "Say, Jack, did you write those pieces in the paper with the name 'Jack London' to them? I always said our Jack London was smart enough to do it, but these mudhens wouldn't believe it."

Jack told his old pals that he was in fact the author of those newspaper articles and, chuckling, whispered to Cloudesley, "Such is fame!" *The Call of the Wild* had been on the bestseller list, receiving national acclaim, for nearly six months, but rather than any fame he had achieved as a man of letters, it was the potboilers he had dashed off for *The San Francisco Examiner* that impressed his former comrades-in-crime. They celebrated the reunion by treating Jack and Cloudesley to a dinner of duck stew and steam beer. London returned the favor by staking the group to a round of Benecia saloons—and by handing them a few extra dollars for "possible emergencies" when he and Johns departed for the *Spray* in the early hours of the following morning.

"I regret none of it," Jack confessed to Cloudesley, speaking of those wild days of his youth and the likelihood he might have wound up in prison, or dead: "They were purple passages of life." He would regret some passages of his life during the coming year, but they would be no less colorful.

16

THE WAGES OF WAR

I am hungry to be where you are and disgusted at being here.
War? Bosh! . . . Never were correspondents treated in any war
as they have been in this. It's absurd, childish, ridiculous, rich,
comedy.

—JACK TO CHARMIAN

Two months of recreational sailing on the *Spray* with Cloudesley had
helped to relieve his stress and enabled London to regroup emotionally;
it had also provided him enough uninterrupted time to finish *The Sea-
Wolf*. But it had not relieved the financial pressures weighing on him.
When he returned to Oakland on December 20, he discovered that
his excesses had reduced his bank balance to less than thirty dollars.
With Christmas coming and a half-dozen mouths to feed, he needed
cash in a hurry. Fortunately for Jack, there was a war on the Far Eastern
horizon, and where there was a war, there would be a cry for war correspondents.

Trouble between Japan and Russia had been brewing for several
years. In 1894, Japan had gone to war with China because the Chinese
government claimed dominion over Korea, a claim vigorously denied
by Japan. Japan won a quick, decisive victory, successfully invading Manchuria and capturing Port Arthur on the Liaotung Peninsula. Japanese
troops would have taken the entire peninsula and stayed in Port Arthur
except for the intervention of France, Germany, and Russia. Meanwhile,

Russia had negotiated with China for the right to extend its Trans-Siberian Railway through Manchuria down to Port Arthur. Both nations, Japan and Russia, wanted control over Korean industry and trade.

This was the golden era of expansionism for the great powers of the West. Russia was not alone in its encroachment on Asian and Pacific territories. Britain had already planted the Union Jack over three-quarters of the globe; France, Belgium, Holland, and Germany were rushing to take what was left of the "underdeveloped" countries. Even the United States had gotten into the act with the Spanish-American War, seizing the Philippines, Guam, American Samoa, Hawaii, and Wake Island.

Despite its military victories in China, Japan was denied its share of the spoils by the Western powers. At the end of the nineteenth century, Russia, breaking a series of treaties with Japan, moved into Manchuria and Korea, establishing a naval base at Port Arthur. Japan was outraged, but the Russian giant was more concerned with the threat of revolution at home than with what seemed a Lilliputian military threat five thousand miles away. By the end of 1903, war was imminent, and newspapers were eager to exploit the crisis. Expecting a quick Russian victory, the editors were frantically looking for big-name correspondents to report the war before it ended. William Randolph Hearst, godfather of the sensational new "yellow journalism," wanted the best in the business for his syndicate. The services of American journalism's beau ideal, Richard Harding Davis, had been bought by *Collier's*. But Jack London, whose name had been even more prominent than Davis's in 1903, would do just as well if not better. Hearst therefore outbid several other editors to make London an offer he couldn't refuse.

On January 7, Jack mailed the completed manuscript of *The Sea-Wolf* to Macmillan, asking Brett "to send each month $127.50 to my wife [and also] $22.50 to Miss Kittredge," who would check proof sheets with "Mr. Sterling, my best man friend, my comrade—and a man with an eagle eye for errors." Later that day he boarded the SS *Siberia* with a score of other journalists en route to Yokohama via Honolulu. The seventeen-day voyage to Japan was an ominous prelude to the sea of troubles he would oppose during the next six months. Within less than a week, he came down with an attack of grippe. Barely recovering from that, he sprained his ankle so badly that he was bedridden for three days and had to be carried on deck by his fellow correspondents for the rest of the week before he could hobble around on crutches.

He had signed on with Hearst for glory as well as for money. The dangers he imagined in the Russo-Japanese conflict made his earlier escapades seem like kids' games. He had set out thinking this would be the most thrilling of all his adventures: "I knew that the mortality of war correspondents was said to be greater, in proportion to numbers, than the mortality of soldiers . . . I had heard of all sorts and conditions of correspondents . . . where life was keen and immortal moments were being lived."

When he arrived from Yokohama at the Imperial Hotel in Tokyo on the afternoon of January 24, he found two scores of correspondents—many of whom had been there for weeks—waiting for permission from the Japanese authorities to follow the armies to Korea before war broke out. The authorities had no intention of allowing the foreign correspondents to get anywhere near the front. "The situation was unique in the annals of journalism," attested Willard Straight, the Reuters representative. "A government holding the rabid pressmen at a distance, censoring their simplest stories, yet patting them on the back, dining them, giving them picnics and luncheons and theatrical performances and trying in every way not only to soften their bonds and make their stay a pleasant one, but siren-like, to deaden their sense of duty and their desire to get into the field."

Jack had no intention of being seduced. He hadn't traveled seven thousand miles to eat Japanese lotus; he had come for action. "I soon found that there were two ways of playing the game," he decided: "either to sit down in Tokio as [they] wanted me to and eat many dinners, or to go out on my own resources." His own resources were, as always, ample, and his efforts to get into battle were nothing short of heroic. Three days after arriving, he pulled out of Tokyo without authorization, heading for the front.

Arriving in Nagasaki only to discover there were no passenger spaces available on the ship to Chemulpo (Inchon), he headed back up to Moji and booked passage on a steamer scheduled to leave on February 1. With some time on his hands before departure, he figured this would be a good opportunity to photograph some local scenes. He didn't know Moji was a fortified city and that photographs were forbidden:

"Japanese police 'Very sorry,' but they arrested me. Spent the day examining me. Of course, I missed steamer. 'Very sorry.' Carted me down country Monday night to town of Kokura . . . Found guilty. Fined 5 yen and camera confiscated," he wrote on February 3. With the help of local newspaper correspondents, buttressed by the intercession of Richard Harding Davis and Lloyd Griscom, the U.S. minister to Japan, he regained his camera, but he was still a long way from gaining the front.

He booked passage again to sail for Chemulpo, but the Japanese commandeered his ship for military purposes. It was on the same day, February 8, that Admiral Togo's fleet launched a surprise attack against the Russian navy at Port Arthur. Though he had no official word, London knew that a battle was at hand, because he had seen a fleet of Japanese warships headed out to the Yellow Sea, and "soldiers had been called from their homes to join their regiments in the middle of the night." Desperate for a ship, he managed to catch a tiny native steamer bound for Fusan (Busan). "Dashing aboard in a steam launch, got one trunk overboard but saved it. Got wet myself, and my rugs and baggage, crossing the Japan Sea." When he reached Fusan, he caught another small steamer for Chemulpo so overloaded with Japanese and Korean passengers and their baggage that it listed to starboard "fully thirty degrees." They got as far as Mokpo, whereupon the ship was commandeered by the military and "all passengers and freight were fired ashore."

At Mokpo he was still several hundred miles away from Chemulpo, where Japanese troops were disembarking en route to the Yalu River and Manchuria. So he chartered a native fishing junk with a crew of three Koreans, doing business "with a 24 word vocabulary and gesticulations." They headed up the peninsula, carrying five Japanese passengers along with them, in freezing weather. "Grows more gorgeous," he wrote to Charmian on February 11, off the Korean coast. "Caught on lee-shore yesterday, and wind howling over Yellow Sea. You should have seen us clawing off—one man at the tiller and a man at each sheet (Koreans), four scared Japanese, and the fifth too seasick to be scared." Despite smashing a rudder and losing a mast in the storm, the frail craft managed to anchor at Kun-san that evening in a driving rain, the icy wind "cutting like a knife."

The reception Jack received ashore was a warm contrast to the ocean's relentless chill. The villagers welcomed with him with "five Japanese maidens," who chatted with each other about his "beautiful white skin etc [sic]" while helping him "undress, take a bath, and get into bed." He was visited the next morning by Kun-san's leading citizens, including the mayor and captain of police, "all in my bedroom . . . while I was being shaved, dressed, washed, and fed." When he left on a different boat with a five-man Japanese crew that morning, they all warmly cheered him off, crying, "Sayonara."

The following week was neither warm nor cheerful: "And maybe you think it isn't cold, traveling as I am, by junk," he wrote to Charmian. There were no stoves on board, and the only source of heat was a tiny charcoal box he had bought. By now the snow had come down to the ocean, and ice was forming along the edge of the beaches. "Still wilder, but can hardly say so 'gorgeous,' unless landscapes and seascapes seen between driving snow squalls, be gorgeous," he wrote on February 13. "Never thought a sampan (an open crazy boat) could live through what ours did." In addition to the freezing weather and what threatened to be imminent shipwreck on a lee shore, he was half-crazed from a blinding headache caused by the noxious fumes of the little charcoal stove on board. "I did not much care what happened; yet I remember, when we drove in across, that I took off my overcoat, and loosened my shoes—and I didn't bother a bit about trying to save the camera."

Had he attempted to swim in those freezing waters, even if he somehow escaped being fatally dashed against the reef, he would have succumbed to hypothermia before getting halfway to shore. They finally made anchor at a fishing village, where the six of them spent two nights with a score of "men, women, and children" all crammed into one tiny room. The villagers were fascinated because he was the first Caucasian they had ever seen. "I showed one old fellow my false teeth at midnight. He proceeded to rouse the house. Must have given him bad dreams . . . for he crept in to me at three in the morning and woke me in order to have another look."

London finally reached Chemulpo late on the evening of February 16. There he met two other correspondents: Robert L. Dunn, a photographer for *Collier's*, and F. A. McKenzie, a reporter for the London *Daily Mail*. Both had sailed there a few weeks earlier, before the Japanese military officials clamped down on foreign correspondents. Now they were waiting for permission to proceed to the front. "I want to say that Jack London is one of the grittiest men that it has been my good fortune to meet. He is just as heroic as any of the characters in his novels," Dunn reported. "He doesn't know the meaning of fear . . . When [he] arrived in Chemulpo [he] was a physical wreck. His ears were frozen; his fingers were frozen; his feet were frozen. He said he didn't mind his condition so long as he got to the front . . . He had been sent to do newspaper work, and he wanted to do it."

Jack's physical condition wasn't the worst of his problems when he arrived at Chemulpo. One of Charmian's letters had caught up with him there—a long letter telling him, among other things, that Bessie now knew her to be Jack's lover. Eliza had apparently given their secret away after seeing Charmian waving kisses to Jack when the *Siberia* weighed anchor on January 7. This news troubled him especially, since he had left his power of attorney with his sister. "Concerning Power of Attorney," he replied to Kittredge on February 17: "The dollars do not amount to anything to me where human relations are concerned . . . So I shall let power of attorney remain in E.'s hands . . . If she has failed me, I have no one to fall back upon but you . . . Oh, my beloved, I pin everything to you—my faith in life, my desire for life."

The impending battle back at home did not deter him from his immediate objective: to get to the battle at hand. Disregarding the ravages of his sea voyage and the restrictions of the Japanese military establishment, he began immediately preparing his outfit to move north toward the Yalu River and Manchuria, where a Japanese army of some two hundred thousand was quietly massing for an attack upon eighty thousand Russian troops. His outfit comprised five horses (two riding horses plus three pack ponies), four men (an interpreter, a cook, and two mapus [grooms] to look after the horses), and enough provisions for the horses and the men.

By March 4 he had reached Ping Yang (Pyongyang), more than half the distance from Seoul to the Yalu. He admitted that he was "saddle-sore and raw" from having ridden nearly two hundred miles on horseback. Four days later, he reached Poval-Colli after bluffing his way past military authorities in Ping Yang: "Arrive at this forlorn village; people scared to death," he wrote to Charmian. "Already have had

Russian and Japanese soldiers—we put the finishing touch to their fright . . . As I write this a cold wind is blowing from the North, and snow is driving. Also, before my door are groaning and creaking a hundred bullock-carts loaded with army supplies and pushing North."

Jack was also pushing north. By March 9 he had reached Sunan, within forty miles of the front. Here he was detained again as thousands of Japanese troops were marching past. "IMPORTANT. ANOTHER VEXATION!" he exclaimed: "Just caught five body lice on my undershirt . . . Lice drive me clean crazy. I am itching all over. I am sure, every second, that a score of them are on me. And how under the sun am I to write for the Examiner or write to you!"

Still, write for both he did. During the past five weeks, while suffering one vexation after another, he had cabled nine dispatches to the *Examiner*. The first, published in the February 27 issue of the *Examiner*, was datelined "SHIMONOSEKI, Wednesday, February 3, 1904" and headlined HOW JACK LONDON GOT IN AND OUT OF JAIL IN JAPAN. STORY OF JAPANESE OFFICIAL RED TAPE THAT SOUNDS LIKE COMIC OPERA. A VIVID GLIMPSE OF JUDICIAL WAR-TIME METHODS IN MIKADO'S REALM. TALE THAT HANGS ON INNOCENT SNAPSHOTS. Its essence is conveyed in the words "comic opera."

There was less humor in the dispatches as his progress brought him closer to the front. "The Russians are boldly and fiercely pushing forward their advance south of the Yalu river. Their Cossacks are scouting far in advance of the main body through Northern Korea," he reported on March 2. "Ping Yang is in a state of panic . . . Ten thousand [natives] have fled the city and others are leaving hourly. From further north, in the direction of the Yalu, tens of thousands of refugees have been driven out. The fear of the Russians has become a blinding terror."

Despite his frustrations with the Japanese bureaucracy, he praised the soldiers themselves as well-disciplined warriors: "They march along without apparent effort under their forty-two pound kits. There is no stooping forward, no slouching, no lagging nor does one see a man continually adjusting straps and pads or hear tin cups rattling or accouterments clattering."

On March 5 he was able to report the first land combat: "A scouting party of Russian Cossacks, crossing the Yalu at Wiju, had ventured 200 miles south into Korea to get in touch with the Japanese and discover how far north they had penetrated . . . splendid looking soldiers, perfect horsemen and mounted on sturdy Russian ponies." He described how the Cossacks, twenty in number, encountered no Japanese troops until "they reached the ancient walled city of Ping Yang." At last, Jack was within hearing distance of the action. As the Russians neared the city, they spotted and gave chase to five Japanese cavalrymen, whom they followed in hot pursuit until fired upon by the riflemen stationed at the walls:

> To Company 7 of the Forty-sixth regiment of infantry, Twelfth division of the Japanese army, belongs the honor of firing the first shots on the land. Fourteen men of this company . . . had watched the chase as it led up to them. At 700 meters (about 2,300 feet) distance, time 9:30 a.m., they opened fire.
>
> The Cossacks promptly whirled their horses and rode away. Thirty shots were fired in all, to which the Cossacks made no reply. They had fulfilled their errand of finding the Japanese and wisely entertained no idea of capturing Ping Yang. It is remarkable that none was killed or wounded by such short range fire. When asked about this, the officer in charge explained that the riflemen were afraid of hitting their own fleeing cavalry. They aver, however, that two Cossacks were seen to dismount from evidently wounded horses and lead them away. So Russian blood was shed at the first land engagement, even if it was only horse blood.

In his dispatch to the *Examiner* written six days later, while stranded in Sunan, he described in detail the festering sores caused by marching endless miles in ill-fitted boots, and the body sores caused by the raw chafing of heavy leather belts overloaded with knapsacks and equipment: "So one pays the penalty of being a twentieth-century soldier, of being unpracticed in the science of footgear and of being compelled to carry his destroying energy in heavy cartridge boxes slung outside his body instead of inside in the arm and shoulder muscles."

Although restrained from moving more than a hundred yards beyond the city, he was able to visit the makeshift hospital the army had set up in Sunan. Here he witnessed some minor horrors of wartime surgery—the major battle horrors were yet to come. Here also he saw the challenges faced by military surgeons who must do enough patching up to keep the army moving. With anesthetics in short supply, one doctor substituted "a running fire of advice and witticism." To a soldier with a hole in his toe worked nearly to the bone by the nail of another toe, he scolded, "'Why do you come to war if you make trouble over a little thing like this?'" To another, whose operation was so painful that he had to be held down by his comrades, the surgeon reproached, "'Why do you cry? A soldier does not cry. You are going to fight the Russians.'" The tactic worked: "The man ceased squirming and composed his face." London now took a step beyond objective reporting: "A pleasing operation, this patching":

> Here is man, a rational creature, a creator of wonder and of beauty, and of marvels. He has enslaved the blind elements and forced them to do his work for him . . . Having done these things, he devotes his intelligence to the manufacture of machines of destruction . . . Also, he takes a man and instructs him in the humanities of medicine and surgery. This man becomes skilled in the alleviating of pain and the mending of injuries. And this man [is] dispatched to Korea [where] he mends the men that they may mar other men.

Three days after sending this dispatch, he wrote to Charmian that he had been ordered back, first, from Sunan to Ping Yang and, now, to Seoul: "the Japanese are disciplining us for our rush ahead and the scoop we made—and they are doing it for the sake of the correspondents who remained in Japan by advice of the Japanese and who have made life miserable for the Japanese by pointing out that we have been ahead gathering all the plums."

He was forced to spend the next month in Seoul. "I'll never go to a war between Orientals again," he vowed in a letter to Charmian on April 1. "Here I am, still penned up in Seoul, my 5 horses and interpreters at Chemulpo, my outfit at Ping-yang, my post at Anju—and eating my heart out with inactivity."

His tedium was broken shortly thereafter when he received word from Eliza that, because of a blunder at the *Examiner*, Charmian's letters had been forwarded to Bessie instead of to him. Apprehensive over the scandal of his separation from Bessie, Charmian had left California on February 20 to visit Edward Payne's daughter, Lynette McMurray, in Newton, Iowa.

Still, he was growing increasingly restive in Seoul. "When I think of all those letters of yours held up I almost go crazy with anger. *Crazy!* I mean it. Everybody in the hotel has noticed my touchiness, & I have 'jumped' everybody on the slightest provocation," he declared on April 5. "I'm going to ride off steam now on a jockey saddle & a spanking big horse, and if we don't kill each other we'll kill a few native babies or blind men." He also grumbled about having to don "a frock coat & top hat" the next night in order to deliver a reading from *The Call of the Wild* for the local YMCA foreign residents: "Custom of the country . . . imagine me in a Prince Albert & a stovepipe."

Frederick Palmer, a fellow correspondent, recalled London's behavior in less than flattering terms:

> Although cheery and kindly, and liking conversation with him at the center of it, he preferred to walk alone in aristocratic aloofness, and always in the direction he chose no matter where anybody else was going. He had his own separate mess and tent: general and private of his army of one, he rode in front of his two pack-donkeys, which jingled with bells, the leader bearing an American flag.

On April 16, having allowed a score of other correspondents to catch up with London in Seoul, the Japanese authorized fourteen of the group to move toward the front with General Tamemoto Kuroki's First Army—under the close watch of an official censor named T. Okada. "I was one of the lucky fourteen that was graciously allowed to travel with the army. But this time it was different," Jack reported. "It was like a party of Cook's tourists with supervising officers as guides. We saw what we were permitted to see and the chief duty of the officers looking after us was to keep us from seeing anything."

After slogging along a road that spring rains had turned into a river of mud, sometimes up to their horses' shoulders, they neared the front line at Wiju a week later. "Here I am, on the banks of the Yalu, waiting for the first big land fight," Jack wrote to Brett on April 24. "Can say I know a lot more about horses than when I started out."

He could also say that he knew a lot more about the Japanese military bureaucracy than when he started out. These officials were determined that only favorable accounts of their troops' performance in battle be conveyed to the world outside. Foreign correspondents were not allowed to view the action firsthand but were required to get their accounts of the action from Japanese officers. Until now, though not involved in battle action, Jack had at least enjoyed some free rein and movement with the army. After he reached Korea, he had also enjoyed considerable freedom to use his camera; and he had sent hundreds of photographs back to the *Examiner*. Especially noteworthy in those pictures is his focus on the human experience. People dominate London's photographs, people in every walk of life: soldiers and other military personnel, of course, but also beggars, coolies, peasants, priests, noblemen, and children. But now that he was under the surveillance of the army in Manchuria, the taking of photographs even remotely related to military operations was strictly forbidden.

Where now was the thrill of adventure and danger he had come halfway around the globe to report? His fuse, never very long, was burning fast. "I am clean disgusted," he wrote to George Sterling on May 8. "My work is rotten . . . so circumscribed am I, so hedged about with restrictions, that I see little, hear but little more [and] in no way can manage to get in intimate touch with officers or men." Two weeks later he wrote to the *Examiner* that he could endure the futility of his situation no longer and that, unless they arranged to assign him to the Russian side or "expressly bid" him to stay where he was, he planned to leave for home within six weeks. He would leave sooner than that.

Less than a week after mailing his letter to the *Examiner*, he exploded. His mapu Manyoungi caught a Japanese officer's groom stealing fodder allotted to London's horses. Furious, Jack strode over to the stable at once to confront the culprit. Instead of apologizing, the mapu scowled and made a threatening gesture. Instantly all the frustrations Jack had experienced over the past months came to a head. Standing before him in the flesh was an insolent representative of all he detested in the Oriental attitude. He straightway decked his offender.

It was not a knockout punch, but it was heard halfway around the globe. The Japanese were very sensitive about what they perceived as an overweening arrogance on the part of the Western world. The groom

Jack hit reported the incident to his superiors, protesting his own innocence. His report was corroborated by fellow mapus. Although the Japanese officers had no qualms about striking their subordinates, they were not about to tolerate such abuse from an outsider. Of all the foreign correspondents, Jack London had been the most obstreperous. He had already been arrested: once at the fortified city of Moji for illegal use of his camera, and again for moving out toward the front from Sunan to Ping Yang without permission. Of late, he had become openly contemptuous. In short, he had worn out his welcome. Time to get rid of the nuisance and make a clear example for the other foreign correspondents. Major General Fuji, chief of staff to General Kuroki, on being informed of the latest incident, immediately ordered that London be arrested and held for court-martial.

Despite London's surliness, his fellow correspondents tried to come to his rescue. They sent a delegation to the headquarters at Antung, "explaining that London was a most gifted writer, with a strong sense of pioneer American *bushido*, which responded with a blow of the fist to an insult." Their plea was rejected: The Honorable Mr. London had violated regulations once too often. "Article 4 of REGULATIONS FOR PRESS CORRESPONDENTS" quite clearly stated that "Press correspondents should look and behave decently, and should never do anything disorderly"; and "Article 5" instructed that "Press correspondents should take care not to do anything harmful to the troops." The evidence was conclusive: Mr. London's misbehavior merited the court-martial.

From all appearances, Jack's good luck had run out with his welcome. The outcome of the court-martial was problematic: at best it would be unpleasant; at worst it could be fatal. Thanks to Richard Harding Davis, that outcome was averted. Hearing of London's predicament, Davis sent an urgent cable to his friend Theodore Roosevelt, alerting him to London's imminent trial. President Roosevelt admired London the man as well as London the writer. Despite their dissimilar backgrounds, they had a good deal in common. Like Jack, "Teddy" had contributed character-building articles for the strenuous young readers of the *Youth's Companion*. More to the point, like Jack, he had created a legend for himself as a man of action. Both had become public heroes in their own time. Nobody was going to bully an American hero while Roosevelt was president. The president acted at once. He cabled an official U.S.

protest to the Japanese government, demanding London's immediate release from custody. In no mood to incur America's wrath while fighting Russia, the Japanese War Office ordered General Fuji to release London and send him back to the United States.

Jack was ready to leave. "Oh, my Darling, if you could only know how happy I am this morning. I arose singing with joy. I had heard from you," he wrote to Charmian on June 1. "Hurrah! I'm coming home— coming home to you, to pillow my head on your breast and sleep for a while I think."

17

THE LONG SICKNESS

The things I had fought for and burned my midnight oil for, had failed me. Success—I despised it. Recognition—it was dead ashes. Society, men and women above the ruck and the muck of the water-front and the forecastle—I was appalled by their unlovely mental mediocrity. Love of woman—it was like all the rest.

—*JOHN BARLEYCORN*

Jack expected Charmian to be waiting on the pier for him when his ship docked in San Francisco. "I cabled you yesterday that I was coming," he had written to her. "I shall arrive about July first, but I think there is a chance for this to beat me home. I shall direct it to Berkeley in the belief that you will be there at that time." But instead of being greeted by Charmian when the SS *Korea* docked in San Francisco at the end of June, Jack was greeted by a process server with "separation and maintenance" papers from Bessie and by the following headline in the *San Francisco Chronicle*:

JACK LONDON SUED BY WIFE
Young Journalist Is Accused
of Extreme Cruelty in
Action for Legal Separation
Woman Collaborator Figures in Trouble

He was stunned. He had expected a fight with Bessie, but he had not counted on this sensational media coverage. More shocking was the denigration of Anna Strunsky, whom he had not seen for nearly two years. Yet here was her name in print for all the world to witness:

> Extreme cruelty is alleged, dating back to the time when Miss Anna Strunsky, a young graduate of Stanford University and student of sociology, collaborated with London in writing the "Kempton-Wace Letters." Although Mrs. London made no complaint for a long time, she suffered in silence from the indifference and coldness of her husband toward her. Gradually she felt that her husband's affections were slipping away from her. Try as she would, she did not win back the ardent love that had filled their early married life with happiness . . . Divorce proceedings were threatened about two years ago when, it was said, Mrs. London accidentally found Miss Strunsky sitting on her husband's lap.

The Strunsky family, one of the most highly respected in the Bay Area, was scandalized. Anna immediately issued a vigorous disclaimer to the press, with no hint of her deepest feelings for Jack:

> Absurd is hardly a word strong enough to be used in regard to the silly stories about the love-making that went on before Mrs. London's eyes. The ridiculous part of the whole thing is the fact that my visit to the Londons' house occurred exactly two and a half years ago. At that time there was not a breath of rumor to the effect that their married life was not happy . . . Immediately after my visit to his home, I went to New York, from there to London, and I have spent the greater part of my time since then in Italy; returning from Naples only four months ago.

Even Flora, partial to Bessie and usually taciturn in such matters affecting her son, came to his defense: "I can hardly believe that Bessie has made such charges," she told the *Chronicle*:

> "Cruelty and desertion" indeed! During my whole life with them I do not recall where Jack once said an unkind word to her or did anything

that could in any way hurt her feelings. He was loving, affectionate and generous to a fault during the first two years of that marriage. Then there began to grow a gradual coolness between them, due to her not understanding the needs of his literary work, and partly caused by the "hero worship" of a lot of silly girls who wrote him letters and veritably dogged his footsteps whenever he left the house. Jack looked upon the latter as a joke, and would often laugh about it. Perhaps he took it all too lightly, for things went from bad to worse between husband and wife, and a year ago, they decided to separate . . . Jack has made her a liberal allowance, and has done all in his power to promote her comfort and that of the little girls.

What prompted Bessie to take such a course of action? She had known for some time that Charmian was "the other woman." So why had she chosen to defame Anna instead? The answer to that question was known to only a handful of people until Joan London published Anna's account sixty-two years later: "As Anna told me the story, Jack kept pressuring my mother to get a divorce. I know that she was very unwilling to do so. She loved him, she wanted her babies to have a father":

I am sure that she sincerely felt that while a woman was undoubtedly involved in my father's wish for a divorce, it was a mere infatuation which would soon pass. Yielding finally to my father's pressure, my mother consulted an attorney, who was also a friend to whom she could open her heart and speak freely. Anna said that it was the attorney who proposed the plan to which my mother agreed: to draw up the divorce papers, name Anna Strunsky, and file the papers in what Anna described as a "sealed" file in the courthouse. The next step in the plan was to tell my father, on his return from the Russo-Japanese War assignment, that he could have his divorce, but at the cost of Anna being named in the complaint.

Bessie and her attorney had no intention of publishing the contents of that sealed file, Anna recalled, because they both believed Jack would never knowingly expose Anna to defamation. Their plan backfired when "a few days before Jack returned, a 'curious' newspaperman somehow managed to gain access to the sealed file and promptly broke the news of the London divorce." As a result, Jack told Bessie, "You have done your worst. Now get a divorce on the obvious grounds—desertion."

Not only stunned by Bessie's mistreatment of Anna, London was devastated by the havoc her course of action wreaked upon his finances. Her lawyer had persuaded a judge to issue an injunction preventing him "from drawing his money from his bank, his salary from his employer, or money due from the firms in the East that have published his books."

Hurtful as these blows were, they were less so than Charmian's failure to meet him when he landed. He had cabled her announcing his return and his ardent expectations, but the woman to whom he had given his heart was nowhere to be seen. Her absence at this critical moment was a crushing disappointment. It initiated a period of emotional chaos that would prove near fatal to his dream of success as well as to his dream of an ideal mate. Three years afterward, Charmian told Blanche Partington that Jack had never quite forgiven her for letting him "fight it out alone."

So why did she—and where was she? On advice from Aunt Netta, she was keeping a safe distance in Newton, Iowa. This was hardly conduct befitting the brave woman of Jack's dreams. "I see no reason why you should not return to California, for my troubles with Bess are bound to continue for a weary long while," he wrote to her on July 6. "You may crop up in the midst of it, you may never be mentioned. But elect to do as you see fit. If you remain away till divorce is granted, you may remain away for years, you may die and be buried away." Aware that he was on the verge of pleading, he pulled up short by telling her that she must decide for herself, for her own good, "and not allow any thought of me and my selfish desire for happiness to influence you." But he could not entirely conceal his bitterness in his postscript: "Write me at Flat if you can see your way to it."

It would be nearly two months before she returned to California. During the interim, he would try to impose some kind of order upon the chaos his life had become. First, he had to come to terms with his wife. For a while, after seeing his two lovely daughters again, he even considered reconciliation. One of the most poignant passages in *Jack London and His Daughters* is Joan's memory of her father's return from the Orient in the early summer of 1904. Not yet four at the time, she remembered the event sixty years afterward as if it had happened only the day before. She also remembered how worried she and her mother had been about Baby Bess, a "sweet-tempered baby who rarely cried, but [who] had never made the slightest attempt to talk" even though she would be two years old within a few months. No "loving device" Bessie tried seemed to work. As Joan recalled, "[Becky] communicated her wishes only to me, in a rich variety of grunts emphasized by gestures, which I unaccountably understood and translated to Mother."

Joan was also concerned that her little sister did not know her father, who had been away for so many months. Each day, she would stand under Jack's picture in the front hall of the house and, as Becky watched, point up to the photo saying, "My Daddy!" But Becky gave no sign of understanding "other than the pleased smile she bestowed impartially on everything that was brought to her attention, from toys to mashed potatoes." However, one evening at the end of June, after the two girls had gone to bed, Joan heard her mother laughing and talking excitedly. "It was Daddy, longed-for and instantly familiar, who had returned, as I had known he would, from the other side of the world!" Eager to see his two daughters, Jack came into their bedroom, and even before Joan could utter the cry of joy that was in [her] throat, Becky "sat up in her crib and gazed at him solemnly. Slowly, her lips curved in her pleased smile. Raising her hand, the chubby index finger pointing, she said clearly, 'My Daddy!'":

> Overcome with astonishment and disbelief, Mother and I watched Daddy leap to the crib and gather Bess up in a tumultuous armful, kissing her, rumpling her silky golden hair, and exclaiming, "Little Bess! Baby B!"
>
> Turning joyfully to us and seeing our stunned faces, he demanded, "What's the matter? Is Baby B the only one who is glad to see me?"

When Bessie and Joan told him those were Baby B's first words, he exclaimed over and over, "It took her Daddy to make her talk!"

His feelings for Charmian were less enthusiastic. His faith in her devotion could not be soon restored. In her copy of *The Faith of Men*, dated July 22, he wrote one of his most laconic inscriptions: "Dear Charmian:—You know, I know, and what the deuce do we care who else knows? Jack." Brought up sharply by this brusqueness when she received the book, she acted without further delay: "Coming" was the one word she telegraphed on July 27. Despite his repressed anger, he had hungered for her too long to risk spoiling her return with a quarrel when she arrived in Oakland on August 1. Instead, he took her to bed that night. "Arrived 1216 [Telegraph Avenue] nearly nine—all well," she recorded in her diary. Indeed all seemed more than well to Charmian as reflected in her next entry:

!!!!!!

After she had gone up to Glen Ellen on August 4, Jack was still under the spell of their passionate reunion: "Dearest—You are with me yet, I almost believe. I cannot shake the vision of you out of my eyes." And a few days after that he exclaimed, "I've the [picture of] the sweet-limbed woman on horseback, & now I've the sweet-limbs, too."

Such delights were limited during the coming months. He harbored a deep resentment of her two-month delay in returning to his arms, and he would find ways to get even while trying to compensate for his own depression. One way was with the old Crowd, particularly with Blanche Partington. The last paragraph of his August 4 letter revealed his ambivalence, and his duplicity: "Sunday, Aug. 14th. I'll take 'our' crowd out on the *Spray*. And you can't come—not till after the interlocutory decree is safe." As he well knew by this time, it was no longer "our" crowd. Unknown to Charmian, her erstwhile friends were working to undermine her relationship with Jack. Jack was neither unaware of the conspiracy nor entirely innocent. His datebook reveals that on Saturday, August 6, just two days after writing to Charmian that he couldn't shake the vision of her out of his eyes, he had a rendezvous with Partington in her apartment at 1822 Fell Street.

One of his few unadulterated pleasures during these months was his reunion with his daughters. "Believe me," he wrote to Charmian, "it has taken all the resolution I could summon to prevent my going back, for the children's sake. They are such joys, such perfect little human creatures." However, years later, he said, "If I had gone back, it would have meant suicide or insanity."

Although these were bleak months for Jack, they were some of the brightest for Joan and Becky. Never again would they see so much of the father they loved. The tension between him and Bessie had lessened when she consented to a divorce and lifted the injunction against his finances with his agreement to build a house for her and their daughters. On August 11 he purchased a lot with the provision that it would revert to him if she remarried. That fall Bessie and the girls moved into their new home along with Manyoungi, who made his quarters in the attic room.

Manyoungi had impressed London with his excellent command of the English language, his neatness and cleanliness, his flawless manners, and above all his good-natured efficiency. Jack arranged to bring him back as his valet, cook, and housekeeper. This arrangement was greeted by London's socialist friends with bemusement—and by his nonsocialist friends with amusement. Here was a self-proclaimed revolutionary—one who had run, and would run again, for political office on the Socialist ticket—who was evidently adopting the self-indulgent habits of the despised bourgeoisie. But Jack had an explanation: "Why tie my own shoes when I can have it done by some one whose business it is, while I am improving my mind or entertaining the fellows who drop in?"

"I had no understanding of 'servant,'" said Joan. "I thought of Manyoungi as Daddy's friend, who helped him because he was so busy, and I was proud because he was my friend, too." She and Becky adored him. Joan remembered particularly Manyoungi's wonderful hands: "small, slim, supple and very strong." They were also loving hands, hands that taught the two youngsters the intricacies of acrobatics. "While he performed prodigies of balance, we grasped his hands—and how tightly we clung to them at first—and, our bodies horizontal, walked up his legs and thighs and torso; then, swinging to the vertical, we stepped lightly onto his shoulders and stood there, triumphant and unafraid."

With their father, the play was rowdier and less graceful, but no less loving. "Always when Daddy came to see us in the afternoon, he romped with us," Joan recalled:

Singly or simultaneously, we would rush him, growling fiercely, and the next instant be tumbled back with one sweep of his arms. Sitting on the floor, he would parry our lunges with lightning-swift jabs, knock our heads together, tease us and taunt us with high good humor until we launched a fresh attack. In the end, the fortress was stormed, four small legs clambered over him and four small fists reduced him first to shouts of laughter, then to prolonged fits of giggles, and finally the three of us sprawled on the floor, breathless and content. For that little while, he was wholly ours and we were wholly his.

Jack was not wholly anyone else's during that unhappy year. Although surrounded by friends, he felt like a stranger in his own land. "I had life troubles and heart troubles," he wrote in *John Barleycorn*, "and descended into my slough of despond." The dream of the better life to which he had committed himself had become a morbid nightmare. For the first, and arguably the last, time in his life, he became seriously suicidal, admitting that he gave his revolver away for fear he might unwittingly shoot himself in his sleep. "In brief, I lost my fine faiths in pretty well everything except humanity, and the humanity I retained faith in was a very stark humanity indeed." In a letter apologizing to Anna for all the trouble he had caused her, he admitted that he was a "changed" man: "Though a materialist when I first knew you, I had the saving grace of enthusiasm. That enthusiasm is the thing that is spoiled, and I have become too sorry a thing for you to remember . . . I wander through life delivering hurts to all that know me."

On September 22, sensing something was still wrong in their relationship, Charmian came down meet him in Oakland, but this brief reunion was somehow different. When she returned to Glen Ellen two days later, she wrote expressing her concern. "No, dear, I have no particular trouble bothering me now," he answered on September 29:

I think, most probably, that you and I are in a very trying stage just now. The ardor & heat & ecstasy of new-discovered love have been tempered by time, on the one hand; and on the other hand we are denied the growing comradeship which should be ours right now. Instead, we must wait another year before we can enter upon this

comradeship of daily intimacy—& the intervening period is bound
to be full of worry & anxiety if we do not understand its significance.

The next few months would "be full of worry & anxiety"—regardless
of their understanding of the significance. Charmian intuited something of the significance and was doing the best she could to make
amends. For one thing, she undertook the task of reading, correcting,
and typing his manuscripts. For another, although she could not maintain the "comradeship of daily intimacy," she had sex with him as often
as circumstances allowed. Within two days after receiving his letter, she
rode the train down to Oakland again so that she might get him back
into her arms and "sweet limbs." This time the results were immediate.
"In many respects, last night was (to me) one of the most satisfying
times we have had together," Jack told her in a letter on October 4.

The next week, he wrote to Brett, apologizing for not being able to
deliver a "spring book" for the coming year. "I expect to potter around
the next couple of months writing several short stories, and trying my
hand at a play—not a serious big effort of a play, though I'd like some
time to write a really big play." The play he would try his hand at was
Scorn of Women, a melodrama based upon one of his Klondike tales by
the same title. But his friend Ethel Barrymore would decline to star in
it, and he would never see it produced. "In the three months since my
return [from Japan], I have written nothing at all, with the sole exception of story enclosed herewith," he also told Brett. The enclosed manuscript was "The Game," the first of London's four pioneering stories
about prizefighting, three of which, including this one, rank among his
best work.

Boxing held a special fascination for London. "I would rather be
heavyweight champion of the world—which I can never be—than king
of England, president of the United States, or Kaiser of Germany," he
declared. His schoolboy scraps and his more dangerous escapades on
the Oakland waterfront had provided an early initiation into the world
of physical aggression, and an appreciation for the practical value of
being handy with one's fists. However, it was not until he trained with
Jim Whitaker, former British army boxing instructor, that he honed his
skills. From that time onward, he boxed whenever and with whomever
he could: friends, visitors, even playfully with Charmian. He also loved

watching a good fight, and here was the chance to make money at the same time. He possessed an exceptional talent for describing physical violence, and he had enough firsthand experience to give his readers an authentic sense of what actually happens when two men struggle to pound each other senseless inside the ring.

The manuscript of "The Game" he mailed to Brett on October 10 was less than fourteen thousand words in length, scarcely enough to make a bound volume. With careful typesetting, copious line drawings and vivid artwork, along with Jack's three-thousand-word expansion, Macmillan was able to publish a handsome edition in 1905. Because of its realistic treatment of this brutal and sometimes deadly sport—the young hero dies in the ring on the eve of his wedding—genteel critics found London's story offensive with its "sheer street-bred sensuality." Some reviewers, however—including the lightweight champion Jimmy Britt—praised the tale as an "intensely graphic portrayal of the prize ring" and "an epic on pugilism."

Except for "The Game," Jack was not doing much that fall to improve his financial situation—and he was doing even less to improve his relationship with Charmian. He spent her birthday, November 27, with Blanche Partington, but any chance that his affair with Partington might have reached full bloom was nipped in the bud when Kittredge came back to town two days later. "Mate's at night," she wrote in her diary. "Sweet visit. Gave me stuff to copy. Also first act play to read." They would be together more frequently during the next three weeks. On December 1 they attended George Sterling's birthday party, at which she played the piano. "Grand time," she recorded, "Dear Mate!"

While Jack was working on his first attempt at playwriting, an article appeared in the Sunday, December 4, edition of the *San Francisco Chronicle* that would result in the production of one of his most successful novels. THE CALL OF THE TAME—AN ANTITHESIS ran the headline. Below the headline were pictures of two large dogs facing each other, captioned: BONES—WHO HEARD THE CALL OF THE TAME and BUCK—WHO HEARD THE CALL OF THE WILD. In the article, Flora Haines Loughead compared the real-life "Bones, the Mahlemuit, bred of the wolf in Alaska," and subsequently brought to California by Mr. and Mrs. Theodore Scharff, with London's fictional hero in *The Call of the Wild*:

Bones was bred to cold and want, to hard labor and abuse. Upon contact with white men he answered the Call of the Tame and became docile, gentle and affectionate beyond nature. He has been rescued from the Arctic terrors to live out his days in comfort and happiness in the lovely Santa Clara Valley, where on warm days he seeks the cool shade of trees or rolls himself in the water for refreshment. Bred the wolf, he has allied himself with man.

London was quick to see the marketing possibilities. He wrote to Brett the next day about the next book he was going to write, an antithesis to *The Call of the Wild*: "Instead of the devolution or decivilization of a dog, I'm going to give the evolution, the civilization of a dog . . . a *proper* companion-book—in the same style, grasp, concrete way . . . it should make a hit." Make a hit it did when it appeared in 1906 as *White Fang*.

In the meantime, Jack was agonizing over his personal issues. Charmian's December diary entries indicate that their relationship was heading for a crisis. She went back down to the city on Thursday, December 15, after receiving a "Letter from Mate." Then, on Monday, "Big understanding with Mate." That understanding is clarified in her correspondence with Blanche Partington three years later. She realized that Jack had been unfaithful, and she was willing to forgive this, but, she explained, "I had to be absolutely satisfied that I was the one woman in the world to him at the time I married him." She told Jack that she would not hold him to any promises: he was free to do whatever with whomever he chose. He listened to her announcement in tight-lipped silence, started to leave without a word, then suddenly turned and exclaimed, "You were never so dear to me as you are this minute!" Her ultimatum put an end to his affair with Partington, but not an end to his depression.

Thinking a change of scenery might help, on New Year's Eve he took the train down to Los Angeles to see Cloudesley and the Tournament of Roses parade. On January 2 they watched the colorful pageant without worry of work. Cloudesley had the task of shielding his celebrated guest from fans and publicity mongers. He allowed only a couple of breaks in Jack's leisure. The first was a lecture, "The Scab," already promised to the speakers' committee of the Socialist Party in Los Angeles and delivered before a packed house of paid admissions at the Simpson Auditorium on January 8.

Attending the lecture was Nathaniel Hawthorne's son, Julian, a distinguished literary critic whom Hearst had sent to Southern California to write descriptive articles on the region. Two years before, Hawthorne had reviewed *A Daughter of the Snows*, labeling the book "a crude and incoherent novel" and concluding that if the author were "satisfied with his present level of performance, there [was] little hope for him." But London's "level of performance" had risen since then, and Hawthorne's treatment of London in the two articles he wrote for the *Los Angeles Examiner* was much more favorable. The first of these, headlined on the front page of the January 10 issue, was a report on London's lecture: "It is pleasant to look upon Mr. London. He is as simple and straightforward as a grizzly bear. Upon his big, hearty, healthy nature is based a brain of unusual clearness and insight. His heart is warm, and his sympathies are wide. His opinions are his own—independent, strongly held, courageously expounded, perspicaciously conveyed."

Hawthorne's second article, appearing on January 12 and headlined JACK LONDON IN LITERATURE, reported his interview with the famous novelist. "Mr. Hawthorne discovers in the young author a rich variety of praiseworthy qualities and suggests that a circumstantial account of Mr. London's own life would make a greater story than he will ever write" was the lead-in. Jack's responses to Hawthorne's inquiries about his philosophy and his literary works reflected the effects of his long sickness: "Talk about surviving in our works has small weight with him . . . We are here today, and gone tomorrow, and that is all . . . He had no paternal tenderness for his literary progeny. They were mothered by necessity, not by love."

"Does all this appear frigid and saturnine?" Hawthorne asked in concluding. "Mr. London himself, his speech, gestures and the look of his eyes, supplied the corrective. In himself he is hearty, genial, honest, simple; no trace of a pose in him; he inspires strong liking from first to last."

Despite the "hearty" impression London made on Hawthorne, he was sick in body as well as soul, suffering intermittent symptoms from something he feared might be cancer or venereal disease. That ailment would warp his view of the world, aggravating his depression. He left

Los Angeles on January 12 and the next evening delivered a lecture, "The Class Struggle," followed by reading from *The Call of the Wild* before a standing-room-only audience at the Normal School in San Jose. Near the end of his reading, some of those who had been standing for nearly three hours began shuffling around, gathering up their coats and umbrellas. A reporter for the San Francisco's literary journal *The Argonaut* described Jack's response:

> Mr. London flashed one look over the big audience and then half carelessly, with no touch of impatience or personal feeling, yet with a fine scorn that disdained even while it took cognizance, said, "Just wait two minutes and then I'll be through." A ripple of approval ran through the crowd, and the burst of applause that followed was indeed spontaneous; for none could but feel genuine admiration for the manner in which "the neatest call down of the season," as the college youth on my left termed it, had been given.

A week later, he caused a much bigger stir when, at the invitation of President Benjamin Ide Wheeler, he delivered his lecture "Revolution" before the student body and faculty at the University of California at Berkeley. His tirade against the abuses of the capitalistic system was a long one, and his audience was unusually quiet: the faculty was stunned, the students fascinated. At noon he was still going strong. Realizing that he had run past his time limit, he turned and asked President Wheeler if he should stop. Told to continue, he went on to this unsettling conclusion: "Seven million revolutionists, organized, working day and night, are preaching the revolution—that passionate gospel, the Brotherhood of Man . . . The capitalist class has been indicted. It has failed in its management and its management is to be taken away from it . . . The revolution is here, now. Stop it who can."

Although faculty reactions were mixed, most of the students were enthusiastic. Shortly afterward they organized a UC Socialist Club. Charmian, who had attended the lecture, reported that while Jack was chatting with members of the faculty, he admonished Professor Charles Mills Gayley for the obsolete literary works traditionally used in the English curriculum: "Dr. Gayley, permit me to make the criticism that English is not being taught the right way. You are giving the students for their textbooks such antiquated authors as Macauley, Emerson and others of the same school. What you need in your course is a few of the more modern types of literature—" Professor Gayley interrupted: "Perhaps you are not aware, Mr. London, that we are using your own 'Call of the Wild' as a textbook at the University?" Realizing the joke was on him, Jack laughed along with the rest of the group surrounding the rostrum.

During the first months of 1905 he lectured frequently throughout the Bay Area on "The Scab," "Revolution," "The Tramp," "The Class Struggle," and "How I Became a Socialist," but his love for the party could not fill the emotional void in his life. To find some solace, he took to the water again. At dawn shortly after the first of February, he loosed the anchor of the *Spray* at Oakland Estuary and set sail on a cruise of the inland waterways of the Sacramento River. Not alone—three other men and a dog were aboard: Cloudesley, Manyoungi, Herman "Toddy" Albrecht, and "Brown Wolf" (a quarter-wolf malamute and sled dog inherited from a Klondiker and later immortalized in Jack's story by that title). All passengers proved to be fit sailors except Albrecht, whose ineptness caused the loss of an anchor and a near loss of the boat. After the *Spray* barely escaped disaster during a storm in San Pablo Bay, Albrecht left the party and went back to Oakland.

On February 4, Jack left the boat at Black Point on the Petaluma River and took the train to Glen Ellen, arriving at Wake Robin late that evening. He found Charmian sick in bed with neuralgia and an abscessed ear, the result of her twenty-two-foot dives under his instruction at the Oakland baths. For the next two days he devoted all his time to her, chatting and reading aloud to her "by the hour," she recalled, adding that she could vouch that "no one ever knew tenderer nurse." Jack's presence was therapeutic, for on the evening of the second day, her appetite returned and she was hungry "for the first time in weeks." The two of them raided Netta's pantry and feasted on "honey and biscuits and sun-dried figs, [giggling] like truant schoolfellows."

Jack returned to Rio Vista to resume cruising on the inland rivers along with Cloudesley, but a strong current kept the *Spray* tied up for a fortnight. The delay allowed Jack time to catch up with his writing and relaxing before they set sail again. They arrived in Stockton on February 26 and were met by members of the local Socialist Party, who had scheduled London to deliver his "Revolution" lecture before the Critic Club, a private group limited to ten of the most prestigious citizens of Stockton. The meeting was held at the home of Johannes Reimers, the writer-horticulturalist whom Jack had met at the Strunskys' in San Francisco three years earlier. Jack chuckled when he saw the headline of the special dispatch sent to *The San Francisco Bulletin* on March 11:

LONDON STARTLES STAID CLUBMEN OF CITY OF STOCKTON
Novelist Charged With Having Read A Paper Before Critic Club
That Was Blood Red, Anarchistic Propaganda.

"Jack London has set all Stockton by the ears by a paper he read before a very select club in this city last Sunday evening," the report began, explaining that "Revolution" turned out to be an unexpected shocker to the members and their guests, which included "several of the foremost citizens of this city and not a few ladies." Because of its elite nature, "nearly all those present were in evening dress," with the notable exception of London, who came in "negligee costume—rich, but exceptionally unconventional—and during the entire evening puffed cigarette smoke." As if the tenor of his lecture were not enough, this alone caused many to gasp. When he concluded his lengthy reading, members and guests were given the opportunity to criticize the paper. It was at this time, in London's rebuttal, that "the real display of pyrotechnics commenced." Pounding the table and puffing cigarette smoke, "he lectured the hearers as though they had been unruly school children . . . all of which so alarmed and befogged his auditors that they subsided into an embarrassing silence, out of which they did not emerge until yesterday and today."

Jack was elated; his Stockton comrades scandalized. "Comrade London," complained one of them, "I believe you have set back the socialist movement at least fifty years." Cloudesley recalled that Jack "simply grinned" at the time, but remarked seriously, some years later, "I cannot believe I have had any such tremendous influence in the socialist movement, but if I have had any influence at all, I believe I have advanced the cause of socialism, the accomplishment of the revolution, by as much as five minutes."

Just before leaving Oakland on the *Spray*, he agreed to run for mayor again, this time polling nearly one thousand votes. It was a symbolic gesture. When Charmian asked him what if he had been accidentally elected, he replied, "I wouldn't let my name be used if I thought there was the slightest possibility of winning. If I did by chance get elected, I guess I'd run away to sea or somewhere with you!" Years afterward he confessed that at the lowest depths of his depression, it was socialism that saved him: "It was the PEOPLE, and no thanks to John Barleycorn, who pulled me through my long sickness. And when I was convalescent, came the love of woman to complete the cure and lull my pessimism asleep for many a long day."

The curative effects of woman's love became manifest in the second week of March. After their Stockton visit, Jack took the *Spray* down the San Joaquin and Sacramento rivers, through the Carquinez Strait, then up to Napa on March 7 to see the Winships. Edward Winship, the "tycoon of Napa County," owned a couple of factories along with several other properties. Jack had met him and his wife, Ida, the year before, aboard the SS *Siberia* on his way to Japan, and they had invited him to come for a visit when he got home from the war. Even though Winship was rich, Jack liked him because he was gregarious and fun-loving— different from typical bourgeois "stuffed shirts." Ed's true vocation was the pursuit of happiness with good company, good food and drink, and wild rides around the county in his shiny new Studebaker.

Jack also loved fun, but there was a greater love waiting for him over the mountain in Glen Ellen. He could forgo Ed's fun and games for a while to pursue his own happiness. As soon as the crew of the *Spray* had settled in at the Winship mansion, he wired Charmian that he was "Coming tomorrow horseback." Her diary entries for the next few days tell a remarkable story:

Wed. Mar. 8—Mate arrived horseback from Napa—tired—lame . . .
Fri. Mar. 10—Dull weather. Bad ear . . . Mate's awful blues—& mine.
Sat. Mar. 11—Mate returned Napa—I rode with him over Nun's [*sic*] Canyon into Napa Co. Raining. Mate decided to come here April lst.

The simplicity of the last sentence is deceptive: It was a decision of major significance, for a transformation had taken place in Jack's attitude during those four days. He had never liked the country. What he loved was excitement and people. "Ah! city life is the only life after all—there you meet people," he had written to Johns six years earlier; "as a rule you meet vegetables in the country. I really become heart-sick, if I mingle too long with our agrarian population."

The same attitude persisted during his March visit with Charmian at Wake Robin. "I don't seem to care for anything—I'm sick," he confessed. "This doesn't seem to be what I want. I don't know what I want. Oh, I'm sorry—I am, I am; it hurts me to hurt you so. But there's nothing for me to do but go back to the city. I don't know what the end of it will be." Once again, hers was the right response: "Very well, then, the thing for you is to do what you feel you must, of course.—And we won't say any more about it." Had she pressured him, he would have drawn back. Instead, he suddenly clasped her hand and exclaimed, "Why—why—you're a woman in a million!"

That night he slept an unprecedented eight straight hours—almost twice the quota he had been allowing himself during the preceding hectic months. Next morning he arose refreshed and deeply changed, though not yet fully aware of the transformation that had taken place. Nor was she aware of the change. She thought at first she had in fact lost him as she accompanied him that Saturday morning, March 11, on the ride up the mountain and through Nuns Canyon toward Napa: "Away we rode together, he and I, one of us with a heavy heart . . . For I felt this was the last of Jack, that he was slipping irrecoverably from us who loved and would have helped him; and, what was more grave, slipping away from himself."

But the Valley of the Moon was working its magical spell. "As we forged skyward on the ancient road that lies now against one bank, now another, the fanning ferns sprinkling our faces with rain and dew, wildflowers nodding in the cool flaws of wind, I could see [him] quicken and sparkle as if in spite of himself and the powers of darkness." Suddenly Jack began talking enthusiastically, saying he would move up to one of the cabins on the property along with his books and furniture, then asking if she would allow him to dictate his "damned correspondence" to her and find him a good horse for the $350 he had just received from a story he'd published in The Black Cat.

She could hardly believe her ears. He stopped, reached over, and put his hand on her shoulder: "You did it all, my Mate Woman. You've pulled me out. You've rested me so. And rest was what I needed—you were right. Something wonderful has happened to me. I am all right now . . . you need not be afraid for me any more."

Two days later he wrote to Brett, "Am going to bring the *Spray* back to her moorings now, & go up into the mountains until next fall—no telephones, no people, no engagements, nothing but work, sunshine, & health." On March 23, back in Oakland, he wrote to Ida Winship to thank her and Ed for their hospitality and told them, "I came home to bed, where I have been lying ever since, awaiting operation. To-morrow I am carted away to hospital, & Saturday the surgeons will be gouging around my anatomy—an old hurt of years' standing, which I hope will now be quite cured." His operation cured the "old hurt." His move to the Valley of the Moon the next month would cure his "long sickness."

18

THE VALLEY OF THE MOON

Part of the process of recovering from my long sickness was to find delight in little things, in things unconnected with books and problems, in play, in games of tag in the swimming pool, in flying kites, in fooling with horses, in working out mechanical puzzles . . . in the Valley of the Moon, I found my paradise.

—*JOHN BARLEYCORN*

Fifty miles north of San Francisco, nestled between Petaluma and Napa—nurturing some of the finest grapes and tastiest wines in the world—the tiny Sonoma Valley is rich both in history and in beauty. *Sonoma*, the Suisun word, has been translated, according to some legends, as "Valley of the Moon" because of the valley's crescent shape and its mystical lunar implications. The valley is seventeen miles long, one to five miles wide, framed on the east by the Mayacamas mountain range, on the west by Sonoma Mountain, and with its southern tip pointing toward the mouth of Sonoma Creek at San Pablo Bay, its northern tip nearly touching Santa Rosa.

The Native Americans who gave the valley its poetic name found it a veritable paradise, moderate in climate and bountiful in wild game and freshwater springs. Although the Native Americans and much of the wild game had vanished from the valley by 1905, Jack was able to find sanctuary there. "These days (during Mate's illness before and after operation) are the turning point in the lives of Mate & me,"

Charmian wrote in her diary on March 25. "We are truly learning each other, our worth to each other."

Part of their mutual learning was recognizing the Crowd's machinations. For some time now, Blanche, Carrie, and the others, feeling Jack slipping out of their grasp, had been at work to undermine his relationship with Charmian, finally resorting to vicious innuendos. She was hardly so faithful as she seemed, they suggested: She had engaged in "affairs" with other men during his long absence overseas. Jack met them head-on. "All right," he demanded, "give me your proof, all of it—names, places, dates—I want it all—and I don't want you to spare my feelings." But they could only give him vague insinuations and gossip. "Mate is secretly occupied with the Crowd concerning me, standing for His Own loyally; but I know nothing of it until later, at Glen Ellen," Charmian confided in her diary.

During his weeklong convalescence at Shingle Sanatorium in Oakland, Charmian visited him daily. He was released on Saturday, April 1, returning to his flat at 1216 Telegraph Avenue. She spent nearly twelve hours with him on Sunday. "Mate improving fast," she wrote on Monday, April 3. "So loving to me." By Friday he was well enough to take her to lunch in San Francisco, buy a saddle for Washoe Ban (the thoroughbred Charmian had bought for him), meet with the Oakland High School boys at 4:00 p.m., and chair the Ruskin Club dinner at Stanford in the evening. The next day he took Joan and Becky to the Barnum circus in Oakland.

Charmian was no less busy herself. She helped Manyoungi with packing Jack's things and, on April 13, ferried Washoe Ban from Oakland to San Francisco, then to Petaluma via the river steamer *Sonoma*. After stabling him there and getting a few hours' sleep at the American Hotel, she set out the next morning for Glen Ellen, riding the last twenty-two miles on horseback over the mountain. No proper Victorian lady would have dared venture out on such an odyssey unescorted and seated, like a cowboy, astride her mount. If sometimes short on propriety, Kittredge was long on pluck. For her the trip was a pleasant adventure. "Not tired at all," she recorded when she got back to Wake Robin. "My heart happy over summer plans." But she had still not learned the full truth about the Crowd. On the evening before leaving Jack in Oakland, the two of them had accepted an invitation to the opera from Blanche Partington. "I felt something wrong with Blanche & Jack & me, but could only feel," Charmian wrote. "Mate was uncomfortable & preoccupied." It would be another couple of weeks before she would learn exactly why.

Monday, April 17, 1905, was a red-letter day in their lives: on that date Jack moved permanently out of the city and into the Valley of the Moon. "Mate arrived with outfit including dog Brown. Very tired. Spent day resting." This was one of the few days in his life he would willingly spend resting. The newspapers clamored for the reasons behind his abrupt move, hoping to elicit juicier items concerning any future matrimonial plans. "I have forsaken the cities forever; winter and summer I shall live at Glen Ellen" was his response.

Try as he might, though, he could not escape the world for long; and the world would in time follow him into the Valley of the Moon—at his invitation. While he often needed solitude, he could seldom bring himself to turn away any visitor, friend or otherwise. He did make this rule: No one was allowed to intrude upon his morning work hours. Having rented one of Netta's two-room cabins for six dollars a month, he asked Charmian to hand-letter two signs, which Manyoungi nailed up over the doors. The notice over the front door read:

NO ADMISSION EXCEPT ON BUSINESS;
NO BUSINESS TRANSACTED HERE.

Over the back door was posted the following:

PLEASE DO NOT ENTER WITHOUT KNOCKING.
PLEASE DO NOT KNOCK.

For the next few months he was free to work and enjoy his leisure without the constant intrusion of guests. Also, the Crowd's tactics had backfired. "The Crowd, trying to separate us, by fair means or foul, drove us together so that nothing on earth but death could drive us apart. And we are finding each other by day & night," Charmian recorded in early May. "It's sad to find dear friends (?) treacherous and small, but there's good in everything if we are true to ourselves. In being true to myself, I have proved true to Jack."

Thanks to Charmian as well as to his new environment, he was now able to settle into his most productive routine. Each morning, he wrote (never less than his thousand-word minimum) while she transcribed his scrawling longhand of the previous day into typescript. This regimen quickly began paying off. On April 22, only five days after his arrival, he mailed off "The Sun-Dog Trail" to *Harper's Monthly Magazine*, from which he received $500. Five days after that, he sent "The White Man's Way" to *Century* magazine. Although rejected by *Century* and subsequently by *The Cosmopolitan*, the story was accepted by the *Sunday Magazine of the New-York Tribune*, which paid him $530. On May 11 he mailed "The Unexpected" to *McClure's* for $655.

These were recreational days for both of them. Charmian, who suffered from chronic insomnia, could sleep late in the mornings while Jack worked. Early afternoons were spent dictating his latest correspondence to her, after which, while she practiced on her piano and rested or rode her beloved mare Belle, he splashed and romped with the neighborhood children in the new swimming hole he had created by putting a small dam across Graham Creek. Within a week after coming to Wake Robin (to the surprise of his doctors), he had started riding again and could be seen astride Washoe Ban cantering into downtown Glen Ellen on his way to the post office, waving cheerfully in response to "Hello, Jack!" from the farmers in front of the general store and the loungers on the porch of the corner saloon.

It did not take him long to discover that country folk were not necessarily the dull "vegetables" he had disparaged in his letter to Cloudesley a few years before. In fact, some were transplanted urbanites like him who had won a new lease on life by escaping the city's miasma. Later he would dramatize their transformations in his fiction through characters such as Ferguson, the wiry little mountain man whom Elam Harnish encounters in *Burning Daylight*, formerly managing editor of a large newspaper who fifteen years earlier had been consigned to premature burial by his city physicians:

"They kept me poor with their bills, while I went from bad to worse. The trouble with me was twofold: first, I was a born weakling; and next, I was living unnaturally—too much work, and responsibility, and strain . . . So I quit, quit everything, absolutely, and came to live in

the Valley of the Moon . . . I persevered, and used my body in the way
Nature intended it should be used—not bending over a desk and swill-
ing whiskey . . . and, well, here I am, a better man for it."

Ferguson's testimonial might easily have been Jack's during the
spring and summer of 1905. "It's too bad that you can only get your
country in the expensive doses of the Sanitarium," he wrote to his
friend Fred Bamford, who was taking health treatments at Burke's, outside Santa Rosa. Burke's was all right, but the main thing was to get
away from all the stress of his life in the city, Jack explained: "The thing
is, to cease being intellectual altogether. To take delight in little things,
the bugs and crawling things, the birds, the leaves, etc., etc."

Jack's delight in country life grew stronger as he and Charmian rode
together over the Sonoma hillside. One spot in particular caught his
eye. He would replicate this vista in *Burning Daylight*, through the eyes
of his city-worn hero, who feels "like a poker-player rising from a night-
long table and coming forth" into the morning's fresh air. Gazing with
wonder at the beauty before him, he takes off his hat "with almost a
vague religious feeling . . . The atmosphere was one of holy calm. Here
man felt the prompting of nobler things . . . It seemed to him that he
had never been so happy."

At the end of May, London wrote to George Sterling that he had
decided to buy land and build a home in the Sonoma Valley. "I am really going to throw out an anchor so big and so heavy that all hell could
never get it up again," he declared. He found out that the plot with the
"three inexpressibly romantic knolls" he and Charmian had lucked
upon was owned by a neighboring rancher named Robert P. Hill. On
Saturday, June 3, they rode over to ask Hill how much he wanted for the
place. Hill replied that he had recently offered the 129-acre plot to
Joshua Chauvet for seven thousand dollars. The next day, Jack and
Charmian picnicked on Hill's ranch with Manyoungi, Netta, Roscoe,
and Edward Payne. "Mate nearly wild over it," Charmian recorded—so
wild he refused to haggle over the price. Some years afterward, when
the Hills had become good friends, Robert confessed that he had been
willing to lower his initial quote if Jack had held out for it.

Four days later London paid Hill a binding fee of $500, then wrote
to Brett asking for a $10,000 advance against royalties. "The place [is] a

bargain, one of those bargains that a man would be insane to let slip by," London rationalized. He described in detail the magnificent natural setting, concluding, "I have been over California off and on all my life, for the last two months I have been riding all over these hills, looking for just such a place, and I must say that I have never seen anything like it."

Brett did not send the $10,000; but he did send London two checks totalling $8,322.28, which enabled him to pay Hill the full amount of the purchase, including an additional $600 for the livestock and farm equipment on the place. "I scarcely see the possibility of any unwisdom entering into my purchase," he wrote in response to Brett's advice against tying himself down with real estate. "I shall always be free to come and go, even to the ends of the earth."

In the meantime, he needed more money. The advance Brett had sent would not keep him financially afloat for long. He had told Brett the previous December about his plans to write another novel, but it was more than six months before he started it. "Ground is broken today for the foundation of [my new] barn," he wrote on June 27. "Also today I have completed the first thousand words of my 'White Fang' story— the companion story to 'The Call of the Wild,' which I mentioned to you some time ago."

Although he claimed he was "anchoring good and solid," his seeking impulse would not allow him to become solidly anchored for long. Within less than two months he had already begun to lay new plans for roaming the world. On the first of August he wrote to Brett that after settling down in his new country home, he intended to build a boat and circumnavigate the globe on a seven-year cruise. "Now, don't think I am joking," he said. "I never more ardently desired to do anything in my life . . . First rattle out of the box, 2100 miles sailing from San Francisco to Honolulu, and then the long stretch down into the South Seas, and some time ultimately, the stretch across the Atlantic to New York City!"

When fall came, London was already on the move again—not west by boat, but east by train to New York City. Badly overdrawn on his Macmillan account, he had devised a plan that would gratify his socialist colleagues as well as his creditors: he would do a lecture tour. This plan was prompted by Upton Sinclair. On September 12, Sinclair had met at Peck's Restaurant on Fulton Street in New York City with several other prominent liberals—including Leonard Abbot, Clarence Darrow, George Strobell, and Charlotte Perkins Gilman—to establish the Intercollegiate Socialist Society. Their aim: the "promoting of an intelligent interest in Socialism among college men and women, graduate and undergraduate, through the formation of study clubs in the colleges and universities, and the encouraging of all legitimate endeavors to awaken an interest in Socialism." Strobell and Sinclair were elected as vice presidents, but neither possessed the necessary charisma for setting the hearts of youth aflame. The ISS needed a president who was a dynamic model of liberal manhood. Jack London, in absentia, was elected unanimously.

Here was an opportunity to get well paid for preaching what he genuinely believed. The Chicago-based Slayton Lyceum Bureau, recognizing London's popular appeal, offered him six hundred dollars a week plus expenses for a cross-country lecture tour. The Bureau provided an itinerary involving some thirty lectures from October to February, and on October 18, he boarded the train east with Manyoungi. Charmian left two days later for Newton, Iowa, where she would wait for him at the home of her friend Lynette McMurray until he came to lecture at nearby Grinnell College on November 25. His first stop was in Lawrence, Kansas, on Sunday, October 22, where he sermonized on "Revolution" for an audience of five hundred at the University Auditorium. He had enough platform savvy to temper the party line with both humor and compassion: "Occasionally he drew a laugh from his audience; once or twice when he talked about the child labor of the Southern states a woman wept quietly," reported *The Kansas City Star*. "He is like his published portraits vitalized," wrote the *Star* reporter. "Personally [he] has a great charm of manner. He is very youthful, ingenuous and friendly."

During a whirlwind score of lecture stops ranging from Iowa to the East Coast and back to Elyria, Ohio—where on November 18 he was guest speaker for the People's Institute writing courses—he received a wire notifying him that he was, at last, legally free to marry again. He and Charmian had initially planned to hold a quiet wedding ceremony at the home of the McMurrays following his lecture at Grinnell, but again his need for immediate gratification prevailed. Rather than wait another week, he telegraphed her to catch the next train to Chicago, where he would wait for her before moving on to his next lecture in Wisconsin.

She arrived at nine o'clock the following evening (three hours late) and found him "pacing the station pavement" with their wedding license in his pocket. Because it was Sunday, they needed help from "Mr. Harstone," city editor for the Hearst-owned *Chicago American*, in finding someone to perform the wedding ceremony. Thanks to Harstone's influence and London's promise of a scoop for his paper, they succeeded in rousing a justice of the peace, J. J. Grant, and were married that night as Jack slipped Dayelle "Daisy" Kittredge's wedding ring onto the third finger of Charmian's left hand. "The informal suddenness and speed of this termination to our courtship savored of the age of chivalry, when knight-errant with doughty right arm slung his lady love across the saddle bow on a foaming black charger," enthused Charmian. "Let none say that ours was less romantic."

According to the newspapers, it was considerably less romantic. When the newlyweds drove to the Victoria Hotel, where Jack and Manyoungi had registered the day before, Charmian quietly walked upstairs by a side entrance to avoid the newspapermen who were lying in wait to get the latest story on her celebrity husband. Reporters were unaware of the change in his marital status. All might have been well enough if Jack hadn't stopped at the front desk to write "Mrs. Jack London" on the register between his name and Manyoungi's.

One of the newsmen spotted the addition, and the chase was on. "Back to Victoria Hotel—night made hideous by reporters!" was Charmian's diary entry. Jack ran up to their hotel room with the news-hungry gang hard on his heels. He won the race, slamming the door behind him, but lost any chance for privacy. He refused to respond to what had quickly become a clamoring mob. "Come on through with the news, old man—be merciful; we've *got* to get it," one reporter pleaded. "You're a newspaperman yourself, you know. Come across and help us out." But Jack stuck to his pledge to give the scoop to Harstone for the *Chicago American*. The mob finally dispersed after Jack, speaking from behind the locked door, promised the full story the next morning, on Monday. "Jack adorable—my perfect bridegroom and lover, at last" was the bride's closing diary entry for November 19.

Furious because they had been scooped by Harstone, the other Chicago papers found something else to sensationalize. A recently passed Illinois law prohibited remarriage until a full year had passed since the granting of the final decree. Returning to Chicago on the morning of Tuesday, November 22, following Jack's lecture in Geneva Falls, Wisconsin, the newlyweds were greeted with an oversize headline:

JACK LONDON'S MARRIAGE INVALID!

"What the hell!" spluttered Jack, laughing in spite of himself. "The other sheets are getting even. We're in for it!"

The Chicago newspapers began trashing the marriage, and across the country the rest were printing the story as if it needed no verification. To Jack those were fighting words. "If my marriage is not legal in Illinois, I shall re-marry my wife in every state in the Union!" he declared, providing more ammunition for the media cannon. As it turned out, the authorities agreed that the marriage was a legal one, but that hardly mattered to a society still muffled under the cloak of Victorian morality. It was now evident that Jack London had abandoned his wife and children, having succumbed to the wiles of a man-stealing homebreaker. Wanting accurate likenesses of Charmian in their files, many papers resorted to sketches or handy photos of other women. One Iowa weekly claimed she was "so ugly that the children on the streets of Newton ran screaming to their mothers whenever she passed by." Several indignant groups cancelled London's scheduled lectures. On balance, the negative publicity, financially speaking, was more asset than liability, and it kept Jack busy.

He was back on the circuit by December 2, speaking before "a good-sized audience of fashionably gowned women" at the Central Christian Church, entertaining the Des Moines Women's Club with his literary and Klondike "Experiences." The Des Moines episode typified the public's ambivalence. On November 30 the *Des Moines Capital* reported that the women who disapproved of London's treatment of his first wife would nevertheless attend his lecture. The next day the headline in *The Des Moines Register and Leader* was PROTEST IS MADE AGAINST LONDON. On December 3 *The Cedar Rapids Republican*, under the headline WOMEN AS HERO WORSHIPPERS, questioned the propriety of London's addressing respectable women's clubs. On that same Sunday, a Des Moines clergyman sermonized "against women for 'fawning' over London." He was particularly disturbed by the behavior of the Women's Press Club and the Women's Club, who had competed with each other to steal London's attention and time before his lecture. WOMEN'S CLUBS WAR OVER JACK LONDON'S VISIT was the headline on the December 3 issue of *The Des Moines Register and Leader.*

The newlyweds left Newton on December 4, taking the night train to Chicago and from there the Lake Shore train to Boston, arriving on the morning of Wednesday, December 6. On Thursday evening, Jack delivered an address to the Bowdoin faculty and student body in New Brunswick, Maine. The audience response here was unequivocally favorable. "One of the strongest and most trenchant addresses that has ever been given [here], it was both inspiring and a revelation to the large audience that filled [Memorial Hall]," the *Lewiston Evening Journal* reported on December 8, explaining that Mr. London "proved as interesting a lecturer as author, moving his audience to laughter by his brilliant humor, while the silence following his realistic description of the darker side of life showed the compelling power of the man over his listeners."

While in Maine with a week and a half to spare, Jack and Charmian took the opportunity to visit her relatives in Ellsworth and Mount Desert Island. After returning to Boston on December 16, he delivered a series of socialistic lectures to packed audiences at Tremont Temple, Faneuil Hall, and Harvard Union. At Faneuil Hall, he preached "Revolution" under Gilbert Stuart's portrait of another celebrated revolutionist, the Father of Our Country. Upon finishing his socialist sermon, he was surprised when the famous activist Mother Jones marched up to the rostrum and, to the crowd's delight, planted kisses on both his cheeks. His reception at Harvard was even more spectacular. Some fifteen hundred young men crowded into Harvard Union—the largest group in history to congregate there, according to *The Boston Globe.*

These university men, the cream of America's bourgeois crop, admired this dynamic avatar of strenuous manhood with his soft-collar shirt, tousled hair, ready smile, and athlete's physique. Perhaps it didn't occur to them that they were the decadent heirs to the system he was attacking with his declarations of red revolution. So well had they been

228 • JACK LONDON

sheltered that when he told his story from *The People of the Abyss* about the old Carter and Carpenter—who, homeless and starving, were reduced to scavenging garbage from the slimy gutters of the East End—they burst out laughing. "It astonished me considerably," he told the young gentlemen at Yale a few weeks later, "when a hall full of Harvard men almost laughed me off my feet upon my telling them of some particularly harrowing experiences I have had with *les miserables* of our society . . . They were good fellows, clean fellows, noble fellows; but they simply couldn't appreciate what I was talking about."

A week following Jack's Harvard appearance the newlyweds were on their way south to the Caribbean aboard the *Admiral Farragut* for an overdue honeymoon. On New Year's morning they landed at Port Antonio, Jamaica, and checked into the Hotel Titchfield, where they met one of Jack's favorite authors, Ella Wheeler Wilcox, and her husband, Robert. They spent the next five days touring what Charmian called this "British-neat island paradise," then took the Spanish steamer *Oteri* to Cuba. After another five days enjoying the "lazy warm airs" of the Caribbean, she "wondered if anything to come in our wanderings could approach the romance that was here . . . We hated to leave Havana—but all the world's before us!"

Florida was next on their itinerary: "Boating, angling for edible fish and hooking outlandish finny shapes, driving in the Everglades, calling at the alligator and crocodile farm, and shopping for curios and snakeskins." But the honeymoon was nearly over. When they arrived at Daytona Beach, Jack was suffering from a splitting headache. "I came to this damned place mainly to see those racing cars," he groaned; "and now look at me." Because of the familiar flu-like symptoms, he thought at first that he was coming down with the grippe, but when he began to weep uncontrollably, he realized that he'd contracted something new. Soon afterward, Charmian experienced the same symptoms, and the honeymooners were shedding a flood of tears. As it turned out, they were both suffering from another virus: dengue fever.

Both were still ailing when they reached New York City at 5:10 p.m. on January 19. Charmian was able to go to bed as soon as they were registered at the Hotel Belleclaire, but Jack—"ill, hollow-eyed, travel-worn, and very miserable"—was scheduled to lecture in less than three hours. He did not even have time to eat before he drove off to the Grand

Central Palace. Representing the Intercollegiate Socialist Society, he spoke to an audience of four thousand on "The Coming Crisis." Vendors sold copies of his latest socialist book, along with candy and little red flags. Many of the ladies in the audience wore red dresses and hats, or red ribbons. Jack had come to awaken, not to entertain:

Consider the United States, the most prosperous and most enlightened country in the world . . . In New York City lived a woman, Mary Mead. She had three children: Mary, one year old; Johanna, two years old; Alice, four years old. Her husband could find no work. They starved. They were evicted from their shelter at 160 Steuben Street. Mary Mead strangled her baby, Mary, one year old; strangled Alice, four years old; failed to strangle Johanna, two years old, and then herself took poison. Said the father to the police: "Constant poverty had driven my wife insane . . . I could get no work. I could not even make enough to put food into our mouths. The babies grew ill and weak. My wife cried nearly all the time."

This was just one of the examples London presented his audience. He was in peak evangelical form. Fever became fervor, captivating four thousand socialistic disciples. "The whole thing with its hubbub of horrors, with its sinister statistics, with its whirling warnings, would be as a dream before me now, did I not remember those four thousand living faces, those shouts of enthusiasm and applause, that hush of awed and terrible expectancy," reported one member of the press.

The next day, Jack lunched with Upton Sinclair. Though only two years older than Sinclair, London's wealth of experience made it seem that a battle-scarred veteran was meeting a raw recruit. The two had the one common cause, but beyond this they could not have been two more different personalities. Sinclair was an abstemious puritan; London was the hard-drinking hedonist. Yet so profoundly moved had been Sinclair by London's lecture that he admitted he was "prepared to give my hero the admiration of a slave." That was before he had been exposed to Jack's less idealistic persona:

[All] day the hero smoked cigarettes and drank—I don't remember what it was, for all these red and brown and green and golden concoctions are equally painful to me, and the sight of them deprives me of the control of my facial muscles. Jack, of course, soon noted this; he was the red-blood, and I was the mollycoddle, and he must have his fun with me . . . Tales of incredible debauches; tales of opium and hashish, and I know not what other strange ingredients . . .

The two men would remain friends, not as hero and hero-worshiper, but, in Sinclair's words, as "two young social dreamers, eager to remake the world." Later that year Jack wrote an enthusiastic review of *The Jungle*, praising it as "The book we have been waiting for these many years! The *Uncle Tom's Cabin* of wage slavery!" Over the next decade they would exchange inscribed copies of their books, as each new edition was issued. In 1915, London wrote an introduction to Sinclair's anthology *The Cry for Justice* that brought him a measure of redemption in the eyes of his idealistic comrade:

Not one ignoble thought or act is demanded of any one of all men and women to make fair the world. The call is for nobility of thinking, nobility of doing. The call is for service, and, such is the wholesomeness of it, he who serves all, best serves himself . . .

To see gathered here together this great body of human beauty and fineness and nobleness is to realize what glorious humans have already existed, do exist, and will continue increasingly to exist until all the world beautiful be made over in their image.

And just three months before his death, Jack sent a cordial letter inviting Upton and his wife to the ranch, adding, "You and I ought to have some 'straight from the shoulder' talk with each other. It is coming to you, it may be coming to me. It may illuminate one or the other or both of us."

A week after his Grand Central Palace appearance, London spoke before a group including another "Sinclair." Legend has it that twenty-year-old undergrad Sinclair Lewis was instrumental in setting up London's Yale presentation and that he interviewed Jack on the morning after his lecture, but both claims lack evidence, though there is some evidence that Lewis had read *The Sea-Wolf* and that he was in the audience when London delivered his address. Four years later, when the two met at Carmel, they entered into one of the oddest business deals in the history of American letters: the veteran author's purchase of plot outlines from an unpublished tyro.

At the conclusion of his lecture, Jack was invited to continue the discussion with a group of students in a dormitory. After midnight he attended a second conference at Old Mory's; following that, he was escorted by students up Chapel Street to another late-hours reception in the socialist parsonage. A few days later one professor said that London's lecture was "the greatest intellectual stimulus Yale had had in many years." According to the *New Haven Register*, "The spectacle of an avowed Socialist standing upon the platform of Woolsey Hall and boldly advocating his doctrines of revolution, was a sight for gods and men. He is rattling the dry bones in a manner to disturb sleep."

Jack continued to rattle the dry bones during the next ten days, preaching—sometimes twice a day—in Chicago, St. Paul, and Grand Forks. While in Chicago, he and Charmian had dinner with Jane Addams at Hull House. His lecture on February 4 to the faculty and students of the University of North Dakota proved to be the last on his tour. "Have been miserably sick, and have canceled a whole string of lectures, including all California lectures," he wrote to Cloudesley. Not yet fully recovered from the virus he had contracted on his honeymoon, he was near total exhaustion from his round-the-clock schedule as evangelist and celebrity. As they were headed home on the 20th Century Limited, "Jack, suddenly, with a sigh, nodded his curly head and as suddenly fell asleep," Charmian remembered. "All strain was erased from his features—it was the face of a dreaming child." Although no longer a child, he was dreaming about what would become the greatest adventure of his life.

19

CATASTROPHE

> I'd rather win a water-fight in the swimming pool, or remain
> astride a horse that is trying to get out from under me, than
> write the great American novel. Each man to his liking . . . That
> is why I am building the *Snark* . . . The trip around the world
> means big moments of living.
>
> —*THE CRUISE OF THE SNARK*

"It was all due to Captain Joshua Slocum and his *Spray*, plus our own
wayward tendencies," Charmian explained. Jack read Slocum's *Sailing
Alone Around the World* aloud to the camp children at Wake Robin in
the summer of 1905 as they "sat in the hot sun resting between water
fights and games of tag in the deep swimming pool," she recalled, and
"when Jack closed the cover on the last chapter, there was a new idea
looking out of his eyes."

On April 24, 1895, Slocum, at the age of fifty-one, had set sail from
Boston in the *Spray*, a thirty-seven-foot sloop rebuilt with his own
hands from a derelict hull. He dropped anchor in Newport, Rhode Island, on June 27, 1898. During those three years and two months he
had sailed forty-six thousand miles entirely alone "without power, radio, money, advertising sponsor, insurance, or hospitalization."

If fifty-one-year-old Joshua Slocum could circumnavigate the globe
in a small boat all by himself, thirty-year-old Jack London could do it
easily with Charmian by his side. Unlike Slocum, London would not

settle for a pre-owned, reconditioned derelict. Neither money nor expertise would be spared in making his boat the best boat of its size ever built. She would be constructed of the finest buttless planking that money could buy; with three watertight bulkheads, she would be not merely unsinkable but unleakable; she would be forty-five feet long (including an extra five feet for an indoor bathroom); her beautiful bow would defy the heaviest storms; she would be stocked with six months' provisions, including dozens of crates of fresh fruits and vegetables; and, unlike Slocum's *Spray*, she would be equipped with a rugged seventy-horsepower gasoline engine for added safety and convenience. She would set sail for Hawaii and ports beyond on October 1, 1906. And she would be fondly called the *Snark*, after the fabled craft in Lewis Carroll's mock epic.

London's *Snark*, when finally ready for launching, cost more than five times the original estimate of seven thousand dollars. Multiple butts were discovered in her cheap planking. The finished product was two feet shorter than London's plans had specified. The powerful gasoline engine broke loose from its bedplate and fell on its side before the boat cleared the harbor. The boat's bottom leaked, the sides leaked, and the "water-tight" compartments leaked, contaminating all the fresh fruits and vegetables with gasoline. The *Snark* did not sail until April, 1907, and even then the boat was not seaworthy.

What went wrong? A number of things, chief among which was the worst cataclysm in recorded California history. "EARTHQUAKE" is the opening entry in Charmian's diary for Wednesday, April 18, 1906. She and Jack were awakened at precisely 5:14 a.m. Throwing on their clothes, they ran to the rented barn on the Fish Ranch, where they discovered that Washoe Ban and Belle "had broken their halters and were still quivering and skittish." By six o'clock Jack and Charmian were on horseback, riding up the mountain to their new ranch. From that height they could plainly see the great columns of smoke rising over San Francisco and, to the north, Santa Rosa. On their way back down to Glen Ellen, they stopped to check the partially finished stone barn that London had contracted to be constructed. Jack had wanted the finest and sturdiest that money could buy. What he discovered was that the quake had shaken down the walls, revealing that they were thin shells filled with debris. "Jerry-built," he murmured, "and I told him the solid, honest thing I wanted—and did not question his price," he said of Martin Pasquini, the contractor he had hired to build the barn.

That afternoon they took the train to Santa Rosa. That smaller city had been hit as hard as San Francisco and was a mass of smoking rubble. From there they went to Oakland and took the ferry over to the inferno that San Francisco had become. "That night proved our closest to realizing a dream that came now and again to Jack in sleep," said Charmian, "that he and I were in at the finish of all things—standing or moving hand in hand through chaos to its brink, looking upon the rest of mankind in the process of dissolution." So shocked were the two of them that Jack declared, "I'll never write a word about it. What use trying? One could only string big words together, and curse the futility of them."

The quake had disrupted the water supply throughout the city, and the fires were burning out of control even as General Funston's men were resorting to dynamite to contain them. The two of them witnessed the condition of one of the injured firemen when they got to Union Square. "His back had been broken, and as the stretcher bore him past, out of a handsome, ashen young face, the dreadful darkening eyes looked right into mine . . . Jack, with tender hand, drew me away."

They spent the night walking through the burning streets. "We must have tramped forty miles that night," Charmian wrote. As dawn began to break, they stopped, exhausted, at a corner house on Nob Hill—not far from the Fairmont Hotel, now beginning to burn. There, on the front steps to the residence, Jack dozed off, while she watched, worn out but too tightly strung to sleep:

> Presently a man mounted the steps and inserted a key in the lock. Seeing Jack and myself on the top tread . . . something impelled him to invite us in. It was a luxurious interior, containing the treasures of years . . . Suddenly, midway of showing us about, he asked me to try the piano, and laid bare the keys. I hesitated—it seemed almost a cruel thing to do, with annihilation of his home so very near. But Jack whispered "Do it for him—it's the last time he'll ever hear it," sent me to the instrument. The first few touches were enough and too much for [him], however, and he made a restraining gesture.

As the flames came closer, they left Nob Hill, making their way through the ruins down Mission Street and taking the ferry over to Oakland. There, in safety, they ate a late breakfast, then collapsed in bed at noon and slept around the clock. The following day, after checking to make sure Charmian's Berkeley property was undamaged, they returned to Glen Ellen on the evening train.

They had little time for resting. *Collier's Weekly* magazine wired Jack that it wanted a twenty-five-hundred-word firsthand account of the San Francisco disaster for its May 5 issue. Despite his assertion that he would never write a word about it, he couldn't turn down this offer: twenty-five cents a word would be the highest rate he had ever received. They started to work: Jack writing, Charmian typing. He considered it mediocre, but "The Story of an Eye-Witness" has subsequently been cited as a model of rhetorical as well as journalistic excellence.

In contrast, London's *Snark* was anything but a model of ship-building excellence. "Spare no money," he had told Roscoe Eames, whom he was paying seventy-five dollars a month to learn navigation and to oversee the boat's construction. "Let the *Snark* be as stanch and strong as any boat afloat. Never mind what it costs to make her stanch and strong; you see that she is made stanch and strong and I'll go on writing and earning the money to pay for it."

Even before the disruptions of the Great Earthquake, he had been writing more furiously than at any time since the creative frenzies of his apprenticeship. On March 2 he mailed off "Brown Wolf" to *Everybody's Magazine*. He was paid $750, but that was hardly enough to keep ahead of the mounting expenses of his latest dream. The *Snark* was exchanging his earnings for debts faster than he could write. Within less than a week after finishing "Brown Wolf," he sent a 3,477-word review of Upton Sinclair's *The Jungle* to *The San Francisco Examiner*. One week after that, he finished "A Day's Lodging," for which *Collier's* paid him another $750. On March 25 he sent "When God Laughs" to *Collier's*, but the magazine rejected it—as did several others. For once, he seemed fully aware of what he had written. "You ask when you are going to see another short story," he wrote to S. S. McClure on April 25. "I sent you a weird decadent one, 'When God Laughs.' I won't get a bit excited if you don't see your way to publishing it. It is preposterous, untrue and impossible." *Smart Set* accepted it for $200—not enough to "make a living out of," Jack later complained. His next effort was another story entirely. Immediately after finishing "When God Laughs," he began jotting down notes for "The Apostate." On April 4 he mailed his 7,673-word manuscript to the *Woman's Home Companion*. This compelling indictment of child labor, based upon his own experiences, would become a classic in the literature of social protest. The editors of *Woman's Home Companion* recognized its merit at once and paid $767.30.

His expenses were now virtually out of control. Four days after finishing "The Apostate," he sent a 1,462-word article to *The San Francisco Examiner*, in protest against the unjust imprisonment of William ("Big Bill") Haywood, Charles Moyer, and George Pettibone, leaders of the Western Federation of Miners, for their alleged role in the assassination of Governor Frank Steunenberg of Idaho. But the *Examiner* was not inclined to print such an open attack against American capitalism. Seven months later the piece was published by the *Chicago Daily Socialist*, but Jack was never paid for it.

Cash was what he needed, and fiction produced cash. Even before his Idaho article, he had started a new novel: "The First Lovers . . . The Long Ago . . . In the Youth of the Younger World . . . The Younger World . . . The First Love Tale," he had scribbled on his notepad. By April 25 he had finished one-third of the novel he had decided to title *Before Adam*. "The situation of this story, in the biological sense, is really before Adam; it is the most primitive story ever written," he explained to S. S. McClure: "It goes back before the cave-man; before fire; before the wearing of clothes; before the use of weapons—to a time when man was in the process of Becoming . . . There is a love-motif! a hero! a villain! rivalry! And a literary reproduction of the landscape and conditions of the Younger World."

By the first of May, halfway through the novel and near exhaustion, Jack decided that he and Charmian needed a break. On May 3 they started on a horseback ride through Northern California astride Ban and Belle, touring the Petrified Forest, Napa Valley, Ukiah, through the redwood forests, over to Fort Bragg, back down to Santa Rosa, and home through a rainstorm on May 14. "Not a tap of work did we perform on this real vacation," she wrote.

Refreshed and back at work again, Jack finished *Before Adam* on June 7. After *McClure's* declined to publish the novel, he turned it over to his agent, Paul Reynolds, who sold it to *Everybody's* for five thousand dollars. The magazine started the serialized version in October, and Macmillan published the book in February 1907.

A few days after completing *Before Adam*, London received a letter from Herbert Stone, editor of *The House Beautiful* magazine, requesting an article on "My Castle in Spain." Mentioning that he was also contacting Edith Wharton, Richard Le Gallienne, and a couple of others with the same request, Stone explained, "What I want is a description of your ideal home and its contents and surroundings."

Jack spent the next several days working on his vision of the ideal home: "My first idea about a house is that it should be built to live in," he explained. "Perhaps it is because of the practical life I have lived that I worship utility and have come to believe that utility and beauty should be one, and that there is no utility that need not be beautiful." His fusion of form and function reflected the principle of "organic architecture" pioneered by Frank Lloyd Wright. The house of his dreams would wed beauty and utility in its every room—including the bathroom. Much of the expense should be devoted to materials that are easily kept clean, with a minimum of ornamental frills. "More delightful to me is a body that sings than a stately and costly grand staircase built for show. Not that I like grand staircases less, but that I like bath-rooms more." The principle of purity would obtain beyond the bathroom. Plain hardwood floors—no carpets to collect dust and to breed bacteria. His dream house would be open to the air, with large verandas and large fireplaces, with sliding doors to keep out the stormier elements and screens to keep out unwelcome "creeping, crawling, butting, flying, fluttering things" but not to keep out "the good fresh air and all the breezes that blow." In sum, this would be "a happy house . . . a house of air and sunshine and laughter." In his letter accompanying the sketch on July 22, he explained, "I think I've given the ethics of my house beautiful. There are lots of people, I'll wager, who do not imagine that ethics and architecture are at all related." Stone responded with a check for $150 and published the article the next January.

While writing every day, Jack confessed that he was now filled with "a great happiness" this summer. "In fact, I never felt so free in all my life," he reassured one of his correspondents. "I swim every day about two hours. I sit on the sand naked in the sun and read for an hour every day. I play a rubber of whist several times a week. And, also, I ride horseback for an hour every day." Charmian's diary entries reflect the same mood: "Lovely days . . . Mate so sweet to me . . . Lollypop days . . . Happy as an angel with my lover-husband!"

Even with Jack's rigorous creative regimen, there was time for recreation and occasional trips to Oakland, San Francisco, and Napa. There was plenty of company, too: Elwyn Hoffman; Xavier Martínez; Felix Peano; Jim Whitaker; the Sterlings; Ida and Jack Byrne; Flora London with Ida's boy, Johnny; and Eliza Shepard with seven-year-old Irving, who was recuperating from a leg broken while "nipping" a wagon ride.

The Londons were now enjoying "a continual honeymoon," Charmian confided in her diary: "Pop-Pop-Pop-morning. Light work . . . Sewing on underclothes while Mate reads aloud to me," she wrote on August 24. These loving days in the Valley of the Moon during the summer of 1906 would become part of the "big novel" she mentioned that Jack was now planning. This project had been on his mind for a long time. Shortly after returning home from the Klondike he had jotted down these notes:

> Perhaps write a novel, a la Wells, out of idea of wage-slaves, ruled by industrial oligarchs, finally ceasing to reproduce. And either figure out new way of penetrating the future, or begin far ahead of the actual time of the story, by having the writing dug up by the people of a new and very immature civilization . . . Novel—CAPTAINS OF INDUS-TRY. Industrial oligarchs controlling the World, terrible struggles of workmen; some big city center of some scene like Paris Commune. Read up.

By the summer of 1906, his idea of writing a "novel, a la Wells," after simmering for almost eight years, had been influenced by several key factors. He had been personally exploited as a factory "work-beast." He had witnessed as a hobo the human tragedies of a major economic depression in America. He had recorded the chronic heartbreaking poverty in the London slums. More recently, while on his lecture trip, he had visited Jane Addams at Hull House and had also seen firsthand the notorious Chicago stockyards indicted in Upton Sinclair's *The Jungle*.

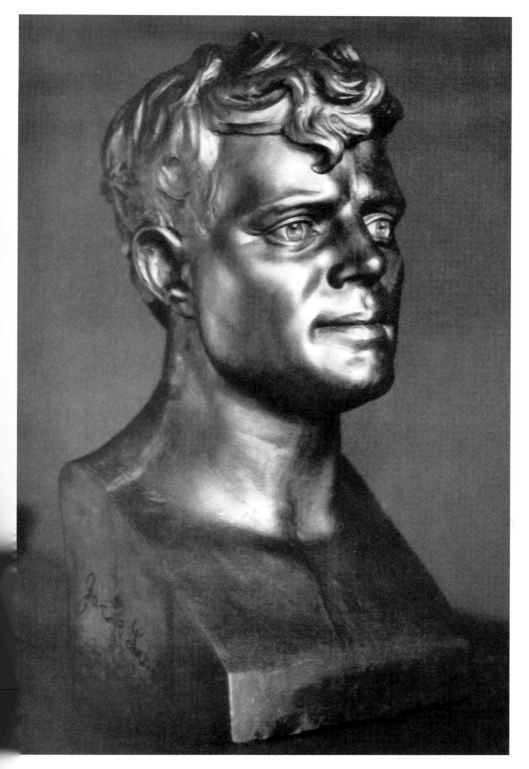

Jack London

(Bust by Finn Frolich; photograph by Earle Labor, courtesy of Irving and Mildred Shepard)

Flora London

John London

Jack and Rollo, ca. 1886

Jack in Yokohama, 1893

(All courtesy of Huntington Library)

Sheep Camp, August 21, 1897 (Dick North has identified London as the second figure from the left in the group on the right side of the photograph)

(University of Washington Libraries, Special Collections, LaRoche 2033)

Marshall Bond and his dog Jack (left), Dawson City, 1897 (Huntington Library)

Cloudesley Johns
(Huntington Library)

Anna Strunsky
(Huntington Library)

Jack and Bessie
London, 1900
(Huntington Library)

To my mother—
— who has trav-
ailed sore with me
in the making of
men & women to
breathe & move &
do things in the
printed pages of
a book.

Jack.

May 22, 1901.

Presentation copy of
The God of His Fathers
(the first book London
inscribed to his mother)
(Royce G. Labor Library)

Macmillan advertisement for
The Call of the Wild
(Earle Labor Collection)

Jack and Bert the Cobbler in
The People of the Abyss, 1902
(Huntington Library; photograph by Jack London)

Charmian Kittredge London
(Earle Labor Collection; gift of Milo Shepard)

Jack London to
Charmian Kittredge, 1903
(Earle Labor Collection)

Russo-Japanese War, Korea, 1904 (Huntington Library; photograph by Jack London)

On Washoe Ban in Glen Ellen, 1905 (Huntington Library)

Nob Hill mansion, 1906 (Huntington Library; photograph by Jack London)

George Sterling's Carmel group, 1906: (top, from left) Charmian London,
Alice McGowan, Grace McGowan Cooke; (bottom, from left) George Sterling, Jimmy
Hopper, Jack London, Carrie Sterling (Huntington Library; photograph by Arnold Genthe)

First crew of the *Snark*, 1907 (Huntington Library; photograph by Jack London)

Snark at Apia, Samoa, 1908 (Huntington Library; photograph by Jack London)

Martin Johnson and Solomon Islander, 1908
(Huntington Library; photograph by Jack London)

Masquerade ball, Guadalcanal, 1908 (Huntington Library; photograph by Jack London)

Charmian at Malaita market, 1908 (Huntington Library; photograph by Jack London)

Muldowney saloon fracas, 1910 (Earle Labor Collection)

Jack with daughters Becky and Joan
(Huntington Library)

Eliza Shepard
(Jack London Museum and Research Center, Centenary College of Louisiana; gift of Milo Shepard)

London one week before his death
(Huntington Library)

The lecture tour was perhaps the major factor. He was never before, or after, so enthusiastic in his public outcries against the evils of capitalism as he had been while evangelizing socialism coast to coast. Within weeks after returning home, he had written to Brett that he was thinking of writing "this summer a book to be entitled *The Iron Heel.*" On August 19, the day after finishing his story "Just Meat," he began making notes for the new novel: "The shadow of the Oligarchy, etc. (make vivid). That stupendous and awful epoch of social evolution, etc. Make a terrific feel. Be sure to bring in Chicago, the 'City of Blood' where the proletariat revolt was drowned in blood—a second and more terrible Commune."

Eight days later, he wrote to Cloudesley, "I'm having the time of my life writing the story." Here was the fictional articulation of London's own private dreams of revolutionary glory. The book's hero, Ernest Everhard, a natural aristocrat with blacksmith's biceps, is Jack's idealized clone. With his Spencerian philosphy and his Marxist rhetoric, he is also Jack's metaphysical replica. Moreover, his mate, Avis Cunningham Everhard, is modeled after Charmian; and her love affair with Ernest reflects that of Charmian and Jack.

Although not his artistic best, *The Iron Heel* is London's bravest book. "I have now finished 32,000 words of *The Iron Heel,*" he wrote to Brett on September 28. "If it hits the American public at the psychological moment, it will make a ten-strike. In many ways, it is the most daring book I have ever attempted." But the American public was hardly "at the psychological moment," and even Jack's socialist comrades were mixed in their responses. While a few leaders such as Eugene Debs and Bill Haywood liked it, the socialist press was at best lukewarm and at worst cold in its reception. *The Arena,* for example, called the novel "a detriment rather than a help to the cause of social justice."

London's initial disappointment with the party's response to *The Iron Heel* grew into bitterness over the years. "It was a labor of love, and a dead failure as a book," he later admitted. Inscribing a copy for one of his friends a few months before his death, he wrote, "This was the stuff I devoted twenty years of my life to, & found the 'People' wouldn't fight for it." Despite the initial response, *The Iron Heel* was hardly a failure.

During the past century it has been praised not only by famous writers such as Anatole France and George Orwell but also by major political figures such as Lenin and Leon Trotsky. Morover, the rise of fascism following the First World War appeared to validate the ominous forebodings of London's work. "Outside the United States Jack London's *The Iron Heel* has had an enormous effect, educating large numbers in Marxism and inspiring generations of revolutionists," Paul Siegel wrote for the *International Socialist Review* in 1974: "Disregarded at its appearance in 1908 by the Social Democratic journals, it was the one American work listed by Bukharin in his bibliography of Communist literature . . . and today it continues to sell throughout the world in the millions in many translations."

On December 13, Jack mailed off his ninety-thousand-word manuscript to Macmillan. By this time he and Charmian had moved back to their Oakland apartment, to be closer to the *Snark*, whose construction had fallen alarmingly behind schedule while costs were moving ahead even more alarmingly. It was now obvious that the ship would not be ready for sailing by the end of the year as originally planned. Besides miscalculating the unforeseen expenses and delays caused by the earthquake, London had also made a serious error in acceding to "Uncle Roscoe" Eames's request to be taken along on the cruise as co-navigator, and an even more serious error in commissioning him to oversee the building of the boat while boning up on his navigation skills. Instead of overseeing and boning up, Roscoe was making the rounds of the local bars bragging that he was captain of the *Snark*.

By the fall of 1906, word of Jack London's latest adventure had been broadcast through all the newspapers. Consequently he had been inundated with applications from aspiring argonauts who believed the Golden Fleece was now somewhere to be discovered in the South Seas and beyond those far horizons: "From every class of society over the wide world we thought to circumnavigate—doctors, lawyers, beggarmen, chiefs, thieves, multimillionaires, sailors single and in crews, poets, historians, geologists, painters, doctors of divinity—in short, men, women and children of every color and occupation, wrote or telegraphed or paid us calls, imploring to sail on any terms, or none," wrote Charmian. Some even offered to pay for the privilege of becoming crew members. Among the hundreds of letters that poured in, one from a lanky eighteen-year-old youth in Independence, Kansas, caught Jack's attention. The author explained that he himself had planned a similar voyage and had, in fact, traveled to Europe and back, "returning by way of New York with twenty-five cents of the original five dollars and a half with which [he] had started." Furthermore, he stated, he was an experienced photographer and wanted no wages for the trip, but merely the chance to share in the great adventure.

Here was a man after Jack's own heart. Indeed, this young Kansan was himself destined to win fame as an adventurer. His name was Martin Elmer Johnson. One week after posting his letter, Johnson received London's reply. Years later he recounted his excitement: "I was standing in my father's jewelry store after supper on the evening of Monday, November 12, 1906, when a messenger boy came in and handed me a telegram. The instant I saw the little yellow envelope, something told me that this was the turning-point of my life." The telegram contained only three words: "Can you cook?"

"Sure. Try me," he lied. Though he couldn't cook, he would quickly learn, and he would prove himself invaluable as a congenial man of many talents. "All right," London responded in a letter detailing his plans for the voyage. The *Snark* would carry a crew of five in addition to Johnson: Roscoe Eames, a cabin boy named Tochigi (Manyoungi's replacement), Herbert Stolz (a Stanford athlete and future Rhodes Scholar), and the Londons. All six, including Charmian, would share in the duties of "sailorizing." They would "expect plain cooking,—in fact, cooking with a minimum of grease [using] oil instead of lard and such things." And "Oh, if you have a bad temper, don't come, for it'd be the only one on the boat!" He should pack very lightly, since the boat was small and they would be in hot weather throughout the trip. "Also, I may say that we should all of us have lots of good times together, swimming, fishing, adventuring, doing a thousand-and-one things."

Three weeks later, carrying just "a small satchel and a camera," Johnson boarded the Santa Fe train west to the coast. He arrived in Oakland on the evening of December 7 in a downpour and immediately called the Londons' apartment. Jack himself answered the phone: "Hello, boy; come right along up," he exclaimed, giving Martin directions. Johnson was greeted at the door by Charmian, who took his wet raincoat, handed him a towel, and said, "Jack's waiting for you":

At that moment a striking young man of thirty, with very broad shoulders, a mass a wavy auburn hair, and a general atmosphere of boyishness, appeared at the doorway, and shot a quick, inquisitive look at me from his wide grey eyes. Inside, I could see all manner of oars, odd assortments of clothing, books, papers, charts, guns, cameras, and folding canoes, piled in great stacks upon the floor.

"Hello, Martin," he said, stretching out his hand.

"Hello, Jack," I answered. We gripped.

And that is how I met Jack London, traveler, novelist, and social reformer; and that is how, for the first time, I really ran shoulder to shoulder with Adventure, which I had been pursuing all my days.

He would not run with Adventure for another four months. Delay after delay in the *Snark*'s construction was playing the devil with the Londons' sailing plans. In the meantime, they were anything but idle. In addition to Jack's occasional lectures and the couple's short trips to Nevada, Southern California, and Carmel, they watched rugby matches at UC Berkeley, attended plays and concerts, and took dinner with friends at the local restaurants. Their daily routine included some physical activities as well: occasional swims at the Piedmont natatorium, biking, and daily boxing. The last of these exercises appalled Flora, who strongly disapproved the couple's ungentlemanly mismatch until one afternoon visit when she saw Charmian knock Jack into the dining room door so ferociously that the redwood panel was cracked.

Construction on the *Snark* crept along at its petty pace while expenses were running amok. The cost of materials had skyrocketed since April, and workers were getting earthquake wages. The original estimate was near tripling, and the job was nowhere near finished. Sinking more deeply into debt, Jack was forced to mortgage both his Sonoma and Charmian's Oakland properties. To make matters worse, *The Cosmopolitan* magazine, which had given him a two-thousand-dollar advance on his promise of sending it his exclusive travelogue, cancelled its agreement and requested a refund when it discovered he was planning to send various other *Snark* articles to its competitors.

Financial necessity dictated not only literary invention but also quick and efficient work. His fictional muse temporarily deflated under

The Iron Heel, Jack turned back to the adventures of his youth. On December 17 he countered *The Cosmopolitan* with a proposition to send it, instead of a cash refund, "a series of tramp reminiscences." Uncertain of ever getting its money back, the magazine accepted. Four days later he finished a five-thousand-word piece, "Confession," the first in a series titled *My Life in the Underworld*. It had been a dozen years since his last hobo adventures, and in his memory these represented a golden youth lost forever. George Brett was hesitant to bring out the book under the Macmillan imprimatur when he received the manuscript now titled *The Road*, which Jack wanted to subtitle "Tramp Reminiscences." Responding to Brett's suggestion that the book would damage both London's reputation and the sales of his other books, Jack wrote a vigorous apologia: "In *The Road*, and in all my work, in all that I have said and written and done, I have been true. This is the character I have built up; it constitutes, I believe, my biggest asset . . . I have always insisted that the cardinal virtue is sincerity, and I have striven to live up to this belief."

Brett and London were both partially right. Brett was correct in anticipating a poor critical reception and weak sales. As one reviewer remarked, "That a man of [London's] unquestionable powers should lead such a despicable existence is strange enough. That he should tell his story with impertinent pride is still stranger." The book sold fewer than six thousand copies in its original edition. Although the public had snapped up *The Call of the Wild* and *The Sea-Wolf*, a lingering genteel readership was not yet quite ready to valorize the hobo. On the other hand, *The Road* was destined to become a classic that inspired such peripatetic authors as Hemingway, Steinbeck, and Kerouac.

As weeks dragged into months, the delay in the *Snark's* departure began impacting more than the Londons' bank balance: it was also affecting their health and their marriage. Charmian recorded ailment after ailment, his as well as hers, in her diary: headaches, backaches, colds, pleurisy, and depression. As he often did when they were in the city, Jack was drinking more. "Mate not looking well," she wrote on February 2: "Drinks cocktails. No exercise. I feel bad about him." A fortnight later she recorded, "Mate takes 3 cocktails before dinner all by himself. I cry." Two days after this, she wrote that Jack had gone out with his socialist friends—then came home "very late, *full*." She had nervous chills and got no sleep that night. "I didn't get up until middle of afternoon," she wrote the that day. "Thank God, I don't have to live in a city always. I almost think that such a life would, in the end, kill that otherwise imperishable thing—the love of Jack and me."

Things brightened in late February when they visited Carmel-by-the-Sea, where George Sterling had recently established a new headquarters for some of his favorite bohemian friends. In the summer of 1905, with the help of his friends Charles Wood and Gene Fenelon, he had built a rustic mansion on a knoll overlooking a beautiful pine forest near the old Carmel mission and just half a mile from the ocean. Here he planned to live off the land, renouncing his decadent, philandering city life along with his well-paying city job. "Carrie and I love the simple life—the simpler the better," Sterling explained to Ambrose Bierce. "I'm going to live on mush-and-honey, which costs little, and what game I shoot. It's extremely plentiful about Carmel. Also I've leased several acres of adjacent land, from which I can get a small income by raising potatoes."

For evening gatherings he had designed an ample eighteen-by-thirty-foot living room finished in oiled redwood and warmed by a huge chalk-rock fireplace. During the day the votaries—when not engaged in tilling, planting, hunting, or writing—would enjoy walking the beach, swimming, fishing, and all forms of wholesome fun and games. To Sterling's sybaritic commune would come, both as visitors and as settlers, the liveliest artistic spirits of California: Ambrose Bierce and his nephew Carlton with his wife, Lora; Mary Austin; Jimmy Hopper; Arnold Genthe; Joaquin Miller; Charles Warren Stoddard; Xavier Martínez with Elsie; and of course Jack London with Charmian. Jack would later memorialize their pagan antics—"their excessive jollity, their childlike joy, and the childlike things they did"—in *The Valley of the Moon*: "It seemed more like some fairy tale or books story come true." The key word here is *seemed*, for Sterling's Arcadian dream would ultimately transform into a nightmare of depression, divorce, and death.

In early 1907, however, Carmel-by-the-Sea provided a welcome if brief retreat for the Londons. Charmian recorded a "lovely walk" with Carrie Sterling to Point Lobos on February 22 and found temporary relief from her chronic insomnia, sleeping comfortably that evening "within sound of surf." Although Jack spent that day, and the next, drinking and playing cards with George, Dick Partington, and "Toddy" Albrecht, he made amends: "Loved me all evening," was Charmian's diary entry. "I felt full of sunshine. Good to be away from Oakland."

They returned to the city two days later, correcting proofs for *The Iron Heel* on the train ride back. And Jack returned to work, still trying to catch up with mounting expenses. He sat down at his desk and began writing a series of weekly potboilers, starting with a Klondike tale ("The Passing of Marcus O'Brien"), followed by four weird socioscientific fantasies ("The Unparalleled Invasion," "The Enemy of All the World," "The Dream of Debs," and "A Curious Fragment"). All five were second-rate, and none were initially accepted by the top magazines to which they were submitted.

By now, the *Snark* had become a national laughingstock, and the newspapers were having a field day at Jack's expense. Where formerly bets were being made about *when* the boat would finally sail, the betting was now changed from "When?" to "If?" More damaging, the project had also become a joke to the workmen, who were also having a field day at Jack's expense. The *Snark* had reached the status of "London's Folly" and "Jack's Sea-Going White Elephant." London wrote to Brett, "the whole building of the boat has been one continuous series of disasters," concluding that the "only thing for me to do is to get away somehow, and finish her as I go along."

On the morning of Tuesday, April 23, with her motley crew waving goodbye to hundreds of friends and curiosity-mongers, the *Snark* sailed out through the Golden Gate for Hawaii. The anchor had been hoisted by hand because the power transmission failed to work. The interior was still unpainted, and the exterior paint was peeling. The broken and useless seventy-horsepower engine was lashed down for ballast on the bottom of the boat, awaiting resuscitation in Honolulu. The lifeboat "leaked like a sieve" as did the watertight bulkheads, while kerosene and gasoline were ruining the fresh produce. All the ironwork on the boat "proved to be mush," snapping "like macaroni" under the slightest stress. The luxurious bathroom, with its fancy sea valves and levers, "was the swiftest wreck of any portion of the *Snark*," handles breaking off short at the first heavy pressure.

The naval officers who were members of the Bohemian Club traded predictions over their Scotch and sodas. "He won't get as far as Hawaii," declared one. "If he strikes the tail of a typhoon, that boat will go down to the bottom in a flash." Overhearing him, Arnold Genthe retorted, "The boat may go down, but Jack London never will!"

20

PARADISE LOST

Life has rotted away in this wonderful garden spot, where the climate is as delightful and healthful as any to be found in the world . . . When one considers the situation, one is almost driven to the conclusion that the white race flourishes on impurity and corruption.

—*THE CRUISE OF THE SNARK*

"Ho! for Honolulu!!" begins Charmian's diary entry for April 23. "Sailed out thru Golden Gate, in fierce tide-rips. 'Snark' behaved beautifully." They were feeling pretty well until later in the day. As the *Snark* was bobbing along on the high seas, the crew began to feel the symptoms of seasickness. "At first, you fear you will die," explains Martin Johnson; "then, after it has a good hold on you, you fear you won't die." It was more than a matter of simple nausea. "Never had I known anything like it! My head ached, my stomach ached, every muscle in my body ached. There were times when it seemed impossible that I should live." One by one, the crew members began to drop, precariously clutching the tiny twelve-inch guard rails as they vomited over the sides, then collapsing into their unsteady bunks, for the boat's sickly rolling was relentless.

By the end of the first week, all except Tochigi had weathered the worst of their vertigo, but on Saturday they encountered their first storm. As the seas grew dangerously higher, the *Snark* was caught in a gigantic trough and refused to heave to, threatening at every great wave to swamp and sink. She managed to stay afloat—but she was far from watertight: "The sides leaked, the bottom leaked . . . Even the self-bailing cockpit quickly filled with water that could find no outlet. Our gasoline, stored in non-leakable tanks and sealed behind an air-tight bulkhead, began to filter out, so that we hardly dared to strike a match." Because the floor of the galley was only two feet above the bottom of the boat, water rose to knee height, and Johnson had to prepare their meals in his rubber boots, while below him saltwater sloshed freely from one "airtight" compartment to another. "Will we ever reach Honolulu alive?" he wondered.

Everyone was black and blue from being knocked about, Charmian the worst hit. She sported a mass of lumps, abrasions, and bruises, the most painful resulting from a spectacular somersault she performed when her wet rubber shoe soles slipped on the top step of the companionway and she landed on her elbow six feet below. Martin openly marveled that she did not cry. "I *couldn't* cry. It hurt too much to cry," she told him—but later at the wheel by herself, she "wailed loud and long."

The crew's bruises were more than physical. Tochigi was heartsick when he found the books he had brought along ruined by saltwater. Roscoe Eames grew increasingly sullen after Jack had dressed him down for his navigational incompetence and shirking of his assigned duties. Bert Stolz went into a funk before they were barely a fortnight out: "No ambition—grouchy, neglectful," Charmian wrote on May 9. And Jack, having promised Charmian he would give up alcohol and cigarettes until they reached Hawaii, was suffering withdrawal symptoms: headaches, insomnia, crankiness—aggravated by delusions that boxes of his favorite Imperiales had been hidden from him somewhere on the boat. By the time they reached port, he was nearing the end of his tether, raising hell with the crew. "Poor fellow is irritable and jumps us all, all the time!" Charmian lamented on May 18. "I feel so sad it should turn out this way."

Her sadness and his irritability vanished the next day when they "were spanking along smartly in a cobalt sea threshed white on every rushing wave, with the green and gold island of Oahu shifting its scenery like a sliding screen as [they] swept past lovely rose-tawny Diamond Head and palm-dotted Waikiki toward Honolulu Harbor." Early the next morning, less than a month after sailing out through the Golden

Gate, the *Snark* was met in Honolulu Bay by a government launch. The morning edition of *The Pacific Commercial Advertiser* was tossed up onto the deck, and the immigration inspector Brown and customs inspector Farmer climbed aboard, jovially pointing out the headline:

LONDON SNARK LOST AT SEA WITH ALL ON BOARD.

Shortly thereafter, they were met by a second launch and boarded by the port physician, who checked their bill of health and declared them free to enter the Port of Honolulu, where the wharves were lined with citizens anxious to welcome them with garlands of orchids. But neither Jack nor the *Snark* was in shape to face the crowd. He apologized that they were headed for Pearl Harbor, where they were expected by Thomas W. Hobron, a Honolulu "artist, merchant, good fellow" who had promised the use of his cottage during their stay. The officials replied that Mr. Hobron had been called to San Francisco but had given instructions that his bungalow was still theirs for as long as they needed it.

Their vision blurred the moment they set foot on the tiny wharf at Pearl Harbor. The miniature gyroscope nestled deep within their inner ear was still regulated by the eternal undulations of the ocean. Charmian staggered and was barely saved from falling back into the ocean by Commodore Clarence Macfarlane, head of the Hawaii Yacht Club, and Albert Waterhouse, a neighbor commissioned by Hobron to make the Londons welcome. Jack tried making a joke about his wife's "sad walk" but then had to grab his host to keep from going overboard himself. When they finally stepped off onto what should have been solid ground, the land seemed no steadier than the wharf. When Jack turned his head too quickly to admire the panorama of tropical flowers, the line of royal palms that made an avenue to the Waterhouse home began "swinging in a great arc across the sky." Only after an intense effort could he stop their dizzy swinging. He felt as if he were drugged, like Odysseus, under some Circean spell. At that point all of them began laughing, Charmian recalled, "very much better acquainted for the fun."

Clinging to each other for balance, she and Jack followed their host "across a spacious, wonderful lawn and down an avenue of royal palms . . . The air was filled with the songs of birds and was heavy with rich warm fragrances—wafture from great lilies, and blazing blossoms of hibiscus, and other strange tropic flowers." After "naught but the restless, salty sea" for so long, they both felt as if they had been magically transported into some kind of beautiful dream land. Compared with their tiny residence on the *Snark*, the Waterhouse home looked like a mansion as they approached it: cool and spacious, "with a great sweeping veranda where lotus-eaters might dwell . . . Couches with grass-woven covers invited everywhere, and there was a grand piano that played, I was sure, nothing more exciting than lullabies." Soft fragrances from a multitude of flowers wafted through wide-open doors and windows from the sea breeze. "Here was no blazing down of a tropic sun upon an unshrinking sea." Housekeepers in lovely sarongs "drifted around and about, noiselessly, like butterflies." After their first real bath in nearly a month, Jack and Charmian were served exotic victuals by the "butterfly maids." It all seemed to be too good to be real: "It was a dream-dwelling."

But the dream was real. The next five months would be happy, relaxing, and productive. Of course Jack had been writing steadily, weather permitting, on their voyage. "Every day, Jack wrote two hours . . . no more, no less," said Martin. "He would get up in the morning and take his trick at the wheel, have breakfast, and then shut himself in his stateroom for just two hours and write . . . He writes it just once, and never goes over it to change it. He writes with a fountain pen, and nobody can read his writing but Mrs. London. He turns his manuscript over to her, and she types it and gets it ready for the publishers."

As soon as they had settled into their Hawaiian bungalow, he finished a forgettable Klondike tale titled "Flush of Gold," and by the end of May he had composed what was to become the most memorable of his two hundred stories. He had written a much shorter story titled "To Build a Fire" six years earlier for the *Youth's Companion*, but that piece—an exemplum for boys, preaching the two-stranded moral lesson "Never travel alone!" and "Mind the wisdom of your elders!"—lacked the subtle characterization as well as the atmospheric richness and thematic depth that distinguish his masterpiece. In 1908, when "To Build a Fire" appeared in the *Century* magazine, someone evidently told the editor, R. W. Gilder, he had bought soiled goods, because he sent a complaint to London. "A long, long time ago I wrote a story for boys which I sold to the *Youth's Companion*," Jack replied: "It was purely juvenile in treatment . . . As the years went by, I was worried by the inadequate treatment I had given that motif, and by the fact that I had treated it for boys merely . . . I do know, I am absolutely confident, that beyond the motif itself, there is no similarity of treatment whatever."

An examination of the later story validates London's statement. Few readers can forget, for example, the concluding image of the frozen figure that a few hours before had been a live human being, the dog delaying briefly and "howling under the stars that leaped and danced and shone brightly in the cold sky [before] it turned and trotted up the trail in the direction of the camp it knew, where were the other food-providers and fire-providers." For more than one hundred years "To Build a Fire" has been universally acclaimed as a superb model of literary naturalism, and the author created his chilling classic while basking in Hawaii's halcyon breezes.

Early on the morning of May 29, while Jack and Charmian were leisurely enjoying their after-breakfast coffee, "a perfectly nice and affable young man" suddenly appeared, striding across the lawn. A reporter from *The Honolulu Advertiser* had caught the first train from the city and was excitedly holding out the latest issue of *Everybody's Magazine*. Jack London had been criticized by the president of the United States! In an interview, Theodore Roosevelt, having read *White Fang*, had branded London a "nature faker" for dramatizing an incident in which a large wolf-dog was overcome in a fight with a smaller animal. "I can't believe that Mr. London knows much about the wolves, and I am certain he knows nothing about their fighting, or as a realist he would not tell this tale," the president declared.

"Why, look here," Jack said, laughing as he glanced through the article, "he says that the lynx in my story killed the wolf-dog. It did nothing of the kind . . . My story is about the wolf-dog killing the lynx—and eating it! . . . I can see myself writing an answer to Mr. Roosevelt later on, in some magazine." Nine months later, he wrote his answer:

President Roosevelt tried and condemned me on two counts. (1) I was guilty of having a big, fighting bull-dog whip a wolf-dog. (2) I was guilty of allowing a lynx to kill a wolf-dog in a pitched battle. Regarding the second count, President Roosevelt was wrong in his field observations taken while reading my book. He must have read it hastily, for in my story I have my wolf-dog kill the lynx. Not only did I have my wolf-dog kill the lynx, but I made him eat the body of the lynx as well. Remains only the first count on which to convict me of nature-faking, and the first count does not charge me with diverging from ascertained facts. It is merely a statement of a difference of opinion. President Roosevelt does not think a bull-dog can lick a wolf-dog. I think a bull-dog can lick a wolf-dog. And there we are.

Roosevelt's criticism did nothing to spoil the Londons' Hawaiian idyll. If anything, it enhanced their celebrity status on the islands. On the evening of May 29, as they were dining in a quiet corner of the Royal Hawaiian Hotel, "a bearded young man" approached their table and said, "You're Jack London, aren't you?—My name is Ford."

Ford was a famous globe-trotting writer who, captivated by the islands, had become their top promoter. "Oh, yes," Jack responded, "Alexander Hume Ford. I heard you were in Honolulu, and have wanted to see you. I've read lots of your stuff—and all of your dandy articles in *The Century*." Ford regaled them for two hours "with information about everything under the sky," including his plans to revive the ancient Hawaiian sport of surfing. After dinner they rode the electric trolley out to the Moana Hotel to join the reception for a visiting congressional party at the home of the territory's delegate, Prince Jonah Kuhio Kalanianaole ("Prince Cupid") and his wife, Princess Elizabeth. Charmian was especially impressed by the "glorious" princess, who stood in the receiving line "touching with hers the hands of all who passed, with a brief, graceful droop of her patrician head, and a fleeting, perfunctory, yet gracious flash of little teeth under her small fine mouth."

Less gracious if no less regal was the dethroned sovereign queen Liliuokalani, seated in a nearby armchair. Charmian recollected that she was glad to be well down the receiving line, for it gave her more time to study the great woman who had fought so vigorously to preserve the ancient kingdom of Hawaii. What she observed was a face "rather thin, strong, and pervaded with an elusive refinement [as the] most striking characteristic [due perhaps] to the expression of the narrow black eyes, rather close-set, which were implacably savage in their cold hatred of everything American . . . Imagine her emotions . . . sitting uncrowned, receiving her conquerors." None of this was lost on Jack, for later he would memorialize the Hawaiian tragedy in one of his finest stories, "Koolau the Leper."

The tension was broken that evening when one of the younger congressmen, hearing mention of the writer's name, blurted out, "That Jack London! Why didn't somebody tell us? Great Scott!" As good-humored laughs went up among the crowd, Charmian turned to her grinning husband and whispered, "That's how you pay for your 'Dream Harbor' seclusion!"

By this time the Londons could find little seclusion anywhere on the globe. They were great newspaper copy, often garnering front-page headlines. Jack had learned early the commercial value of his exploits, and by 1907, he had become expert in transmuting his personal experiences into cash. "Funny way to make a living!" he told Charmian shortly after their arrival in Hawaii. "I carry my office in my head, and see the world while I earn the money to see it with."

A few afternoons later, while lounging in the shade on Waikiki Beach, they suddenly became fascinated by a distant vision. Several hundred yards out on the ocean was a tiny figure riding the crests of mountainous mile-long waves. As the waves grew nearer, they saw the bronzed body of a man: "And straight on toward shore he flies on his winged heels and the white crest of the breaker. There is a wild burst of foam, a long tumultuous rushing sound as the breaker falls futile and spent on the beach at your feet; and there, at your feet steps calmly ashore a Kanaka, burnt golden and brown by the tropic sun."

Here was another challenge Jack couldn't resist. As a mere youth he had been crowned "Prince of the Oyster Pirates," had earned the coveted title "Profesh" among the hobos, had proved his mettle as an ablebodied seaman, had performed the backbreaking work of two men in the Oakland power plant, had out-backpacked native porters over the Chilkoot Pass, and, full grown to manhood, had sailed a frail little boat more than two thousand miles across the wide Pacific. Now he was compelled to master the surfboard.

From the perspective of the casual observer, surf-riding may appear to be the simple matter of keeping one's balance on a buoyant board atop a big wave—a playful exercise in childlike fun. From the standpoint of the surfing tyro, it is a different matter, difficult and precarious—as Jack and Charmian soon discovered. Captivated by the graceful spectacle they had just witnessed, they quickly borrowed a couple of small surfboards. For the next hour they kept working at it, trying to emulate the little Kanaka boys they saw surfing in the shallow waters near the beach. Kicking and paddling furiously, they tried time and again to ride the small waves—time and again failing before the grinning youngsters.

"Get off that board," a voice shouted. Alexander Hume Ford, who had been watching from a distance, came to their rescue. "Chuck it away at once. Look at the way you're trying to ride it. If ever the nose of that board hits bottom, you'll be disemboweled. Here, take my board. It's a man's board." Handing over his seventy-five-pound surfboard, he spent the next half hour carefully instructing the couple in the rudiments. Following several attempts, Charmian finally "accomplished one successful landing, slipping up the beach precisely to the feet of some stranger hotel guests, who were not half so surprised as myself." But after being knocked in the head by her overturned surfboard, and fearful that she might receive an even worse blow, Charmian had had enough. Jack also had beginner's accidents, including a spectacular one in which he flipped over in a complete somersault.

But he was determined to master the surfboard, even if it killed him. Within half an hour, under Ford's tutelage, he had discovered how to catch the waves and stay afloat. Next, his mentor explained how he must use his legs as a rudder. That piece of advice, Jack claimed, saved him not only from suicide but also from homicide. As he was riding a huge wave in to the beach, he suddenly spotted dead ahead a woman in the water waist high. "How was I to stop that comber on whose back I was?" he wondered in horror as he rushed toward her. In his mind's eye, he saw a dead woman, fatally bludgeoned by a surfboard. "The board weighed seventy-five pounds, I weighed a hundred and sixty-five. The added weight had a velocity of fifteen miles per hour. The board and I constituted a projectile."

An instant before the projectile reached its target, Ford's last monition flashed into his brain: "Steer with your legs!" Quickly executing this maneuver, he managed to divert the projectile from its target at the last second. His heroic feat was not without lesser consequences:

The wave gave me a passing buffet, a light tap as the taps of waves go, but a tap sufficient to knock me off the board and smash me down through the rushing water to bottom, with which I came in violent collision and upon which I was rolled over and over. I got my head out for breath of air and then gained my feet. There stood the woman before me. I felt like a hero. I had saved her life. And she laughed at me . . . She had never dreamed of her danger.

"Tomorrow," announced his mentor, seeing that his pupil was a quick learner, "I am going to take you out into the blue water." Shading his eyes, Jack looked out to the "great smoking combers that made the breakers [he] had been riding look like ripples." After a moment's hesitation he responded bravely, "All right, I'll tackle them to-morrow."

The next day, he followed Ford out into the "deep water where the big smokers came roaring in." He had always been a good swimmer, but this was something new. Simply to get through and over these monstrous waves was a battle. Man, puny man, versus Nature, mighty Nature: here was the primal challenge that underscored London's personal code.

While London and Ford were battling the big combers in the deep water, they were joined by a third man: George Freeth, a native-born one-quarter Hawaiian, arguably the world's greatest surfer. He would eventually move to Los Angeles and initiate Californians into the sport. That day he served as high priest of the high waves for Jack London. He taught Jack how to survive the big breakers by sliding off his board and going underwater to avoid being brained by the board. He also taught him that the key to surf-riding was nonresistance: "Relax. Yield yourself to the waters that are ripping and tearing at you. When the undertow catches you and drags you seaward along the bottom, don't struggle against it. If you do, you are liable to be drowned, for it is stronger than you . . . Swim with it . . . swim upward at the same time. It will be no trouble at all to reach the surface." To survive against the "really ferocious" waves far out in the deep water, one needed to be an expert swimmer with a fearless respect for the water. Had he lacked this expertise, Jack "could have been drowned a dozen different ways." Instead, when he finally emerged from the ocean, having caught the big waves, he was filled with pride and an "ecstatic bliss."

His bliss was short-lived. While outsmarting the ferocious power of the tropical sea, he had forgotten the insidious power of the tropical sun. For more than four hours during the heat of the day he had exposed his body to the devastating rays of that sun. Charmian was shocked when she saw the broiled figure limping back up to their tent-house: Both his face and his body were covered with "large swollen blotches, like hives," she said, "and his mouth and throat were closing painfully." The backs of his legs were so badly grilled that he couldn't stand erect. As the burning pain increased, he could no longer crawl much less walk. The only way he could get around without help was face upward, with his back raised, creeping on his heels and the palms of his hands. "Don't let me laugh," he moaned to her; "it hurts too much."

Dr. Charles Cooper was baffled when he arrived to examine his broiled patient. He recognized the second-degree sunburn immediately, but the mysterious swollen blotches that covered the body and face were beyond his medical experience. The key to an accurate diagnosis could have been Jack's recollection that the blotches resembled those he had suffered with the shingles aboard the *Sophia Sutherland*. It would be almost ninety years, however, before London's symptoms were diagnosed as lupus.

His painful broiling failed to diminish Jack's enthusiasm for surf-riding. He vowed to turn to the big waves as soon as his legs and blisters allowed. Recovery took several days, and though he couldn't stand or walk, he could still write. Even while Charmian applied cool cloths to his parched skin, he was sitting up in bed on June 3, composing a tribute to the "Royal Sport," which was published that fall in the *Woman's Home Companion*. Mark Twain had devoted a paragraph to surfing in *Roughing It*, after his own futile attempts yielded nothing but "a couple of barrels of water in me," concluding that "None but natives ever master the art of surf-bathing thoroughly." London proved otherwise, and his article helped open American eyes to the excitement of this sport.

Three more days passed before Jack could move well enough for the couple to return home to their bungalow. While confined to the bed, he could not only read and write but also enjoy sex. "Jack a rapturous lover, in spite of his pain with sunburn," Charmian confided. He managed to get dressed on June 6, "the operation (not an inappropriate word) accompanied by running commentary on things as they were, which would be both interesting and instructive in a biographical sense, did one dare the editorial censors."

The next day they toured the fifty-thousand-acre Ewa Plantation, southwest of Pearl Harbor. The plantation manager, H. H. Renton, devoted his entire day to guiding their tour. They were fascinated. Beyond the technological complexities of the plantation's operations, Charmian was especially impressed by the cultural mélange: Here were foreign villages of "Japanese, Chinese, Portuguese, Norwegians, Spanish, Swedish, Korean—even Russians." And here they were born, married, worked, and died "within its confines." She noticed that there were no Hawaiian workers: "for they are proud and free creatures, and it would seem pity to bind them on their own soil." This last observation would become a major theme in London's Hawaiian masterpiece, "Koolau the Leper"; furthermore, his own critical assessment of this great commercial enterprise would be central to his first Hawaiian tale, "The House of Pride," which he started shortly following their tour.

On Monday evening, July 1, the couple boarded the *Noeau*, the "ship of despair, ferry of human freight, condemned," bound for the leper colony on Molokai:

> We are not merry, Jack and I, for what we have witnessed during the past two hours would wring pitying emotion from a graven image . . . None of it did we miss—the parting and the embarkation of the banished; and never, should I live a thousand fair years, shall I forget the memory of that strange, rending wailing . . . Shrill, piercing, it curdled the primitive life-current in us, every tone in the gamut of sorrow being played [as each] loved one stepped upon the gangplank, untouched by the officers and crew.

What had prompted Charmian and Jack to undertake this voyage of the damned? Lucius E. Pinkham, president of the Hawaiian Board of Health (and later governor of the territory), urged them to visit the island and see the situation for themselves. In light of the "considerable misrepresentation of the Settlement," he trusted London to "write a fair picture." They spent five days on Molokai, freely mingling with the patients. Jack then proceeded to write a landmark sketch that would change the world's misconception of that alleged "pit of hell." He stated up front that "the horrors of Molokai, as they have been painted in the past [have been distorted] by sensationalists who have never laid eyes on [the colony and that] neither the lepers, nor those who devote their lives to them, have received a fair deal."

Chief among those who devoted their lives to them were Jack McVeigh, superintendent of the settlement, and Dr. William J. Goodhue, resident surgeon of the colony. In the spirit of Father Joseph Damien de Veuster, who had sacrificed his life ministering to those ravaged by the disease, both McVeigh and Goodhue (along with wife and family) had settled on Molokai. Realizing that there was no known cure for the bacillus *M. leprae* and fully aware of the terrible consequences of infection, they nevertheless worked tirelessly to make as comfortable as possible what remained of life for their condemned patients, all the while exposing themselves to those bodies carrying the insidious bacterium.

Regarding McVeigh, Charmian noted that "he carries a heart as big as the charge he keeps, and a keen gray eye quick to the needs of his children as he calls them." She and Jack were invited to observe these gruesome operations, in which Goodhue excised infected areas from the patients' bodies to prevent gangrene. Both were shocked by the horrors they witnessed. Concerning one young patient with a running sore under his shoulder, Charmian saw that what had "appeared on the surface was nothing to that which the knife revealed." While sparing her readers further details, she said, "I wish I could picture the calm, pale surgeon, with his intensely dark-blue eyes and the profile of Ralph Waldo Emerson, whose kinsman he is, working with master strokes that cleansed the deep cavity of corruption; for it was an illustration of the finest art of which the human is capable."

The next day brought less depressing images, as it was Independence Day, and a loud motley crowd of the "horribles," as they labeled themselves in their various grotesque homemade costumes and masks, had risen at dawn to parade before the superintendent's house. It was a brave spectacle, as if they had chosen to counter the horrors of their disease through joyous parody. "Some of the actors in this serio-comic performance were astride cavorting horses, some on foot; and one, an agile clown in spots and frills, seemed neither afoot nor horseback... for he traveled in company with a trained donkey that lay down peaceably whenever it was mounted." Another, in harlequin dress, "exhibited with dramatic gesture and native elocution a dancing bear personified by a man in brown shag to represent fur." Following this group was "a cavalcade of pa'u [horsewomen] who thundered past, brightly costumed in long skirts of varying colors, including the patriotic red, white, and blue."

This was only the first act of their play. As the day progressed, the celebrations continued with footraces, sack races, horse races, and even a donkey race in which the slowest donkey won first prize. The most impressive spectacle was the reappearance of the horsewomen racing by: "the flying horses with their streaming beribboned tails, the glowing rides, long curling hair outblown, and floating draperies painting the track with brilliant color—all mortal decay a thing forgot of actors and onlookers alike in one grand frolic of bounding vitality and youth."

"Can you beat it! Can you beat it!" Jack cried as he joined in the fun, snapping picture after picture with his Kodak. Charmian could see that he was thoroughly enjoying the spectacle. He tried to check himself, thinking it shameful, "under such circumstances, to be so lighthearted . . . But it was no use," he confessed. Jack concluded his report with a plea for help in finding a cure: "Carnegie libraries, Rockefeller universities, and many similar benefactions are all very well; but one cannot help thinking how far a few thousands of dollars would go [in enabling] the medical world to exterminate the bacillus leprae. There's a place for your money, you philanthropists."

Following their visit to Molokai, the Londons would spend another three months touring the plantations and ranches on Hawaii (the Big Island) and Maui and enjoying the hospitality of their Honolulu hosts while the *Snark* was being made seaworthy again. During those months, Jack was also trying to find a seaworthy replacement for Roscoe Eames, who had failed miserably in his assigned duty to see that the boat was properly serviced once in safe harbor by repeatedly lying when asked about the boat's condition.

Shortly after dismissing Eames, Jack signed on Andrew A. Rosehill as new sailing master of the *Snark*. Rosehill, "a roaring bucko of old Pacific days" who bragged about capers such as discovering guano-rich Marcus Island only to be cheated of his twenty-million-dollar find by the Japanese navy, appeared to be Jack's kind of man. But Rosehill was more swagger than skill. Despite his efforts to conceal his ineptness under a blanket of bullying profanity, his combination of irascibility and incompetence reached its climax when, during a temper tantrum, he bumped the *Snark* on her trial run into two ships, causing several holes in the stern. As soon as they reached shore, Martin phoned the news to Jack, who discharged Rosehill "with neatness and dispatch, as soon as a cab could bring him from the hotel."

Next, James Langhorne Warren was hired as the new sailing master for the *Snark*. Warren was a convicted murderer who had been pardoned by Governor George E. Chamberlain of Oregon. Because of his own prison experience, London was always inclined to give ex-convicts the benefit of the doubt. Persuaded that Warren was innocent and, moreover, that he was "a good navigator, a thorough seaman and a pretty manly man," Jack wanted to give him "every chance to rehabilitate himself in the eyes of the world."

Five months after they landed, the *Snark* was finally ready for the "long traverse" to the Marquesas. Of the original crew, only Johnson remained. Bert Stolz had returned to his studies at Stanford, and Tochigi had decided that he could not survive any more seasickness. Martin was promoted to chief engineer, Tsunekichi Wada was hired as cook, Yoshimatsu Nakata as cabin boy, and Hermann de Visser as ablebodied seaman. On October 7, the *Snark* departed from the Happy Isles, sailing out of Hilo, Hawaii, toward Tahiti on what would prove to be the most precarious leg of their Pacific odyssey.

"Sandwich Islands to Tahiti. There is great difficulty in making this passage across the trades. The whalers and all others speak with great doubt of fetching Tahiti from the Sandwich Islands." Jack read this admonition from the sailing directions for the South Pacific Ocean only after they set sail. "There is not a word more to help the weary voyager in making this long traverse," he wrote, "—nor is there any word at all concerning the passage from Hawaii to the Marquesas, which lie some eight hundred miles to the northeast of Tahiti and which are the more difficult to reach by just that much. The reason for the lack of directions is, I imagine, that no voyager is supposed to make himself weary by attempting such an impossible traverse."

But Jack London was never one to be deterred by the impossible. The greater challenge meant the greater adventure. For the next two months, over two thousand miles of ocean sighting neither land nor ship, there were challenges aplenty: uncertain winds and variables, unpredictable calms and squalls, the doldrums—but most critical, the shortage of drinking water. One night a water tap was inadvertently left open, and the accident was not discovered until the next morning. By that time all the deck tanks had been drained, and only ten gallons of water remained. Ten gallons of water for seven people, and the boat was caught in the doldrums not yet halfway to the Marquesas. Jack immediately put those precious ten gallons under lock and key, rationing each crew member to one quart a day—one quart a day in the tropical heat. As day after day passed with no rain nor hint of rain, "Our thirst grew almost unbearable," wrote Martin. "We spoke of nothing but water. We dreamed of water. In my sleep, a thousand times I saw brooks and rivers and springs. I saw sparkling water run over stones, purling and rippling, and a thousand times I bent over to take a deep draught, when—alas! I awoke to find myself lying on the deck of the *Snark*, crying out with thirst."

How did Jack deal with his own thirst? Martin says that "he went into his cabin and wrote a sea story about a castaway sailor that died of thirst while drifting in an open boat." Two nights later a drenching downpour enabled them to fill all the water tanks, and Jack announced, "I'll not kill that sailor; I'll have him saved by a rain like this; that'll make the yarn better than ever!" That was the only rain during the remainder of their voyage to the Marquesas. Had that particular squall missed the tiny boat, the *Snark* might never have been heard from again.

Compared with that one close call, the other challenges of the "long traverse" seemed inconsequential. No matter that the fresh provisions spoiled and the flour turned weevily; there was seafood in abundance: bonito, flying fish, shark, dolphin, and even a giant sea turtle "served up in various forms, each better than the last—broiled, fried, soupwise, and in chowder." No matter that the gasoline engine had proved useless; there would be wind enough to carry them along. No matter that they kept finding evidence of the many ways the builders had cheated Jack in the construction of the *Snark*; they loved the little craft all the more with her flaws. No matter that they were confined week after week; they had plenty to do to keep the boat shipshape, as well as boxing and games of cards to play in their leisure hours. And reading. With the *Snark*'s five-hundred-volume library, there was no lack of reading material: Conrad, James, Kipling, Stevenson—these familiar names, and many more, are mentioned in Charmian's diary. In addition to her diary entries, she was also keeping her log of the voyage. Her entry on October 15, 1907, is especially noteworthy: "It is nine o'clock, and Jack has just gone below to write his thousand words of the novel under way. (I cannot call the novel by name because the author hasn't been inspired as promptly as usual in his choice of title.) The hero, Martin Eden, has been waiting to make his first love to Ruth [because] all this week the author has been under the weather." Two years later, Macmillan would publish this most intensely personal of all London's novels with the hero's name as title.

Shortly before midnight on December 6, 1907, after sixty days across the "impossible traverse," the *Snark* dropped anchor in the harbor of Nuka-Hiva, the largest of the Marquesan Islands. "At last we are at anchor. It seems that we must be in paradise," wrote Johnson. "The air is perfume. We can hear the wild goats blatting in the mountains, and an occasional long-drawn howl from a dog ashore." After all those days at sea, the land seemed truly paradisal. "In the morning we awoke in fairyland," wrote Jack. "It is a cyclorama of painted cardboard," elaborated Charmian: ". . . the rugged scissored skyline, the canyons and gorges, sun-tanned beaches, grass-huts under luxuriant plumy palms, and the rich universal verdure . . . It is an astonishing scene, and cannot be compared with any place I ever saw."

As their fascinated gaze wandered far up the towering walls of this great natural amphitheater, they could faintly discern "the thin line of a trail, visible in one place, where it scoured across the face of the wall." Jack and Charmian exclaimed, "The path by which Toby escaped from *Typee*!" Ever since as a boy he had read Herman Melville's romantic tale of youthful adventures in the South Seas, Jack had dreamed of visiting the marvelous setting of *Typee*. He had shared this dream with Charmian. He had brought along a copy of the book, and soon after sailing from Hawaii she, too, had been caught under the spell of Melville's prose. Now the dream had come true, and now, perhaps if their luck held, they might even glimpse the great-great-granddaughter of Fayaway, the lovely pagan sweetheart of young Herman. But then they saw Fayaway's twentieth-century progeny:

We were immediately struck, upon landing, with an ominous narrow-
ness of chest and stoop of shoulders among the natives, only a few
showing any robustness. And the explanation came from moment to
moment in a dreadful coughing that racks the doomed wretches. The
little that is left of the race is perishing and it is not a pretty process.
The men and women are victims of asthma, phthisis, and the sad "gal-
loping" consumption that lays a man in two months or less—to say
nothing of other and unnameable curses of disease that "civilization"
has brought.

On December 10, eager to see Melville's beautiful Typee Valley, they
left the village of Taiohae "astride ferocious little stallions that pawed
and screamed and bit and fought one another quite oblivious of the
fragile humans on their backs [on] an ancient road through a jungle of
hau trees. On every side were the vestiges of a one-time dense population." But there were only vestiges, for once-magnificent stone mansions
were now vacant, "and huge trees sank their roots through the plat-
forms and towered over the under-running jungle . . . In valley after
valley the last inhabitant has passed and the fertile soil has relapsed to
jungle." Melville had been impressed by the strength and the beauty of
the Marquesans, remarking that he had seen no evidence whatever of
any natural deformities among them. But strength and beauty were
nowhere to be seen by Jack and Charmian, and the Valley of Typee in
which Melville estimated a population of two thousand had become
"the abode of some dozen wretched creatures, afflicted by leprosy,
elephantiasis, and tuberculosis."

Riding on out, they found another valley near the ocean, where
were a dozen grass dwellings and "a profusion of cocoanuts, breadfruit
trees, and taro patches." That evening they feasted on old-time Marquesan hospitality. They were sated on fruits, raw fish, stewed chicken
in coconut milk, breadfruit, taro, and roast pig (rather than "long pig,"
the cannibal delicacy that prompted Melville's escape). "The feast ended,
we watched the moon rise over Typee," Jack wrote.

The air was like balm, faintly scented with the breath of flowers. It was
a magic night, deathly still, without the slightest breeze to stir the foli-

age; and one caught one's breath and felt the pang that is almost hurt, so exquisite was the beauty of it. Faint and far could be heard the thin thunder of the surf upon the beach. There were no beds; and we drowsed and slept wherever we thought the floor softest. Nearby, a woman panted and moaned in her sleep, and all about us the dying islanders coughed in the night.

Although the Marquesans were a vanishing race, dying from the pernicious gifts of white invaders, there was no hint of resentment in their treatment of the visitors. In contrast to the "civilized" world, "They do not steal, gossip about one another, nor carry grudges," Martin noted. "Instead, they sing, dance, hunt, fish, and live together as brothers in a life of perfect peace." A few months after their visit, London would memorialize their attitude in his story "The Heathen."

"We hated to get up this our last morning in the Marquesas," Charmian wrote on December 18. Fugitives from a fallen world, they found their reprieve necessarily short-lived. Three months of mail and news awaited them in Tahiti. When word of their departure was spread, the natives came all day in canoes, bringing bountiful loads of oranges, pineapples, yams, taro, coconuts, and bananas. That evening, the *Snark* sailed away from this Lost Paradise toward Tahiti, and beyond that to the Solomon Islands, where the crew would encounter a more sinister hospitality.

21

PARADISE MOMENTARILY REGAINED

> On the arrival of strangers, every man endeavored to obtain
> one as a friend and carry him off to his own habitation, where
> he is treated with great kindness by the inhabitants of the dis-
> trict: they place him on a high seat and feed him with abun-
> dance of the finest food.
>
> —*POLYNESIAN RESEARCHES*

On the evening of their hauling anchor at Nuka-Hiva, Charmian felt a twinge of fear. "Then I remembered that fear is only a word to us of the *Snark*—a word without meaning." If *fear* had been a word with meaning for these natural-born seekers, the *Snark* might have been no more than a clever pun in a Lewis Carroll poem. If *fear* had been meaningful in any context other than the fear of failure, Jack London might have been delivering mail in Oakland instead of receiving mail in the South Seas.

Nine days after leaving Nuka-Hiva, after braving the treacherous currents and reefs of the Tuamotu Archipelago, the *Snark* reached the "Paris of the Pacific": Papeete, Tahiti. As if on cue, the crew of the American cruiser *Annapolis*, in port from Tutuila, Samoa, ran to the rails and cheered while their ship dipped her flag in tribute. Soon after the port doctor had come aboard to check their health and determine that the boat was rat-free, there appeared alongside an outrigger canoe sporting a blood-red flag. Standing at the helm was "a tall, tawny blond man with russet gold beard and long hair, and great blue eyes as earnest as a child's or a seer's." He was dressed in a sleeveless fishnet shirt and a red loincloth.

"Hello, Jack!—Hello, Charmian!" he greeted them.

It was Ernest Darling, the famous "Nature man."

"What's the meaning of the *red*?" Jack asked.

"Socialism, of course," Ernest answered.

In addition to his socialistic greeting, Darling also delivered a tasty welcome basket: "a small jar of clear white honey, two bursting-ripe mangoes, a tiny jar of heavy cocoanut cream, and two small, perfectly ripe alligator pears." When Darling visited the Londons' cottage, he took special note of the boxing gloves hanging on the wall, and Jack asked him if he enjoyed "the game." Ernest answered that he had given boxing lessons at Stanford. That was all Jack needed to hear, and the two donned the gloves. Here was a different man from the ninety-pound weakling whom doctors in Portland, Oregon, had given up for dead a few years earlier. During their spirited match, they traded blow for blow, Jack's tall, lean opponent with his "long, gorilla arms" giving as much damage as he received. But Ernest's hands were adept at healing as well as hurting. Later, he ministered massages to both Jack and Charmian to relieve their recurrent headaches, the worst of which were precipitated by what they found in their waiting mail.

Roscoe Eames's malfeasances were trivial compared with those of his wife. Before departing from San Francisco, Jack had turned his business affairs over to Netta's management, granting her power of attorney and full control of all financial arrangements. In the pile of correspondence and newspapers held for his arrival at Papeete, Jack discovered that since the *Snark*'s departure, the United States had suffered another financial panic and that during this time, without consulting him, Netta had spent hefty unauthorized funds in renovations at the ranch, doubled her salary as his business manager and literary agent, continued charging him rent at Wake Robin for lodging he would never use, and closed several bank accounts on which he continued to write checks. Furthermore, newspaper reports that the *Snark* was lost at sea prompted the Central Bank of Oakland, which held the mortgage on his mother's house, to foreclose.

Again George Brett came to the rescue, cabling funds in time for

Jack and Charmian to catch the *Mariposa* for San Francisco on January 13. "I shall only be in San Francisco eight (8) days," he told Brett, outlining their plan to take the *Mariposa* on her return run to Tahiti so that they could resume their around-the-world cruise.

The *Mariposa* docked in San Francisco on the morning of January 25, and the ensuing week was necessarily busy. In addition to their first priority to bring some kind of order out of the financial chaos Netta had created, Jack visited Bessie and their daughters, Charmian caught up on her shopping, and the two dined with Eliza and visited with other relatives and with members of the old Crowd. Three days later they took the train to Glen Ellen. "Things are rather cold and sad," Charmian recorded. "Getting a lot of business and letters etc. This lasts into evening. Sleep over ten hours. Both of us. Glorious!" Those hours of sleep were restorative. "We get out about noon and ride to the blessed ranch and see everything that we can between showers," she wrote the next day. "The dear ranch! So good to see it. Wiget [the foreman] splendid. Eat cheese and bread and onions there. Visit barn and house site [the future site of Wolf House, the 'dream home' Jack was planning to build]."

On January 30 they left for Oakland, bidding a sad goodbye to the "blessed ranch" they imagined they wouldn't see again for another half-dozen years. Neither realized they would return in less than two years. The prolonged stress was now taking its usual toll on Jack's fragile immune system. "Mate very grippy," Charmian wrote on February 1. Despite worsening symptoms, he met again and had a "good understanding" with Bessie on the next morning. That afternoon he and Charmian boarded the *Mariposa*, bidding farewell amid bouquets of "violets and carnations [to a] big crowd," which included the Sterlings, the Partingtons, Fred Bamford, and Eliza. Charmian's February 6 diary entry reveals an uncharacteristic self-pity:

> Wretchedly ill these days. J's vaporings about taking care of me go glimmering and I spend my hours in loneliness and sleeplessness and tears and pain . . . Can't eat—no taste, or smell—just in dreadful condition, mentally and physically—awfully unhappy. I think J. is sick sometimes, mentally, or he wouldn't do as he does. This reflection helps me thru some hopeless, loveless times,—seldom. Thank God.

She continued in the same spirit throughout the trip as both of them suffered the symptoms of viruses contracted in the cold, damp air of the Northern California winter. She confessed that she was "a sick miserable unhappy woman" and spent most of the days in bed bemoaning her fate in signing on for the voyage. In the meantime, Jack dealt with his ailment by drinking and spending half the nights playing poker, unwilling to take care of himself: "looks sick . . . no exercise; cocktails and poker . . . and violently ill," she wrote on February 12. He apparently showed symptoms of lupus, for she noted the same kind of "swelling" he had suffered in Hawaii after being so badly sunburned from the long afternoon of surfing. "I am nurse again," she complained. "I seem to have lost my man. My new outlook and the sadness it brings me . . . Sick. Tears."

Charmian's mood, as well as Jack's, underwent a dramatic change when they reached Tahiti on February 14. Within two days after landing at Papeete, they enjoyed an "orgy of love," and on the morning after that, Jack awakened her with beautiful pearls brought from Alexander Drollet, the socialist friend and merchant whose cottage they were renting. He was now her "sweet love" protesting his faithfulness since their marriage. "Such days of love! Even work has to succumb. Mate the rapturous lover." February 20 was "Another day of love—such a honeymoon! Mate begins last chap. of 'Success.'"

One week later Jack wrote to Brett that he was shipping by express the manuscript for his new 142,000-word novel: "I don't know what you will think of this novel," he added. "I don't know what to think of it myself. But at any rate, I think you will find it fresh and original." In the same letter, he mapped out his itinerary for his planned voyage around the globe, estimating that he would reach Cape Town, South Africa, "just about a year from now."

Instead, the Snark would sail no farther than the South Seas, and "just about a year from now," Jack would not be in Cape Town but in Sydney, Australia, trying to recover his health. Added to the recurrent lapses in his immune system were the dental problems that had plagued him for years. These were especially severe during their stay on Tahiti. "Still here, and having all my teeth overhauled and gold-capped, while waiting for the engine to be finished," he wrote to Eliza on March 19. "There's no news, and I am too sick with my teeth to write any if there were!" Charmian's diary entries for the last three weeks in March underscore the intensity of his pain: "He is in agony from teeth . . . Mate goes dentist again, and is having a nerve killed . . . suffers with dying nerve . . . He has awful time at dentist's, and reels home like a drunken man . . . Mate's agony in dental chair, and how he clings to me." Finally, on March 29, dentist and patient—both of them "nervously exhausted"—called it quits.

The *Snark* weighed anchor on April 4, headed toward the western boundary of French Oceania (later French Polynesia) and the Society Islands at Bora Bora and, beyond that, to the westernmost edge of Polynesia at Samoa. They stopped en route the next night at the island of Raiatea. Early on the morning of April 6, as they were getting ready to go ashore, Jack's curiosity was roused by the spectacle of a "tiny outrigger canoe, with [an impossibly large] spritsail, skimming the surface of the lagoon." Although it appeared at first glance to be nothing more than a foot-wide shallow canoe, it was in fact "a sailing machine. And the man in it sailed it by his weight and his nerve—principally by the latter."

The temptation was too much to resist for one who had spent the happiest hours of his boyhood sailing a small boat on San Francisco Bay. "Well, I know one thing," Jack exclaimed. "I don't leave Raiatea till I have a ride in that canoe!"

A few minutes later, he was greeted by the owner of that canoe: a tall, handsome young man "with clear, sparkling, intelligent eyes" and dressed "in a scarlet loin-cloth and a straw hat." In his arms were welcoming presents of fish and vegetables. He spoke almost no English, but by means of sign language Jack gained permission to be taken for a ride in his boat. "Come on for a sail," he called below to Charmian. "But put on your swimming suit. It's going to be wet!"

The ride was a new adventure: "It wasn't real. It was a dream," Jack recalled. "That canoe slid over the water like a streak of silver." Tehei was the sailor, and he invited the Londons to visit his home on the little neighboring island of Tahaa. "Shoes, a shirt, a pair of trousers, cigarettes, matches, and a book to read were hastily crammed into a biscuit tin and wrapped in a rubber blanket, and we were over the side and into the canoe."

As they neared the beach across the lagoon, they saw Tehei's house, "erected on stilts, built of bamboo, with a grass-thatched roof," and "a slender mite of a woman" running to greet them: his wife, Bihaura. Here they discovered the kind of hospitality that had prompted William Ellis a century before to declare that these Polynesian islanders had an unequalled reputation for courtesy. Because the visitors had been drenched with seawater on their flying trip across the lagoon, their hosts provided a tub of freshwater and bath towels, then a dry shirt for Jack and a clean white muslin dress for Charmian. "It is not so much what Tehei and his mate do; it is the way they do it, without apparent unusual effort," she wrote. "We were entertained with a solicitude that lacked servility, a friendliness in which there was no obtrusiveness."

The Londons quickly learned not to openly admire any of the couple's belongings, for it was customary to make gifts of those objects to the guests. Immediately upon Charmian's admiring a lovely Polynesian sewing basket, Bihaura gave it to her; likewise with a thirty-foot roll of straw sennit and an artfully carved poi bowl. Jack made similar mistakes in looking too fondly upon a "gigantic coconut calabash [and] a poi-pounder that dated back to the old stone days." Both were immediately his.

Their visit continued throughout the day and into the early evening, when they were served a sumptuous dinner, starting with "glorious raw fish, caught several hours before from the sea and steeped the intervening time in lime-juice diluted with water. Then came roast chicken," followed by "bananas that tasted like strawberries and that melted in the mouth" and "banana-poi that made one regret that his Yankee forebears ever attempted puddings." All of this was washed down with "sharply sweet" coconut milk. But there was still more to come: "boiled yam, boiled taro, and roasted *feis*" (big, juicy, red-colored bananas). The gustatory climax came in the form of a whole "sucking pig, swathed in green leaves roasted upon the hot stones of a native oven, the most honorable and triumphant dish in the Polynesian culture." The meal was topped off with "coffee, black coffee, delicious coffee, native coffee grown on the hillsides of Tahaa." Jack remarked in his article describing the meal, "We were certainly in the high seat of abundance." Charmian, in her own account, slyly observed, "Tehei did the main cooking (an excellent custom in Polynesia that carries no onus with it)." That night they slept on a "big high bedstead, made up with clean sheets and pillow-cases, with a downy red and white steamer-rug spread across the foot," under a canopy of Bihaura's handcrafted quilts "that would put a New England county fair in the shade."

Describing this idyllic interlude in their voyage, Jack attested that "of all hospitality and entertainment I have known, in no case was theirs not only not excelled, but in no case was it quite equalled. Perhaps the most delightful feature of it was due to no training, to no complex social ideals, but that it was the untutored and spontaneous outpouring from their hearts." Tehei would become the model for his hero in "The Heathen," the story of a noble Polynesian who saves the life of his white "blood-brother" by sacrificing his own.

By mid-April the *Snark* was once again at sea on a fifteen-hundred-mile journey, from Tahiti to Samoa, provisioned abundantly with fresh fruit, vegetables, chickens, and eggs. The boat was also provisioned with a new crew member: Tehei had persuaded Jack to take him to Samoa. He proved himself "a jewel" not only as a host but also as an exceptionally "good sailor—keen, willing, with sharp eye for disorder, and a good hand at the wheel."

The crew worked hard during the next few days out: cleaning, painting, and making the *Snark* properly shipshape. When their chores were done, they would lounge around on deck and eat fruit or play cards. Jack boxed daily with Charmian or Martin. In the evening, Charmian played the ukulele she had brought from Hawaii and sang while Tehei, Nakata, and Wada performed native dances. Included in the *Snark*'s recreational equipment were skipping ropes and tops. "The ropes gave us much needed exercise; and we all took boyish pleasure in spinning the tops," Martin recalled. "I have seen Jack London squat down and spin his tops by the hour, thoroughly absorbed in the fun. He said that this, like his cigarettes, soothed his nerves."

On April 23, Charmian recorded the first anniversary of their departure through the Golden Gate. "I know more about geography than I did a year ago, to say nothing of human nature," she noted in the *Log*, adding that "Outside of the dawns and sunsets, and Jack's indignation over my impertinent suggestion from below that my ventilator was not a deck ash-tray, the only other special incident I can think of is the bleaching, or attempt at bleaching Nakata's hair." However, her diary gives an interesting glimpse into "human nature," particularly Jack's: "Beat Mate 50 points casino. [He takes] a ride on bowsprit after throwing dinner and dishes overboard. A very *bad* boy!"

Three days later they came within sight of the Manu'a Islands, the eastward section of American Samoa. Here, once again, was evidence of Western colonialism. Nine years prior to the Londons' arrival, Germany, Great Britain, and the United States had signed a convention by which the paramount interests of the United States in those Samoan islands east of longitude 171° W. long. were recognized, and Germany's interests in the other Samoan islands were similarly recognized. In return, Great Britain withdrew any claims to Samoa in consideration of rights in Tonga and the Solomon Islands. Time would prove that the Americans got the best of this bargain, with Tutuila and its excellent harbor at Pago Pago, a vital naval base during the Second World War.

The *Snark* dropped anchor on April 29, at Tau Island, where for the next couple of days the Londons were treated royally as guests of King Tui-Manu'a and Queen Vaitupu. Tui-Manu'a had initially objected to American authority, but after a visit to the United States, realizing that opposition would be futile, he wisely submitted. According to Martin Johnson, because the United States wanted the island of Tutuila mainly as a coaling station, not as a colony, the king still governed "with nearly as much authority as he had before." The hospitality with which they greeted the famous American author, his wife, and crew indicated that the Manu'ans were disinclined to hold grudges. When the *Snark* appeared off Tau looking for anchorage, she was met by two whaleboats full of heavily muscled and tatooed Samoan warriors, who towed her in to the best holding ground, singing all the while. "After dark several boatloads came out through the surf, and passed by in the starlight, singing, always singing," Charmian recalled; "and in the night we awoke and heard them in the distance, fishing by torchlight under the Southern Cross."

The next morning they were carried ashore on "the mighty shoulders of the tattooed, red-headed Samoans" and "set high and dry" on the magnificent beach. There they were ceremoniously welcomed in native tongues by "the high men" of the island, whose eloquent greetings were translated by "Viega, the teacher, [who] was able to do their high-flown language into very good English, with admirable grace and dignity." Although the king and queen were visiting a neighboring island, Viega capably served as master of ceremonies, introducing the visitors to 'ava.

This ritual involved the drinking of a stringent beverage squeezed from the grated kava root by "pretty maidens whose hands are first punctiliously washed." As Charmian describes it, when the mixture has achieved the "proper amount of flavour and colour of the root, the 'ava makers all stand up and clap their hands. This signifies to the household that the flowing bowl is prepared, and is also a signal that the house is taboo to intrusion until the drinking is accomplished." In the olden days, she explains, the clapping was a warning against evil spirits. "A cocoanut calabash is now dipped into the bowl and brought by one of the pretty maidens to the guest of honor," then to each of the others in descending order of rank. In this case the cup was passed first to Charmian and second to Jack. Each recipient was expected to drain the cup before passing it along. Charmian described the taste as "the freshest, most mouth-cleansing of drinks, leaving an effect on the tongue like a gargle of listerine." To Jack it was a "delectable toothwash that cleanses all the way down." Both were happy that the manner of preparation had changed from olden times when the kava root was chewed by the pretty maidens.

Having duly passed through this rite of hospitality, they were free to tour the village. Charmian was especially impressed by the beautiful Samoan houses—"far superior to those of Tahiti [with their] lofty and roomy and cool" interiors and exquisite workmanship in beams and thatch and sennit. She was also impressed by the general physical attractiveness of the Samoans, except for the "prevalent disfiguring blindness" (the cause of which was apparently unknown) and the remarkable "number of men without hands" (the cause of which *was* known: dynamiting fish).

She and Jack spent considerable time looking for curios and souvenirs to send back home. Throughout their tour they were followed by crowds of fascinated natives. Especially persistent were the children who, quickly learning that Charmian was attracted to some purplish-red cat-eyes (with which she hoped to make a girdle) and that Jack was willing to pay ten cents apiece, came in droves bringing handfuls of the semiprecious gems. That evening, as they stretched out on the veranda of their guesthouse after supper, they were joined by a half-dozen girls who, seeing that the lovely American lady was very tired, proceeded to give her a relaxing *lomi-lomi* (massage). A little later, a choir of boys from the local school drifted over to serenade the honored guests.

The king and queen returned home on May 1. The Londons were royally impressed: Tui-Manu'a, tall and handsome with his "noble profile and head, firm mouth, slender sensitive hands, and the first fine feet [they had] seen in Polynesia—long, slim, classic, even to the long second toe"—appeared "every inch the part." And his queen was "just the dearest of solid, lovable, wholesome women, with dignity and fine manners." She was also the most generous. After the traditional 'ava ceremony, taking the honored guests by the hand, she led them into the royal bedroom, which was to be their quarters for the night: Here the great "black and gilt four-poster was made up snowily, fresh mats laid on the floor, a reading-stand ready by the bed, bearing a good lamp, and upon the floor a heap of Samoan treasures, all for us . . . while from her own finger the Queen took three turtle-shell rings, inlaid with silver, and placed them on my fingers."

On May 2 they did their best to return a bit of Samoan hospitality by inviting Tui-Manu'a and Vaitupu aboard for a noonday dinner, prepared royally by Wada. When the *Snark* set sail later that afternoon, the king and queen circled the ship three times in their royal whaleboat, waving and singing "I nev-ver will for-ge-ett you!"

The *Snark* made the ninety-mile trip to the island of Tutuila that night and entered the harbor of Pago Pago the next morning very unceremoniously. Because Captain Warren blundered in his choice of anchorage, the *Snark* almost drifted into an old schooner; then, losing his head, Warren came close to crashing the boat into a wooden pier. They were saved from disaster when several officers from the battleship *Annapolis*, spotting their imminent danger, jumped into one of their boats and towed the *Snark* to safety. "We [were] a grinning spectacle to the nautical shore, from the Governor in his high mansion down to the least bluejacket on the beach," said Charmian; "and it had to happen in our own naval station, of all places." Jack, who prided himself on his nautical expertise, felt that they had been made a laughingstock by his pigheaded captain.

Now safely anchored, the *Snark* was besieged by a horde of "perky and impudent" young Tutuilans, who paddled out in canoes and swarmed over the rails. Only after Jack grabbed one and threatened to throw him over the side did the gang retreat. A couple of pretty half-caste coquettes also climbed aboard, but quickly retreated back to their canoe when they spotted Charmian. Once ashore as guest in the governor's mansion, she was immensely pleased "to bathe in a real bathroom in hot running water and cold shower, and to sleep in a bed the rolling and pitching of which exists only in the mind."

Because Jack was eager to visit the grave site of Robert Louis Stevenson and move on ahead of the hurricane season, they sailed from Pago Pago on May 6, having taken on board "a new sailor, one Henry, a Rapa [Easter] Islander." The *Snark* came to anchor at Apia, Upolu, the next evening, and they checked into the luxurious International Hotel, where, at least for another fortnight, they could enjoy the comforts provided by twentieth-century plumbing and electricity. "Such a sleep, and such a rejuvenated sailorwoman this morning!" was Charmian's *Log* entry after she had managed eight hours of uninterrupted rest.

Starting out early the next afternoon, they made their pilgrimage up the mountain to Vailima, Stevenson's home, and then on up the dense jungle path to his grave at the summit. For Martin Johnson the ascent was "nearly ten miles of toil." For Charmian and Jack, it was a labor of love. "Driving over the roads he rode. Road of the Loving Heart," she wrote in her diary. They were profoundly moved when they saw the gravestone with Stevenson's famous epitaph:

Under the wide and starry sky
Dig the grave and let me lie
Glad did I live and gladly die
And I lay me down with a will

This be the verse you grave for me
Here he lies where he longed to be
Home is the sailor home from the sea
And the hunter home from the hill.

As they started back down the trail, Jack said in a subdued voice, "I wouldn't have gone out of my way to visit the grave of any other man in the world."

In the days following their pilgrimage, the Londons were fêted by several plantation owners. They learned that Apia had been a notorious slavery post in previous years and that, in addition to Chinese coolies, natives from the Fiji and Solomon islands had been abducted to work the copra plantations. Though the German government had officially outlawed such practices, some five hundred natives were still being imported every year under the veil of "signed and authorized" recruiting papers.

The next morning Jack started one of his most trenchant exposés of colonialism: "Koolau the Leper," a story that would outrage many members of the white establishment who had given their unqualified blessings to the Londons when the *Snark* landed in 1907. Principal among these was Lorrin Thurston, editor of *The Honolulu Advertiser*, who had introduced them to the members of the new Hawaiian aristocracy. He was pleased with Jack's account of the visit to Molokai, but when he read "Koolau the Leper," he felt betrayed. Writing under the pseudonym of "The Bystander," Thurston branded London as "a sneak of the first water, a thoroughly untrustworthy man and an ungrateful and untruthful bounder [because] he has made the worst out of the leprosy situation here, distorted facts, invented others when the truth was not enough to suit his purpose and thoroughly misrepresented conditions."

Jack was quick to respond that his stories were "things of fiction," having nothing to do with his visit to Molokai, about which he had written an article "that was so satisfactory to the authorities that the stamp of approval was given to it for publication to the world." He was right in contending that the theme of "Koolau" had nothing to do with conditions on Molokai as he had witnessed them, but the underlying theme struck a deeper chord in sounding the somber refrain of exploitive imperialism. A few weeks before his death, Jack remarked, "The white man is a born looter. And just as the North American Indian was looted of his continent by the white man, so was the Hawaiian looted by the white men of his islands." Echoing throughout his "things of fiction" is the dying whisper of Kurtz in Conrad's *Heart of Darkness*: "The horror! The horror!" Jack and his crew would witness greater horrors when they sailed west from Samoa to the "raw edge of savagery."

22

INFERNO

If I were a king, the worst punishment I could inflict on my
enemies would be to banish them to the Solomons. On second
thought, king or no king, I don't think I'd have the heart to do it.

—*THE CRUISE OF THE SNARK*

On May 14 the *Snark*—laden with fruit, a hundred-pound sea turtle,
and four dozen fresh eggs—set to sea once again, headed for Savaii,
their last port of call in the Samoan group. What happened en route
was an omen of what lay ahead of them in the Solomons.

"We have just passed through our worst thunder squall, the most
terrifying thunder I ever heard," recorded Charmian. "It was overwhelming, the silken-blue suffusion of the lightning followed by
frightful crashing of rended elements . . . very interesting for a while,
especially when one is within several feet of a thousand gallons of in-
flammable gas-engine fuel, to say nothing of a tank of kerosene and
two tanks of lubricating oil, as well as 15,000 rounds of ammunition."
They survived the fireworks—only to behold a more ominous spectacle
as the storm abated and the clouds lifted. Ahead of them was the island
of Savaii, "a huge squat shape, warted with volcanoes. And from one
living crater . . . flowed a stream of red lava, the venous blood of the
squat and knobby shape." Although several miles inland, the fiery
eruption and its consequences were clearly visible from the *Snark* as
pillars of fire spewed from the lip of the crater and streams of red-hot
lava oozed down toward the shore, raising great geysers of steam as

they reached the sea. So awestruck were the crew that they could hardly eat dinner that evening. Charmian and Jack slept on deck that night—or tried to sleep but kept rising to watch the spectacle.

The sun opened the next morning like the "gate of heaven, with freight of golden angels. And by day, a pillar of gold to guide us," she wrote. "It is so wonderful, so unbelievable—sailing in a white-speck boat in the tropic sea, steering by a volcano." Curious as always, Jack wanted to see how hot the sea had become. He told Martin to start the engine in case the wind failed. As they edged slowly toward the steaming shore, he stationed Wada at the bow with a thermometer and told him to cry out the temperature every few minutes. "Eighty," the cook announced at the first lowering. "Ninety!" he shouted a few minutes later. As they neared the boiling waters where the fiery serpent was slithering into the breakers, the crew—apprehensive that the heat would ignite the thousand gallons of gasoline in the hold—did their best to fight off panic. By now the boat, enveloped in scalding clouds of steam and suffocating smoke, was within two hundred yards of the flowing lava. Breathing was difficult, and the heat was becoming unbearable. Jerking the thermometer out of the water, Wada, his thin voice choking, spluttered, "One hundred!" At this moment Jack ordered retreat. For once, the capricious engine behaved as they chugged back out of the cauldron.

Freed from immediate danger, they eased farther along the coast seeking safe harbor and witnessing the devastation. The view was appalling. They saw some villages totally destroyed, others deserted. "The lava was all-destructive," Martin recalled:

> We would get nearly to the shore, only to see a reeking stream of lava, further back and creeping down to the sea. Then on we would go again. Everyone else in the boat [was] leaning over the rail in wonder, without any idea of the possibility of the engine's stopping, but my heart was in my mouth all the time, for the wind had dropped, and had the engine ever stopped, it would have been all up with us—nothing could have kept us away from those cascades of lava.

On the afternoon of May 16 they found temporarily safe anchorage at the village of Matautu. Taking the launch to shore, Jack, Charmian, and Martin heard native voices a few hundred yards up from the beach. They followed the sounds and came upon a small white church, where several hundred natives were gathered, praying to be spared from the awful catastrophe that had destroyed their villages. But this village was likewise doomed. "On all sides the red-hot lava was creeping down, though they had managed to divert the flow by building stone walls; but they knew that [was] useless unless the volcano [calmed] down," said Martin. "It was dark when we prepared to go back to the *Snark*. We were stopped just as we got to the launch by a white man, calling to us on the beach. We went back and found a big, jolly Irishman, waiting for us in company with a tall German."

The "big, jolly Irishman" was Dick Williams, administrator of Savaii, and the "tall German" was a trading agent named Barts. Governor Williams was putting his best face on the tragic circumstances. Inviting the group to his big concrete house nearby, he amiably called, "Come on in—the 'ava's just made!" Charmian noted that "this fatherly soul was trying to hide from us a deep anxiety for his people, now being driven out of their homes faster than he can find shelter for them."

When they had finished the customary 'ava, Williams piloted their launch inside the reef to get a closer look at the flowing lava. They landed on a sandy beach within a few hundred feet of the evil-smelling monster that crawled inexorably toward the water. "Eyes smarting, breath coming painfully" from the sulfurous fumes, they "walked hand in hand" toward the fiery stream. Here they witnessed the destruction of all living things on the old land—and the dark creation of new land as the molten mass oozed out into the sea. "And then," wrote Charmian, "I saw, close at hand, what I have all my life dreamed of beholding— living, flowing lava from the heart of a volcano, sluggish, pushing, sticky stuff that forced out through a cooled crust of clinker, like rose-madder from a tube—such a terrible, devastating liquid, growing thicker and more darkly red, more heavily sluggish as we watched, under the cooling of the air." Even though the heat was singeing their hair, like curious children they took sticks and, shielding their faces, tried poking the hot mud for lava souvenirs—but it had already become too thick to adhere.

Panting for fresh air, they made their way back to the launch and found themselves shivering in the soft tropical sea breeze. By this time it was dark except for the lurid glow filtering through what was left of the jungle behind them. Then the moon began to rise "slowly, redly, like a round world of blood . . . Very quiet we were, overcome by what we had seen and were seeing, and touched by the trouble and apprehension of this man who [had] the care and keeping of the island in his hand."

Dick Williams's true character was demonstrated the next day. Before the *Snark*'s crew had finished their breakfast on deck, a boat came out from the shore, and one of the governor's khaki-coated native assistants climbed aboard bearing a bouquet of "creamy blumerias, scarlet double hibiscus, and a fragrant fluffy mass of tiny blossoms and grasses and ferns." Before going ashore, Charmian decorated her big Cook Island hat with hibiscus as a visible gesture of her appreciation. During their chat later that afternoon, she asked Williams if he wasn't lonely on this island so remote from his native land, without wife and family. "Bless me—what would a wife-woman do here," he answered. "Women like luxuries, and society, and diversion—what!—If a woman loved me, she would be happy here? Yes—well, well; but where is the woman to love me? . . . Besides, my children need me. They're all my children, these men and women and young folk . . . They know I am strong, and they respect me. But I rule by love." The Londons would presently discover that the white men in the Solomons ruled by harsher methods.

On the morning of May 20, the *Snark* set sail for the port of Suva, nearly a thousand miles southwest in the Fiji Islands. The first three days were spent in angry gales so strong they threatened to swamp the boat and wash all her crew overboard. Because it was impossible to light a fire in the galley, they ate hardtack when not too seasick. When the weather finally cleared, they discovered that they had been blown off course and that Captain Warren had no idea where they were. In fact, they were apparently trapped within a vast circle of reefs and islets known as the Ringgold Islands—and in danger of crashing against the breakers.

Warren was growing more irascible by the day—so much so that in one fit of temper he lashed out at poor, defenseless Wada, breaking the cook's nose and threatening worse damage before Charmian intervened. Her May 23 diary entry reflects the state of affairs: "Boat untidy. Everybody going to rack and ruin." She concluded that Warren was crazy—"an emotional maniac"—and dubbed him "Captain Blight." The *Snark* reached Suva on May 27, and Jack fired him the next day. When Warren complained that it was because of his prison record, Jack replied that the only reason he hadn't been dismissed earlier was his employer's consideration of that record.

One of the most pleasant surprises after reaching port was a cable from Netta that *The Pacific Monthly* had agreed to pay seven thousand dollars to serialize *Success* under the title *Martin Eden*. After a week of being fed, entertained, and rested by their English hosts, the crew of the *Snark* headed for the New Hebrides, six hundred miles due west from Fiji. Their joy now that the "Blight had been wiped out" was short-lived. Jack caught a bad cold, which he passed along to Charmian, thence to Martin. They slept fitfully. Particularly bothersome were the hordes of cockroaches that gnawed their fingernails and toenails during their fitful dozings. "When I am in my bunk and they crawl over me I don't even bother to brush them off," moaned Martin; "but, of course, we have to skim them from our coffee and chase them out of the food." They suffered infections from scratching all the fresh mosquito bites they had acquired in Fiji; the diabolical sores worsened as the *Snark* sailed deeper into Melanesia. Jack described the sores as "excessively active ulcers": "A mosquito bite, a cut, or the slightest abrasion, serves for lodgment of the poison with which the air seems to be filled. Immediately the ulcer commences to eat. It eats in every direction, consuming skin and muscle with astounding rapidity. The pin-point ulcer of the first day is the size of a dime by the second day, and by the end of the week a silver dollar will not cover it." He resorted to drastic measures, dosing his own sores liberally with corrosive sublimate—an effective treatment but one with insidious aftereffects because of its mercury base. Martin held off for a while, finally surrendering to Jack's cure when his shin had swollen to twice its normal size as the voracious spirochete of yaws ate its way to the bone. At first Charmian seemed to be the only one immune to the infection, boasting that "it was all a matter of pureness of blood"—until she acquired her own little badge of common humanity, "the size of a silver dollar." By the end of the month, to aggravate their miseries, all were suffering the chills and blinding headaches of malarial fever.

There was one bright event during this voyage into hell: Martin recalled that one morning as they were sailing westward through the New Hebrides, several miles away from land, "an animated ball of variegated colors" dropped from the sky onto the deck directly at the feet of Charmian. "Lookie, lookie, what I've got!" she cried as she picked it up. What she held in her hand was a beautiful little bird that had evidently flown too far from its home and had fallen to the deck completely exhausted. The crew stood looking in fascination as Charmian "chirped and tried to talk bird-talk to it." After several minutes' calculation, Jack declared, "If it's a land-bird you are, to the land you go," altering their course and sailing as close as safe to shore of the nearest island. "Critics of the man, Jack London, may call him an infidel," Martin remarked, "but I have little doubt that this is the only time a captain ever went twenty miles out of his way when his fuel was low . . . just to put a poor little bird ashore to go back to its mate and its young."

Later that day they landed at Port Resolution on Tana, one of the southernmost of the New Hebrides. "Hitherto I have told of the gentle, big, brown inhabitants of the eastern islands, known as Polynesia," Martin wrote. "But now we have come into Melanesia [and I find it difficult] to describe a race living in absolute savagery, unwitting of those rules of conduct we have laid down for our guidance, a race whose social relations are vastly different from ours." Totally different in every way from the handsome Polynesians, Charmian observed, the Melanesians were "strange little men" who displayed "Poor bodies with little beauty . . . crooked legs. Bulges in the wrong places." When she asked Jack how she could describe them in her Log, he advised, "'Worse than naked,' and let it go at that."

It was not the absence of physical attractiveness that most repelled the passengers of the Snark: it was the absence of what other cultures generally upheld as moral probity and ethical decency. Here were the antitheses of Rousseau's noble savages: these were treacherous, bloodthirsty cannibals, and worst of all were the Solomon Islanders. They would inspire London's darkest stories. "There is no gainsaying that the Solomons are a hard-bitten bunch of islands" begins "The Terrible Solomons":

It is true that fever and dysentery are perpetually on the walk-about, that loathsome skin diseases abound, that the air is saturated with a

poison that bites into every pore, cut, or abrasion and plants malig-
nant ulcers, and that many strong men who escape dying there return
as wrecks to their own countries. It is also true that the natives of the
Solomons are a wild lot, with a hearty appetite for human flesh and a
fad for collecting human heads. Their highest instinct of sportsman-
ship is to catch a man with his back turned and to smite him a cunning blow with a tomahawk that severs the spinal column at the base
of the brain. It is equally true that on some islands, such as Malaita,
the profit and loss account of social intercourse is calculated in
homicides.

One recipe for "long pig" called for breaking the bones and crushing the joints of victims (most commonly female), then staking them,
still living, up to their necks in running water, often for days, until they
were considered sufficiently tenderized for cooking.

Reprehensible as these customs were, they were scarcely worse than
the actions of the men who had invaded this infernal land. Here London was to witness, just as Conrad had done a generation before in the
Congo, the most damning evidence of colonial rapacity. The Solomons
had been discovered in 1568 by the Spanish explorer Álvaro de Mendaña.
By June 28, 1908, when the Snark docked at Port Mary on Santa Ana,
the southern tip of the Solomons, the Caucasian colony had become
firmly entrenched, and the islands were governed efficiently and profitably, if not always safely, under British protectorate. The natives,
usually outsmarted and outgunned, were nonetheless loath to submit
meekly to the iron rule of the white invaders, the worst of whom were
the "blackbirders." Blackbirding was a racist euphemism for slave trading. Under the pretext of hiring the islanders as paid laborers, the
meanest and toughest of the whites raided native villages and "persuaded" their captives to make their mark on contracts requiring them
to work one to three years on the copra plantations for six British pounds
sterling per annum. At the end of their term, the workers seldom received their pay, having been fined for misconduct and variously charged
for tobacco and other items purchased at the company store. "I saw
[them] at work, and they did not look enthusiastic," recalled Charmian:
"These men work hard and long hours, on a fare of sweet potatoes (ku-
mara), nothing but sweet potatoes, boiled. Some of them have to walk

half an hour to the midday meal—sweet potatoes. Sometimes they may catch a fish, or come by a few bananas. But sweet potatoes form practically their exclusive diet. Any stealing of cocoanuts is severely punished."

Despite bouts of malaria, dysentery, and ulcerating sores, Jack and Charmian were venturing into territories where few white men and fewer white women had ever been. On July 2 they sailed northwest from Santa Ana to the island of Ugi, located barely a stone's throw across the channel from the most dangerous island of all: Malaita. When the *Snark* neared the coastline of Ugi, they were greeted by a whaleboat carrying a white man and three natives. The white man was Frederick A. Drew, a missionary of the Melanesian Society, Church of England; the others were three of the islanders he had succeeded in converting to Christianity. Charmian described him as "the slight, strong blond type of wiry young English rover who has grit enough to go anywhere and do anything. He met us with frank blue eyes and friendly smile, and immediately he stepped aboard everybody was laughing in the best of fellowship because he wore the familiar badge of Melanesia—a white rag about the shin."

Drew guided them in toward the village of Eté Eté, and as evening approached they were met by an Australian trader named Hammond, who piloted them to safe anchorage next to his own small ketch. Both Drew and Hammond had managed to survive several years in the Solomons for two reasons: they had taken enough time and effort to understand the alien psychology of the natives, and unlike the blackbirders and plantation managers, they neither exploited nor otherwise victimized the islanders. In his story "The Inevitable White Man," London remarks, "If the white man would lay himself out a bit to understand the workings of the black man's mind, most of the messes would be avoided."

Dozens of Christian missionaries had lost their heads in Melanesia because of cultural ignorance and religious hubris. In his story "The Whale Tooth," for example, London tells of a Christian martyr named John Starhurst who, armed only with his Bible and his faith that "no man can withstand [the weapons of] Truth and Right," challenges in open combat a native chief armed with "an enormous war-club." At the end of the story, in answer to the question "Where is the brave man?" a chorus of savage voices bellow, "Gone to be dragged into the oven and cooked."

Wiser than Starhurst, Drew had spent a full year studying the customs and learning the language of the Melanesians before attempting any conversions. He "helped them lay out streets, and the dirty village, with its houses stuck anywhere they could find ground to put them, gradually took on a healthful, systematic look." He then rewarded them for building clean new houses, with one yard each of blue calico. Martin noted that "Dr. Drew went no further toward dressing them, for he realized that as soon as a native puts on white man's clothes he begins to imitate the white man, and to imitate the white man in that part of the world is bad policy."

Both Drew and Hammond stayed on board for supper on the evening of the Snark's arrival, enlightening the crew with tales of the dark Solomons. The next morning the newcomers were awakened before breakfast with gifts by Hammond: papayas, limes, and an item Martin said he had almost forgotten came in anything but cans: "the best treat we had had for ages—milk, sweet, fresh cow's milk!" The trader kept a healthy herd of cows and provided "generous gallons of fresh milk, rich and spicy-flavored," along with fresh fruits and vegetables throughout their stay on Ugi.

Later in the day, they accompanied Hammond into the village of Eté Eté, where they recognized the salutary results of Drew's careful work: "the native houses similar but superior to those at Port Mary, and the natives generally of a better class." Even so, the ancient chief Ramana had not forgotten the good old days, eloquently boasting in pidgin English "with cackling glee and horrible grimaces, of the numerous white men he had killed in his day, when 'him fella white man gammon along him fella mouth too much.'" While Ramana delighted in thus impressing the white visitor's attractive wife with his war stories, he refused to let her shake his "sacred hand." According to Melanesian custom, women were "foolish cattle" and he was "taboo to the touch of lesser animals." Noting the accumulated filth on his hands, Charmian took no offense.

Both Hammond and Drew cautioned the crew that despite the missionary's gallant work, there remained many unconverted islanders. Taking this warning in earnest, they marked America's Independence

Day with a celebration dramatically different from the year before with the friendly lepers on Molokai. "We haled forth every dispensable bottle, match-box, piece of cardboard, cocoanut shell, and went at a demonstration of marksmanship that ought to make us taboo from any 'monkeying' in these parts. Mausers, automatic rifles, Colt pistols, Smith & Wesson revolvers, and Mr. Hammond's Sniders [rifles]." Thus, feeling relatively safe, they spent the afternoon sightseeing and shopping for souvenirs to send back home, including not only battle shields, barbed spears, and poison arrows but also a luxurious black skirt and matching bra made from lengthy strands of unpalatable human hair.

That evening, after the rest of the crew had retired, Jack and Charmian managed to steal some precious moments to themselves sitting on the rail of the *Snark*, talking quietly "in the starred darkness of sky and water" about the romance of their great adventure, and joying in the destiny that had prompted them to follow "'the old trail, the out trail, our own trail,' that calls us over the world."

On July 7 the *Snark* dropped anchor at Penduffryn, the largest plantation on the island of Guadalcanal. Most of this twenty-five-thousand-square-mile island was terra incognita to white men in 1908; thirty-five years later it would become very familiar to the outnumbered U.S. marines who fought desperately against entrenched Japanese forces to win the first major land battle in the massive island-hopping campaign of the Second World War. Although the plantation was only four years old, it already showed the marks of an advanced civilization in the midst of a primitive culture. "Here I find myself in the queerest situation, in a big house with a retinue of servants culled from cannibal tribes, on a copra plantation in the heart of the Terrible Solomons," wrote Charmian. "In my charmingly furnished boudoir there is a rack of rifles, always loaded and ready, and I am to keep my revolver with me night and day."

Penduffryn was owned by two Britishers, Thomas Harding and George Darbishire, who, with the help of a manager named C. L. Bernays, had already brought five hundred acres of copra under profitable cultivation. Charmian was struck by Harding's singular appearance in this alien setting:

[He was a] handsome Englishman, of medium height and weight, with blue eyes and black lashes and hair, a cupid-bow mouth with even teeth and a small moustache . . . clad in a white "singlet" and white lava-lava with coloured border, and barefoot [while on] his head is an enormous Baden-Powell, and in his ears are gold rings which lend a Neapolitan touch, [and] from his neck depends a gold chain with a locket in which he carries a miniature of his wife.

Because his wife was in Sydney when they arrived, Charmian was given her rooms and personal servant until her return. So excited were the hosts by the visit of the celebrated *Snark* that they proposed that the Londons consider this plantation their home while exploring all the surrounding islands. "You and Jack will make the mistake of your lives if you do not stay around here a few months, making Penduffryn your base for cruises that are unmatched by anything left in the world," Harding cajoled Charmian. So charmed was she by his proposal that she made him an unusual promise: "to do something I seldom attempt— coax my husband."

Coax him she did, and under the misapprehension that his tropical ailments were on the mend, Jack agreed to the proposition. "The *Snark* adventure is only just beginning—indeed, to-morrow we do our first real exploring, a trip up the Balesuna in canoes, to a village where no white woman has been, and, a few miles beyond, a place where no white man has ever set foot," Charmian wrote. It had been only a few years since a group of explorers from an Austrian warship fatefully named *Albatross* had ventured inland and "made friends" with the bushmen, who then proceeded to kill and "kai-kai" all but a couple who escaped to tell the gory tale. Until now, nobody else had felt curious enough to repeat the adventure.

"Sun he come up!" was the call from Vaia-Buri, their Solomon servant, on Sunday morning, July 12. Despite a vicious attack of malaria, Jack dosed himself with quinine so that he, along with Charmian and Martin, could canoe upriver with Harding and Bernays into the heart of the island. Well armed for battle, they encountered no openly hostile natives. What most impressed them was the lush beauty of virgin Nature as yet undefiled by the white man's touch: "vivid flame-red blossoms and vari-colored morning glories . . . great black velvet butterflies, accompanied by flocks of little blue ones."

When they returned to Penduffryn, they were met by Darbishire, who had just returned from Sydney, Australia, aboard the steamer *Moresby*. "Darby" was a striking contrast and complement to his partner Hardy. Charmian described him as "a big blond Englishman, vastly tall, very pink, and so lovable that to shake his long, kind, freckled hand is to find a friend." Like the Londons, he was a Kipling fan who could recite their favorite poems while they lounged on the veranda.

He was also an inveterate party animal. Within a day of his return to the plantation, he had instigated an elaborate entertainment. "Everyone was so happy," Martin recalled, "and we acted like children. We had big card games and even a masquerade ball. Darbishire, who was always the life of the plantation, dressed as an English lady, and I was his partner to the dance." Charmian provided music with her ukulele. When the fun lagged as the players began to wind down, Darby jump-started them again with hashish. A mock funeral replete with coffin, skulls, flowers, and candles was staged over the semiconscious body of Bernays as Darby groaned loudly through a horn during the funeral march. "A circus" was Charmian's succinct diary summary. The circus was still in progress two days later when she decided to dress up Darby "in rouge and garters and pantalettes" while Martin painted his face.

"So tired. Mate also tired," Charmian wrote on July 20—but the party was not over. Darby was up early the next morning, "rouged to kill, eating doughnuts and doughnuts and then some." That evening, Jack decided to try hashish—with a repeat of the effects he had suffered a few years earlier when he made a hashish sandwich at George Sterling's prompting: "He went clear off his head, acted so wild that Mrs. London was frightened; and no one else would take it," Martin recalled. He was "sick, 3 times," Charmian noted. "Put him to bed about midnight, and sleep hard." He was "sitting up and reading" the following day but admitted that "he could never become a hasheesh fiend."

By the early morning of July 22 the party was over and the revelers were paying the penalty. Harding was in a rotten mood with a bad hangover. Charmian remarked "Poor Darbishire's sad and silly condition." In addition to his sores, fever and malaria, Jack was now suffering from a rectal fistula and diarrhea, "keeping his bowels in check with cholera-pills and opiate." Two days later, Martin declared he had suffered his own fill of Solomon miseries and was ready to go back home to Kansas. His fever and yaws had worsened, and the daily dosings of quinine, corrosive sublimate, and blue vitriol had nearly driven him crazy: "I was looking forward to getting out of this particular part of the world. It was too wild and raw, too full of sickness and sudden death." Fortunately, Jack persuaded him to change his mind.

Fun-loving Darby's "shadow," or darker self, now appeared. After word reached the plantation that several Malaitan workers from a station fourteen miles south had run off to the jungle vowing to take some white heads back home as trophies, a thorough search for weapons was made among the huts at Penduffryn. When spears were discovered in one of the huts, the two culprits were stripped and whipped in the presence of all the other workers. Using a big boar-hide whip, Darbishire "gave them the worst licking I ever saw anyone get," said Martin. "He made deep cuts in their hide, from which the blood spurted. It nearly made me sick, but I knew the whipping was necessary; for it is solely by intimidation that the white man rules in the Solomons."

On August 8, Captain Jansen of the *Minota*, a notorious blackbirding yacht, invited the Londons to join him in returning to their home islands a boatload of native workers who had completed their tours of duty on the plantations. Charmian and Jack were interested in seeing for themselves the kinds of extreme situations they had been hearing about. Originally built as "a gentleman's yacht in Australia—a beautiful rakish thing of teak and bronze and lofty cedar, fin-keeled [and] very fast," the *Minota* had been intended for finer use. The beautiful teak door to the main cabin was disfigured by tomahawk marks, left there a few months before by a party of rampaging Malaitans who had broken in "for the trove of rifles and ammunition locked therein after bloodily slaughtering Jansen's predecessor, Captain McKenzie."

The present complement of the overcrowded yacht included, along with Captain Jansen and First Mate Jacobsen, a double crew of fifteen Solomon Islanders. The passenger list comprised some two score homebound recruits, the Londons, Nakata and Wada, plus a surprise passenger: Jansen insisted that Charmian and Jack take his quarters, and when she opened the door she met "the shy, half-wild eyes" of a native girl. She was the daughter of a Malaitan chief who had given her in order to curry favor with the white recruiter. He had assured Jansen that she would be a delectable morsel if the captain decided to "kai-kai" her. "She's an embarrassing parcel," Jansen said, "but I thought too much of my neck to refuse her." Virtually the entire near-naked body of the terrified girl was covered with *bukua*, an infection caused by a loathsome "vegetable parasite that invades the skin and eats it away. The itching is intolerable. The afflicted ones scratch until the air is filled with fine dry flakes." Jansen had vowed to take the miserable girl to a Christian mission as soon as he finished this recruiting trip. "It's all I can do . . . If I leave her anywhere else, ten to one she'd be kai-kai'd before I'm out of sight. The fleshy parts of a woman's forearm and leg are the favorite feast-bits . . . But they wouldn't get so much off her," he said, looking at her infected body.

Even though Jansen had given the Londons the captain's quarters, this was anything but a luxury cruise. "It was insufferably hot in our bunks," Charmian wrote, and the incessant shrill chatter of the recruits, many of whom were suffering from seasickness, continued throughout the night. In addition to their nausea and *bukua*, many of the natives were afflicted with Solomon sores, some "with holes in their legs so terrible that a fist could thrust in to the bone . . . Whenever we see a particularly horrible case, we retire to a corner and deluge our own sores with corrosive sublimate," Charmian confessed. "And so we live and eat and sleep on the *Minota*, taking our chance and pretending it is good."

Nor was this a normal "seeking" cruise. They were taking their chances, and no amount of pretending it was good could obscure the fact that the diseases and even graver dangers were real. That reality became more evident when, before dropping off their first group of recruits, Jansen ordered a double row of barbed wire erected around the deck. It was further evident when each landing was managed with two whaleboats: one carrying recruits, the other guarding with loaded rifles in case the bushmen decided to attack. As they entered one bay after another, Charmian found herself fascinated by "the primeval stillness of jungle that grew to the water." In some instances there would not even be "the whistle of a 'watch-bird'" to break the silence. "You wouldn't dream that a hundred pairs of eyes or so were looking right at us now, would you?" Jansen observed. "They're not missing an eye-winker—I know them," he added grimly. At some places, although the beaches seemed clear, he refused to land his passengers. At others he dynamited fish, flushing out the natives to share the easy catch. At an occasional village he felt it might be relatively safe for Charmian to go ashore to mingle with the native women at market—wearing a Colt .32-caliber revolver on her hip.

A blond, blue-eyed New Yorker of Dutch stock who had abandoned an uncongenial home life to follow the lure of the sea at the age of eleven, Jansen had not totally abandoned his culture. Like Charmian and Jack, he loved good music, and he had brought along a tiny Edison phonograph with some of his favorite records for relaxing at the end of a hard day. There is something both ironic and strangely touching in the image of the three of them—Charmian, Jack, and Jansen—lying around on deck after supper in the darkest heart of Melanesia "listening blissfully" to the thin, scratchy lyrics of Gilbert and Sullivan emerging from "cracked and much-worn records," while below them, First Mate Jacobsen lies in his "insufferably hot" cabin silently enduring an attack of malarial fever, and a miserable bunch of passengers crowded into the main cabin bemoan their seasickness and other ailments.

Within a week of their sailing from Penduffryn, Charmian had also been laid out with fever. As the Londons' sores continued to multiply, so did the horde of cockroaches that had selected their cramped quarters for "a combined Fourth of July and Coronation Parade," Jack testified. "They were from two to three inches long; there were hundreds of them, and they walked all over us. When we attempted to pursue them, they left solid footing, rose up in the air, and fluttered about like humming-birds." Charmian's diary entry on August 13 reveals her miseries: "Mosquitoes, and not much sleep . . . Weak from fever, I cry at the least provocation, or none, weep hard and long." The worst was yet to come.

On the next day, Captain Jansen landed the last of his cargo of recruits at Malu, on the northern tip of Malaita. There they were greeted by George Caulfeild, "a slenderly built, sandy-haired man, one of the sweetest and most unaffectedly righteous souls we ever knew." This mild-mannered missionary had managed to survive longer than any of his predecessors on the most savage of all the Solomon Islands. Veteran that he was, Caulfeild was fully aware of the precariousness of his situation. And just as Jack had listened to the tales told in the Northland by the sourdoughs and *chechaquos*, so he listened, mentally recording and

assimilating, as this missionary and Captain Jansen traded horror stories about massacres, severed white heads, and cannibal feasts.

But he had no need to rely on secondhand experience for one near-
fatal incident. On August 19, Captain Jansen prepared to leave Malu
Bay with a fresh load of recruits bound for Penduffryn. It was a sunny
day, and all omens seemed favorable for sailing. It would take only a
few minutes of careful steering to ride the strong current through the
narrow entrance of the encircling reef. But just as they were about to
clear the entrance, a sudden storm hit them, driving the ship onto
the reef and breaking the anchor chain.

"Bedlam reigned. All the recruits below, bushmen and afraid of the
sea, dashed panic-stricken on deck and got in everybody's way. At the
same time the boat's crew made a rush for the rifles." The helpless boat
was now completely at the mercy of the storm, being lifted up and
down by the swelling waves like a child's plaything. The deck rolled almost perpendicular to one side, then to the other, while the crew tried
desperately to dodge as "trade-boxes, booms, and eighty-pound pigs of
iron ballast rushed across from rail to rail and back again." At the same
time, all hell was breaking loose below: the recruits "were screaming
and making frantic rushes to the deck—only to clamber back down
when they encountered greater dangers topside."

The chaos on board was not the worst of their troubles. Although no
natives had been in sight when the *Minota* hit the reef, suddenly, "like
vultures circling down out of the blue, canoes began to arrive from every quarter." Jansen and his crew, holding steady with their rifles, kept
the canoes at bay, but the rest of the tribesmen now began "flocking
down from the hills, armed with spears, Sniders, arrows, and clubs,
until the beach was massed with them." The situation was critical. The
Minota, firmly in the reef's grasp, was absorbing blow after blow from
the heavy seas. In hours, or perhaps less, its beautiful teak hull would
be pounded into splinters. If the crew attempted to escape in the
whaleboat, all their rifles and ammunition would not be enough to
hold off the surrounding horde.

In this hour of direst need, Mr. Caulfeild was sent to deliver them
from their enemies. The encircling canoes parted just enough to let the
missionary's boat through. Jansen had already written an SOS to

Captain Keller of the *Eugenie*, another blackbirder, anchored five miles to the south, but could find no way to deliver the note. He offered a half case of tobacco to anyone who would run the errand. None of the surrounding cannibals were interested. They simply "grinned and held their canoes bow-on to the breaking seas." They knew it would be just a matter of waiting patiently out of harm's way until everything and everyone on board would be theirs for the taking.

Caulfeild broke through the black wall of resistance: "I know what you think," he shouted at the crowd. "You think plenty tobacco on schooner and you're going to get it. I tell you plenty rifles on schooner. You no get tobacco, you get bullets!" Finally, after several minutes of silence, one lone savage paddled up and accepted the offer. Within three hours, "a whale-boat, pressing along under a huge spread of canvas, broke through the thick of a shrieking squall to windward":

> It was Captain Keller, wet with rain and spray, a revolver in his belt, his boat's crew fully armed, anchors and hawsers heaped high amidships, coming as fast as the wind could drive . . . The vulture line of canoes that had waited so long broke and disappeared as quickly as it had formed . . . And down below in the wreck of the cabin the missionary and his converts prayed to God to save the *Minota*. It was an impressive scene: the unarmed man of God praying with cloudless faith, his savage followers leaning on their rifles and mumbling amens.

Later, after sunset, believing they would be safer in his own shack, Caulfeild took Charmian, Nakata, and Wada—along with all their luggage and the ship's money and mail—ashore in his whaleboat. One of his own devoted followers volunteered to stand guard while the missionary scouted out the situation on the beach. Too keyed up for sleep, Charmian decided to pass the time writing a letter home to Aunt Netta: "I am writing on a little green-topped table on which lie my five-shooter and a Winchester automatic rifle . . . Wouldn't it be funny if I actually should have to fire on some one? Well, if it is necessary, I'll call up a firm New England jaw, and go to it; and if I fire, I'll not miss, I promise!"

Fortunately, she did not have to fire on anyone. The *Minota* somehow withstood three days of heavy pounding and was finally pulled free on August 21. On the next afternoon, the *Eugenie*, which had come to their rescue, sailed out of the bay with the Londons aboard. "Almost homesick at leaving Malu," Charmian wrote. Four days later, safely aboard the *Snark*, she maintained, "I *am* having a good time— the time of times; for I am doing what I want to do, in the company I crave, with 'life and love to spare,' and too absorbed in the potentialities of being to be more than superficially arrested by the flip of little irks or fears."

Those "little irks and fears" would become very large during the next couple of months. Their dream voyage around the globe was falling apart along with the crew of the *Snark*. The whole crew, not just Jack, was suffering from a variety of tropical maladies: fever, dysentery, yaws, plus a fresh dermatological nightmare called *gari-gari* ("scratch-scratch"), which made the miseries of poison oak seem like child's play. Jack learned that the entire crew of the *Sophia Sutherland* had been wiped out a few years earlier when they had contracted the disease in the Solomons and, failing to get proper medical aid, died from blood poisoning. As if all these were not enough to discourage him, he was also suffering from hives, the painful rectal fistula, and a weird ailment that caused his hands to swell so badly that he could not grasp the wheel to steer the boat; moreover, his fingernails and toenails began to grow prodigiously thick, while the skin on hands and feet flaked off like fish scales. Both he and Charmian began to fear that he had contracted leprosy from their visit to Molokai.

Regardless, they were reluctant to give up their dream. Back aboard the *Snark*, they continued their Melanesian explorations for another two months. Jack's medical problems continued to worsen. "'Tis the witching hour of midnight, when tired wives yawn; and I have just watched Jack fall uneasily asleep in a copious sweat, after a raving period of intolerable fever-burning," Charmian wrote as they were headed toward the Lord Howe Atoll. "[He] is sleeping with one eye half open, and I wish he would either close it or wake up, he looks so ghastly . . . But he takes his attacks easier than I do, for at their height his mind wanders, and in the easement of temperature he falls asleep, and so misses the conscious nerve-suffering that I endure because I cannot go out of my head." On September 28 she confessed in her diary, "Not much sleep, shaky in nerves. I cry and cry." She entered a slightly different note in her *Log* on that date: "I do not feel well any of the time—am tired and listless; but a strange elation of happiness possesses me, and all's well."

All was far from well. "I have just returned from a voyage on the *Snark* up to Lord Howe and Tasman Islands," Jack wrote to George Brett four weeks later: "We were gone over two months on the trip, during which the *Snark* was a hospital ship. There was never a time when some of us were not sick, and most of the time most of us were sick . . . And all the time I think I've been the sickest of anybody on board." On November 4 he and Charmian sailed aboard the *Makambo* for Sydney, Australia, arriving there ten days later. On November 30 Jack was operated on for two fistulas. The doctors knew how to treat his malaria and his yaws, but they were baffled by the affliction that resembled leprosy:

> No case like it had ever been reported. It extended from my hands to my feet so that at times I was as helpless as a child. On occasion my hands were twice their normal size, with seven dead and dying skins peeling off at the same time. There were times when my toe-nails, in twenty-four hours, grew as thick as they were long . . . It did not mend, and it was impossible for me to continue the voyage. The only way I could have continued it would have been by being lashed in my bunk, for in my helpless condition, unable to clutch with my hands, I could not have moved about on a small rolling boat.

When he told Charmian his decision to abandon their cruise, she "broke down and sobbed unrestrainedly." Still suffering from the mysterious skin ailment, he was released from the hospital on December 18. Five days later he hired the veteran sea captain Charles Reed to go with Martin and bring the *Snark* down to Sydney.

Though "miserable and weak" and "crazy with hands and threatened feet," he was able to report the heavyweight boxing match for the world championship between Jack Johnson and Tommy Burns on December 26 for *The New York Herald* and *The Australian Star*. Because of his celebrity status, the officials bent the rules prohibiting women as spectators and allowed Charmian to watch the bout. "Inside, only woman among 20,000 men," she noted in her diary. "It seemed like a funeral to have Burns beaten so terribly. Johnson merely played with him."

In mid-January 1909 the couple traveled down to Tasmania hoping that the cooler climate would hasten the healing process. While improved, they continued to suffer from occasional spells of fever, and Jack's hands refused to heal completely. They returned to Sydney a month later, and on March 3 Captain Reed and Martin brought the *Snark* into the harbor. They spent the next few weeks bringing closure to this, their greatest adventure. Jack advanced enough money to Martin so that he could fulfill his ambition to circle the globe back to Kansas. Tehei and Henry returned to their homes. Wada worked his way back to Honolulu as a ship's cook. Nakata would be their most cherished helpmate for the next half-dozen years. On April 8 the three of them left Australia aboard the *Tymeric*, a 330-foot tramp steamer bound for Guayaquil, Ecuador. Because the ship was not authorized to carry passengers, Jack signed on as purser, Charmian as stewardess, and Nakata as cabin boy.

The *Snark* had been sold for a mere fraction of the original cost to an English syndicate to be used for blackbirding. Charmian and Jack learned later how lucky they had been to escape the Solomons alive. Both Captain Keller of the *Eugenie* and Claude Bernays of Penduffryn plantation had been murdered and beheaded, while jolly Darbishire had died from dysentery.

Charmian concluded her *Log* on the hopeful note that she and Jack would "fit out another and larger boat, and do it all over again, and more—and do it more leisurely, more wisely under the tropic sun." They would sail in larger boats; however, their next adventure would be on land, furrowing the rich earth in the Valley of the Moon.

23

THE AGRARIAN DREAM AND LOSS OF JOY

> I am rebuilding worn-out hillside lands that were worked out
> and destroyed by our wasteful California pioneer farmers . . . I
> believe the soil is our one indestructible asset.
>
> **—LONDON TO GEDDES SMITH**

Once out in the open sea, away from the humid climate of Sydney,
Jack's health, and particularly his swollen hands, began to improve.
Both he and Charmian still suffered from intermittent bouts of fever,
but within a week they were strong enough to resume their daily exercise: she walking a mile back and forth on deck, he boxing with the
ship's mates. They were both working regularly again now—Jack on
the home stretch of his novel, Charmian typing up his chapters—and
relaxing the way they had in the past—writing letters home and playing the ukulele, both playing casino and cribbage in the evenings,
catching up on their reading and their lovemaking. He finished his
Solomon novel on April 22, and the next day—the second anniversary
of their sailing the *Snark* out through the Golden Gate—they celebrated by reading *Adventure* aloud.

He immediately began work on two of his most uncharacteristic
stories. "I enjoy listening to the flow of yarns Mate and Capt. keep
going," Charmian wrote. She was not merely listening, but also tran-
scribing Captain McIlwaine's Scottish brogue, which Jack would use
as dialogue. The first, "The Sea Farmer," would be "the tragedy of the
farmer who, for economic reasons, must be a sailor." The story was

rejected twenty times before being accepted by *The Bookman* for seventy-five dollars, a tenth of what his stories made in *The Saturday Evening Post* and *The Cosmopolitan*. As one editor explained, this was not "the sort of story one would expect to find should we advertise in advance a 'Jack London Story.'"

Next he began jotting down notes for his second "steamer story": "Island McGill folk . . . Try all manner of ways of working in the peasant psychology—be deft & delicate." He titled it "Samuel," but as with "The Sea Farmer," his accurate portrayal of Scottish local color and dialogue made it too different from a "Jack London Story." After a score of rejections, it was finally accepted by *The Bookman* for one hundred dollars.

Writing to Jim Whitaker on May 2, London bragged about how well he was sparring with all three of the ship's mates. "I took the third clean off his feet yesterday with a left hook. All I can say, despite two game thumbs and a dozen face bruises, that I'm the least marked of any of them. They are all husky young English fellows and they are not afraid of taking punishment nor are they afraid to give it." Jack's daily sparring matches brought to mind the several bouts he had witnessed in Australia, and immediately after finishing "Samuel," he began writing "A Piece of Steak," destined to become a classic of the ring. Featuring the hard-fought contest between an aging former champion and an aspiring young contender, the story is a brilliant dramatization of physical action; it is also a moving allegory of the timeless theme of Youth vs. Age.

On May 19 the *Tymeric* docked at Guayaquil, Ecuador; and two days later the Londons departed by train for Quito. Built alongside the Andes mountain range, and opened for traffic in 1908, the 288-mile zigzag railroad from Durán to Quito was called "the most dangerous railway in the world." Earthquakes, landslides, rockslides, and washouts were a constant threat to the trains shuttling along the narrow-gauge tracks. Charmian mentions that a big rock fell on the roof of their car but apparently did no major damage.

They reached Quito on May 23, in time for dinner at the Posada Royal Hotel—which was less than "Royal": chickens were roosting outside in the vegetable garden, a green cockatoo had made his home in Nakata's room, native women were doing their washing on the same floor with the guests, someone discharged a revolver in the early hours, the beds were infested with fleas, and the "Toilet, 'excusado'—*Used paper in box*."

The highlight of the two-week stay in Quito was their introduction to the bullfight. "A cowardly sport" was Charmian's succinct verdict. Jack cheered for the bull and elaborated her verdict in the story he began the next morning, vigorously indicting what he considered the sport's gratuitous cruelties. He said he wanted also to dramatize "the essential differences between the Spanish and Anglo-American temperaments." He titled his story "The Madness of John Harned," and his protagonist goes into a murderous rage upon witnessing the horrible goring of a horse in the bullring.

Charmian noted that they were "not sorry" to leave Quito when they boarded the train on the morning of June 8. Two weeks later they sailed on the SS *Erica* for Panama, having decided "to return home by way of Colón via New Orleans." They arrived in Panama on June 25 and, during the following week, caught up with their correspondence, shopping, and loving: "Such adorable things! Such silks and pongees, linens and embroideries! . . . We spent over $200.00 . . . Mate the lover. Never-ending charm and novelty of each other . . . He's so in love with my love for my things."

On the morning of July 2 they took the train to Culebra to view the area where U.S. forces were constructing a canal that would join the Atlantic and Pacific oceans: "Evidence of work everywhere, engines puffing everywhere. Excavating, and tons of dirt going along . . . Wonderful piece of engineering." They celebrated Independence Day at the Hotel Tivoli, Panama. "*The Glorious Fourth!* Last 4th we spent at Ugi, Solomon Islands, and made great noise with our guns and revolvers. Dear lost *Snark-Days!*" Charmian lamented.

They would find better days ahead. On July 18, after a brief layover in New Orleans, they boarded the Texas and Pacific Railway for "home-sweet-home" via the Grand Canyon, arriving in Oakland on July 21. While in Oakland, they united again with friends and family. Three days later they took the train to Glen Ellen: "The *dear* ranch. We ride all over it," she wrote. "Sleep well."

The ranch had expanded considerably during their absence. To the original 129 acres of the Hill Ranch, Netta had negotiated to add the

127-acre La Motte Ranch, the 24-acre Caroline Kohler Ranch, and the 9-acre Fish Ranch. The additional acreage was separated from the Hill Ranch by the 700-acre Kohler and Frohling Ranch, which Jack would purchase in 1910. Because of the disastrous physical consequences of his *Snark* voyage, his "seeking" was no longer aimed seaward, but landward. During the next seven years, with the help of Eliza Shepard, who became his ranch superintendent and business manager in early 1910, he worked to fulfill an agrarian dream that had perhaps been latent in his vision ever since his childhood on the land John London had successfully farmed.

"I go into farming because my philosophy and my research have taught me to recognize the fact that a return to the soil is the basis of economics," Jack declared. "I see my farm in terms of the world, and the world in terms of my farm . . . I adopted the policy of taking nothing off the ranch. I raised stuff and fed it to the stock. I got the first manure spreader ever seen up there, and so put the fertilizer back on the land before its strength had leaked out." He also applied the practices of tillage, crop rotation, and terracing he had observed during his trip to the Far East. "You increase the organic content by levelling, preventing the destructive erosive effects that draw from it the organic content—so that instead of one-tenth of one meager crop a year you can grow three rich crops a year."

He erected the first hollow-block silo in the West and invented a circular rock-and-concrete "pig-palace," devising a system of flushing and sanitizing his piggery and barns so effectively that one English visitor said the premises were "sweet as a nut." He subscribed to more than a score of agricultural journals, which he read intensively, along with reports issued by the U.S. Department of Agriculture. He also kept in touch with the horticultural work of his Santa Rosa neighbor the famous "plant wizard" Luther Burbank. As Burbank recalled, "Jack London was a big healthy boy with a taste for serious things, but never cynical, never bitter, always good-humored and humorous, as I saw him, and with fingers and heart equally sensitive when he was in my gardens."

Jack's good humor may have been due to another factor. On January 30, Charmian wrote, "Send off $10.00 order to W. H. Companion for baby patterns, flannels, embroider patterns etc. Mate cheerfully gives me checks and lovingly joshes me." A month earlier she had confided, "There really can't be a doubt about it. Mate's proud as a peacock, and I'm pretty interested and happy myself tho' I tire easily, and begin to wish I'd nothing to do—for a change." This was all that was needed to make their marriage complete. As much as he loved his two daughters, he also wanted a son, but it didn't really matter that much to him. If a son, they would name him "Mate." If a daughter, that would be just fine: "Joy" would be her name. The next half year would be one of the happiest in their lives.

"Mate so sweet and tender and 'loves' me every time I come near him" was a typical diary entry during these early months of 1910. "Mate dear love, tells me, tries to tell me what this all means to him. 'But for the woman I love to be carrying our baby.' In his sleep he touches it, passes his hand over and over it with infinite gentleness. Last night, only half awake, he got me on his shoulder: 'Dear sweetheart—I do love you!' I am so happy."

Their connubial idyll was briefly interrupted by a trip down the coast to George Sterling's colony. "Pleasant crowd,—and lovely day," Charmian wrote at Carmel-by-the-Sea on February 27. "Mate so kind and helpful—assists me around. Baby is calming down a bit." Members of the group, with Sterling serving as master of ceremonies, included Arnold Genthe; Herbert Heron, Cloudesley's half brother, with whom Jack would later collaborate on the play *Gold*; Ernest Untermann, German-born painter and one of the founders of the Socialist Party of America; and (Harry) Sinclair Lewis, "a tall, gangling young man in his early twenties," as described by Genthe.

In early 1910, "Hal" Lewis was still a literary comer struggling to make a name for himself. Sensing opportunity, he quickly latched on to the big-name author. He was hungry for cash, and Jack was hungry for fresh plots to keep his own literary mill turning. On March 10 the two sat up until one o'clock, according to Charmian, "discussing plots for plays." She might have added "and stories," in light of the plots Jack decided to use: "Mate bought $70.00 worth of them, at $5.00 apiece." He would ultimately buy another baker's dozen before deciding that he'd provided the young writer enough financial aid.

A fortnight on the "Seacoast of Bohemia" was enough for Jack. It was more than enough for Charmian, who repeatedly complained in her diary not only about the maddening tobacco poisoning and poison oak but also about the maddening bohemians: "I am tired—tired of people, and deadly tired of seeing 'em *drunk*. How I truly *hate* all that!" By March 13 she was physically ill, running a fever. They left for Oakland the next day, and on the Ides of March she fainted while getting her hair done at Marvin's Salon. "I am 'all in,' and wish I were 'all out.' I want to be a woman again," she complained. "This is not my day." It was not her nature to indulge in self-pity. Back home a few days later, she was again her old (*new*) self: "*ME* Charmian Kittredge, making baby-clothes for my *own*! Mate is adorable."

At the same time, Mate was beginning a second attempt to become "Jack London, Playwright." On January 25 the Londons had gone to the MacDonough Theatre in Oakland to see Olga Nethersole in William Hurlbut's *The Writing on the Wall*. Nethersole's agent told Jack, "[She] is much interested in social questions and Socialism and thinks if you two could get together you would have a soul fest." After the play, he and Charmian took the celebrated English actress to dinner at the Saddle Rock. "A gracious & beautiful woman," Charmian noted. "Crazy to have Mate write a play for her, etc. It would be a great thing."

Theft, the play he wrote for her, was not "a great thing"—and was never performed in either of their lifetimes. It was far too pedantic to make for good theater. Time and again the hero and the heroine interrupt the action to belabor the audience with long-winded diatribes against exploitive capitalism. London sent the manuscript to Olga on July 12, giving her permission to "cut, slash, alter, do what you please with it." She first responded that she liked the play, but a few months later changed her mind, placing the onus on her production company. It probably occurred to her that *Theft* would be too financially risky to perform before genteel bourgeois audiences. "Nethersole fell down, because she signed a 2 yrs. engagement with the Schuberts, & they had other plans—in spite of the fact, after reading the play, that she wrote me 'how much money' *she was going to make for me*," Jack wrote to Blanche Partington. "Show me an actress, & I'll name her as cheaper than the woman on the street."

On April 28, Jack took the train down to watch a boxing match between Tommy McCarthy and Owen Moran at Dreamland Rink in San

Francisco. The bout was fairly even until the sixteenth round, when Moran landed an overhand right that decked his opponent, causing McCarthy to strike the back of his head on the ring floor. McCarthy died shortly thereafter with a fractured skull. That tragedy and the events of the following week served as the genesis for one of London's most interesting short stories, "The Night-Born," in which he dramatizes the contrast between the "Man-Mean City," exemplified in the death of a young boxer, and the virginal purity of Nature-in-the-Wild.

Jack brought three notorious guests with him when he returned home on Sunday: "Red Emma" Goldman; her "erstwhile attorney," E. E. Kirk; and her fellow anarchist "partner" Ben Reitman. "I had met [London] with other young socialist students at the Strunskys' on my first visit to California, in 1897," Goldman recalled. "I had since read most of his works and I was naturally eager to renew our acquaintance." There was another reason she wanted to renew their acquaintance: she wanted him to support her educational project, the Modern School of the Ferrer Association in New York, and she invited him to attend her fund-raising lecture in San Francisco.

"Dear Emma Goldman," he answered: "I have your note. I would not go to a meeting even if God Almighty were to speak there. The only time I attend lectures is when I am to do the talking. But we want you *here*. Will you not come to Glen Ellen and bring whomever you have with you?" As Goldman later reflected: "Who could resist such an amiable invitation? I had only two friends with me . . . but even if I had brought a whole caravan, Jack and Charmian London would have welcomed them, so warm and genuine was the hospitality of those two dear people."

> Here was youth, exuberance, throbbing life. Here was the good comrade, all concern and affection . . . We argued about our political differences, of course, but there was in Jack nothing of the rancour I had so often found in the socialists I debated with. But, then, Jack London was the artist first, the creative spirit to whom freedom is the breath of life . . . In any case it was not Jack London's politics that mattered to me. It was his humanity, his understanding of and his feeling with the complexities of the human heart.

Goldman was no less complimentary in her praise of Charmian, whom she remembered as "a gracious hostess, gentle and loving in her expectant motherhood," a hostess who, during their three-day stay at the ranch, "hardly rested, except after dinner, when she would sew on the outfit for the baby while we argued, joked, and drank into the wee hours of the morning."

Charmian regarded Emma as "not remarkable intellectually but is a good, clean, wholesome, lovable woman—tho' many might never guess it." Reitman, on the other hand, she found "rather impossible, but interesting for a *short* spell." In her biography, she recounted one of Jack's practical jokes. Near Reitman's dinner plate was placed a small red volume titled *Four Weeks, a Loud Book.* His curiosity roused, Reitman opened it—and it exploded like a firecracker. Recalling the incident, Jack exclaimed, "Never did any one jump so high as that red anarchist!"

Goldman and Reitman left on May 2, and Lucy Parsons arrived the next evening. The Londons were "delighted with her. Part Aztec, Mexican, and what else? . . . very delightful and refreshing, and she's never let the Haymarket die from the memory of the people. How she has *worked.* Jack takes her on horseback to the ranch and is pleased with her grit." In her diary entry Charmian was referring to the infamous Haymarket Affair of 1886, which had resulted in the unjust conviction and hanging of Lucy's husband, Albert Parsons, along with three other anarchists. Albert's crusading widow subsequently earned the title "Jeanne d'arc of the Chicago anarchists." London would use Lucy's name for the heroine in "The Night-Born."

The next month, Jack got a disheartening letter from Lorrin Thurston, who had flayed him earlier that year in *The Honolulu Advertiser* as "an ungrateful and untruthful bounder" because of the gruesome depiction of leprosy in his Hawaiian story "Koolau the Leper." Hardly dissuaded by Jack's rejoinder, Thurston now took a cheap shot at London's latest novel:

> If Martin Eden had taken a fresh hold on himself; discovered that there is life and hope in the world, as well as death and despair, and taken hold and worked out—at least tried to work out—the problem of improving the world and its conditions, the story would have done

some good, by suggesting to discouraged souls that there is something in life worth living for, and helping themselves as well as others.

Thurston had missed the main point of the novel—an indictment of the protagonist's fatal self-centered individualism—and it was a very sensitive point with Jack: "I dare to say that I am more continually happy than you. I laugh more than you," he replied. "You are ideal, I am more ideal. Your ideal has consisted of conventional statecraft, conventional morality, and conventional material exploitation. My ideal, on the other hand, has been that of a cleaner, better, nobler world, more immediately accessible for all humanity than you could ever dream or hope for." Jack would find it hard to laugh during the coming weeks, however.

In April, John J. Burke, news editor of *The New York Herald*, had approached him with an irresistible offer: to report "The Fight of the Century" scheduled for July 4 in San Francisco. This was a fight for the World Heavyweight Boxing Championship between the seemingly unbeatable current champion, Jack Johnson, and the former unbeaten champion, James J. Jeffries, whom a clamoring public and press had managed to coerce out of retirement as "The Great White Hope." Burke asked Jack, "Do you think it would be possible for you to go up to the training camp before the fight and let us have a daily story of your impressions of the fighters, to be wired every night?"

Jack would have been willing to pay his own way to witness what promised to be an epic battle between these two giants of the ring. Like the rest of white America, he idolized "Big Jim." Also like the rest of white America, he yearned to see the arrogant black man dethroned. Unlike most in America, who lacked the opportunity to see either fighter in action, Jack had seen them both. In San Francisco on November 16, 1901, he had reported the battle wherein Jeffries brutally demolished Gus Ruhlin. And in Sydney, Australia, on December 27, 1908, he had reported the championship fight wherein Johnson effortlessly lifted the heavyweight crown from the head of Tommy Burns. Jack's was the lone white voice granting Johnson his due as the new reigning champion. He promptly answered Burke that he would take the assignment for one hundred dollars per day plus expenses. He and Charmian were expecting the arrival of their new baby at about the same time.

That posed no problem for Jack, since the training camp would be close at hand, and the proud father could be with mother and child within an hour's time.

On June 13, Charmian moved from the ranch to Oakland in anticipation of what she described as the "Great Event." Three days later, Jack learned that the Fight of the Century was probably going to be moved from California to Reno, Nevada. And three days after that, at one thirty in the morning, "came my hour," Charmian wrote. Jack drove her to Fabiola Hospital as soon as she was dressed:

> Mate arrived about 2:30 [p.m.] and napped on couch while I got busy with preliminary pains. After a while he came beside me, and laid his dear curly head beside me, and we napped together—I from exhaustion. Then came on the terrible hours, when he helped me, breathed with me, loved me and praised me, until I could stand no more, and made no headway, and they gave me Ether, and took my baby from me.

The newborn infant was a beautiful blue-eyed girl, apparently perfect in every way. "We named her Joy, Mate and I—our Joy-Baby." Their Joy was short-lived. The placenta had not come, and the mother was placed again under the ether for surgery. "Long afternoon fighting nausea. Oh, the numbness of my broken body! And yet, the pain." The greater pain came the next morning, when Jack and Eliza stood on either side of her bed and told her that her lovely firstborn had not survived. "Our own baby, our little daughter, ours, our Joy-Baby—gone at 4 in the morning, only 38 hours old—in the twilight of the morning. The birth had been too hard." The infant's spinal cord had been mangled during the difficult delivery. "How broken one can be. But I had my Mate, and he loved me, loved me."

On June 22 her loving Mate appeared at her bedside again, this time with a badly swollen black eye and matching story. Following the tragedy, the distraught father had walked downtown to make final arrangements for his trip to Reno. Passing the office of *The Oakland Tribune*, he saw on display in its window Jim Jeffries's new autobiography. He stopped and bought four extra copies to share with fellow reporters at the fight. With these under his arm, he continued his walk—still preoccupied with the loss of his daughter—wandering into the city's seamy underside. Strolling along, he realized that this area, which had been a wholesome and respectable neighborhood during his youth, had degenerated into an urban tenderloin. Needing a rest stop, he headed into the first of several saloons and made his way to the lavatory, past a table where the proprietor, Timothy Muldowney, was finishing an early supper. Before Jack could close the lavatory door behind him, Muldowney jumped up, jammed his foot in the door, and ordered him out, mistaking the bright covers of Jeffries's book for some gaudy advertisements the carrier intended to tack up on the wall. He then proceeded to vent his own bad mood on his unsuspecting trespasser.

Half sick with grief, Jack himself was in no mood for a fight. Rather than seizing the gauntlet, he apologized as he turned to exit—but that fired Muldowney to greater fury. Thinking Jack was an easy target, he swung a mighty roundhouse right. His target was neither easy nor helpless. However, instead of counterpunching, Jack clinched his assailant and called for help from among the half-dozen barflies who had encircled the brawl. But they had no intention of helping. They wanted to see this well-dressed gentleman thoroughly manhandled. Each time he broke free and headed for the door, they encircled and pushed him back into the raging fists. Those fists he could counter. Muldowney's raging head was a harder challenge as he resorted to butting Jack's face with his skull, at first hitting then missing his target as his victim ducked, causing him to butt the top of London's head with his own face and suffer some telltale bruises of his own.

It took Jack nearly fifteen minutes to escape to the street, and into the arms of a passing policeman. Badly shaken, nose bloodied, one eye black and swollen shut, he demanded that the officer arrest the saloon keeper for assault and battery. Instead, the cop turned to Jack's assailant: "Hello, Tim," he said. "What's the mix-up?"

"Hello, Charley," Muldowney answered. "I'm settin' in me kitchen eatin' a bowl of soup, when this guy comes in drunk and starts gettin' smart wid me. I never seen him in me born days before. He was drunk—and I got witnesses to prove it, so help me God." A half-dozen voices chimed in unholy testimony. The result was that London was arrested.

True to form, the Bay Area newspapers sensationalized the incident, hinting at "the vilest construction upon his presence in the low resort." The media were not interested in publishing an accurate report; Muldowney's story made much livelier copy: EMINENT AUTHOR JAGGED AND JUGGED was the first headline Jack read the next morning. HEARD THE CALL OF THE WILD! was another. Others were equally sensational: NOTED NOVELIST ATTEMPTS TO CLEAN OUT TENDERLOIN CAFE; "JACK LONDON ASPIRES TO CHAMPIONSHIP HONORS . . . He wants to be the challenger if Jeffries takes the count."

Released on bail, London appeared in police court later that morning as both plaintiff and defendant. The prosecuting attorney for the *People v. Jack London* counseled him to drop his charges: "Shake hands with Mr. Muldowney and make it up, and we'll drop the case right here. A word to the judge, and the case against you will be dismissed." But Jack was in no mood to shake hands, nor did he want the case dismissed: He wanted to prosecute Muldowney for assault and battery. "Oh, I'll prosecute you both," the prosecuting attorney retorted. Because of the priority accorded by the press to Jack's highly publicized role as reporter in the upcoming Fight of the Century, the London-Muldowney case was postponed until after July 4.

"You have no chance," advised Jack's friend Joseph Noel, editor of the Oakland *Bulletin*: "Everybody knows you were beaten up by this man. His reputation is most unsavory. But it won't help you in the least. Both cases will be dismissed. This will be because you are you. Any ordinary man would be convicted. You are now up against the local police and political machine. You haven't a vote of your own here. Much less do you swing any votes. This dive proprietor swings a string of votes in his precinct—a mighty long string."

Meanwhile, bearing the rueful blessing of his hospitalized wife, who insisted that he fulfill his commitment to *The New York Herald*, Jack boarded the train to Nevada. "Everybody is arriving in Reno," he telegraphed the paper on June 23. "Never in a war, at any one place, was congregated so large a number of writers and illustrators." For the next week and a half Reno would be the center of the boxing universe, and two Herculean fighters would stand at the epicenter.

The contrast between the two was striking. At Jeffries's training camp, Jack witnessed "a big bear, heavy and rugged . . . physically a man that one may well say occurs no oftener than once in a generation."

His manner was as fearsome as his physique: "His brusqueness is astounding, and he is just as brusque to the Governor of the State as to the latest cub reporter away from his home for the first time. I shall never forget the first time I met him . . . At the moment our hands gripped, he gave me a deep, solid, searching look straight in the eyes. There was no geniality in his eyes, no kindliness."

No less impressive physically, Jack Johnson was a dramatic contrast personally, as London described him:

> His voice was just as jovial, his handshake as hearty, his smile as dazzling as when I last saw him in Australia. Like Jeffries, he, too, is every inch a big man. But they are vastly different types of man . . . Possibly a good conception of [the] difference between the two may be gained from my own feelings about them. If Johnson should rush upon me in anger and with full intent to do me bodily injury, I feel that all I would have to do would be to smile and hold out my hand, whereupon his hand would grip mine, and he, too, would smile. On the contrary, I am certain, if Jeff rushed at me in wrath, that if I did not die of fright there and then, I should bite my veins and howl in maniacal terror.

Jack favored Jeffries to win the fight, but he was sufficiently versed in the art of boxing to appreciate the skills of this mighty warrior's opponent, noting Johnson's virtuosity as a defensive boxer and his exceptional coolheadedness. "Another of his remarkable attributes is an instinct for a blow that is positive genius . . . A wonderful fighter, indeed, is Johnson, utterly unlike any other fighter, a type by himself."

On Independence Day the crowd of twenty thousand devotees of the Great White Hope witnessed not the fierce battle of giants but merely a game of cat and mouse. For fifteen rounds Johnson played with his opponent as he had played with a score of others before him, feinting and striking at will, all the time carrying on a witty repartee with the former heavyweight champion Jim Corbett, who figured that his abusive patter from Jeffries's corner would distract Johnson enough to ensure his favorite's success. It ensured, instead, Jeffries's failure. For every stinging epithet hurled by Corbett, a sharper blow was administered on Jeffries, until his face was one bloody mass—and all the while, round after round, the black champion matched Corbett's insults with cheerful retorts.

"Round fifteen, and the end. It was pitiful," London wrote. "He who had never been knocked out was knocked out. Never mind the technical decision. Jeff was knocked out. That is all there is to it." The bitterly disappointed white crowd shouted their angry plea to the referee: "Don't let the negro knock him out, don't let the negro knock him out!" Before the referee could finish his count, Jeffries's corner men jumped into the ring and held him up so that only a technical decision instead of a knockout could be declared in favor of Johnson.

London was the only white reporter to openly recognize Johnson's greatness. He concluded his final report with a question: "And where now is the champion who will make Johnson extend himself, who will glaze those bright eyes, remove that smile and silence that golden repartee?" It would be another five years before a challenger, from the Kansas farmlands—a six-foot-seven, two-hundred-sixty-pound young behemoth named Jess Willard—answered that question after twenty-five sweltering rounds in Havana, Cuba.

Back in Oakland, Jack did his best to comfort a badly broken Charmian. She was trying bravely to recover from the double shock of a near-fatal delivery and the death of their firstborn. A week after Joy's death, she had cried to herself:

> Oh, the luxury of letting down a little from this iron control—of letting the tears run and run . . . I don't think now of my empty arms, and my unused breasts, and of the dear rotundity that was mine so many sweet months, in which lived and moved the little body that died in getting out. Such a *beautiful* baby, they all tell me—Perhaps I'm glad I never saw it. It would have been harder now. And it's quite hard enough as it is.

Three days later, after a particularly excruciating surgical procedure, she wrote, "It must have been today that Dr. Nelson tried to 'return' my worst *hem'd,* and I yelled like a good one, but he didn't get any tears out of me . . . My—but I can't stand any more pain now."

True to character, in spite of her own suffering, Charmian worried about Jack's health. He had been hit with a summer cold that had turned into bronchitis: "It was mainly grit that carried Jack through the Reno period. He was miserably ill, probably from the effects of the Muldowney struggle, and coughed incessantly," Charmian recalled. Fearing that he had tuberculosis, he had his sputum examined. The test results were negative but did reveal a bronchial scar. Though she does not mention it, the years of heavy smoking, aggravated by stress, were taking their toll on his health.

Charmian was right in diagnosing the effects of the Muldowney affair. On July 6, London appeared in police court determined to prosecute Muldowney on charges of assault and battery. Noel had been right: Jack had no chance; under no circumstances was this judge going to jeopardize his reelection by undercutting his Tenderloin constituency. After hearing testimony from each party, Judge George Samuels's decision was to dismiss the case, giving both "the benefit of the doubt."

Jack was indignant. Not only had he been publicly misjudged, but he had also been publicly humiliated. "Some day, somewhere, I'm going to get him," he told Charmian; "I don't know just how—perhaps it will be in thwarting his dearest ambitions; but mark my words, I intend to get him." It didn't take him long to decide how. First, he would use his creative talents to produce a story about the episode, changing enough names to protect the guilty and exonerate the innocent. A week after the courtroom fiasco, he wrote to Blanche Partington that he had already written four thousand words on a "a short story involving how I got my black eye and how the political and police machine worked." His story would be printed for the entire nation to see that fall in *The Saturday Evening Post*.

But this was not enough; he wanted more immediate justice. Finishing his story, he wrote an open letter, asking Charmian to type and mail copies special delivery to Samuels and all the Bay Area newspapers. He reviewed the "unfair, bullying game" Samuels had played before the court, concluding, "Someday, somewhere, somehow, I am going to get you. I am going to get you legally, never fear. I shall not lay myself open to the law. I know nothing about you or your past. Only now do I begin to interest myself in your past and to keep an eye on your future."

Charmian followed his instructions, but she was concerned about potential legal repercussions, and told him so. "Using my common sense, in that open letter I strove to make something strong enough to encourage newspapers to publish it, and at the same time I strove to avoid anything that could be construed as criminal or civil libel or as contempt of court," Jack reassured her. "I'm only doing it because of a sober fun. It's not really serious; it is interesting. Sometimes it's dreadfully satisfying to squash a slimey worm."

But it was serious. His quarrel with judicial bullying could be traced back seventeen years earlier, when he was summarily sentenced to thirty days in the Erie County Penitentiary—and was aggravated perhaps by a less traumatic judicial encounter in 1903, in the Oakland Police Court, when the same Judge Samuels pronounced him guilty and fined him five dollars for riding his bicycle after dark without a light.

On August 2, Jack confided to Charmian that Noel had discovered some kind of connection between Samuels and "Muldowney's dive." Two days later he received a letter from J. S. Smith of Oakland revealing that Samuels owned the property on which the saloon was located. Eliza's verification of this information at the Office of the County Assessor prompted a second open letter to Samuels: "According to the records in the Assessor's Office of the County of Alameda, 362-7th Street is assessed to George Samuels," London wrote. "If you are not the George Samuels in question, I apologize here and now for entertaining even for a moment the idea that a judge of rectitude should own such a low place and derive revenue from it, and at the same time try a case between a non-resident like me and a revenue-paying vote-swinging resident like Muldowney." Samuels tried to exonerate himself by claiming that the affair looked "like a political plot engineered by my enemies," but London had succeeded in hoisting him on his own legal petard: Judge Samuels was removed from his bench at the next election.

Jack now turned his attention to realizing his dream of a model ranch. As always, he required more money, and despite his plans to make big profits from other ventures, he could most easily acquire more money by selling his literary goods. Short fiction remained the quickest way to get cash, and during the next months, he produced a score of stories, some of them clearly hackwork, but a few representing his creative genius at its best. During this same period, he also wrote *The Abysmal Brute*, a mediocre novel about prizefighting based on one of the plot outlines purchased from Lewis.

Charmian was strong enough to return from Oakland to Wake Robin on August 3. This was a healing time for both of them. Her diary reveals that they had resumed their regular lovemaking. By mid-September she could also resume horseback riding; she and Jack were once again riding old trails and exploring new ones on the ranch. The next month, he bought the *Roamer*, a thirty-foot yawl, and they set sail across the bay from Oakland's City Wharf, the same wharf from which they had left on the *Snark* three and a half years earlier. This time they would spend their days and weeks cruising the myriad rivers, creeks, and sloughs of Northern California. "My old, old dream come true—to see Jack with this stage of his youthful performances!" said Charmian: "He looked much like his piratical early self . . . in the blue dungaree and time-honored 'tam' pulled down with a handful of curls, over his sailor-blue eyes that roved incessantly for changes and found comparatively few."

These brief *Roamer* voyages provided both of them welcome escape from the ever-present stress of ranching, financing, and hosting. Away from land, he could do his morning writing stint without distraction and use his afternoons and evenings in recreation: cards, music (particularly Charmian's ukulele and singing), and reading or studying articles and government pamphlets on scientific agriculture. "I am so restfully happy," she wrote, "I guess this trip is exactly what I've been looking for."

By mid-November they were back home from their cruise, and Jack was again focusing his energies on building the finest ranch that money, enhanced with scientific intelligence, could buy. But again, funds were getting low. "I've got five hundred dollars in the bank, and an eight-hundred-dollar life-insurance premium due," he confessed to Charmian a few weeks after their return to Glen Ellen. "But never fear—'Smoke Bellew' will pull us even with the bills."

"Smoke Bellew" was a series of Klondike stories he had contracted to write for *The Cosmopolitan* magazine at the guaranteed rate of $750 apiece. The editor had asked for "a series of six stories, each story complete in itself but containing the same principal character throughout the series. [The stories] should be virile, in your best style, throbbing with reality but not likely to repel with too gross an expression or too brutal a realism."

The result was profitable hackwork, as Jack himself admitted, but nonetheless popular—so popular, in fact, that *The Cosmopolitan* subsequently asked for another half-dozen tales in the series. During this same period, he also contracted with *The Saturday Evening Post* to write a series of eight "Sun Tales" featuring Captain David Grief, a white superhero immune from the devastating rays of the tropical sun and all those tropical ailments that had so sorely afflicted his creator. More hackwork, but equally popular, and the two series provided enough funds to launch yet another new adventure.

24

FOUR HORSES FOR A CHICKEN THIEF

I read in today's paper that your son-in-law has given me a black eye, and that my wife has deserted me! In yesterday's paper I read that I had been fishing in a Washington lake for Beardslee trout with a diamond stud attached to my troll for lure. One reads very many things.

—LONDON TO H. L. RICKS

By the time Jack reached the age of thirty-five, he was firmly established as headline copy for every newspaper in the country. In that era before radio, television, and the Internet, accurate reportage was at best erratic, and one did in fact read "very many things" as the legend grew.

His newsworthy career notwithstanding, London's financial condition remained critical in 1911. During a visit in December 1910, Felix Peano had invited Jack and Charmian to spend the next month at his home in Los Angeles. As Jack told Charmian, "It'll be a nice winter change, and I can forget my creditors easier at a distance while I'm slaving to pay them." The month they spent in Southern California gave them some pleasurable respite from both the damp, cold Sonoma winter and the pressures of his creditors.

"One of my commissions while south," Charmian recalled, "was to look up a suitable four-in-hand of light horses for a summer trip to northern California and Oregon." Their "seeking" drive was now in full force again. They had already seen more than half of the Pacific world;

it was time they saw at least half of their own country's Pacific states. Jack would hire his friend Bill Ping, a veteran stagecoach driver, to train him to drive a four-horse team with fitting harness and eleven-foot whip. He would hire a second stagecoach driver to train the four horses.

Despite his busy schedule, Jack could still find time to support the Socialist Party. At this time the party's most dramatic struggles were taking place in Mexico, where Ricardo Flores Magón and Emiliano Zapata were leading the revolution against the murderous regime of Porfirio Díaz. In early February, Mexican revolutionaries, along with members of the Industrial Workers of the World, seized Mexicali and set up the Socialist Republic of Lower California. Concurrently the Socialists in Los Angeles held a rally at the Labor Temple to express support for the Mexican comrades. They invited London to speak at the rally, but he was unable to do so. According to the newspaper headlines, he was south of the border riding at the head of a band of revolutionaries:

JACK LONDON LEADS ARMY OF MEXICAN REBELS. DIAZ AROUSED BY ACTIVITY OF WRITER OF WARFARE was the two-inch February 4 headline of the *San Francisco Post*.

JACK LONDON, THE NOVELIST, LEADING A BAND OF INSURGENTS IN MEXICO, declared the New Orleans *Times-Picayune*.

"JACK LONDON IS WITH REVOLUTIONARY ARMY. It is reported here tonight that the Mexican Government has learned that London is an active participant in the revolution and has protested to Gov. Sloan of Arizona," announced the *Boise News*.

London was indeed "an active participant in the revolution," but he was not leading an army of insurgents. Instead, he was still in Los Angeles interrupting his hackwork by writing, first, this letter, "To the dear brave comrades of the Mexican Revolution":

We socialists, anarchists, hobos, chicken thieves, outlaws and undesirable citizens of the United States are with you heart and soul in your efforts to overthrow slavery and autocracy in Mexico . . . All the names you are being called, we have been called. And when graft and greed get up and begin to call names, honest men, brave men, patriotic men and martyrs can expect nothing else than to be called chicken thieves and outlaws . . . I subscribe myself as a chicken thief and a revolutionary,

JACK LONDON

He also took time to write one of his finest short stories: "The Mexican," in which a dedicated Hispanic youth defeats a highly favored white boxer to win enough money to buy needed guns for the revolution. This was London's last major hurrah for the revolution—and for the party as well.

As soon as he mailed off "The Mexican" in early June, he returned to his "Sun Tales." He also returned to building what he called his "Beauty Ranch." He had invited Eliza Shepard to move up to Fish Ranch with her eleven-year-old son, Irving, the year before. Now separated from her husband, she was free to devote her managerial energies wholeheartedly to supporting London's rapidly expanding enterprises.

Knowing that he finally had a reliable business manager and ranch supervisor, Jack was ready to launch his "road boat" for a three-month, fifteen-hundred-mile voyage north. "I have written *The Call of the Wild* which some of my friends refer to as my 'best seller,' but the thing nearest my heart is the 'Call of the North'—of Northern California—the natural God-made paradise, which equals only the paradise inhabited by Adam," he announced. Someone less adventurous might have preferred a comfortable train ride, but Jack preferred a more exciting challenge: He would load a wagon and drive a team of horses up the coast.

"HUH!" snorted one veteran rancher, "Drive four horses! I wouldn't sit behind you—not for a thousand dollars—over them mountain roads." Pulling London's carriage would be four different horses with four very different personalities, no one of which had ever been broken to harness. Prince was "a many-gaited love horse from Pasadena"; Milda was a fourteen-year-old "unadulterated broncho [with] mule and jack-rabbit blended equally"; Maid was Charmian's favorite riding mare, whose legs "would be ruined forever [Charmian feared] if she were driven for three months"; the fourth was the aptly named "Outlaw," a rambunctious mare who for seven years "had defied all horse-breakers and broken a number of them" until one lanky, strong-willed cowboy had finally "got her goat [with a] fifty-pound saddle and a Mexican bit." She was Jack's favorite riding horse.

Training those four horses was a snap compared with mastering an eleven-foot whiplash. "If any tyro thinks it is easy to take a short-handled, long-lashed whip, and throw the end of that lash just where he wants it, let him put on automobile goggles and try it," Jack advised: "On reconsideration, I would suggest the substitution of a wire fencing-mask for goggles." By June 12 he had brought the horses and whiplash sufficiently under control to begin their odyssey. Judging from his account, they were wandering happily through Paradise. According to him, the "coast weather was cool and delightful, the coast driving superb" and, contrary to warnings about bad roads, they never found any:

> At every stream, the road skirted dizzy cliff-edges, dived down into lush growths of forest and ferns and climbed out along the cliff-edges again. The way was lined with flowers—wild lilac, wild roses, poppies, and lupines. Such lupines!—giant clumps of them, of every lupine-shade and color. And it was along the Mendocino roads that Charmian caused many delays by insisting on getting out to pick the wild blackberries, strawberries, and thimbleberries which grew so profusely.

Charmian's diary entries were less ebullient. They make it clear, among other complaints, that she had never quite recovered from the trauma of losing her baby. Joy's birthday is noted every month. "Wonder if I'll ever be real strong again—my hands are still weak and it's been over a year!" she lamented on July 3. Her entries brightened with a note of nostalgia the next day as she remembered previous Independence Days: "Last 4th July was in Fabiola, Mate in Reno. 4th before that, Panama; 1908, Ugi, in Solomons, and we fired off our automatics. 1907, Molokai, at the Leper races. Quiet 4th at Eureka." But she was feeling worse two weeks later, after coming into contact with poison oak during one of their roadside stops. "Eyes swollen now—can't hang my arms down at all."

She was more critical of the roads than Jack had been: "Much dust . . . One gets so dirty." She was happy that they were not camping out; because of this, she was never forced to wear the dust and dirt more than a day. When they stayed in hotels more than one day, she was not forced to wear anything at all. "Spend day undressed, except for lunch," she noted on August 27 in Redding. "Dine naked as usual!"

she wrote in Orland two days later: "Orland Hotel full of mosquitos, and hot! Hardly sleep at all. Lovers just the same—all bitten up." She could also sleep late in their hotel rooms if she needed the extra rest while Jack wrote his thousand words each morning. "Watching him in this phase, exhilarated with the youth and beauty of the summer world of out-doors," she wrote years later, "I caught myself thinking of him as driving a team of stars; for he harnessed the very stars to do his work—his lines reaching to the stuff of which the stars are made."

They were greeted as celebrities in each town, and sometimes they stayed in the homes of friends rather than in hotels. As always, the newspapers were publicizing their latest adventure. WHERE IS JACK LONDON? ANSWERING THE CALL OF THE WILD? demanded *The Eureka Herald* when the couple was a week later than anticipated. "Have you seen him?" asked the Humboldt *Times* on July 2. "If you see a big, broad-shouldered fellow, with a cowboy hat and a yellow outing suit, you will know it is him" was the answer. "When it was announced in town that 'Jack London had arrived,'" said *The Port Orford Tribune*, "an electric thrill shot through every heart, eyes sparkled with delight, boys shouted through the streets, and even the oldest and coldest stand-patter in town joined in the demand for a proper recognition of Jack London in our old town. Not a man in town but had read some of his wonderful books."

The four-horse adventure, unlike that of the *Snark*, ended healthily and happily. The Londons reached Wake Robin just in time for lunch on September 5. "Later, go up to cottage and then to big house. Everything surpasses expectation," Charmian noted in her diary. Eliza had done very well during the three months since their departure, renovating an old California Wine Association cottage as a temporary home for her brother and his wife until their dream house was ready for occupancy.

Wolf House would be the fitting name for their "big house." The celebrated architect Albert Farr of San Francisco had been engaged to draw up the plans according to London's vision—a vision articulated five years before in his essay "The House Beautiful." By early June the construction was already well under way. "House—*Big House*—My! It looks great!" exclaimed Eliza. "The teams are busy with scrapers, digging out the space for the last foundation walk by redwoods—and everybody who has seen the walls already up—men who know—material men—coming for orders—workmen & etc—say they are simply splendid."

"Simply splendid" was the right description for Wolf House: "a unique building, embodying ideas which the author himself has thought out, as well as hobbies which he has for a long time been eager to promulgate and enjoy," announced a major architectural journal. Albert Farr called the style "American rustic," explaining that the materials used in construction were to be gathered, wherever possible, from the surrounding countryside: redwood logs and stone from a nearby quarry. The foundation was to be one massive floating concrete slab, earthquake proof and strong enough to support a forty-story building. The living room would be eighteen by forty-five feet, two stories high, with an "immense stone fireplace [enhancing] the cheerfulness of the room." In addition to enough space for entertaining their frequent visitors, Charmian would have a room large enough for her Steinway grand piano, her own beautifully appointed private bedroom, insulated from noisy drinking-and-smoking guests, and Jack would be insulated for his work and have ready access to his personal library of fifteen thousand books, currently stored in various places.

Wolf House would take another couple of years to complete. In the meantime, they would make the renovated cottage their home. "Up early—such a raft of things to do. Such plans for the carpenter! Such shelves, and a wood box and milk-closet, and a shelfboard around dining-room molding, and little stepladders to be made, etc. Mate has an orgy of book-arranging," Charmian wrote on September 6. The following days were "Busy, happy, loving days. Very tired from unusual hard work on my feet; but everything so interesting—settling in our first home together and the first Jack ever had."

The next four months would be one of the longest periods uninterrupted by travel they ever spent together on Beauty Ranch. Once again, the latchstring was out full time: Guests included Blanche Partington, whom Jack enjoyed baiting with her Christian Science convictions; George Wharton James, Jack's longtime editor friend who subsequently published a reminiscence of his visit; Ed and Ida Winship, the Napa aristocrats who delighted in driving the Londons around in their latest-model touring car; Daniel Sydney Ayres, who served as agent in trying to sell Jack's works to the burgeoning film industry; the Sterlings; Ed Morrell, whose alleged out-of-body experiences while a prisoner in San Quentin inspired London's *The Star Rover*; and Spiro Orfans, a young immigrant from Greece who spent several weeks on the ranch painting Charmian's portrait. All these and more visitors came to Beauty Ranch during that autumn.

Those last four months of 1911 were not their happiest. Aside from tiring work and tiresome guests, Charmian as well as Jack suffered from various ailments. For instance, she mashed her left little finger in a door—a minor injury for some, perhaps, but major for a typist and pianist. The two of them contracted colds, Jack's being the more severe because of his smoking, which aggravated his chronic coughing spells; hers aggravated by her chronic insomnia. There was also his heavy drinking, aggravated by George Sterling's visits. On November 9, after George and Jack had spent a boozy afternoon down in the Glen Ellen saloons, finally coming back up to the ranch in pouring rain, Charmian pulled Jack aside and talked to him in private: "I spring 3-drinks a day and baby proposition and it looks as if it might go thru'. Feel happy about it and like getting baby clothes from barn. Mate falls for the less drink and more baby. Takes me up on it."

December found them packing for another voyage: from New York to Baltimore and from there around Cape Horn to Seattle and back to Glen Ellen seven months later. Jack spent the afternoon of Christmas Eve with Joan and Becky. That night he, Charmian, and Nakata boarded the Western Pacific, arriving in New York on January 2, 1912. The next couple of months would be even unhappier than the preceding four. Judged from Charmian's perspective, New York was the City of Dreadful Night. "Almost any passage in our companionship I contemplate with more pleasure than that 1912 winter in Gotham," she admitted later. "Nine-tenths of the two months' time we made our headquarters in Morningside Park East, he was not his usual self . . . Coincident with our arrival, he warned that he was going to invite one last, thoroughgoing bout with alcohol, and that when he should sail on the Cape Horn voyage, it was to be 'Good-by, forever, to John Barleycorn.'" He was true to his warning if not to his vow. Her diary entries are rife with undisguised despair:

Very cold. Beastly cold, with cutting wind. Sick and miserable. Wish I were anywhere than in New York . . . My nerves are titillating like the innards of an electric bell . . . [Jack] says he'll come home early, but I know he won't, & go to sleep. He doesn't either. Strange dreams, all of him. Everything so broken . . . Sort of nightmarish state I'm in . . . I have scared feeling all the time . . . I don't feel spirited enough to fight.

She worried not only about Jack's carousing but also about his health. His cough had worsened, and despite her cautioning, he stubbornly insisted on wearing his thin silk socks and low-cut, thin-soled oxfords when tramping about at all hours in the Manhattan snow.

There were a few pleasant interludes for her. On January 11 they strolled down Fifth Avenue for a visit to the studio of their friend Arnold Genthe. January 17 was "A sweet day of love, [staying] in bed till nearly noon, reading LeGallienne's Rubaiyat [sic]." Next evening they enjoyed a supper of fine ducks (sent by Rex Beach) with Liebfraumilch. On January 21 they had a "good time [at the] charming home of Ella Wheeler Wilcox in New Haven." The night of February 7 was spent with the Wallings in Cedarhurst, Long Island: "Slept on couch in den . . . Help bathe baby Anna . . . Splendid talk with Anna, in which she tells me several things." Two weeks later they attended the Empire Theatre, enjoying the performance of a very pregnant Ethel Barrymore in Hubert Henry Davies's *Cousin Kate*. On the following day, Charmian visited the Strunskys' East Side wine shop: "Feel lifted out of the filthy unhappiness of New York for a few hours," she confided.

Jack did manage some important business during those weeks in New York. Because of his urgent need for cash, he severed his ties with Macmillan and contracted with Doubleday, Page and Company to publish *A Son of the Sun*. The most considerable transaction was his new contract with the Century Company, who agreed to give him a hefty advance of one thousand dollars monthly for the next six months for his projected "Alcoholic Memoirs."

Despite his profitable business transactions, he was scarcely fonder of Gotham than his wife was: "Rome in its wildest days could not compare with this city," he declared. "I must have the open, the big open. No big city for me, and above all not New York. I think it is the cocksure feeling of superiority which the people of the metropolis feel over the rest of the country that makes me rage."

They left New York on February 25, spending three days in Philadelphia before going on to Baltimore, where their ship, the *Dirigo*, was docked. "Not a very merry Leap Year Day for me," Charmian wrote on February 29. "Went shopping—lot of things for ship. Took a lone sandwich & glass of beer in café at one; writing letters later, in room, when Jack came in, head clipped close. I cried for a couple of hours. Awful shock. He laughed." His head wasn't "clipped close": it was shaved "naked as a billiard ball." Charmian recovered enough to visit Poe's grave, making Jack keep his hat pulled down, but refused to go out to dinner or the theater with him that evening. The next day was no better: "Don't want to look at Jack. He's awful. He drinks pretty steadily all morning. Throws up some of it."

The one bright spot in the day was Possum, a three-month-old fox terrier who would be given roles to play in London's next two novels and who would continue to delight them for years to come. The four of them—Possum, Jack, Charmian, and Nakata—boarded ship on the first of March, having paid a thousand dollars for their passage. The *Dirigo* was a three-thousand-ton, four-masted steel barque. Because the ship was not registered for passengers, Jack was signed on as third mate, Charmian as stewardess, and Nakata as cabin boy. Setting sail on March 2, they would spend the next one hundred and forty-eight days at sea. It was a time for unwinding, playing, reading, writing, and mending emotional fences. It was a time especially for writing, and Jack would resume work on the novel he had described to George Brett ten months before:

> I think it is going to be a popular story. Its motif is *back to the land* ... I take a man and a woman, young, who belong to the working class in a large city. Both are wage-workers, the man is unskilled—a driver of a brewery wagon, or something of that sort. The first third of the book is to be devoted to their city environment, their meeting, their love-affair, and the trials and tribulations of such a marriage in the working-class. Comes hard times. The woman gets the vision. She is the guiding force. They start wandering penniless over the country of California. Of course, they have all sorts of adventures, and their wandering be-

comes a magnificent, heroic, detailed pilgrimage. After many hints and snatches of vision, always looking for the spot, they do find the real, one and only spot, and settle down to successful small-scale farming. Not only will it begin as a love-story, but it will end as a love-story.

The *Dirigo* voyage provided an ideal opportunity for completing that story: no visitors, no reporters, no bill collectors, no carousing.

As often happened, what London was writing interacted with what he was planning to do. During breakfast on the morning of April 13, he told Charmian he couldn't get the ranch out of his head: "First time he's ever had anything of his own that he couldn't get out of his head," she remarked. For the next three months he would plow steadily through his back-to-the-land story. *The Valley of the Moon* would be his longest novel. In an interview a year before his death, London said, "Among all my books, I think, 'The Call of the Wild' is the most popular one, but 'The Valley of the Moon' is [the] more ideal one to me."

During the intervals between typing Jack's big novel, Charmian found time to write a story of her own, a publishable sea tale titled "The Wheel." Both she and Jack found time for boxing, practice with their rifles, card playing, puppy playing, and reading the half-hundred books they had shipped. They delighted in climbing high up the masts—even up the mainmast, swaying dizzily with the deck ninety feet below: "Here, remote, ecstatic, above the 'wrinkled sea' and the slender fabric of steel, we lived some of our finest hours, enthralled by the recurrent miracle of unbored days, love ever regenerate, and contemplation of our unwasted years."

Not all the hours on their voyage were fine, however. Shortly after embarking, Charmian was afflicted with a terrible case of "hives," only to discover after several miserable days and sleepless nights that the cause was bedbugs. She also suffered a painfully infected finger for a fortnight or so (a hindrance in her typing routine), but darkest was her worry about her husband's drinking. He had first told her he would stop all alcohol not only during the voyage but ever after. Then came the rationalization: "One evening, about three months out, at table, the mate Fred Mortimer remarked, "I never drink on duty. I drink very little anyway; just a glass now and again onshore with the fellows."

Charmian's heart sank when Jack replied that he was not an alcoholic "in any sense of the word" and that he would never be mastered by alcohol. "Therefore," he declared, "when I am on land again, I shall drink, as you drink, occasionally, deliberately, not because I have to have alcohol in the economy of my physical system, but because I *want* to, we'll say for social purposes . . . It has never mastered me . . . it never shall."

Early on the voyage, Charmian had complained that Jack didn't understand how worn out she was: "I actually believe he has forgotten the past two months, or, that he never realized what they were meaning to me." Typing the notes for *John Barleycorn*, his next major book, in mid-April made her "blue and foreboding." And a month later she confessed, "The uncertainty of the alcohol future depresses me unspeakably." Her depression lifted a fortnight later, after she determined once more to bring a child into their marriage:

> I don't waste any time, for to-day, ripe & willing & desirous, I laid myself in my husband's arms & told him, if *he* was strong & willing & ready, we would "send" for another baby. He ready? and strong? and willing? *He* wasted no time either, at this timely time. And so, on this Great Day, I, Charmian Kittredge, the same old girl, deliberately went after a child, to replace the child that happened, & that left so great a lonely desire in me.

When the *Dirigo* docked in Seattle on July 26, the Londons were greeted by Martin Johnson and his new wife, Osa. That evening they attended the theater to hear a lecture by Martin, who was now on tour with his own presentations about the exciting *Snark* adventures. Charmian noted that "Mate had 2 cocktails & some wine during afternoon & evening." On July 30 they boarded the small steamer *City of Puebla* along with Nakata and Possum, arriving in San Francisco three days later.

Back home at the ranch on August 4, they plowed into the mass of letters that had piled up over the past five months. Four days afterward, Jack left to join George Sterling at the Bohemian Grove for the club's annual High Jinks celebration, and Charmian took the train down to their apartment in Oakland to get a medical exam. She was pregnant now, and they were eagerly anticipating another child—they hoped a son this time—but on August 10 she noted "a discoloration on my person." This untimely bleeding portended a miscarriage.

More heartrending than her worries about Jack's drinking was her diary entry for August 12: "Another Hope Lost . . . About quarter of 3, went to bathroom, and promptly bore a month-old child!" The pains of her miscarriage lasted for three days. Dr. Larkey, her new physician, told her that the lacerations from her previous delivery had apparently never healed properly. Aunt Jennie was called in to help care for her. Martin and Osa Johnson visited and tried comforting her the next day—but at least for a while she had lost her radiant persona along with her baby: "Feel very unsmiling, & rather bitter—One can't lose 2 children thru' one doctor's ignorance, or carelessness, or fear—whatever it was—without feeling feelings . . . Mate phones & is sending Eliza down. I am glad. I feel so *bereft*. She comes, & cheers me with account of how Mate picked out the pretty things he wanted her to bring down."

It would be several months before she regained her full strength. Although Jack had been exceptionally caring during the first days following her trauma, he was less than understanding during the next month, lecturing her on the subject of "hospitality" when meeting the constant crowd of visitors at the ranch.

One of the few bright spots for her during those months was the presence of a talented Australian pianist named Lawrence Godfrey-Smith, who was their ranch guest from the end of September until the first week of 1913. He arrived "full of enthusiasm" and immediately bonded with Charmian. "He praises my Steinway very highly, especially for its unusually good treble. Laurie plays beautifully and he's a *man* before he's a musician—an all-around man," she wrote next day; "Mate takes Laurie (on King) over trail to Wolf House, where I meet them. Laurie is splendid rider and likes his horse, too. He's crazy over the new house." And the day after that: "Work some and go in frequently to hear Laurie practice. Such good things. I sing for him and he says nice things."

After Charmian's operation to repair the effects of her miscarriage, it was Laurie who first sent her flowers. Jack quickly picked up his cue. On that same day, "Mate himself sends chrysanthemums, and then white roses, and finally, he would shoulder the door open and appear with an armful of violets—a great head of packed blossoms. He felt awkward about bringing flowers, but my joy reassured him. The ice was broken by our picking out a bouquet for poor little Joan." His daughter had been stricken with typhoid fever just a few days earlier but had managed to fight off the fever and the debilitating effects of the illness long enough to go with her father and little sister on an excursion to Idora Park. Typhoid was often fatal, and her life hung in precarious balance: "Days and weeks, nights and days vanished from my awareness in an endless, icy nightmare," Joan wrote. "But it seemed very often that, coming briefly to consciousness, I found Daddy beside my bed, anxious-eyed but warming me with his quick, encouraging smile as I sought his face."

Charmian's recovery from her operation took another month. On November 7 she moved from Merritt Hospital to stay at the home of her friend Elizabeth Bull. While she had visitors aplenty, she missed the ranch and, most of all, her husband. The feeling was mutual, as evidenced by Jack's frequent letters. Deeply disappointed as he was by their second loss of a child, he gave no sign of this in his letters to her:

> Miss you? I've got to have you away from me for a couple of days truly to appreciate you. To myself, all the time, these days, I keep swearing: "She's a wonder! She's a wonder!"
>> For you are. You're the best thing that ever happened to me . . .
>> Your man.
>> P.S.—When are you coming home? I miss you so dreadfully.
>> WOLF.

He phoned her on November 20 that he was readying the *Roamer* for another voyage, this time with their friend Laurie as boat guest. The next week, she celebrated her forty-first birthday aboard ship—"Very tired and lazy, but so contented. The tiresome, painful, useless past few weeks fall from me . . . I feel like a new person in body and spirit, but my desire to get around exceeds my ability." It was another month before she felt that she was her old vibrant self again.

During their monthlong idyll, they fished, read, played pinochle, and stopped over at some towns to shop, visit friends, and tour historic sites ("Sutter's Fort. Worth the whole trip!"). Laurie impressed them with his daily dive into the cold December waters, and Possum took a plunge "on purpose, or by accident" twice a day. Jack resumed his daily writing stint on his "Alcoholic Memoirs," the somber notes of which rang in the unluckiest year of his life.

25

UNLUCKY THIRTEEN

Gone? I am going now. In my jaw are cunning artifices of the dentists which replace the parts of me already gone. Never again will I have the thumbs of my youth. Old fights and wrestlings have injured them irreparably . . . My lean runner's stomach has passed into the limbo of memory. The joints of the legs that bear me up are not so adequate as they once were, when, in wild nights and days of toil and frolic, I strained and snapped and ruptured them . . . Never again can I run with the sled-dogs along the endless miles of Arctic trail.

—JOHN BARLEYCORN

London mailed the final installment of his "Alcoholic Memoirs" to *The Saturday Evening Post* on January 13, 1913. Despite his open rejection of all forms of superstition and paranormal phenomena, his private dreams must have been haunted at some point during this particular year by the weird significance of the number thirteen. He called it his "bad year": "My face changed forever in that year of 1913," he told his wife. "It has never been the same since." In view of what happened to him during those months, that change is fully credible: "It seemed as if almost everything that could hurt him befell him," said Charmian.

"First, there was the death of a woman friend, an invalid," Charmian wrote in her biography. "Never had I observed him so stirred by the passing of any adult person. That this one so bright, so brave, should have ceased, for once made his philosophy waver. 'I did something last night I never did before,' he confessed. 'I concentrated every thought and actually tried to call that girl back . . . Of course,' he smiled half-foolishly, 'there was no answer.'"

Close to dying during the early weeks of 1913 was Eliza Shepard's thirteen-year-old son, Irving. He had been critically burned while climbing a tree and coming in contact with a 220-volt electric line on December 13. His life still hung in precarious balance during the early weeks of 1913. He was placed in the Londons' cottage during these weeks so that Charmian as well as Eliza could minister to his wounds.

Nature itself seemed to mirror the dark mood of 1913. "Weather is bitter cold—regular snap-ice, frost, wind," Charmian recorded. Snow-falls are exceptional in the Sonoma Valley; there were three during the year 1913. A false spring "brought out blossom and young fruit un-timely, only to be frosted after belated showers." A plague of grasshop-pers destroyed many of Jack's "baby eucalyptus trees, which were supposedly immune from pest and blight. 'Certainly,' he would groan in unison with his harassed sister, 'God doesn't love the farmer! Look at that beautiful half-grown cornfield scorched and withered by sun and north wind!'"

As if Nature hadn't provided troubles enough, Eliza's estranged husband, evidently drunk, showed up at the ranch on May 3 and de-manded money from Eliza, threatening to kill her. "Old Shepard shoots up the ranch," Charmian noted. "Irving comes running in evening cry-ing 'Come quick! Papa's trying to hurt Momma. Papa's got a pistol!'" Jack immediately came to her rescue, disarmed Shepard, and ordered him off the ranch. Eliza gave Shepard ten dollars. He used the money the next day to go to Santa Rosa and swear out a warrant for the arrest of Jack London and Jack Byrne, Ida London's husband, who was work-ing for Jack. The case was thrown out of court the following week.

Another shooting proved fatal: "One of the most valuable draft brood-mares, in foal, was found dead in pasture, from a bullet." This bullet was fired accidentally by a hunter on London's property—resulting in Jack's posting of No Trespassing signs.

On July 6, Jack complained to Charmian that he was suffering from "suspicious pains" in his abdomen. They took the train down to Merritt Hospital in Oakland, where Jack's physician, W. S. Porter, diagnosed appendicitis. Dr. Porter performed an appendectomy two days later and discovered that Jack's kidneys were also diseased. London recovered from his appendix operation in record time; his kidneys would not recover.

With his bank balance down to three hundred dollars, on August 18, Jack mortgaged the Hill Ranch property to get enough funds to finish the Wolf House before winter. Four days later—"At midnight Eliza comes to tell us of fire, and our Wolf House is destroyed. Mate and I are cheerful enough until we get back, at almost 5 a.m. Mate breaks down completely." The new home that was built to last a thousand years had been reduced to a huge stone shell and pile of rubble in less than six hours. Because it was supposed to have been virtually fireproof, Jack had taken out an insurance policy of only six thousand dollars; the bank had added a second policy of ten thousand dollars to cover half the loan on Hill Ranch; an additional policy of at least fifty thousand dollars would have been needed to cover his total financial losses due to the fire. No amount of money could have covered London's emotional loss. What pained most deeply was the suspicion of arson. "We never did learn whose hand applied the torch. I had all but written 'assassin,'" Charmian wrote. "For the razing of his house killed something in Jack, and he never ceased to feel the tragic inner sense of loss."

For years after London's death, the question of arson remained unanswered until finally, in 1995, a group of experts from the American Academy of Forensic Sciences meticulously examined the ruins and concluded that the conflagration was started by spontaneous combustion. The redwood paneling and other flammable fixtures within the house had been rubbed down that day with linseed oil, and the workers had neglected to remove their oil-soaked rags; the temperature had been unusually hot that day and evening—very hot even for August in the valley—and once the rags ignited, fire spread throughout the structure, virtually exploding within minutes. The massive rock walls only served to hold inside and intensify the inferno. The walls, reinforced by steel rods and wires, are still standing. Poet William Everson has called Wolf House "the most impressive ruin in the American West."

A month after the fire, Jack confessed to Charmian that the pain in his heart was more than emotional heartbreak over the loss of their dream house: "Haven't you noticed that I have got into the habit of laying my palm over my heart?" he asked. "I didn't realize I was, until I happened to catch myself at it." He also told her that, after an examination by Dr. Porter, he had been denied insurance by "a certain life insurance firm to whom he had applied some time back for an additional policy." Charmian suggested that excessive smoking might be the cause, but "he did not take to the diagnosis."

Regarding pain, he spent two hours in the dentist's chair on October 23 as Dr. Granville Shuey pulled out all his remaining upper teeth. As if this were not enough dental agony, he admitted in a letter to his brother-in-law Ernest Matthews that he "suffered hell" until six days later, when he had a wisdom tooth pulled. Charmian noted that, even with his excruciating pain, he managed to "bravely tackle his 1000 words."

Earlier that year, Jack had suffered an equally painful emotional challenge following the arrival on February 27 of a guest named Joseph Allan Elphinstone Dunn. As a reporter and war correspondent, Dunn had impressed London as a "man's man." He had interviewed Jack for *Sunset* magazine prior to the *Snark* launching in 1907, and in early 1913 he sent Jack an inscribed copy of his *Care-Free San Francisco*, which prompted an invitation to the ranch.

Dunn was also something of a "lady's man." No sooner had he arrived than he started courting Charmian. She obviously enjoyed his flirtation because her diary entries during the next several days were filled with references to "Allan." "He has sweet ways—'dear' & 'dear heart'" was her first comment about him. His charm was taking its full effect within the week: "Feeling fine, and sleeping well. Happy as a lark [with] Allan" was her March 2 entry. Two days later she was "having a lovely experience" riding to the top of Sonoma Mountain with Allan. The day after that they spent another "glorious morning on horseback," then rode down to the Southern Pacific Depot to watch the unloading of Neuadd Hillside and Cockerington Princess, the two magnificent shire horses Jack had bought. They "fool around in forenoon, watching for stallion to come back from exercise" on March 6, and he reads her his "Kahuna story" after lunch. "Later he paints at bridge I walk over." Two days after this, they "fool around in sunshine, with goats, and Neuadd Hillside, etc., lie about in grass, etc." On this day "Mate" accompanied them. Jack was evidently becoming aware of his wife's exceptional fondness for their guest, because that night she heard her "dear love groaning, and moaning, and [trying] to sleep."

Dunn departed on March 10, and that evening Charmian and Jack had "one grand powwow" concerning her attraction to Dunn, after which he declared, "'I am the proudest man in the world. I have found that I have a heart, and I have nearly died.'" She admitted on the following day that she felt "very much of a battle ground. But what men! I can't help pouting out my chest! But I am heartbroken over the realization of Mate's suffering. Just the same—he has learned about women from me, and can appreciate some of my 'white nights.'"

Allan Dunn's special attentions to Charmian, like Laurie Smith's the year before, served as another wake-up call to Jack: "Mate is so sweet to me . . . He lies against me all he can, and loves me." However, their "grand powwow" had neither completely cleared the air nor cured her infatuation with Dunn. Three days after his departure, she complained that he had not written to her: "Rather expected to hear from [Allan]. Guess he's keeping 'sober' counsel with himself." She received a "perfectly serious letter" from him the next day, after which she and Jack had "some wonderful talks on the subject." She didn't divulge the specific details of either the letter or their talks, but on March 16 she noted: "Nerves have been shaken quite a bit—Mate's too, for that matter. [He] loves me to death these days. My own dear man."

This was not the last of Allan Dunn. There are no decipherable entries in Charmian's diary for the first several days in April, until the second week. On April 10, however, Dunn had evidently returned to the ranch, charming as ever: "Great days—full of beauty of interest and situation. Blue eyed men." He was still there three days later, and she was as infatuated as ever: "Allan finishes redwood picture. Beats any redwood painting I ever saw."

There is no clear indication in the diary of either Dunn's further presence or his departure, and two weeks later Charmian and Jack were in Los Angeles on film business. If Dunn was not physically present during this time, however, he had become a major presence in their marital relationship. Both Charmian and Jack were deeply affected. On April 29 she wrote: "Stay in bed all day and sleep and rest and think." He, too, was thinking—more sharply aware than ever that his wife was an exceptionally attractive woman whom he could not afford to take for granted. When they returned from Los Angeles to Oakland the next day, he bought her "the most glorious string of corals."

Charmian's diaries during the first three weeks of May provide no apparent clues about the Dunn affair, but the issue had not been resolved. Jack feared that his wife had been guilty of infidelity—something more serious than mere infatuation—and he confronted her with his suspicions on May 24. Judging from her diary entry, he grilled her mercilessly until she finally broke down, convincing him that she had been a faithful mate who had never dreamed of having sex with Dunn. "Awful headachey," she wrote that evening. "Terrible thing to be doubted when one is innocent."

"From Pathos to Bathos" might be a fit heading for the final chapter of the "Jack/Charmian/Allan Affair." June 24 is the last diary entry referring to Dunn, which reads simply, "A.D. in papers." A.D. was indeed in the papers—sensationally so. He had been arrested for filching jewels from a hostess at a weekend party and trying to pawn them under the name of "Elbert Hubbard." He confessed to the crime, telling the authorities that he had committed it in desperation because he'd suffered a run of bad luck in selling his stories. "I don't think it was kleptomania," his victim attested. "I think it was just a plain case of robbery." Among other articles the police found in Dunn's possession were some of London's monogramed silk pajamas, which proved a windfall for the newspaper cartoonists. Because the loot was recovered and Dunn confessed, and because his record appeared to be otherwise clean, charges were dropped.

Dunn never appeared again on Beauty Ranch or in Charmian's diary, and their brief fling was never consummated. Regardless, it had a serious impact on her marriage, making it very clear to her husband that she was the most important woman in his life. It also provided material for *The Little Lady of the Big House*, London's next major novel, which would be based upon the theme of ménage à trois.

Compounding the emotional turmoil of London's "bad year" were problems with his role as a father, a role he was never satisfactorily able to fulfill. During 1913 he wrote a series of letters to the older of his two daughters that painfully revealed this ineptitude. Perhaps it was because he himself had never had a fitting childhood that he was unable to grant it to his own children. More likely, it was because he had never had a fitting marriage to their mother. He had admittedly married Bessie even though he did not love her. In the years following their divorce, he had come to hate her, and that hatred boiled over, scalding his daughter Joan particularly. It was Joan who bore the brunt of his implacable resentment toward Bessie and his frustration because Bessie refused to allow the two daughters to visit their father at Beauty Ranch. It was Joan who was caught most directly in the middle of the bitter feud between her two parents, and it was she whom he unwisely forced to declare her allegiance in the war. As she wrote many years afterward, "His longing for his daughters was deep and true, his need for them was desperate. But did anyone ever bungle more badly in trying to realize that desire?"

On May 7, Joan wrote to him requesting thirty dollars to help cover expenses for moving into the new house he had built for them and for cleaning and laying the carpets. Even though he was struggling to keep up with expenses, Jack did not object to her request. What he did object to was his daughter's ill-advised argument for making the request. First, she was patently covering for Bessie in telling him she was writing the letter without her mother's knowledge. Second, she said that her mother's funds had been exhausted in covering medical bills for their daughters' illnesses, but that he shouldn't be angry with her mother because his daughter was asking for more money. Third, and most provocative, she told him, "Mother has borne everything on her shoulders for the past twelve years and now I am trying to help her. I am trying to drive away those nasty wrinkles in her face." She concluded by saying, "Now don't forget—don't scold mother but scold me."

Ultimately she would get far worse than a scolding. Her father's response to this letter was reasonably mild, however, compared with what was coming down the line during the next several months. "Dearest Joan," he replied on May 9, "Yes, but, my dear daughter, your Daddy also is getting old, and wrinkled, & tired . . . It happens that I am your Daddy, & that I pay a lot of bills for you and your sister and mother." He enclosed a check for thirty dollars, asking her to show his letter to Bessie, and signing it "Your loving Daddy."

His next two letters were brief but affectionate, congratulating her on their move into the new Piedmont house and on her forthcoming graduation from Durant Grammar School (also advising her which courses to take in high school). Then, on August 17, he wrote a long letter warning her against taking advice about writing from English teachers, because they themselves "can't write salable English . . ." He pointed out that because he knew more than most teachers of English, she as his "first-borne" would be well advised to come and visit him on the ranch so that they could have a good long talk about her "whole life welfare . . . that the greatest thing in the world right now for you would be to have this talk with me." He asked Joan to share his letter with her mother "and talk the whole matter over with her."

Here was an open plea to Bessie as well as to his daughter. Bessie undoubtedly sensed the implications of such bonding and rejected the invitation for her daughter. A week later, literally ill from his loss of Wolf House and having received no response, Jack unloosed his bitter self-pity in another letter:

> Dear Joan:—, I feel too miserable to write this at my desk. I am sitting up in bed to write it . . . My home, as yet unoccupied, burns down— and I receive no word from you. When you were sick I came to see you. I gave you flowers and canary birds.
>
> Now I am sick—and you are silent. My home—one of my dreams— is destroyed. You have no word to say . . .
>
> Don't you think it is about time I heard from you? Or do you want me to cease forever from caring to hear from you?

Joan had evidently written her condolences about the Wolf House fire on the same day Jack sent this letter, and the two letters crossed in the mail. To make matters worse, she unwittingly undercut her sympathy when she explained that she was unable to visit his ranch "so long as it meant seeing people other than him [namely Charmian]." She asked if he could not see and understand her situation, closing her letter with "Your sorrowful and repentant Joan."

"No; I neither 'see' nor 'understand,'" he replied. "Now just what is it that you see, and you understand, which prevents you from coming to see me on my ranch?" His tone was moderated a couple of days later when he received a long letter from Joan telling him about her new experiences at Oakland High School and enclosing a poem she had just written. "Dearest Joan," he wrote. "Your poem, for a first attempt, is dandy! splendid!"

Then, in October, their relationship took another turn for the worse when he met with her and her mother at their Piedmont home with the proposition that Joan come to live with him and Charmian on the ranch. The maneuver was doomed to failure. Joan could not accept such an invitation without her mother's blessing, and that blessing would never be forthcoming. Now openly vindictive, he wrote a long letter rashly denigrating Bessie as a "little person [who] out of her female sex jealousy against another woman, has sacrificed your future." He warned Joan furthermore that "if you join with your mother in this little sex jealousy of a thwarted female, you will doom yourself to grow up in the little environment of a little place called Piedmont, which is populated by little people."

This letter would settle the matter forever—in Bessie's favor. "Well, Dad, I've read over your letter, read it twice carefully," Joan replied on October 28.

> So this is to say, I am perfectly satisfied with my present surroundings and do not wish to change them. I resent your opinions of my mother . . . she is a good mother, and what is greater in the world than a good mother? . . .
>
> And now, Daddy, since we have thrashed this question out together, may we not leave it? . . . I shall stay with my mother, and I shall keep my promise to do so, until I'm old enough to support myself. Please, Daddy, please let me feel that this is the last of these awful letters you force me to write to you; it hurts me so to write them . . .

Bitter though his October letter had been, Jack's relationship with his elder daughter had not reached its nadir. That was yet to come.

In the meantime, his financial situation was growing more precarious. Although his monthly income was now upward of ten thousand dollars, his outgo exceeded that amount. He was pouring more money than ever into Beauty Ranch—paying dozens of workers, planting thousands of eucalyptus trees along with several orchards, and buying purebred livestock. As with any farm, a full payback would take years.

To make matters worse, he was embroiled in lawsuits trying to protect the rights to his works. "At the present moment I am up against it hard, and fighting for my very life—my financial life, I mean," he wrote to Ernest Matthews on October 11. "A bunch of financial pirates and robber lawyers have joined together, and are at the present moment trying to take away every bit of copyright I possess in everything I have ever written."

This was not all. According to Charmian, he was "out of pocket about ten thousand" on a scam by the Fidelity Loan & Mortgage Company and a deal gone bad in Mexican land stocks. Nor was this all. His delegated literary agent, Joseph Noel, had persuaded him to invest another hefty sum in the Millergraph, a lithograph process that promised to return enormous profits but would fail expensively to fulfill that promise. Noel was also bungling his literary assignment in New York City, where he was appointed to get contracts for placing *The Sea-Wolf* and London's other works into the theaters. On December 17, Jack told Noel that his bank balance was down to $10.60.

Twelve days later he wrote to Joan, apologizing for not sending any extra money for Christmas. "I did not have it," he explained. "Let me tell you my Christmas. I sent only 2 presents all told, one was to you, one was to Bess. So far I have received one Christmas present—it was an advertising calendar . . . Daddy."

26

NEW YORK, MEXICO, AND HOME AGAIN

I have always been a fighter. I have never said anything nor
written anything that I have failed to back up afterwards . . . At
the end of it all, I shall go down into the darkness standing by
my opinions, and fighting for my opinions.

—TO THE EDITOR, *ARMY AND NAVY JOURNAL*,
JUNE 22, 1914

Charmian and Jack celebrated the birth of 1914 aboard the *Roamer* anchored in the mud off Richmond. "Storming. Cozy in mud," she wrote.
"A true Happy New Year for Mate & me. Our 1913 financial troubles
are somewhat carried over—Noel's funny situation as regards 'Sea
Wolf' . . . Mate and I are full to overflowing with love for each other,
and all's well. We're praying we won't have to go to N.Y. about Noel."

Their 1913 financial troubles were indeed carried over, and their
prayers were answered—but the answer was not quite what they had
prayed for. Jack had no viable option, such was the extremity of their
financial predicament: He must take another trip to their least-favorite
city. Charmian wrote that he was "almost sick," and she was "paralyzed
at the thought." Noel had so badly entangled the dramatic and cinematic rights to London's works, particularly those of *The Sea-Wolf*, that
Jack was faced with the possibility of losing all rights and facing legal
battles that could cost him everything he owned. It took every cent he
could borrow and scrape up to pay for his travel expenses. Charmian
was forced to borrow $107 from Martin Johnson until a promised $500

from Brett had been wired to the Merchants Bank of San Francisco. Even Nakata had to ask Martin for a loan.

On January 12 Jack arrived in New York City, hardly the ideal place for celebrating his thirty-eighth birthday. Without fanfare, he quietly checked into a hotel in the Theater District in downtown Manhattan. Here he could avoid the usual crowd of reporters and get his work done without interruptions. He had a number of pressing business items on his agenda, but topping the list was *The Sea-Wolf* issue. A combination of legal naïveté (with a touch of chicanery and greed) and the vagueness of new copyright laws had allowed Noel to sign over half the dramatic rights for London's novel to the theatrical agent George Pelton for a paltry advance of $700—only to discover afterward that film rights were included in the contract. Realizing what had been virtually given away, London was hoping to buy back his rights for $3,100—less than a tenth of what Pelton was demanding. "He swears he has absolute trump cards: I say produce them," Jack wrote to Charmian. "At present moment I am playing a ticklish game of bluff in lieu of any legal backing."

Faced with what looked like disastrous defeat, Jack resorted to what he called "play-acting," his euphemism for calculated intimidation. Since Pelton had called his bluff, Jack's only chance now was somehow to force him into a tolerable compromise: he would try to scare the hell out of him. This performance would be a more sophisticated version of his showdown with the editors of the *Overland Monthly* fifteen years earlier. A major difference was that, instead of an unknown tyro, he was now America's most popular author, and instead of playing the bully for five dollars, he was playing for thousands. His shabby hotel provided another advantage: the proper stage for his act. By careful manipulation, he managed to lure Pelton up to his room. Here's the "play" as he related it to Charmian:

> You should have seen me . . . For two days I purposely let my beard grow, and you know how black it comes out. I opened my pajama-coat so that the mat of hair showed on my chest. And of course I left out my upper teeth, mussed up my head and wore an eyeshade. I was not pretty.
>
> So, when the clerk 'phoned up that he was below, I said "send him right up." He answered, "he's stepped outside." "Outside," says I, "what

for?" "I don't know—he said he'd wait for you there." "Tell him I'm in bed, and can't come down."

Well, when his tap came, I sat up in bed, and the high-arm chair I had placed for him had its back to the door so that if he tried to escape me he'd be in an awkward position getting out of his chair to do it . . . He came in, trying not to look queer when he saw the object I was—haggard from the dark growth on my chin and neck, hair showing on my chest, and a ghastly toothless smile of welcome! In his hand was the document, which I took from him and glanced over. And every little while I looked aside to one or the other of my fists, as if gloating over them. As I talked with him without appearing to study him I took in his sick, scared face and soul. He'd have given anything not to have got himself into that chair.

And then, I went over the whole business again, all we had talked in our many interviews, and he finally consented to release for a tithe of his original claim. He said:

"I'll go right to my office to make the change, and send you the agreement immediately."

I had waited for just that, and didn't mean that he should elude me again. Said I:

"You'll sign that paper right here on that table, before you leave this room!"—and when he protested, I went on, closing and unclosing my fists, to tell him just exactly what I would do to him if he refused. He looked this way and that, at the telephone, and half around at the door, and knew his situation for precisely what I had made it. He signed the release and left it with me.

Jack's performance in *The Sea-Wolf* business signaled a change in his attitude toward New York. "I no longer say 'To hell with New York,'" he wrote to Charmian. "I am here to master New York & to enjoy New York." And he did enjoy this visit more than any previous ones, probably because he no longer felt intimidated by the city and was free to appreciate its uniquely rich gifts. In addition to personally negotiating better terms with his publishers and magazine editors whose offices were located in the city, he admitted he had fun "mixing up with the 'Billtoppers,' with the booking agents, the girls creamed from all the country who are succeeding or who are eating out their hearts on

Broadway ... with Tammany men, prize-fighters, street walkers, managers of theatres, also directors & producers, also leading ladies, kept women, etc., etc., etc. More room for scandal, I guess."

A major highlight was seeing Anna again. She came several times to visit him at his hotel. When he kissed her, she quipped, "Another Scandal, Jack?" She made sure the reporters would be hard-pressed to sensationalize their meetings: she brought along her babies and her sister Rose. At one of their meetings he read to them sections from the new novel he was writing. This was the book inspired in large measure by the prison experiences of Ed Morrell. It would be published the next year in Britain as *The Jacket*, in America as *The Star Rover*. Anna described it as "the best thing ever written on capital punishment." Writing to her husband about her renewed acquaintance, she remarked, "I found this visit with my old friend very stimulating. He is not a philosopher as you are, but his mind is agile, and his nature generous and practical . . . He insists that nothing in the world matters but love, therefore a woman (and a man) ought not to care about anything but love."

That he was practicing what he preached is evident in the letters he was sending back home to Charmian—a far cry from his attitude during their previous visit to the city:

Do you know, I look at the women I encounter these days, and always, as I look, is a vision of your sweet, beautiful body, of the spirit that informs it to such quick eagerness, to such sureties and certainties of will. Oh, I know your thoroughbredness that is at the one time an irk and the highest joy to me. No man may ride a thoroughbred mare without tenseness & irritation along with the corresponding joy that is aroused by the very tenseness & irritation . . . Ergo?—my arms are around you, as they shall always have to be around you for love of you & appreciation of you—you damned thoroughbred!

He dodged a hot scandal on January 30 after attending a burlesque show with Frederick McCloy, business manager of the Columbia Theatre and editor of the Burlesque Department of the *New York Star*. On January 31, the *New York Journal* published an article titled "Three Women Hurt in Auto Wreck Refuse Surgical Attention." The name of Jack

London did not appear in the article. He explained what happened in his letter to Charmian: "Met all the performers after show (cracks made at me by players during show), & then McCloy, leading lady, soubrette & a singer, & a dancer, had supper at a huge Harlem Pabst café." After supper, at about 1:00 a.m., the six of them piled into a taxi and as they were speeding down Broadway suddenly saw another two taxis collide and turn over in front of them. In order to miss the wreck, their driver swerved his taxi, which rolled over and "flew into pieces as if it had been exploded by a bomb." The passengers were tumbled and piled on one another, with Jack at the bottom spitting out broken glass. Amazingly, no one was badly hurt. "Maybe 1914 has started its lucky turn," he said. This incident was indeed lucky: Although he suffered multiple bruises and abrasions, he could have been critically injured or killed. Furthermore, he managed to catch another taxi and escape the crowd of spectators, police, and reporters without being recognized.

On February 20, Charmian met his train in Sacramento, then rode back to Oakland with him, noting, "Great time & good talk on the New York business affairs." Her euphoria over his return after so many weeks was short-lived: the next day he relapsed into one of his dark moods. He was drinking again, loosing the old demon "White Logic" to bully her. "Wonderful morning till 11," she wrote on February 21. "Good afternoon at John Barleycorn."

Charmian always insisted that Jack never became tipsy or lost control when he drank, but that he became more coldly and rationally intense. In other words, he never abused her physically, only intellectually and emotionally. He was still in his dark mood back at the ranch two days later, for he evidently berated her for not bearing a child and announced that he had given up any hopes of her ever bearing another child. Although she didn't specify her husband's comments, his tirade was obviously bitter and abusive: "Learning more and more," she wrote; "And then the Deluge—the baby matter. Mate turns down a page. I grieve." She was still crying the next day: "Feel sick & miserable—and I was so well."

On that same day, he lashed out at his elder daughter in a four-page letter more coldly if not rationally intense than anything he had written before. He had apparently decided to "turn down a page" not only on babies but also on his elder daughter. He began by saying he was sending her a check for $4.50, "according to account presented by you. When I tell you that this leaves me a balance in the bank of $3.46, you will understand how thin the ice is upon which I am skating." He went on to say that she must not charge schoolbooks or any other items to his account without his or Eliza's permission. But that was only a minor issue he had decided to address. The major issue was far more critical:

> All my life has been marked by what, in lack of any other term, I must call "disgust." When I grow tired or disinterested in anything, I experience a disgust which settles for me that thing forever. I turn the page down there and then. When a colt on the ranch, early in its training, shows that it is a kicker or a bucker or a bolter or a balker, I try patiently and for a long time to remove, by my training, such deleterious traits; and then at the end of a long time if I find that these vicious traits continue, suddenly there comes to me a disgust, and I say Let the colt go. Kill it, sell it, give it away. So far as I am concerned I am finished with the colt . . .
>
> Years ago I warned your mother that if I were denied the opportunity of forming you, sooner or later . . . I would develop a disgust, and that I would turn down the page . . . If you should be dying, and should ask for me at your bedside, I should surely come; on the other hand, if I were dying I should not care to have you at my bedside. A ruined colt is a ruined colt, and I do not like ruined colts.

He did not sign this letter "Daddy," but "Jack London." Long after his death, Joan confessed, "Even today, rereading his letter of February 24, 1914, I am appalled by the relentless, calculating cruelty with which he wrote to me, his daughter, just turned thirteen." Yet, despite her heartache, and to her credit, Joan did not let his letter destroy their relationship forever:

> I rejected his rejection simply because I could not possibly accept it. Little by little, with the initiative on my side for each cautious easing of the tension, but with its immediate acceptance by Daddy, an affectionate correspondence was resumed . . . And yet, Daddy was different . . . Except on rare occasions, his old exuberance was gone. Fewer letters were exchanged than before, but they were loving letters, and

when we were together, he expressed his love for us and his interest in what interested us in ways I shall never forget.

In spite of London's financial problems, deteriorating health, and darker mood, his seeking spirit was as strong as ever in 1914. While in New York, he had negotiated with *Collier's* to write a series of travel articles for a trip around the world, starting west to Japan in April. This time he would sail as a tourist with his wife on conventional commercial vessels. They changed their plans when the editor asked him to go south instead, to report American involvement in the Mexican fracas. Here was a much hotter prospect than writing promotional tourist articles. "And now," he said to Charmian, "I may redeem myself as a war correspondent, after what I was held back from doing by the Japanese Army."

Here, too, was a rare opportunity to join forces with his country as it flexed its newfound military muscles. Much in the same manner as President McKinley had believed himself divinely ordained to uphold American interests in Cuba after the sinking of the battleship *Maine* in 1898, so President Wilson felt compelled to defend the integrity of the American flag when the dictator Victoriano Huerta refused to order a twenty-one-gun apologetic salute to that sacred icon following an arrest of American sailors in Tampico. More was at stake than respect for the American flag, of course—such as American investments in Mexican oil. Heeding the call to action, Wilson sent all available warships to Mexican waters and ordered the navy to seize the port of Veracruz to prevent arms shipments from reaching Huerta. The operation turned into an actual battle on April 21, and 19 Americans and 126 Mexicans were killed.

Anticipating action, Jack had left Glen Ellen with Charmian and Nakata on April 17 for Galveston. He would not reach Veracruz until April 27, too late to report any battles. He might not have reached Veracruz at all without the help of his fellow war correspondent Richard Harding Davis, who once again came to his rescue. All the correspondents in Galveston had received their credentials from Washington and were preparing to sail aboard the transport *Kilpatrick* on April 24 with General Frederick Funston—all the correspondents except Jack London. On the morning of the scheduled departure, he was still nervously waiting and wondering. "I can't understand it, I can't understand it," he complained to Charmian. "Each time I've called on General Funston, his aide has courteously put me off. I know the General is not well, with that abscess in his ear, poor devil; but that isn't the reason. So there seems to be simply nothing I can do."

Nothing would have been done in time without the intervention of Davis, who told Jack what was going on. "It's that 'Good Soldier' letter," Davis explained. "The General thinks you wrote it." As soon as he heard it, Jack could understand why he had been put off. This was a scathing antiwar letter distributed and attributed to his authorship several years before. Despite his disclaimer, the belief in his authorship persisted. The military establishment would never grant any special privileges to its author. However, with Davis's support, Jack was able to persuade General Funston that he was innocent of the charge. "I gave him my word of honor that I did not write a line of that canard," he reported to Charmian, "and upon that word he takes the responsibility of adding me to his already filled quota of correspondents." London left along with the rest of the correspondents later that day aboard the troopship *Kilpatrick*.

Four days later Charmian and Nakata debarked at Veracruz from the *Atlantic* in company with other correspondents' and officers' wives. By this time the atmosphere was more festive than war-torn. Only the heavily bombarded naval academy and the unrepaired damage to their hotel rooms indicated that a battle had taken place scarcely a week before their arrival. "Hot inside room and Mate can't work," Charmian noted. "Spend much time on sidewalk café, absorbing long, cool drinks. Plaza full of people, band playing—Mexicans enjoying the show. Quite a number of American and English women."

Once again, Jack's plans of personally experiencing the dangerous excitement of warfare would be frustrated, and once again he would describe as best he could what he personally witnessed at the wartime scenes. "Ashore all is peaceful and as markedly on its toes as is the sea," he reported on May 23:

> Everywhere marines and blue jackets are cooking breakfast . . . American women . . . are breakfasting on the cool arcaded sidewalks of hotels bordering on the Plaza . . . In the Hotel Diligencias's bedroom

where I write these lines under lofty, gold-edged beams, there is a splatter of fresh bullet holes on the blue wall . . . The wrecked door shows how our sailors entered behind the butts of their rifles in the course of the street fighting and house cleaning.

The most violent action London witnessed during his Mexican adventure was not at a battlefront but in a saloon—and he never reported the incident. It was his fellow correspondent Oliver Madox Hueffer who, in a tribute following Jack's death, rendered the account as "most characteristic of the man." The two reporters, bored with the lack of action in Veracruz, decided one morning to board a small steamer bound for Tampico, "the Mexican oil center." Jack said he wanted to go and find out "what oil smells like." However, before visiting the oil wells, he and Hueffer checked into one of the local saloons:

[The town was] a chosen haunt for the cowardly type of tough . . . who drifts to any part of the world where a strike may be expected . . . In the bar, in which a large number of those gentry were assembled, some kind of quarrel took place. I became aware of it on seeing most of the assembled loungers at the bar take refuge under tables or behind columns . . . Two large and very drunken men remained afoot, swaying as they stood. After a dramatic pause they produced revolvers, fired, emptied them into space and the surrounding mirrors, without hitting each other, and thereafter lurched solemnly out of opposite doors. I had not realized what was afoot, and with London remained quietly sitting at our table. And I can still remember the look of childish glee and the raised hand with which he implored me to do nothing to interrupt the scene, while for all comment came, characteristically: "Now, what do you think about *that*?"

Hueffer considered Jack's response to this episode "delightful and romantic," but London's reports of the effects of the war were neither delightful nor romantic. Particularly moving were his descriptions of the battle casualties, American and Mexican alike. "I want to register my protest right now that modern war, for the man who gets bullet wounded, is not at all as romantic as old-time war. Furthermore, a modern bullet, despite its steel jacket which keeps it from spreading, is a terrifically disruptive thing to have introduced into one's body." Even though designed to spin, this bullet "wobbles" during the initial and final phases of its flight. If the target is hit during either of these phases, the damage is extraordinary:

> The effect of such bullets on human bone can be readily imagined. There is no reason, with modern antiseptic surgery, why a clean-drilled hole through flesh and bone cannot be healed nicely. Unfortunately, such being the terrific impact and wobble of our high-velocity bullets of to-day, the bone is shattered for too great a distance into too many minute fragments. The only thing to do is to take off the limb.

Making his way out of the hospital through its vacant chapel, now devoid of altar and holy statues, he paused for a moment, still haunted by what he had just witnessed: "And as I stood in this place whence the worship of the gentle Nazarene had departed, strong on my vision were the amputated limbs, gaping wounds, and ruined bodies caused by our wobbling bullets."

Although London reported that amebic dysentery was relatively rare in Veracruz, he was hit hard by the microbe on May 30. By the following day he was already passing blood. "Feel pretty anxious—drugs fail to check Mate's condition," Charmian wrote on June 1. Within twenty-four hours his medication had begun to relieve the bleeding: "Improvement, but a very miserable Mate Man." Now she and Nakata were preparing all his food in their hotel room: boiling all their water, feeding him rice water, cocoa, and malted milk, and giving him three irrigations a day. By June 8 he was strong enough to go out for his first shave in more than a week, and also to go with Charmian and Nakata to the quarantine office for the health certificates they needed before they could leave for home.

London's attitude toward the Mexican Revolution had changed radically during the three years since writing the letter to his "dear, brave comrades." In an article for the socialist *Appeal to Reason*, John Kenneth Turner declared that London had been effectively courted, subsidized, and corrupted in producing "a brief for the oil man, a brief for intervention, a brief for what Mexicans call 'Yankee Imperialism.'"

The principal source of Mexico's problem, according to London, was the mongrelized *mestizo* (the "breed"), part Spanish, part native. Although this breed constituted only 20 percent of the Mexican population, it was this "class that foments all the trouble, plays childishly with the tools of giants, and makes a shambles and a chaos of the land. [They] are the predatory class":

> They produce nothing. They create nothing . . . "shake down" the people who work and the people who develop . . . raise revolutions or are revolutionized against by others of them, write bombastic unveracity that is accepted as journalism in this sad, rich land, steal pay rolls of companies, and eat out hacienda after hacienda as they picnic along on what they are pleased to call wars for liberty, justice, and the square deal . . . Honor is one thing to them, another thing to an American; so likewise with truth, probity, and sincerity.

It was not his denigration of *mestizos*—nor his blatant Anglo-Saxon racism—that infuriated the socialists so much as London's support of American intervention, his endorsement of the capitalistic spirit of enterprise and efficiency, and what they viewed as his subversion of the Marxist spirit of revolution. As he viewed the situation, Mexico was "a great, rich country, capable of supporting in happiness a hundred million souls, being smashed to chaos by a handful of child-minded men playing with the tragic tools of death made possible by modern mechanics and chemistry." What was needed was the disciplined hand—disciplining fist, if necessary—of their civilized, efficient "big brother" north of the border to bring civilized order, peace, and prosperity out of this chaos. "Mexico must be saved from herself," and it was the intervention of American military and industrial power that London saw as working toward that salvation.

Jack's split with the party was assured when he came out openly in support of Britain and the Allies in the Great War. "Either we believe in the brotherhood of the working class, or we do not believe in it," declared the socialist manifesto he had signed in 1908: "We cannot carry in one hand the bloody sword of war, and in the other the gospel of solidarity." However, the consequences of the chaos and carnage he witnessed in Mexico tempered his socialist idealism. He said that while he preferred to settle conflicts through peaceful and legal arbitrament, he nevertheless felt compelled to carry an automatic pistol to protect himself from men who would rob him by violent means: "I hope for the day to come when it will not be necessary for any man to carry an automatic. But in the meantime, preferring to be a live dog rather than a dead lion, I keep thin oil on my pistol and try it out once in a while to make sure that it is working . . . so it is with nations . . . it behooves nations to keep thin oil on their war machinery and know how to handle it."

"No one could be more shaken than Jack, in July, by the beginning of war in Europe," Charmian remarked. Although he was devoted to building Beauty Ranch, the war weighed heavily on his mind: "More staunchly than ever before he reiterated his faith in England. 'England is fighting her first popular war,' he would say; and he could not forgive Germany, over and above her sworn Frightfulness, for having been stupid enough to think that England would not fight." His response was unequivocal two years later, when the editor of *The Cosmopolitan* solicited "a brief Christmas message to the American people from the ten most distinguished and representative citizens of this country": Jack replied, "I believe intensely in the pro-ally side of the war. I believe that the foundation of civilization rests on the pledge, the agreement, and the contract . . . Civilization at the present time is going through a Pentecostal cleansing that can only result in good for humankind."

Would he want to join forces with the Allies as a war correspondent? Perhaps, if the call came—and if the price was right. On September 23 he telegraphed *Collier's* that he was willing to cover the European front at the same rate that he had received in Mexico. The editor, Henry Forman, replied that he was reluctant to repeat those terms and, furthermore, that foreign journalists were having difficulty reaching the Franco-German front. So London continued writing fiction. By this time, he was thoroughly tired of the job, but he had no other option. It was write or face financial collapse, bankruptcy, and failure: failure to care for all those dependent upon his support, failure of his plans for rebuilding Wolf House, failure of all his dreams for Beauty Ranch, failure, in sum, of his lifelong commitment to the American Dream of Success.

He was hoping that the success with his ranch would free him from the burden of his daily thousand words and the daily chatter of

Charmian's efficient typewriter. However, as with any farming venture, the process would take years. In the meantime, none of his investments were panning out. The gold mines in Mexico and Arizona into which he had poured thousands proved to be false claims. The Millergraph lithographic process, hyped by Joe Noel as a sure thing and costing Jack additional thousands, was another gamble destined never to pay off.

One of his several exercises in financial futility was the Jack London Grape Juice Company. The prohibitionist Eugene Chafin visited Beauty Ranch and suggested to Jack that he use the grapes from his vineyards to make grape juice instead of wine. London agreed to let his name be used, and a group of investors consequently formed the Jack London Grape Juice Company to market "The Drink That Knocked Out John Barleycorn." Newspaper headlines announced, LONDON WILL FIGHT BOOZE BY MAKING GRAPE JUICE! Eliza, to whom he had given power of attorney to exercise while he was in Mexico, wisely refused to sign the contract with the directors of the company because they would not guarantee that London would not be held responsible for any of the company's debts. Her refusal was fully justified when the company went bankrupt the next year: suits for fraud brought against London totalling $31,250 were dismissed because the contract had not been signed.

London's investment in eucalyptus trees was another story. This was the real thing, according to certified agricultural authorities, not a gamble at all. Since the middle of the nineteenth century, this allegedly fast-growing, fire-resistant, disease-resistant, disease-preventive tree with its aromatic leaves had been promoted as a remedy for a plethora of human ailments (including bronchitis, cholera, and constipation) as well as for the country's dwindling hardwood reserves. Here seemed a material for all seasons. According to promotional broadsides and to government bulletins as well, eucalyptus was patently serviceable in the multifarious uses of lumber: not only such larger structures as houses, barns, piers, and ships but also farm implements, furniture, and objets d'art.

Jack believed that here at last was a profitable way out of his unremitting daily grind. Shortly after returning home from his *Snark* cruise, he had written to Grant Wallace, proprietor of the Eucalyptus

Agency in Monterey, for advice on planting trees that would grow on high-dry soil. Wallace responded with advice on the variety of trees to plant and the proper methods of planting, concluding, "If you will set out say 200 of your broad acres to eucalyptus, you will have a bonanza which will have most of the gold mines lashed to the mast." This was encouragement enough. "I know of no legitimate investment that will compare," Jack wrote to Bessie's cousin Minnie Maddern Fiske. "I plan, in ten years, to plant 500,000 trees. By the time that the last 50,000 are planted, I can cut the first 50,000 planted, and, from then on, yearly, I can cut 50,000. This means, at present most conservative hard wood prices, a net profit of $50,000 a year . . . I have read endless volumes & pamphlets & forestry bulletins on the subject, and am confident that my conclusions are correct."

But those "pamphlets & forestry bulletins" failed to recognize that out of the hundred-and-some-odd varieties of eucalyptus, only a couple were suitable for lumber, and it took just as long for those to grow as an oak tree. The rest were relatively useless as building materials— worse than useless: they were filthy and, because of their penchant for shedding limbs as well as bark, potentially deadly. This serious error notwithstanding, most of Jack's agricultural ventures were ultimately successful, and he spoke truly when he inscribed *The Valley of the Moon* to his ranch manager in 1914:

Dearest Sister Eliza:—
We know where lies the Valley of the Moon, you and I; and the Valley of the Moon, in our small way, yours and mine, will be a better valley for our having been.
    Your loving brother,

JACK LONDON

27

A SEA-CHANGE

I have had a very fortunate life, I have been luckier than many hundreds of millions of men in my generation [and] while I suffered much, I have lived much, seen much, and felt much that has been denied to the average man. Yes, indeed, the game is worth the candle.

—LONDON TO ETHELDA HESSER, SEPTEMBER 21, 1915

In many of his agricultural enterprises London was ahead of his time. However, his deteriorating health made it increasingly apparent that he would not live to see his agrarian vision fully realized. As he passed his thirty-ninth birthday, even the unpracticed eye, looking closely, might see that he was far from well; the practiced eye might see that he was dying. In public, he was determined to maintain his celebrated smile and legendary image of robust good health. In private, when he dared to relax, the picture was very different.

While he might conceal the truth from the world outside, he could not hide it from Charmian. She saw it all too clearly: "There was something inimical working in Jack's blood in those days," she noted. During their January excursion to Truckee for the winter sports, he complained that it was his "smashed ankles" that prevented him from joining the skiing and ice-skating parties. "Getting old, getting old," he would grit through his teeth as she massaged his cramping feet and legs. But it was more than smashed ankles that was bothering him. By now he was also suffering from not only cramps but also chronic gout. Nor was that all:

"Severe pyorrhea of long standing contributed its quota of poison; and, in his acid condition, his yachting fare of twelve-minute-roasted canvasback and mallard, and red-meated raw fish, was hazardous menu."

Something even more inimical was working in his diseased kidneys and collapsing urinary system, as manifested in his bloated body. "Look at the size of my ankles, Irving, I can hardly stand on my feet today," he said to his nephew one morning as he dismounted from his horse and limped up to visit Eliza. Worse yet were the excruciating spasms induced by kidney stones. Even a man with Jack's iron will would have been hard-pressed to bear these attacks; he needed the help of medication. That help was readily available in the form of morphine and comparable analgesics. These could temporarily mask the pain: they could not cure the malady.

Still, he must keep going, and he must keep writing. Income from magazine and book sales, enhanced by movie contracts, continued to mount. As of December 31, 1914, Macmillan Company alone had sold more than one million copies of his books. He was now the highest-paid author in America, but, as usual, outgo threatened to exceed income. If he could only hold on until his investments in the ranch began to pay off, until cinematic copyright laws were regularized, until royalties from his foreign editions reached expectation. But this was a formidable *if.* A major problem: the Great War that had begun just as his European sales were beginning to take off. This conflagration knocked "a poor fellow's plans into a 'cocked hat,'" London complained to one correspondent. "The war has hit the whole writing game, and hit it hard," he wrote in answer to a letter from the playwright Walter Kerr, who had asked for financial help in placing his scenarios. "It is sink or swim with me at the present time, and at the present time I am floundering hard."

As a means of getting at least temporary relief from stress, he took Charmian and Nakata aboard for another *Roamer* cruise during the first weeks of 1915. Here was an opportunity for him to help Charmian put the finishing touches on her *Log of the Snark* while he wrote a three-act play at the request of San Francisco's Bohemian Club for the 1916 "Jinks" at their summer retreat in the redwood grove near the Russian River: *The Acorn-Planter* was to be his last attempt at drama. The subtitle gives some hint about the work's peculiarity: *A California*

Forest Play—Planned to Be Sung by Efficient Singers Accompanied by a Capable Orchestra. Composed mostly in verse form to be chanted, it begins in "the morning of the world" and concludes with "the celebration of the death of war and the triumph of the acorn-planters [as] The New Day dawns, / The day of brotherhood, / The day of man!" The club rejected the play because of difficulties in finding "Efficient Singers" and a "Capable Orchestra." Although a theatrical failure, the play is an important final testament to London's agrarian vision. He believed that the roots of humanity's social ills and conflicts were basically economic and that wars would end only when all had enough to eat—through the universal conversion of swords into plowshares.

As a courtesy to London, Brett authorized Macmillan to print 1,350 copies of *The Acorn-Planter.* Although a fine copy in dust jacket is now worth several thousand dollars at auction, the play was scarcely worth a pittance in royalties. Jack needed a book he could bank on. "You know what kind of a dog writer I am," he telegraphed Edgar Sisson of *The Cosmopolitan* on January 30:

> Remember *Call of Wild* and *White Fang* were both serial successes as well as big book successes. I have two crackerjack dog books I want to start writing right away. Shall I go to it? Wire me. Each will be about seventy thousand words and they are bound to make a hit with my dog public which is the biggest public I have. The announcement of a dog serial by me should fetch subscribers.

Sisson approved the publication of both projects, though London would not be around to see their serialization in 1917. Before then, however, he would attempt to put some further distance between himself and his various creditors.

"I am leaving the ranch tomorrow on my way for a short trip with Mrs. London to Hawaii. I am taking my work with me and shall roll it off steadily day by day," he wrote to Brett on February 18, telling him of his plan to write two new dog stories: "I am making fresh, vivid, new stuff, and dog psychology that will warm the hearts of dog lovers and the heads of psychologists, who usually are severe critics on dog psychology. I think you will like these two books and there may be a chance for them to make a good impression on the reading public."

That the stuff of *Jerry of the Islands*, first of the two novels, was "fresh, vivid, new" is arguable. The novel's setting is none of these: it is a return to the Solomon Islands as a canine version of *Adventure*. That it would "warm the hearts of dog lovers" may have been true in the early twentieth century. As its dust jacket boasts, "Never was a dog more lovable, more courageous and resourceful than the Irish terrier Jerry— never has a dog had a more adventurous, colorful life." But it would hardly warm any twenty-first-century hearts when readers discover that Jerry's "adventures" principally consist of helping to round up "kinky-haired cannibals" recruited to work the copra plantations managed by the "white lords."

By contrast, *Michael, Brother of Jerry*, the second novel, was not only "fresh, vivid, and new" but is still relevant today. Especially noteworthy is London's indictment of the training of animals to perform onstage. "Cruelty, as a fine art, has attained its perfect flower in the trained-animal world," he explains in his foreword. *Michael* was Jack's last written word on dogs, but that word had far-reaching consequences. Following its posthumous publication, his call for "local and national organizations of humane societies and societies for the prevention of cruelty to animals" was answered with the formation of the Jack London Club dedicated to this crusade. The club achieved an international membership of nearly one million before its disruption by the Second World War.

London did not finish his sequel to *Jerry* until after he and Charmian returned from their Hawaiian vacation, which lasted from March 2 to July 16, 1915. Those four and a half months seemed to have been a return to paradise. The couple were even greater celebrities than they had been during their visit eight years earlier. The furor aroused among the members of the establishment over Jack's leprosy stories had subsided. As proof, his sometime friend Lorrin Thurston now greeted him with open arms. Within a fortnight of their arrival, the Londons had already met in "informal audience" at her royal request with Queen Liliuokalani. Jack and Charmian discovered that—thanks in considerable measure to his own widely published praise of the islands—Hawaii was no longer terra incognita for the tourists.

The social and economic problems that had troubled the Londons so deeply during their earlier visit now seemed to be ameliorating. The

owners of the great sugar and pineapple plantations still ruled the islands, but theirs seemed to be a benevolent oligarchy, and everyone,
including the workers, appeared to be reasonably healthy and happy.
Moreover, there was a remarkable lack of racial friction.

These changes encouraged Jack, at the invitation of Alexander
Hume Ford, to deliver one of his most interesting lectures, before the
Hands-Around-the-Pacific Organization, which met in Honolulu on
May 5. His talk, "The Patriotism of the Pacific," was published three
months later as "The Language of the Tribe." In it he envisions a
"world tribe" united by a universal language, not merely in words but
in actions and attitudes. "I began studying the language of the tribe
when I was very young," he says. "My first lesson was in my own home,
and I then began to find out how hard it is to speak and understand that
great tribal language of the world people. First you must have sympathy, then you must study out, not what the other fellow says, but what
he means, for the language of the world tribe is not always reducible to
words."

London gives as the example of this first lesson a misunderstanding
with Jennie Prentiss. "I loved her almost as I loved no one else, for it
was from her black breasts I drew the milk of life. In her I had all faith."
But that faith was badly shaken when, after reading Paul du Chaillu's
story "The Gorilla Hunters of Africa" at the age of seven, he asked if she
had ever seen a gorilla before being brought to America as a slave.
Knowing that there were no gorillas in America, he was devastated
when she replied that she had seen many of them on the plantation. His
faith was not fully restored until five years later, when he discovered
that she had meant "guerrillas." He therefore advocated the establishment of an organization for bringing the various peoples of the world
together so that they could meet personally and "get down deep under
the surface and know one another." His address was instrumental in
the formation of the Pan-Pacific Union the following year.

Throughout their six-month stay, London's health apparently improved. Except for a two-day bout of food poisoning in early April,
Charmian recorded no medical problems for him. What she did record
was their daily basking in the warmth of the Hawaiian sun and their
"celebrity sunshine." Added to lunches, dinners, and lectures, Jack
hosted evening poker parties for his University Club friends. Several

years afterward, one of the participants commented that the group's favorite beverage was one made from oranges "with ample powdered sugar, cracked ice, and bar soda from a syphon bottle," and he never saw London "take a single drink of anything intoxicating."

While Charmian kept regular entries about their activities in her diary, one noteworthy Hawaiian episode is missing because she was not there. In mid-May, Jack accompanied a congressional delegation to Kauai, which enabled him to personally view the setting he had described so vividly in "Koolau the Leper." During his visit, he was guest at the home of the Reverend John M. Lydgate, renowned Christian missionary and founder of the recreational mecca Lydgate Park. Pleased to be host for "the Prince of the world's story-tellers," Lydgate described London as "about 40 years of age, though looking much younger, boyish offhand, natural and unassuming." He was surprised by London's attitude toward his chosen profession: "Literature is the last thing, apparently, that he wants to talk about. If left to his own resources, he unfailingly drifted round to the interests and problems of his great ranch in California, where the difficulties of practical farming have been impressed upon him." The two men discussed such similar problems as cultivation, crop rotation, and labor shared by the Hawaiian "sugar estate."

Later in their meeting, London talked about "the experiences of deep-sea sailing [and] the thrill of continuous adventure" on his *Snark* voyage. Lydgate was impressed that, in his conversation, London was so "easy, natural, direct, and simple . . . More remarkable, perhaps, considering what he [had] gone through, [was] the absolute freedom from slang and profanity." Finally, when his host pressed him to discuss his writing, London recounted his daily two-hour stint of working "in the morning, rain or shine, Sundays or holidays, the only exception being when he [was] off on a trip like the Congressional outing." Lydgate noted that Jack was "somewhat of a radical, or even an iconoclast" in his attitude toward literature: "He holds very lightly to the accepted canons and rules of literary practice. He claims that literature was made for man and not man for literature."

Jack's claim that literature was made for man is underscored by an introduction he wrote during his stay in Hawaii for Upton Sinclair's *Cry for Justice: An Anthology of the Literature of Social Protest*. If he had by now become disenchanted with the Socialist Party, he had clearly not lost his faith in humanity: "It is so simple a remedy, merely service. Not one ignoble thought or act is demanded of any one of all men and women in the world to make fair the world . . . The call is for service, and such is the wholesomeness of it, he who serves all, best serves himself." In his memorial tribute following Jack's death, Alexander Hume Ford affirmed: "As I ask myself, 'Why did I like Jack London from the start?' I know it was because I intuitively guessed that he loved Humanity more than he loved himself, his work, or life itself."

Paradise being ephemeral, Jack was compelled to fulfill his mortal responsibilities: Beauty Ranch for one. Even under the capable management of Eliza, this project could not succeed indefinitely without his occasional hands-on involvement. But the marketing of his works in the inchoate film industry needed his immediate personal intervention. Joseph Noel had made a mess of the dramatic and cinematic rights of *The Sea-Wolf*. Worse, Frank Garbutt—a millionaire entrepreneur who had turned his perverse energies into moviemaking and who had turned London's popular fiction into moneymaking (for himself)—had succeeded not only in alienating Jack's favorite actor/director, Hobart Bosworth, but also in swindling London out of countless thousands by claiming that box-office receipts were far below expectations.

Consequently, on July 16, Jack and Charmian boarded the SS *Sonoma*, arriving in San Francisco six days later. On July 28, he took the night train down to Los Angeles to discuss financial matters with Garbutt directly. Charmian did not disclose the details of his meeting, but on July 30 she noted, "Mate returns from Los Angeles with $5,000.00 and a good interview and experience with Garbutt." Except for this succinct entry, neither she nor Jack mentioned what had occurred in Los Angeles on July 29—and thereby hangs a tale that London might have written had he lived long enough to appreciate its significance. Instead, it did not appear in print until nearly six decades later, in the autobiography of one of Hollywood's most famous directors, Raoul Walsh.

On the dust jacket of *Each Man in His Time*, Walsh is described by the actor Gregory Peck as "one of nature's noblemen . . . a rousing, colorful roughneck"—characteristics that fit Jack London as well. Like London, Walsh was a natural-born seeker who loved adventure, especially when it involved taking risks. Knowing this, D. W. Griffith commissioned him to film the *Life of Villa* on location during the revolutionary leader Pancho Villa's epic march from Juárez to Mexico City. Shortly after Walsh had finished editing that "good and bloody" five-reeler, according to his account, Jack London and Wyatt Earp showed up at the studio one afternoon wanting to meet "the man who rode with Villa."

There is no reliable record of when and how the two men got together. They may have met accidentally on the studio lot. After he had retired from law enforcement and moved to Los Angeles, Earp spent much of his time around the film studios looking for work as a consultant. London had read about Walsh's daring film work in Mexico and was naturally curious to meet him personally. "London was getting on in years, but his seamed face was still as rugged as his stories," Walsh recalled. "For a man who had only a year or more to live, he appeared to be in vigorous health ... The legendary Earp was tall and a little stooped, but I could still see him as the marshal of Tombstone."

They wanted to talk about his Mexican escapade, but Walsh managed to get a few details from London about his Klondike adventures and from Earp about the O.K. Corral shootout. Although he describes Earp as "legendary," the word would have fit London better than Wyatt Earp in 1915. It would be another dozen years before Earp's biographers conferred this distinction upon the onetime peace officer and longtime gambler/saloon keeper—and a decade beyond that before Hollywood canonized him and elevated the half-minute gunfight in a dusty Tombstone back lot to the status of Homeric epic.

Back home at Beauty Ranch, summer and fall witnessed visits from the usual crowd, including old friends such as George Sterling, Cloudesley Johns, Ed and Ida Winship, Blanche Partington, and Finn Frolich (who sculpted busts of both Charmian and Jack during those months), along with dozens of new visitors—too many for Charmian, who was plagued with poison oak, fatigue, and insomnia. "I feel (as usual) tired, with all the noise and confusion," she privately confessed. "First day we'd been alone for 3 months—in fact, since our return from Hawaii," she wrote on October 11. However, there were two welcome new guests that day: "Sisson of *Cosmopolitan* arrives, bringing another Hearst man—Goddard—movie picture—both sent to see Jack about movie serial. Looks like good business."

It was very good business—if not the best art. Hearst wanted London to collaborate with the scenarist Charles Goddard (of *The Perils of Pauline* fame) to produce an episodic novel for both serialization and cinematic production. The pay was twenty-five thousand dollars, enough to persuade Jack to interrupt at least temporarily his work on *Michael.* It was also enough to compel him to double his customary thousand-words-a-day regimen. This book, titled *Hearts of Three,* was "a new departure," he explained. "I have certainly never done anything like it before; I am pretty certain never to do anything like it again." Wisely, he never did, for *Hearts of Three* was not even successful movie material, much less good fiction.

Charmian's diaries during these months contain repeated comments about her fatigue and depression. Both she and Jack were evidently homesick for Hawaii and wanted to return there by the year's end. Meanwhile, two of her diary entries are particularly notable: "Sekinè, the new boy, being broken in by Nakata," she wrote on August 24. Nakata had informed them while still in Hawaii that he had fallen in love and wanted to get married and enroll in dental school. He pledged to stay with them until they could find a suitable replacement—or, more accurately, "successor," for they would never find anyone they would love as deeply as they loved Nakata. His successor was Tokyo-born, twenty-three-year-old Tokinosuke Sekinè, who had immigrated to America four years earlier after graduating from the Okura Shogyo College. He was destined to play a significant role not only in the last year of London's life but also in response to his death.

The second particularly noteworthy entry in Charmian's diary appears three months later. On November 25 she mentioned someone destined to play a significant role in her own life after Jack's death: "Go Oakland afternoon. Orpheum—Houdini. See him in dressing room. Take him to Saddle Rock." The Londons loved vaudeville as well as the traditional theater, and Houdini was a major attraction. On the next evening, Jack added distinction to Houdini's performance by appearing onstage with him. After the show, he and Charmian met Houdini's wife, Bess, and took them both to supper at the Saddle Rock restaurant.

"Charming Houdini. Shall never forget him," Charmian wrote. Nor would he forget her: in fact, she would be hard-pressed to escape the "Magic Man's" ardent courtship in 1918.

By mid-December she and Jack had endured more than enough of friends, visitors, and financial pressures. It was again time to get away. On December 16 they boarded the *Great Northern* for Hilo and Honolulu. "Seems impossible we're really off," Charmian noted the next day. "Been so rushed for so long. Stanford Glee Club aboard and we dance on the glassed-in closed deck and lots of fun. I am 19 again!"

One member of the glee club was Joseph Maltby, who later became a distinguished California judge. Many years after that voyage he recalled his encounter with the two great celebrities aboard:

> I am afraid we did little but meet & observe Jack London. We saw him at meal times & occasionally on deck in the afternoons. He brought a book to each meal & read while he ate. About the middle of each meal he would leave the table, go outside & smoke a cigarette. He kept strictly to himself. However I didn't get the impression that he was morose or taciturn. Rather, that he didn't want the usual hovering, simpering females around a celebrity.
>
> Charmian was a small woman, vivacious & intelligent. Because she was short, & so was I, I had many dances with her aboard ship. Jack never came to any of the dances or functions on ship.

What young Maltby did not know, and what few others realized at the time, was the true extent of London's physical ailments. His smashed and swollen ankles had prevented him from dancing for many years. His failing kidneys and general malaise had put a damper on his gregarious persona. This would be his last cruise to Hawaii.

After a brief stop at Hilo on December 22, the *Great Northern* docked in Honolulu two days before Christmas. The Londons were met at the wharf by their friends Alexander Hume Ford and Harry Strange, who drove them to a spacious old bungalow they had rented at 2201 Kalia Road, Waikiki. The next seven months would seem to be a return to paradise. There was the usual round of social functions. Charmian reveled in the dinners and dances; Jack, in the evening card parties; both of them, in the heartwarming luaus and the Charlie Chaplin movies they were fond of attending. He was now more than ever enchanted by these special islands, bound and determined to win the prestigious accolade of "Kamaaina":

> Kamaaina means not exactly old-timer or pioneer. Its original meaning is "a child of the soil," one who is indigenous. But its meaning has changed, so that it stands to-day for "one who belongs"—to Hawaii, of course . . . It applies to the heart and the spirit . . . Kamaaina must be given to one. He must be so named by the ones who belong and who are best fitted to judge whether or not he belongs.

Jack made his hopes for receiving this accolade very clear in a three-part series of articles he wrote for *The Cosmopolitan*, articles that would do wonders for the Hawaiian tourist industry: "Hawaii and Hawaiians are a land and a people loving and lovable. By their language may ye know them, and in what other land save this one is the commonest form of greeting, not 'Good day,' nor 'How d'ye do,' but 'Love'? That greeting is Aloha—love, I love you, my love to you . . . It is a positive affirmation of the warmth of one's own heart-giving." His love was affirmed when he was anointed "Keaka Lakana," the Hawaiian name for "Jack London." He had finally earned the coveted degree of Kamaaina. As one native of the islands attested after hearing of London's death, "The news came to Honolulu—and people, they seemed to have lost a great friend . . . They could not understand . . . They could not believe. I tell you this: Better than any one, he knew us Hawaiians." That special knowledge would inspire a half-dozen exceptionally fine stories after Jack returned home in midsummer.

Meanwhile, his failing kidneys were taking an ominous toll on his health. According to Charmian, he was limiting his consumption of hard liquor: "Sometimes I think I'm saturated with alcohol, so that my membranes have begun to rebel," he told her. But he was not limiting his consumption of cigarettes. He had also forgone the exercises that would help flush the lethal poisons from his system. Any activity involving his arthritic feet and swollen ankles was too painful. "Not a block would he walk to the electric tram, but called an automobile three miles from town whenever he wanted to go in for a shave," Charmian recalled. "If he were not going out, and expected no company, he spent the day in bathing-trunks and kimono and sandals, not only for coolness at work, but because it was too much effort to dress."

His oft-boasted "cast-iron stomach" had also begun to rebel. "You're never up in time to see the huge breakfast I tuck away—three cups of coffee, with heavy cream, two soft-boiled eggs, half of a big papaia!" he reassured Charmian when she chided him for not taking proper nourishment in the mornings. What he neglected to tell her was that he was now vomiting most of these breakfasts. At the frequent dinners to which they were invited, when remonstrated by his host that he had scarcely touched the food on his plate, he would repeat the story of his breakfast and add that he preferred talking to eating in the evenings.

One morning Charmian awoke to find him standing at her open door, his face distorted with pain. She realized he must be suffering terribly to have broken his pact of never disturbing her in the morning if she had managed to overcome her nightly insomnia. "I had to call you, Mate—I am sorry—but you must get a doctor. I don't know what it is, but it is awful!" This was the first of a series of kidney stones that would make his final months agonizing. But he "made little or no effort to put off his day of dissolution," she lamented. "The friendly physicians exhorted in vain: he clung to his diet of raw aku (bonita), and, aside from the breakfast fruit and occasional poi, which he termed a 'beneficent food,' quite neglected the vegetable nutriment his malady demanded."

London's health was not the only thing failing during his last years. His enthusiasm for the Socialist Party had been declining for some time, and he had been waiting for an excuse to take action. He was provided with this excuse when Netta's husband, Edward Payne, resigned from the Glen Ellen local. As soon as word reached him in Honolulu, he dictated his own resignation for Charmian to type:

Dear Comrades:
I am resigning from the Socialist Party, because of its lack of fire and fight, and its loss of emphasis on the class struggle.

I was originally a member of the old revolutionary, up-on-its-hind-legs, fighting, Socialist Labor Party. Since then, and to the present time, I have been a fighting member of the Socialist Party . . . I believed that the working class, by fighting, by never fusing, by never making terms with the enemy, could emancipate itself. Since the whole trend of Socialism in the United States during recent years has been one of peaceableness and compromise, I find that my mind refuses further sanction of my remaining a party member. Hence my resignation.

Please include my comrade wife, Charmian K. London's, resignation with mine.

Having vented his frustrations with the socialists, he dictated at least a half-dozen other letters on March 7. Three were especially noteworthy. The first was addressed to Joan, acknowledging her thanks for furs he had bought for her and Becky. "Some day, will you take the time off and tell me what books of mine you have read, and what books you have not read," he said. "Also, some time, personally, with you, I should like to have you tell me—and I make this as a challenge and a preparation in advance—to tell me what you think about me . . . Lots of love all round." Many years after his death Joan would tell the world what she thought of her father in *Jack London and His Daughters*.

The second letter was addressed to Edgar Sisson, editor of *The Cosmopolitan*, assuring him that *Hearts of Three* was nearly finished and informing him that he was gathering data for "a crackerjack Hawaii article" and planning "a short story which I shall entitle 'The Hussy,' and which will be a story of love, jealousy, and gold—the last being the largest nugget ever found in the history of the world."

The third letter, addressed to "Dearest Greek," reveals that he had paid George Sterling a hundred dollars for his plot outline of "The Hussy" but had to totally rewrite the story, adding that he'd paid Sinclair Lewis only five dollars for similar work. London then mentioned another Sterling plot: "Do you remember another wonderful story you told me a number of years ago—of the meteoric message from Mars or some other world in space, that fell amongst isolated savages, that was recognized for what it was by the lost explorer, who died or was killed before he could gain access to the treasure in the heart of the apparent meteor?" With Sterling's plot in mind, Jack immediately started his greatest work of science fiction and, regardless of genre, one of his most remarkable creations: "The Red One." Charmian sensed the psychological significance of this story when she wrote, "Sometimes I wonder if it can be possible, in the ponderings of the dying scientist, Bassett, that Jack London revealed more of himself than he would have been willing to admit—or else, who knows? more of himself than he himself realized."

A fortnight later he opened the pages of the most exciting book he had encountered since his discovery of Herbert Spencer two decades earlier. "I am standing on the edge of a world so new, so terrible, so wonderful, that I am almost afraid to look over into it," he exclaimed to Charmian. Her entry for June 14 underscores his enthusiasm: "Mate says this is the happiest day he ever spent in Hawaii." He had begun reading C. G. Jung's *Psychology of the Unconscious*, which had just been published. His reaction was a shock of recognition, for his "primordial vision"—Jung's term for this creative gift—had distinguished much of London's best fiction from the start.

It was an instance of what Jung termed "synchronicity" that Jack's discovery coalesced with his growing interest in the folklore and myths of Hawaii. "Much he read aloud, calling me to him, or following me about to instill certain passages," Charmian recalled. "As I came to look with him over that brink into the possibilities of that new world which was as old as Time, I began to see what it was beginning to mean to him who had sensed its abysses as long ago as when he wrote 'The Call of the Wild.'" During the following months, a period of intense creative activity, he would explore that new world in a half-dozen stories.

Their Hawaiian idyll came to a close on July 26 when, "loaded with leis by friends" and "standing ankle-deep in flowers," the couple looked down "into the upturned faces of the people from [their] Aloha Land" from the deck of the SS *Matsonia*. Five days later they reached San Francisco and a world very different from the one they had left behind.

The next four months would be anything but idyllic. Among the problems awaiting their homecoming was a legal game in which Netta and Edward Payne (along with Joshua Chauvet's son, Henry) were major players. This imbroglio involved riparian rights for Beauty Ranch. In order to provide irrigation for his crops, Jack had planned the construction of a dam at the headwaters of Wildwater Creek with the installation of a pipeline for diverting the water to his new lake. A few weeks before leaving Hawaii, he had received letters from both Paynes proclaiming their dismay at the project. Netta—who had brought Jack's finances to the brink of ruin during the *Snark* voyage—fretted that his latest agrarian venture might threaten her own economic security. "It is impossible," she wrote, "to conceive of anything but straight financial ruin to all of us who are dependent upon Wildwater." Wildwater was the subsidiary creek that flowed by Wake Robin Lodge. Despite her previous insistence that Wake Robin was part of Beauty Ranch, she was negotiating to sell to a stranger without consulting either Jack or Charmian.

"I have just reread your letters," Jack replied. "What is the idea? What do you want? I'll tell you what I want. I want an address. Can you give it to me? It is the address of the Tavern of Morality, where the unswerving schedule of equity is fifty-fifty. Has man merely dreamed of this tavern? Or does it exist? Come. Tell me. Where is the tavern?"

The Paynes pushed forward with their injunction against construction of the dam. This despite the fact Eliza had made sure the dam would not interfere with their water supply. They would persist with this legal exercise in futility until losing their case in court eight days before Jack's death.

Shortly after returning to the ranch, Jack completed "The Kanaka Surf," which he had started on the voyage home from Hawaii. No matter how ill he was, he still possessed the willpower to maintain his writing regimen. But both Charmian and Eliza could tell that his health was failing. While in Hawaii, Charmian had noted the failure of two major sources of his physical pride: his "cast-iron stomach" and his ability to sleep soundly whenever he liked. She was particularly worried by the latter development and the insidious effects of insomnia on Jack's temperament.

He might continue to put on a happy face in public, but he could not maintain that persona among those closest to him. Eliza had noted the "telltale face" of dissolution on the day he returned from Hawaii. "Our Jack has not come back to us," she told Jack Byrne, London's secretary. He was now in his fortieth year, and the progressive miseries of clogged arteries, diseased kidneys, arthritis, rheumatism, chronic nausea and dysentery, edema, and insomnia were taking their inevitable toll on his emotional as well as physical well-being. Charmian, being closest of all, was most often the target of his erratic moods. "Sometimes he was very calm, and evenings were of our sweetest," she recalled. "Again, over-intense, on hair-trigger to snap up any word as a pretext to start an argument if he caught me trying to placate or turn him into smoother channels, he flew into a mental fury, at times hot, at others deadly cool."

Charmian managed to endure but confessed that near the end she "was on the verge of nerve-collapse" from the constant strain caused by Jack's unpredictable outbursts of temper. Most dismaying was the effect of such outbursts on his elder daughter. On September 3 he had lunch in Oakland with Joan and Becky. What occurred that day marked, in Joan's mind, the "last crisis" in her relationship to her father. A fifteen-year-old wanting more financial independence not only for herself and her sister but also for her mother, whose monthly allowance "sufficed only for necessities," Joan asked London for an increase in their monthly allowance. Her mention of Bessie triggered his deep-seated animosity. Although Joan "immediately withdrew" her request, her father, "furiously angry," refused to drop the issue. According to Joan:

> Whatever I tried to say was cruelly twisted into its opposite intention. Frustrated at every attempt to get through to him, stung by the injustice of his accusations, I felt the beginnings of anger and then, to my horror, tears. I struggled to hold them back, but he saw them.
>
> His tirade ended at last. He asked me to send him some figures to help him make up his mind, and said he would let me know. Bess and I walked down Twelfth Street with him to the Orpheum where he was to meet Charmian and some friends. None of us had much to say. In front of the theater he kissed us perfunctorily and moved toward the glass doors that led into the lobby. With one hand on the door, he looked back for a long moment at us, still standing disconsolately on the sidewalk. My impulse to run to him, to fling my arms about him, died at the sight of his set, unsmiling face. He turned then, pushed open the door and went inside. We were never to see him again.

A month later, responding to a conciliatory letter from Joan in which she carefully itemized family expenses, he acceded to her request for an increase in their monthly allowance and signed off "With lots of love, Daddy," seemingly oblivious to the emotional wound he had inflicted.

After that final meeting with his daughters, he joined Charmian and Eliza at the state fair in Sacramento. He had heretofore resisted the temptation to show his prize stock at this annual event. This year, however, Eliza, aware of their blue-ribbon promise, persuaded him. As usual, her judgment proved correct: both Neuadd Hillside and his shorthorn bull Roselawn Choice won grand championships.

Jack was unable to witness the blue-ribbon ceremony. The best he could manage was to watch the display of fireworks from his hotel window. On the second day after arriving at the fair, he was stricken so severely with gouty rheumatism in his left foot and ankle that he was bedridden for the next week. His principal enjoyment between the intermittent attacks, besides watching the festivities out the window, was reading aloud and playing cards with Charmian, who spent hour upon hour massaging his swollen ankle and foot. During those few days, he followed doctors' orders to limit his intake of fats and proteins, contenting himself with the vegetable dishes she ordered for him.

On September 11, because he was able to hobble, they were planning to take the train back to Glen Ellen. Their plans were changed by Dr. Martin Van Buren Turley, an acquaintance they had met in Honolulu. He had just bought a Dodge touring car and offered to drive them home. Accompanying them was Turley's young friend Bill Davis, a negotiator for the Railroad Telegraphers in Portland, Oregon.

The drive over the gravel roads should have taken little more than four hours except for two incidents. First, when they reached Dixon, Jack, feeling he'd restricted himself to his moderate drinking regimen long enough, decided it was time for "a breather" and a cocktail. Upon entering the saloon, he and Bill encountered one of London's old Klondike pals among the loungers, and Jack ordered drinks for all. The bartender set up a second round of drinks "on the house" in honor of their famous guest, after which Jack and Bill rejoined Charmian and Turley, waiting patiently outside.

Jack was in fine spirits by this time, regaling the others with his Klondike adventures as they got back on the road. They ran into trouble just outside Fairfield when the right front tire got a puncture. Fortunately they managed to get into town before the tire was ruined.

During the repairs, Jack spotted a group of small boys spinning tops. At once his own lost boyhood returned. Borrowing a top from one of the youngsters, he began showing off: "But don't you do this, and this?" he said as he made the top spin up the trunk of a tree. They didn't and couldn't. But they could do things he couldn't. Hearing the sound of an automobile in the twilit distance, one of the youngsters quickly identified the make and model. "Well, I'll be damned! How did you know what was the name of that machine?" Jack asked him. "Know its engines of course—I can tell most of 'em a long way off," the boy answered, getting even in the game of one-upmanship. "I'm getting old. I'm out of touch with the younger generation," Jack said as he got back to Charmian. "All they know is gasoline—but I will say they know it pretty thoroughly!" The moon was well up over Sonoma Mountain by the time they reached home.

London's health seemed to be improved over the next few weeks, as the usual parade of guests enjoyed visits to Beauty Ranch. Feeling better, Jack was again in denial of his serious medical condition. At the beginning of the duck-hunting season in October, he resumed his high-protein diet, consuming two mallards a day cooked according to his own recipe. It was a mouthwatering delicacy, but hardly appropriate for someone with failing kidneys. Charmian did her best to dissuade him, with little success: "Oh, I love them so," he rationalized. "I've been good as gold ever since Sacramento, you've seen; and now it won't hurt me to fall off my diet."

Although protesting that he hated writing, he still managed his daily quota. During the month after returning home from the fair, he mailed off four very remarkable stories, including "When Alice Told Her Soul" and "Like Argus of the Ancient Times," both inspired by his recent discovery of Jung; and "The Princess," prompted by one of George Sterling's jokes about three one-armed tramps who tell each other varying versions of their accidental amputations.

Most impressive was "The Water Baby," finished on October 2. It was the last story he would write before his death, and one of the most revealing. Almost entirely without physical action, the story is principally a dialogue between two characters: John Lakana (London's Hawaiian name), a world-weary materialist, and Kohokumu (Hawaiian for "tree of knowledge"), a lively old fisherman who claims the sea as his mother and chants the adventures of Maui, "the Promethean demigod of Polynesia." Responding to Lakana's skeptical remarks, Kohokumu retorts:

"But listen, O Young Wise One, to my elderly wisdom. This I know: as I grow old I seek less for the truth from without me, and find more of the truth from within me . . . Man does not make truth. Man, if he be not blind, only recognizes truth when he sees it . . . Is this thought that I have thought a dream? . . . There is much more in dreams than we know . . . Dreams go deep, all the way down, maybe to before the beginning."

Charmian was impressed by her husband's fascination with Jungian theory during these last few weeks of his life, noting Jack's newly awakened interest in folklore and mythology, and his "comprehension of how to raise lower desires to higher expressions." She notes that in his personal copy of Jung's *Psychology of the Unconscious*, Jack "underscored Jesus' challenge to Nicodemus, cited by Jung: 'Think not carnally or thou art carnal, but think symbolically and then thou art spirit.'" Clearly, the combined influences of Hawaii and Jung had wrought "a sea-change into something rich and strange": London the avowed rational materialist, after coming through the game of life, was a philosophical work in process. At the end it would be neither mind nor spirit, but body that betrayed him.

28

SILVER SPEECH, GOLDEN SILENCE

I would rather be ashes than dust.
I would rather my spark should burn out in a brilliant blaze
    than it should be stifled by dry-rot.
I would rather be a superb meteor, every atom of me in
    magnificent glow, than a sleepy and permanent planet.
The proper function of man is to live—not to exist.
I shall not waste my days in trying to prolong them.
I shall use my time.

—"CREDO"

Although "The Water Baby" may have revealed something "rich and strange" in Jack's philosophy, it was not his final work of fiction. Within a week after mailing his short story manuscript to *The Cosmopolitan*, he was jotting notes for a new novel featuring a beautiful Japanese girl as its heroine. Under his various outlines for projected works, he had jotted down the following:

HAWAIIAN STORIES. Adopted Japanese Baby. Wealthy couple adopt pretty Japanese baby (explain reason why) in Honolulu. Educated, refined, above par of white girls of same class. Peculiarly beautiful. Walked, talked, looked straight out of eyes, etc., like a white girl. Problem: What was to become of her? Who would marry her? Japanese doctor who wanted her. Coolies and servants worshiped her . . . She was essentially sensitive, artistic, a creator of beauty in her way—also an emotional genius in the sense used by Saleeby, a la Anna Strunsky...And yet, always in the roots of her mental process, in spite of training, up-bringing, etc., was the baffling enigma of the oriental mind . . . *Motif*: Desire for understanding; baffling enigma of her own mind; and call of kind. Be sure to elaborate her Japanese innate traits.

On October 12 he wrote to his editor at *The Cosmopolitan* that he was already "five thousand words along and in full swing on an Hawai-ian novel, the heroine of which [is] named CHERRY." He had not yet determined the title but was considering "*Cherry; The Screen-Lady; The Screen-Gazer*; and *Fire Dew*." Despite diminishing vitality, he contin-ued work on his new novel until a crippling emotional disaster brought him down: "Come here and sit beside me. I have bad news for you," he told Charmian on the morning of October 22, "your Great Gentleman is gone . . . Good old Neuadd died last night."

Both of them broke down in tears. "Aside from the monetary loss, this was an incalculable set-back in [Jack's] far-seeing plans, already under way, for breeding," noted Charmian. More than this, the horse's death was an incalculable psychological setback. Neuadd had been the model for Mountain Lad, the stallion in *The Little Lady of the Big House*, whose libidinous trumpeting to Fotherington Princess signifies the virile, ever-young life force, potent even in the midst of death. "Crying unashamedly," Charmian said, "he followed me around much that day, telling more than I have ever dreamed of what the glorious animal had meant to him."

Vowing that the great horse should not have died in vain, London stopped his work on *Cherry* and began jotting down notes for a novel about Neuadd: The owner of the great horse is a "strange scholar man, a rheumatic invalid on his bed of perpetual pain who knew the dirt of all the world, who loved books." In answer to those who questioned his wisdom in paying ten thousand dollars for a horse, he would ex-plain, "I wasn't buying a horse. I was buying a man, and I think I've bought a whole lot of man." When he received news of the horse's death, "pain-wracked on his back among his books and memories of the sensate world in which he had once been a sensate being," the frail scholar determined to write down the facts about this champion stallion so that all would know that "horses were like men."

After sketching out an outline for his horse novel, Jack resumed work on the manuscript at hand. On the day after Neuadd's death, he wrote to Edgar Sisson requesting a six-thousand-dollar advance and bragging that he was "swinging along on *Cherry* at a rate of over two thousand dollars per month." To prove his point, he enclosed fifteen thousand words of the novel. He had not lost the self-discipline that had characterized his writing career from the start, but he was losing something of greater value: his vitality. Charmian mentioned his occasional listlessness, and he admitted that he was having trouble sleeping at night for the first time in his life. He spent his afternoons trying to nap instead of riding with her. More ominous, he was now suffering from chronic kidney stones, nausea, and diarrhea. His physical deterioration was accompanied by temperamental breakdown and the attendant symptoms of depression: "It's a pretty picayune world, Mate—what *am* I to think? Are they all alike?" he repeatedly complained as she recalled how he looked, his back to her with head in hands and elbows propped on his desk. "Every person I've done anything for—and I've not been a pincher, have I?—has thrown me down, near ones, dear ones—and the rest."

"Some of us are still standing by," she reminded him.

"Oh, I don't mean you, of course, nor Eliza. But the exceptions are so rare—friend and stranger alike."

His depression was hardly relieved by the lawsuit over riparian rights to Wildwater Creek. During his last month, while suffering through the multiple miseries of uremia, no less than five times he was forced to ride over to Santa Rosa and spend hours at the trial, "in which my own mother's sister is arrayed in court against me and my husband," Charmian lamented. True to character, at the first session Netta refused to shake Jack's hand. However, also true to character, after their injunction had been dissolved, London drove around and personally invited the plaintiffs for lunch and a tour of the ranch.

To the end he seemed to be in denial of his life-threatening medical symptoms. He had resumed his high-protein intake of rare ducks within a week after returning home from the state fair in Sacramento. Recurrent attacks misdiagnosed as ptomaine poisoning and "an increasing tendency to dysentery" only prompted him to admit to Charmian that "he was shockingly out of condition." He confessed to her that his system "had never been quite right since my sickness and operation in Australia—and Mexico didn't help matters any." His glimpse of reality was momentary. "But don't worry," he quickly rationalized, "I'll be all right, my dear!"

On November 5 he wrote to A. E. Heath of Curtis, Brown and Massie that he expected to be in New York later in the month and that he planned to discuss with the editor of *The Wide World Magazine* an autobiography about his writing career: "My idea, would be to give my writing experiences from my first attempt at writing right on down the line to the present date, I mean my experiences with newspaper editors, magazine editors, book publishers, etc., etc."

On that same day, he answered a letter from the editor of *The Seven Arts*, Waldo Frank, who said that he had heard through several friends, "Nina Wilcox Putnam and Theodore Dreiser among others—about some short stories which are so good that you have been unable to sell them." Word may have reached Frank about London's difficulties in selling stories such as "Samuel," "War," and "Told in the Drooling Ward." Jack replied:

> First, there ain't no such short stories. Second, if there were, my contracts, which are exclusive, and blanket, would prevent me from permitting any one to publish such stories . . .
>
> I do not mind telling you that had the United States been as kindly toward the short story writer as France has always been kindly, from the beginning of my writing career I would have written many a score of short stories quite different from the ones I have written.

One year before this he had written a much longer letter in a similar vein to Mary Austin, responding to her complaint that everyone had missed the point of her book *The Man Jesus*:

> Your letter strikes me that you are serious. Now, why be serious with this bone-head world? . . . I have again and again written books that failed to get across. Long years ago, at the very beginning of my writ-

ing career, I attacked Nietzsche and his super-man idea. This was in *The Sea Wolf.* Lots of people read *The Sea Wolf,* no one discovered that it was an attack upon the super-man philosophy. Later on, not mentioning my shorter efforts, I wrote another novel that was an attack upon the super-man idea, namely *Martin Eden.* Nobody discovered that this was such an attack . . .

Heavens, have *you* read *my* Christ story? I doubt that anybody has read this "Christ" story of mine, though it has been published in book form on both sides of the Atlantic. Said book [*The Star Rover*] has been praised for its red-bloodedness and no mention has been made of my handling of the Christ situation in Jerusalem at all . . . The world feeds you, the world feeds me, but the world knows damn little of either of us.

London's mood was growing darker during the fall of 1916, and his closest friend, George Sterling, was the victim of his irascibility. Although he refrained from directly confronting Jack, Sterling complained to others later on—telling Upton Sinclair, for instance, he felt that London toward the end "had departed from his principles and was becoming violent and irritable and unreasonable."

Jack's behavior was clearly taking its toll on Charmian. "Feeling ill toward night," she wrote on November 17. "Very sick all day" was her entry on November 18. "Can't make it out. Last night. All night up and down. Sore and shaky." She was sick for three days and later remarked, "I was on the verge of a nerve collapse. I must have been laboring under too great anxiety." On the day before the onset of her illness, she had a premonition of impending disaster. Ernest Hopkins, a reporter for *The San Francisco Bulletin,* had spent that day at the ranch with two photographers who took both still and moving pictures. Judged from most of the film, her husband appeared to be in fine spirits, "full of vivacity, with all that he could command of charm and aliveness . . . laughing from the high seat of the water cart, or driving two monster Shire mares in the manure-spreader." But Charmian "had suddenly, in one or two of the poses, noticed something in Jack's face, or an accession of something more than dimly felt of late, that struck fear into me. It might be described as a *deadness*—or an absence of life; something that no face, upon an upright figure, should be." The look she saw is evident in the still photographs of Jack sitting alone on the steps of the house, momentarily off guard and showing only a faint ghost of his famous smile.

She remained in bed all day on Saturday, November 19, their eleventh wedding anniversary: "Mate rubs my back in early evening. The dear! The sweet!" She was still feeling too weak to accept his invitation to accompany him up to the top of Sonoma Mountain on Sunday afternoon, "looking at new land he wants to buy, good land, watered [by springs]." Jack was in a bright mood when he returned later that day from his long ride: "I could develop the springs, and that would mean bigger crops, bigger and better cattle and horses, life, more life," he enthused. "Oh, it's big, and I have so many plans and so much to do . . . I'm going to take up the matter as soon as I can land the prospect of some money in New York. Maybe that autobiographical stuff will pay for it. I'm planning to go on the twenty-ninth. And you're *still* not coming with me?"

Charmian would not be coming with him. She'd had more than her fill of New York during those miserable weeks prior to their *Dirigo* voyage, and in view of his dire medical condition, Jack had no business in going to New York or anywhere else. He slept very poorly that night and vomited his breakfast the next morning—"stomach badly out of order," Charmian noted. "Sleeps in afternoon. Complains much of short sleep." He stayed inside napping fitfully the rest of the day, but roused himself when Eliza came in to talk about ranch business that evening. Once again he became excited telling her his plans to make the ranch an entity to itself with post office, general store, and even a school for the ranch children. "The ranch people can have their houses here, trade here at better prices, be born here, grow up here, get their schooling here, and if they die they can be buried on the Little Hill, where the two Greenlaw children's graves are."

That evening, still ignoring the seriousness of his condition, Jack ordered another nine-minute duck, cooked to his recipe. Joined by Charmian on the veranda of their cottage, he continued raving about his grandiose plans for Beauty Ranch. "Your duck was perfection half an hour ago," she interjected, seeing that he had barely touched his meal and trying to calm him down. "I'm afraid it is far from that now." But instead of calming down, he began declaiming about "the dirty business game" in real estate.

After another half an hour of this ranting, his mood began to shift again in the cycle that had by this time become chronic. Sitting down on the couch beside Charmian, he told her, "You're all I've got, the last straw for me to cling to, my last bribe for living . . . If you don't understand, I'm lost." Even while feeling a note of panic, she tried to reassure him: "I *do* understand . . . You are going too fast . . . Something will snap if you don't pull up. You are *tired*, perilously tired, tired almost to death. What shall we do? We can't go on this way."

He didn't answer, and she couldn't see his eyes because the green eyeshade he was wearing had slipped down over his face. She could see only the corners of his mouth, which "drooped pathetically." They "lay there for perhaps an hour, he resting, sometimes sighing, saying little except by an exchange of sympathetic pressures," when abruptly he turned, put his arms around her neck, and said, "I'm so worn out from lack of sleep. I'm going to turn in." Struggling to his feet, he startled her with this remark: "Thank God, you're not afraid of anything." These were his last words to her.

That night, after he had gone to his little sleeping room off the front porch of the cottage, she decided to calm her "distressed head" by taking a starlit stroll outside. When she returned, she saw that the light in Jack's bedroom was still burning: "Peeping across from my own quarters, I saw that his head had fallen upon his chest, eyeshade down. As I looked, he made a slight movement, as if settling to sleep; and knowing his sore need of repose, I did not venture a chance of disturbing his first slumber." She herself was worn out "from emotion and lack of rest." That night she slept for eight straight hours, the longest in weeks.

The next morning, she was awakened a few minutes past eight o'clock by Eliza, standing beside her bed with Sekinè. She immediately knew that something was badly wrong for them to break the rule of never disturbing her sleep in the mornings: "Sekinè could not wake Jack, so came right to me," Eliza said. "I think you'd better come in and see what you can do."

They could hear his stertorous breathing even before they entered his sleeping porch. What they saw was "Jack, unconscious, doubled down sidewise." Remembering his recurrent gastrointestinal attacks, they thought he was suffering again from food poisoning. Because the ranch telephone was out of order, they sent Jack Byrne down to Glen

Ellen to summon professional medical help. In the meantime the two women tried unsuccessfully to revive him "by means of strong coffee." Failing that, they enlisted the help of ranch hands in walking him up and down the hall, but "equilibrium of the heavy and nerveless figure was maintained only by sheer strength of his supporters."

The first doctors to arrive were A. M. Thomson and W. B. Hays from Sonoma. At that point "the real battle for Jack's life began." According to the newspaper reports, they first suspected ptomaine poisoning and tried "washing out" his stomach, another exercise in futility. Shortly after noon they were joined by Dr. J. Wilson Shiels from San Francisco. At midafternoon, London's own personal surgeon, W. S. Porter, arrived from Oakland. Well aware of his patient's chronic kidney ailments, Porter advised changing the diagnosis to uremic poisoning. At six thirty, Shiels, Thomson, and Hays issued the following bulletin to the press: "Mr. London is in a state of uraemia following an error in diet, causing a faulty elimination of the kidneys. His condition is serious. Further bulletins will follow."

The *San Francisco Chronicle* reported that the medical team had administered the "usual remedies" for such comatose cases: "A hot mustard pack and hot water bottles were applied to his body [and] his skin was rubbed [vigorously]." Still, there was no response. Charmian recalled that, now desperate, they resorted to a different tactic, yelling into his ears: "Man, man, wake up! The dam has burst! Wake, man, wake!"

"This caused a shudder in the congested, discolored countenance, the head jerked, the fixed and awful eyes made a superhuman effort to focus. There was a glimmer of consciousness, evanescent as the dying light along the wires of an electric bulb that has been snapped off." After repeated shoutings of the disaster, "to the point of intolerable agony of rousing from so deadly lethargy," recalled Charmian, "we were rewarded by observing that he protested with the leaden vigor of one half-thralled in nightmare, by slowly beating the mattress with a loosely clenched right hand. The left was never raised." As a last resort, she pleaded, "Let me try something."

They held his limp body up on the side of the bed while she grabbed him by the shoulders and, looking him directly in the face, cried, "*Mate!*

Mate! You must come back! Mate! You've got to come back! To me! Mate! Mate!"

For a brief moment, he seemed to be coming back to her. "Slowly, as something rising from the unfathomable well of eternity, full knowledge brimmed into these eyes that drew to mine in a conscious regard, and the mouth smiled, a fleeting, writhen smile." This, and nothing more, but she felt that he had responded to her call.

Jack's fleeting smile reminded her of a promise he had made long ago: "Death is sweet. Death is rest. Think of it!—to rest forever! I promise you that whensoever and wheresoever Death comes to meet me, I shall greet Death with a smile."

That evening Porter, Thomson, Hays, and Shiels issued the following bulletin: "At about 6:30 p.m., November 21, 1916, Mr. Jack London partook of his dinner. He was taken during the night with what was supposed to be an attack of acute indigestion. This, however, proved to be a gastro-intestinal type of uraemia. He rapidly entered coma and died at 7:45 p.m., November 22, 1916."

It is worth noting that none of the persons present during Jack's last hours, including the four physicians, reported anything other than a natural cause of death. The official death certificate, signed by William S. Porter, MD, states, "The CAUSE OF DEATH was as follows: Uraemia following renal colic." Two decades later, in order to sensationalize his "Biographical Novel," Irving Stone incited the rumor that London had ended his life with a calculated overdose of morphine. Notwithstanding the persistence of this canard, the consensus of medical and pharmaceutical experts in diagnosing London's final symptoms as related to his medical history is this: "Contrary to the assumption that Jack London committed suicide, it seems far more likely that he died naturally from the consequences of his poor health . . . manifested as cardiopulmonary and renal disease and ultimately stroke or heart attack."

On November 23 the shock of the celebrated author's death spread across the nation and around the world. The United Press bulletin gave London nearly an entire page, and *The New York Times* devoted two columns with an inset of London's portrait by Arnold Genthe with the headline DEATH OF JACK LONDON ENDS A LIFE AS ADVENTUROUS AS

HIS NOTED STORIES. *The San Francisco Bulletin* featured a full-page eulogy by Ernest Hopkins headlined:

Jack London Is Dead!
He of All Men
Was Supremely Alive!

"Death is always somehow incredible, but the death of Jack London is peculiarly so," wrote Hopkins: "Just one week ago it was my fortune as a newspaperman to visit the Glen Ellen ranch to be greeted by Jack London with all that exuberance that set him apart and made other men, by contrast, seem colorless . . . London, last Thursday, was brimming over with life, full of plans and anecdotes and jokes and playfulness. He was tremendously alive." Hopkins had obviously missed the momentary look of "deadness" witnessed by Charmian.

On November 23, dressed in his favorite gray suit, Jack's body lay in a gray casket at the Cottage while ranch folk and neighbors paid their respects. "Little as he would have approved of exhibiting the discarded shell of him, it would have been needless affront to the tribute these people were accustomed to pay to the dead," recalled Charmian. One of them remarked, "I tell you, the death of Jack means a sorry day to many. He gave away a meal ticket and added to it a bit, too. His heart went out to the fellow who carried a roll of blankets—or no blankets."

As the hearse was preparing to take the body down to Oakland, Sekinè found Charmian in Jack's workroom and handed her a few keys, the chamois coin sack London had carried since returning from the Klondike, and some notes from Jack's ranch suit. He also whispered something about a note he'd placed in the breast pocket of Jack's suit, together with a pencil and pad—"Just as he always had them, Missie," he added. "What note?" Charmian asked, apprehensive that something her Mate had written would be forever lost. "I wrote, 'Your Speech was silver, your Silence now is golden,'" Sekinè explained. "That was all. It was my Good-by."

Among the letters London had left on his Dictaphone for his secretary, Jack Byrne, to type was the following addressed to his daughter Joan:

Next Sunday, will you and Bess have lunch with me at Saddle Rock, and, if weather is good, go for a sail with me on Lake Merritt. If the weather is not good, we can go to a matinee of some sort.

Let me know at once.

I leave the Ranch next Friday.

I leave Calif. Wednesday following.

He did leave the ranch on Friday, not for New York but for the Oakland Crematorium. A month earlier he had received a letter from Dr. Hugo Erichsen, president of the Cremation Society of America, soliciting his opinion on cremation, to be used in a booklet advocating this practice. "Cremation is the only decent, right, sensible way of ridding the world of us when the world has ridden itself of us," London replied. "Why should we clutter the landscape and sweet-growing ground with our moldy memories? Besides, we have the testimony of all history that all such sad egotistic efforts have been failures. The best the Pharaohs could do with their pyramids was to preserve a few shriveled relics of themselves for our museums."

Following his cremation, a funeral service was held, attended by Frederick Bamford and a few other friends from the old Ruskin Club. "A short address was delivered by the Rev. Edward B. Payne, who was familiar with Jack's unorthodox views; and a poem, which had been asked of George Sterling, was read above his friend." Charmian did not attend. As she explained, "I was not ill, as the report went out. I preferred to remain away from a funeral which represented Jack's idea so little, but which I felt should be accorded to his daughters and their mother." Bessie declined to attend, but Dr. Porter brought Joan and Becky to the service.

"On Sunday morning, November 26th, Ernest Matthews, accompanied by George Sterling, brought the urn from Oakland," Charmian recalled. "We wreathed it with ferns and with yellow primroses from the garden. With the primroses, as a tribute to Jack's adopted home, Hawaii, I wound the withered rust-colored *leis of ilima* once given Jack in Honolulu by Frank Unger and Colonel Sam Parker." She was faithful in honoring his wish to be buried on the hill near the graves of the two Greenlaw children, beneath a giant lava boulder rejected by the builders of Wolf House:

When we had all gathered upon the dripping slope, Mr. G. L. Parslow, our oldest ranchman, received the urn from Ernest Matthews, and set it, with its flowers, in the tile already cemented into the ground. At that moment a great flood of sun-gold spilled upon us from a break in the leaden sky . . . No one stirred the hush. No prayer, for Jack London prayed to no God but humanity. The men, uncovered, reverent, stood about among the trees, and when their senior had risen, the stone was rolled into place.

The giant stone still rests in place a century later. Since that quiet Sunday morning, pilgrims from all four corners of the globe have gathered upon the same slope, paying homage to one whose silver words have proved forever young and vital.

EPILOGUE

Among the fisher folk of Scandinavia and Finland it is rumored that Jack London is still alive.
He has gone away in a boat of his own making, or is breaking trails in the snowfields of the North.
He has left his Valley of the Moon, and no one knows the port for which he has sailed, nor the goal toward which has set his face.

—ANONYMOUS

NOTES

I have used the abbreviations listed here for frequently cited works. See the bibliography for full citations. Aside from the Stanford editions of short stories and letters, unless otherwise noted, references to London's published works are keyed to first U.S. editions. Such popular titles as *The Call of the Wild, The Sea-Wolf*, and *White Fang*, as well as numerous London stories, are accessible in various inexpensive editions; however, several special editions of his works are recommended in the bibliography. While I have cited a number of references to articles about London's career and individual works, please bear in mind that these are intended only as representative examples of the massive scope of important scholarly and critical London studies published during the past half-century.

ASW   Anna Strunsky Walling Collection, Yale University
BJL   Charmian London, *The Book of Jack London*
Call   *The Call: The Magazine* [formerly *The Newsletter*] *of the Jack London Society*
CCL   Centenary College of Louisiana
CSSJL   *The Complete Short Stories of Jack London*
EL   Earle Labor Private Collection
EL/JCR   Labor/Reesman, *Jack London*, revised edition
HL   Huntington Library
JB   Jack London, *John Barleycorn*
JLD   Joan London, *The Daughters of Jack London*
JLFQN   *Jack London Foundation, Inc., Quarterly Newsletter*
JLFRC   Jack London Foundation Research Center
JLJ   *Jack London Journal*
JLN   *Jack London Newsletter*
JLR   *Jack London Reports*
JLRL   Reesman, *Jack London's Racial Lives*
JLSSF   Reesman, *Jack London: A Study of the Short Fiction*
JLT   Joan London, *Jack London and His Times*
LJL   *The Letters of Jack London*

NJL   Charles N. Watson Jr., *The Novels of Jack London*
SSJL   Martin Johnson, *Through the South Seas with Jack London*
UC/B University of California, Berkeley, Bancroft Library
USU   Jack London Collection, Merrill-Cazier Library, Utah State University

Epigraph

vii "The truth about its men of genius": Letter to Joan London, August 3, 1937, 3 p, TLS (typed letter signed), HL.

Preface

xi "It is easy to criticize him": Letter to William English Walling, January 30, 1914, quoted in Boylan, *Revolutionary Lives*, 201, ASW.

xi The canards about London's alleged drug addiction and suicide: See Earle Labor, "A Biographical Hydra: The Myth of Jack London's Suicide," *JLFQN* 23, no. 2 (April 2011): 1–2, repr. at www.jacklondons.net.

xi "vowed to have one thousand women": Headline on the cover of *True: The Man's Magazine*, April 1962. Article by Peter Michelmore and Al Stump: "Wild life of the Iron Wolf: Jack London was drunk at the age of 5, took his first mistress at 16, was famous by 24, burned out and dead at 41," p. 123. For a balanced perspective, see Nuernberg, "Introduction: Jack London's Literary Reputation," *Critical Response to Jack London*, xxiii–xxxvi; Tavernier-Courbin, "Introduction: Jack London: A Professional," *Critical Essays on Jack London*, 1–21; and Labor, "Biography of Jack London," in Berkove, *Critical Insights*, 25–35.

xi "his kaleidoscopic personality": Charmian London, *Our Hawaii*, 244.

xii "Ask people who know me today": *LJL*, 366.

xii While he rejected all forms of the supernatural . . . a thoroughgoing materialist: See, for example, Per Serritslev Petersen, "Jack London's Dialectical Philosophy Between Nietzsche's Radical Nihilism and Jules de Gaultier's *Bovarysme*," *Partial Answers: Journal of Literature and the History of Ideas* 9, no. 1 (January 2011): 65–77; and Lawrence I. Berkove, "On Jack London: Darwinism and the Evolution of Jack London," *Critical Insights*: "[As London] worked with central themes in his literature . . . his understanding of those themes *evolved* from simple to more nuanced and surprisingly more complex conceptions . . . [He] found in Jung a kindred spirit that enabled him to make an extraordinary breakthrough to optimism [and he] appears to have been one of the first to conceive of the possibility of evolutionary ethics," 3, 20.

xii "though the attributes of the lion were there": "To the Man on Trail," *CSSJL*, 159. Also see Clarice Stasz, "Androgyny in the Novels of Jack London," *Western American Literature* 11 (Summer 1976): 121–33; repr. in Berkove, *Critical Insights*, 218–32.

xii "Jack London had a poignantly sensitive face": Arnold Genthe, *As I Remember* (New York: Reynall and Hitchcock, 1936), 74.

xiii a rare genius: For the common denominators of genius, see Malcolm Gladwell,

"A Gift or Hard Craft," *The Manchester Guardian Weekly Review*, December 19, 2008. Extracts from *Outliers: The Story of Success* (New York: Little, Brown, and Company, 2008); and Michael J. A. Howe, "The Expertise of Great Writers," chapter 7, *Genius Explained* (Cambridge, UK: Cambridge University Press, 2001), 157–59, 172–77. Both authors contend that countless hours of intense practice are a common denominator in successful geniuses, regardless of their field of expertise. Howe points out, moreover, that great writers have been great readers as well. London qualifies in both respects, as well as in the less definable genetic factor.

xiii "greatest story": Alfred Kazin, *On Native Grounds: An Interpretation of Modern American Prose Literature* (New York: Reynal and Hitchcock, 1942), 111.

xiii E. L. Doctorow remarks: "Jack London and His Call of the Wild," *Jack London, Hemingway, and the Constitution: Selected Essays, 1977–1992* (New York: Random House, 1993), 5. Also see Jacqueline Tavernier-Courbin, "Jack London in Context," in Berkove, *Critical Insights*, 58; and James Williams, "Commitment and Practice: The Authorship of Jack London," in Cassuto and Reesman, eds., *Rereading Jack London*: "Any attempt to historicize the authorial figure of Jack London . . . will first have to confront the traditional summary of events of his time" (230n7).

xiii his apparent indictment of the myth: London insisted that his primary target in *Martin Eden* was rampant individualism. See his letters to Charles R. Brown, Philo Buck, and Mary Austin, *LJL*, 837, 1210, 1513.

xiii The literary historian Kenneth S. Lynn: "Jack London: The Brain Merchant," *The Dream of Success: A Study of the Modern American Imagination* (Boston: Little, Brown and Company, 1955), 84.

xiv my personal connection with Jack London: For a more detailed account, see Jeanne Campbell Reesman, "The Call of Jack London: Earle Labor on Jack London Studies," *Studies in American Naturalism* 5, no. 1 (Summer 2010): 21–36.

xiv *Jack London's Stories for Boys*: New York: Cupples and Leon Company, 1936.

xv I began writing the first extensive study of London's craftsmanship: Earle Gene Labor, "Jack London's Literary Artistry: A Study of His Imagery and Symbols in Relation to His Themes," Thesis (PhD), University of Wisconsin, 1961, Microfilm and Microform, OCLC Number 321778208.

xv friend and coeditor King Hendricks: See *Letters from Jack London* and *Jack London Reports*. In addition to coediting London's letters and articles, Hendricks published two noteworthy monographs: *Creator and Critic: A Controversy Between Jack London and Philo M. Buck, Jr.* (Logan: Utah University Press, 1961), and *Jack London: Master Crafstman of the Short Story* (Logan: Utah State University Faculty Association, 1966). Also see Earle Labor, "Jack London and King Hendricks at Utah State University," *The Call* 23, nos. 1–2 (Fall/Winter, 2012): 4–7.

xvi "An Open Letter to Irving Stone": *JLN* 2, no. 3 (September–December 1969): 114–16. Also see "My Long-Standing Quarrel with Irving Stone: A Pseudo-Biography Postmortem," *JLFQN* 20, no. 2 (April 2008): 4–7; and Clarice Stasz, "Charmian London, Eliza Shepard, and the Jack London Biographers," *JLJ* 5 (1998): 219–40.

xvi Russ Kingman . . . Thanks to his invitation: In August my wife, Betty, and I were invited to a dinner party hosted by Russ and Winnie Kingman in their Oakland apartment. The gathering included not only Becky and her husband, Percy Fleming, but also the Jack London aficionados Tony Bubka, Edwin Erbentraut, Sal Noto, Jim Sisson, Franklin Walker, and Dick Weiderman.

xvi "When he was with us he was always happy": Quoted in my "Beautiful Becky: Some Reminiscences," *Jack London Echoes* 2, no. 1 (January 1982): 44–45. This short-lived journal, edited and published by D. Michael Bates from 1981 to 1984, contains a wealth of information by London fans and scholars, along with regular columns by Becky London devoted to her father and his works. A comparable view of London is expressed by Yoshimatsu Nakata in his memoirs: See "A Hero to His Own Valet," transcribed by Barry Stevens and edited by Clarice Stasz, *JLJ* 7 (2000): 4–103: "He was so big and fine, with such a wonderful smile. I thought, My! Everybody must love this man" (26). Also included in this article is "Sekine's Account," 94–103. Tokinosuke Sekinè succeeded Nakata as London's valet in 1915, when Nakata married and enrolled in dental school.

xvi Londons' "Cottage": This house where Jack and Charmian lived while awaiting the completion of Wolf House has been restored and is now part of the Jack London State Historical Park in Glen Ellen, California. Thanks to the Shepard family, Charmian's diaries are permanently housed in the Huntington Library. Diaries from the years 1903–1904 are missing, possibly having been destroyed by Charmian.

xvii "She thought that he was the most beautiful young man": July 11, 1995, interview with Anna Walling Hamburger at her summer home on Cape Cod, arranged by Andrew Furer. Examination of the Anna Strunsky Walling collection at Yale University corroborates her daughter's statements.

xvii intensely passionate letters he wrote to Charmian: For a perceptive treatment of this phase of their relationship, see Stasz, chapter 6, "God's Own Mad Lover," *American Dreamers*, 109–25.

xvii "the other Jack London scholar": As a matter of fact, there were several others— King Hendricks, Gordon Mills, Clell Peterson, Alfred Shivers, and Franklin Walker—all of whom were making important contributions to London studies during the decade. Especially worth noting is Hensley C. Woodbridge, who published *Jack London: A Bibliography* in 1966 and inaugurated the *Jack London Newsletter* in 1967, published through December 1988.

xvii the "Ivy Mafia" . . . an astonishing increase in scholarly activities: Eric Miles Williamson, *Oakland, Jack London, and Me* (Huntsville: Texas Review Press, 2007), 132. See Earle Labor, afterword, in Cassuto and Reesman, eds., *Rereading Jack London*, 218–23, which surveys London scholarship from the 1950s to the mid-1990s; and, more recently, Donna M. Campbell, "The Critical Reception of Jack London," *Critical Insights: Jack London*, 106–15. On significant trends in London scholarship during "recent decades," particularly those influenced by the "cultural revolutions of the late 1960s," check Christopher Gair, "Writing

Americans: Author, Race, Nation, 1865–1910," *JLJ* 4 (1997): 173–97; and Paul Lauter, "London's Place in American Studies," *Call* 14, no. 1 (Spring–Summer 2003): 11–17.

xviii a natural-born "seeker": Neuroscientists have located the "seeking drive" in the most primitive area of the brain. Jaak Panksepp explains that when aroused, the seeking impulse "makes animals intensely interested in exploring their world," sometimes overwhelming other primal circuits such as fear and hunger. He suggests furthermore that "this may be one of the brain systems that generate and sustain curiosity, even for intellectual pursuits." See *Affective Neuroscience: The Foundations of Human and Animal Emotions* (New York: Oxford University Press, 1998), 51–55, 145–68. Also see Temple Grandin and Catherine Johnson, *Animals in Translation: Using the Mysteries of Autism to Decode Animal Behavior* (New York: Scribner, 2005), 94–139; and Roz Carroll, "Panic, Seeking and Play in Psychotherapy," www.thinkbody.co.uk: Carroll cautions that there is also "the shadow side of seeking" and that overactivation of this system produces negative results such as frustration and disappointment—which may shed some light on Jack London's darker moods.

1: Mothers and Fathers

3 "I was impotent": Letter to Jack London from W. H. Chaney, June 4, 1897, reproduced in Kingman, *A Pictorial Life*, 18. Most of London's biographers, including Kingman, have identified Chaney as London's probable father. Jack's daughters, Joan and Becky, evidently believed this, as do their descendants. Joan's granddaughter Tarnell Abbott attests that "from looking at family photographs I see the physical resemblances in my sisters, my sons, my grandchildren, my nephews and nieces and cousins to Flora Wellman, William Henry Chaney, Jack London, Joan London, and Bart Abbott." I quote from "In the Shadow of the Wolf: The Jack London Family Legacy—Searching for Truth among the Myths and Mists of Time, Draft 2, January 14, 2011," given to me by the author; the paper was originally presented at the Jack London Society 10th Biennial Symposium in Santa Rosa, California, on November 4, 2010. Also see Joan London, "W. H. Chaney: A Reappraisal," *American Book Collector, Jack London*, Special Number 17, no. 3 (November 1966): 11–13: "Flora was the fourth of what was to be a total of six Mrs. Chaneys; as far as it is known, with the one exception, all these unions were childless . . . Chaney's paternity can never, of course, be firmly established, but the probability is very strong." Joan was unaware that Chaney had fathered three other children by his second wife, Mary Ann Jordan, whom he abandoned when he left Ellsworth, Maine, in 1860. See Allan R. Whitmore, "Jack London's Three Unknown Half-Siblings: Strengthening the Case for a Virile William Chaney's Paternity," presented at the Jack London Society 11th Biennial Symposium, Utah State University, October 4, 2012. I am grateful to Professor Whitmore for sending me this impressively researched article.

3 During the first few weeks: In a November 4, 1931, letter to Fulmer Mood, Joan London says her mother told her that after two months the infant was starving to death, unable to take baby foods. Copy, JLFRC.

3 Mrs. Grantly: *CSSJL*, 1053–54. For Flora's likeness and other autobiographical parallels, see my "Jack London's 'Planchette': The Road Not Taken," *The Pacific Historian* 21, no. 2 (Summer 1977): 138–46. Also see Charles N. Watson Jr., "Jack London: Up from Spiritualism," in *The Haunted Dusk: American Supernatural Fiction, 1820–1920*, ed. Howard Kerr, John W. Crowley, and Charles L. Crow (Athens: University of Georgia Press, 1983), 197–200.

3 "It is her face": *JLD*, 114.

4 a celebrity of considerable distinction: For this and the following information on Chaney, see Fulmer Mood, "An Astrologer from Down East," *New England Quarterly* 5 (October 1931): 769–99. Also see W. H. Chaney, *Chaney's Primer of Astrology and American Urania* (St. Louis: Magic Circle Publishing Company, 1890), 64–165. "Marriage is said to be a divine institution and that matches are made in heaven. Judging from my own experience I should sooner think they were made in the other place," 163.

8 Chaney replied to both: Chaney's letters are reproduced in Kingman's *Pictorial Biography*, 18–21. Copies, JLFRC. Chaney says that, according to the detective's report, "The pistol was second-hand & had not been discharged since being oiled. It smelled of oil & had no smell of gun powder. A carpenter within 20 feet of her at the time heard no report of a pistol . . . Some boys on the other side of the fence heard no report. Her face would have been filled with powder had she shot as she said, but there was no mark of powder about her, etc."

10 "John Griffith Chaney": The middle name was "in memory of Griffith Everhard, a favorite nephew"—son of Flora's sister, Mary Everhard. *BJL* I, 25. Jack would later memorialize the name of Mary's son Ernest in *The Iron Heel*.

11 A vital connection was established: A significant account of London's close relationship to Jennie and the Prentiss family, as well as to the African American community of Oakland, is provided by Eugene P. Lasartemay and Mary Rudge, *For Love of Jack London: His Life with Jennie Prentiss—A True Love Story* (New York: Vantage Press, 1991). Jennie said that "the little fellow was so squirmish and jumpy he reminded her of a jumping jack" (38).

11 "I loved her deeply": *JLD*, 52–53.

12 pneumonia . . . "followed by measles": Department of the Interior, Pension Office, Western Div. No. 566-66-9, March 24, 1886. Copy CCL.

12 "Surely, he must be the bravest man": Frank Irving Atherton, "Jack London in Boyhood Adventures," *JLJ* 4 (1997): 39. This journal publishes for the first time the complete Atherton manuscript on file in the Huntington Library, prefaced by Mark Zamen's informative summary of Atherton's career.

12–13 "their mutual dreams . . . He was always protecting some one": *BJL* I, 18–20.

13 Biographers differ . . . first meeting between John and Flora: Ibid., 21–22, and *JLT*, 13.

14 Recalling the neighbors' gossip . . . one scholar has speculated: See Jim Riefenstahl, "John London: His Legacy of Wanderlust," *JLFQL* 24, no. 2 (April 2012): 2–5, which corrects several errors in Charmian London's biography, including John London's birth date, birth place, and height. Particularly noteworthy is Riefenstahl's information that "John arrived in California in 1874, not 1875 as biographers relate. [Therefore] one can speculate that John and Flora could have met well before Jack's approximate conception date . . . I am not asserting that John London was Jack London's biological father, but neither am I confident that William Chaney was."

14–15 "Can the two of them be buried" . . . "My father was the best man": *BJL* I, 28–31.

15–16 "We had horses" . . . "bleak, barren and foggy": Quoted by George Wharton James, "A Study of Jack London in His Prime," *Overland Monthly* 69, no. 5 (May 1917): 365–66.

16 "It was a wild, primitive countryside": *JB*, 22–34.

17 "Everything was squalid": James, "A Study of Jack London," 367.

17 "The Irish ranchers twitted me": *JB*, 36.

18 "My body and soul were starved": *LJL*, 24.

18 "Here Jack has written": *BJL* I, 37.

18 "I was a dreamer": *LJL*, 136.

18 "One unversed in such matters": *The Triumph of the Egg* (New York: B. W. Huebsch, 1921), 47–48.

2: Childhood's End

20 "Somewhere around my ninth year": *LJL*, 149.

21 "Duty—at ten years": Ibid., 24.

21 "life of toil" . . . "At eight I was deep in Ouida": Ibid., 149, 148.

21 "which he proceeded to bolt": *BJL* I, 47–48.

22 The first was finding a tattered copy . . . "It was this world": *LJL*, 1392.

22 "Do you know": Ibid., 650. For additional information about Coolbrith, see Josephine DeWitt Rhodehamel and Raymond Francis Wood, *Ina Coolbrith: Librarian and Laureate of California* (Provo, UT: Brigham Young University Press, 1973).

23 "I read mornings": *JB*, 41–42.

23–24 "It was recess" . . . "If it were boxing": Atherton, "Jack London in Boyhood Adventures," 16–20.

24 "Jack London was an extremist": Ibid., 141.

24–25 "two good-sized books a week": Ibid., 24.

26 "dream was smashed": *BJL* I, 50.

26 "My mother believed in spirits": *Star Rover*, 161.

26 "Her idea was Utopian": *BJL* I, 53.

27–28 "a dingy little cottage" . . . "We don't try to put on any style here": Atherton, "Jack London in Boyhood Adventures," 27–30.

28 "Hello, Frank, come and sit": Ibid., 74–75.

29–30 "Let me carry your suit case" . . . "And we became eager and restless": Ibid., 82–84.

3: The Apostate

31 "Now I wake me": This and succeeding quotations are from "The Apostate," CSSJL, 1112–29. "Johnny," the protagonist's name, was what Jack was called during his boyhood. He insisted on "Jack" after reaching his teens.

32 "For months at a time": LJL, 25.

33 "not the average": The Human Drift, 52.

34–36 "I wanted to be" . . . "He had Berserker rages": JB, 63–77.

36 "one bright vision" . . . "He and my father talked long": Ibid., 37–38.

37 "'Whisky,' I said": Ibid., 71.

37 "Better to reign": Ibid., 112.

37–38 "In truth" . . . "He talked and acted": Atherton, "Jack London in Boyhood Adventures," 128.

38 According to London . . . California Fish Patrol: London's name does not appear in any of the records of the California Fish Patrol, including the Biennial Report of the California Board of Fish Commissioners that listed regular patrolmen and deputy patrolmen, nor do the names of other patrolmen London mentions as serving under. See Dan Wichlan, "Wake of the Reindeer," JLFQN 23, no. 2 (April 2011), 7–9. Also see Margie Wilson, Oyster Pirates on San Franciso Bay/A History of San Francisco Bay, plus an Overview of Oysters and Their Historical and Cultural Significance (Sonoma County, CA: Wordsworth Publishing, 2013): "Some [Fish Patrol] reports include extracts from the deputies' enforcement reports, and others—but not all—list Deputy Patrolmen," 27. Both Charmian London and Frank Atherton mention some of these men in their memoirs.

38–39 "I had longer spells" . . . "I knew the end was near": JB, 113–19.

39 "respectfully suspicious": Ibid., 124.

40 "These wanderers": The Road, 159.

40 "And let me say": Ibid., 38–39.

41 "I have often thought": Ibid., 10.

4: A Boy Among Men

43 "A sailor is born": "Small-Boat Sailing," The Human Drift, 52.

43–46 "I drank every day" . . . "All my will": JB, 129–40.

46 ten "hard-bit Scandinavians . . . After a bit of strife": "That Dead Men Rise Up Never," Human Drift, 90–93.

48–49 "'I never taste it'" . . . "reeled and stumbled": Ninetta Eames, "Jack London," Overland Monthly 35, no. 209 (May 1900): 420. Eames records another significant episode in her interview with London: When defending his paper route at the age of thirteen, he was repeatedly bullied by another carrier three years older. They finally exchanged blows in a fight lasting more than two hours, Jack finally winning despite multiple bruises and a strained wrist. London dramatizes this fight in his hero's epic battle with "Cheese Face" in *Martin Eden*, chapter 15, 130–38 (Martin keeps fighting despite a broken arm).

49 "Ah! the very remembrance": "The Run Across," *Jack London's Articles and Short Stories in THE AEGIS*, ed. James Sisson III (Oakland, CA: Star Rover House, 1981), 55–57. First published December 2, 1895.

49 "[The] manifest charm": "Bonin Islands," ibid., 3–4. First published January 18, 1895.

50–51 "I had won" . . . "caroused somewhat more discreetly" after that: *JB*, 147–56. London explains that the "square faces" contained some fiery native concoction poured into the empty Holland gin bottles labeled "Anchor Brand."

52 In the sober light: This butchering is vividly described in *The Sea-Wolf*, chapter 17, 155.

52–53 "a true helpmate" . . . Late that afternoon: *CSSJL*, 11–12. Also see Haruo and Clara Furukawa, "Sakaicho, Hona Asi, and Hakadaki," *JLFQN* 17, no. 2 (April 2005): 1–8; and Métraux, *The Asian Writings of Jack London*, 4, 37–40.

53 "When I returned": *LJL*, 25.

5: The Dream as Nightmare

55 "I still believed": *JB*, 187–88.

55 "American social development": "The Significance of the Frontier in American History," *The Turner Thesis Concerning the Role of the Frontier in American History*, ed. George Rogers Taylor, rev. ed. (Boston: D. C. Heath, 1956), 17.

56–59 "Nelson was gone" . . . "I know I loved her": *JB*, 168–81.

59 "Haydee" may have been Lucy Ann Cauldwell: See Lasartemay and Rudge, *For Love of Jack London*, 111, 132. The account of the love affair between Lucy and Jack, including Lucy's photograph, matches London's memoir.

60 "It was four bells": *CSSJL*, 1. James Williams has provided a critically edited version of this story based upon the newspaper text rather than the book publication: Jack London, "Story of a Typhoon off the Coast of Japan," *JLJ* 6 (1999): 113–24.

60 "in a wakeful trance": *BJL* I, 137.

60 "To my mother": *With a Heartful of Love: Jack London's Presentation Inscriptions to the Women in His Life*, ed. Sal Noto (Berkeley, CA: Two Windows Press, 1986), 57.

61–63 "The superintendent beamed" . . . "The thought of work was repulsive": *JB*, 187–201.

6: The Open Road

64 "I became a tramp": *The Road*, 152.

65 a "mild-mannered young man": "Jack London and Kelly's Army," Special Jack London Issue, *The Palimpsest* 52, no. 6 (June 1971): 298–99.

66 "FRIDAY APR. 6.": *Jack London on the Road: The Tramp Diary and Other Hobo Writings*, ed. Richard W. Etulain (Logan: Utah State University, 1979), 30. This and subsequent quotes from the *Tramp Diary* are taken from Etulain's edition, 30–56.

67 "Up I climbed": *The Road*, 144–45.

68 "a young man of about twenty": Etulain, *JL on the Road*, 39–40.

68 "I have made some tough camps": *The Road*, 149–51.

71–72 "the fat Iowa country" . . . "Two of the latter caught me": Ibid., 179–88.

72 "opposed to violent exercise": Quoted by Joan London, *JLT*, 77.

72 "When I heard this": *The Road*, 193.

73 "Dear Son": *BJL* I, 160–61.

75 "Mother was greatly pleased": Ibid., 162. London would use the name of Harry's brother Ernest for the hero of *The Iron Heel*.

75 "On June 29, 1894": *Erie County Penitentiary Records* (Buffalo, NY), 282. Reproduced in Kingman, *Pictorial Life*, 55.

75–77 "It would take a deep plummet" . . . "It was a swift sneak": *The Road*, 107–21.

77 Joan London asserts: *JLT*, 90.

77–78 "On rods and blind baggages" . . . "I ran back to California": "How I Became a Socialist," *War of the Classes*, 272–78.

7: A Man Among Boys

79 "The other students were not impressed": Georgia Loring Bamford, *The Mystery of Jack London: A Reminiscence* (Oakland, CA: Georgia Loring Bamford, 1931), 21.

79 "The teacher rapped vigorously": Ibid., 17

80 "Are you going to the old Oakland High School": *LJL*, 1419.

81–82 "Opposite the big bed" . . . "And I wouldn't brag about it": *BJL* I, 188–92.

82 Some thought him "awful conceited": Bamford, *Mystery of Jack London*, 21.

83 "A Night's Swim in Yeddo Bay": In his *Aegis* story London attributes this incident to "a grizzled old merchant seaman" (*Aegis*, 27). He fictionalizes it again in "In Yeddo Bay" with "Alf Davis . . . a young sailor, just turned sixteen, on board the *Annie Mine*, an American sailing-schooner, which had run into Yokohama [with] its season's catch of skins" (*CSSJL*, 794). However, in *John Barleycorn* he says, "I managed a real exploit by swimming off to the schooner one dark midnight and soundly going to sleep while the water-police searched the harbor for my body" (161). See Métraux, *Asian Writings of JL*, 44–46; and Charles N. Watson Jr., "Jack London's Yokohama Swim and His First Tall Tale," *Studies in American Humor* 3, no. 2 (October 1976): 1–11.

83 "The little middle-class boys": *JLT*, 95.

83 "Arise, ye Americans": *Aegis*, 10.

83 "The Christmas week exercises": Bamford, *Mystery of Jack London*, 23.

84 According to Joan London: *JLT*, 99–100.

84 "She was a pale, ethereal creature": *Martin Eden*, 4.

84 "He was extraordinarily receptive" . . . "He had starved for love": Ibid., 4, 14.

85 "He knew, now": Ibid., 395.

85 "a remarkable man": Quoted by Joan London, *JLT*, 183.

85 "A Canadian gentleman": Ibid., 95–96.

86 "Any man is a socialist": Carolyn Johnston, *Jack London—An American Radical?*, 31.

8: Higher Education

88 "HURRY! Faster": *JLT*, 92.

89 "There were three months": *JB*, 211–12.

89 On July 29 . . . the *Oakland Times*: *LJL* 3–5.

89–91 "I was in full possession" . . . "the craving for the anodyne that resides in alcohol": *JB*, 212–19.

91 George Sterling's bohemian colony: See Franklin Walker, *The Seacoast of Bohemia*.

92 "wild things and romantic things": *BJL* I, 210–12.

92–94 "Another time when we met" . . . "Life from my point of view": Bamford, *Mystery of Jack London*, 27–30. For her remembrance of the cool reception Jack gave her when she and her husband visited the ranch in 1914, see 138–45.

94 When the crowd of onlookers gathered to hear him: *JLT*, 136.

95–96 "Heavens, how I wrote!" . . . "We sweated our way": *JB*, 221–25.

96 two letters he had received from Chaney: see chapter l.

96 "What is significant": *JLT*, 135.

96 "I hardly know what to write": *LJL*, 10.

97 "let career go hang": *JB*, 231.

9: The Golden Dream

98 "It was in the Klondike": Macmillan promotional pamphlet (1913); repr. in *JLJ* 5 (1998): 160.

98 "There had been": Berton, *Klondike Fever*, 100.

99 "the Great Barbecue": Vernon Louis Parrington, *Main Currents in American Thought, III, The Beginnings of Critical Realism in America: 1860–1920* (New York: Harcourt Brace and Company, 1930), 23. Also see Worth Robert Miller, "The Lost World of Gilded Age Politics," *Journal of the Gilded Age and Progressive Era* 1, no. 1 (January 2002): 48–67.

99 "I believed": Hamlin Garland, *The Trail of the Goldseekers: A Record of Travel in Prose and Verse* (New York: Macmillan Company, 1906), 8. Garland was disillusioned when he made the mistake of taking the overland trail to the goldfields through British Columbia. Misled by promotional literature that promised quick and easy travel, he spent more than four months on the trail before reaching his destination.

99 "Klondike or bust!": *BJL* I, 223–24.

100 "His weight was probably ninety pounds": "In a Far Country," *CSSJL*, 212–13.

100 "strong, vital man": *The Oakland Tribune*, August 14, 1938. Sloper is described in this article as "still erect and vigorous, [showing] little evidence of the strenuous life he has led." According to the California Department of Public Health Certificate of Death, Ira M. Sloper (Conn Valley Ranch, Napa County) was born December 5, 1855, and died June 17, 1942.

101 "the back door to the Yukon" . . . "The rest was ashes": Berton, *Klondike Fever*, 231–43.

102 "with Indians and canoes": *To the Yukon with Jack London: The Klondike Diary of*

Fred Thompson, ed. David Mike Hamilton (Los Angeles: Zamorano Club, 1980), 10. Subsequent entries refer to this edition.

103 "I am laying": *LJL*, 11.

104 "Like Argus of the Ancient Times": *CSSJL*, 2437–60. London wrote this story after his discovery of C. G. Jung in 1916. Reesman says that this story "is nearly as important to the Klondike fiction as 'To Build a Fire,'" *JLSSF*, 48. See also McClintock, *Strong Truths*, 156–58; and Earle Labor, "Jung at Heart: Jack London's 'Like Argus of the Ancient Times,'" *A Voyage Through American Literature and Culture via Turkey: A Festschrift for Sam S. Baskett's 90th Birthday*, prepared by Belma Otus Baskett and Oya Basak, edited by Nur Gokalp Akkerman (Istanbul: Bupress, 2011), 125–40; revised and reprinted in *Call* 22, no. 1 (Spring–Summer, 2012): 1–5. Among other significant differences, London's hero returns home as a bonanza king, but Martin Tarwater died at Fort Yukon in 1898 from "acute asthma" without striking it rich. See Dale Walker, *The Wolf*—'03 (January 2003): 7–10, and "Jack London: The Stories," www.jacklondons.net.

105 "the most important photo La Roche ever took": See North, *Sailor on Snowshoes*, 62–68.

105 "The midday sun": *A Daughter of the Snows*, 39–40.

106 "Their hearts turned to stone": *CSSJL*, 485.

107 "like a man boarding a comet": "Through the Rapids on the Way to the Klondike," *Jack London's Tales of Adventure*, 39.

107 They spotted a deserted cabin on Split-Up Island: They may also have been influenced by Miner Bruce's *Alaska*, which London had packed along with Darwin's *The Origin of Species* and Milton's *Paradise Lost*. According to Bruce, "Gold in considerable quantities was found at Cassiar bar on the Stewart River [in 1886]. The richest, by the way, so far located in the Yukon country," 54.

108 "One of these men": Marshall Bond Jr., *Gold Hunter: The Adventures of Marshall Bond* (Albuquerque: University of New Mexico Press, 1969), 38–39.

109 "The Alaskan gold hunter": "The Gold Hunters of the North," *Revolution and Other Essays*, 200.

109 London's "manner of dealing with dogs": Bond, *Gold Hunter*, 39.

110 "the outlook for grub": Berton, *Klondike Fever*, 172.

110 a "vast white silence": Quoted in Franklin Walker, *Jack London and the Klondike*, 118.

110 "There's no drama up here": Quoted in Berton, *Klondike Fever*, 203.

110 "The afternoon wore on": *CSSJL*, 143–44.

111 "Business appointments and deals": *A Daughter of the Snows*, 94.

111 "without imagination": *CSSJL*, 1302.

112 "The table was of hand-hewn": Ibid., 2089.

112 "I remember well" . . . noted a glint: *BJL* I, 235–40.

113 "In my personal medicine chest": *JB*, 232.

113 "One quarter of the bottle": Quoted in Franklin Walker, 140, from Jensen's "Jack London at Stewart River," HL.

113 "In the absence of fresh vegetables": *CSSJL*, 216.

114 "Given some fresh potatoes" . . . "Leave St. Michaels": *BJL* I, 254–57.

10: Breakthrough: *Overland* and *The Black Cat*

115 "And here is the funny thing": *JB*, 237–38.

115 "the head and the sole bread-winner": Ibid., 232.

115 "shocked Flora": *JLT*, 166.

116 "sole legacy in this world" . . . "My honest intention in writing that article": *JB*, 235–38.

116 "I have returned": *LJL*, 18.

117 "Forgive me for not writing": Ibid., 21–22.

118 "NO. 1 MAGAZINE SALES": USU.

118 "reasoned out the perfect formula" . . . "an impassioned realism": *Martin Eden*, 246–47, 232.

119 which he said taught him: "Eight Factors of Success," *The Silhouette* 2, no. 1 (February 1917): 2; repr. in *The Portable Jack London*, 512–13. See also London's advice to Cloudesley Johns, *LJL*, 191.

119–21 "In a general, vaguely general, way" . . . "I wonder what they'll pay": *LJL*, 23–36. For London's dramatization of collecting his pay from the *Overland*, see *Martin Eden*, chapter 33, 190–96. Ninetta Eames Payne gives a more congenial version of the incident in her preface to Payne's *The Soul of Jack London*, x–xii.

121 "devoted exclusively to original": *The Black Cat* 44 (May 1899): 1.

122 "He saved my literary life": THE RED-HOT DOLLAR and Other Stories from THE BLACK CAT (Boston: L. C. Page and Company), v–ix.

122 "First money I ever received": Evidently London did not know that while he was in the Klondike his story "Two Gold Bricks" had been published in *The Owl* 3 (September 1897): 43–48. See *CSSJL*, 49–54, 2500.

123 "I'll never be able to forgive": *JB*, 239.

11: Best in Class: *The Atlantic*

124 "You look back": *JLT*, 184.

124 "I am afraid I always was" . . . "They wanted the 1899 truck": *JB*, 240–42.

125 "Good easy reading": Frank Munsey, "The Publisher's Desk," *Munsey's Magazine* 21, no. 1 (April 1899): 157.

126 "I would never [have] written": *LJL*, 216.

126 "*That man of us is imperishable*": "These Bones Shall Rise Again," *Revolution*, 222.

126–27 "groping" . . . "I am sure a man can turn out more": *LJL*, 83, 96–97, 117.

127–28 "Dear sir" . . . "I can't reconcile the two": Ibid., 45, 48–49, 98. For London's difficulty in reconciling the two, see his "preoccupation with purity" in Stasz, *American Dreamers*, 74; and Lawrence I. Berkove, "London's Developing Conceptions of Masculinity," *JLJ* 3 (1996): 117–26.

128 "Virility in a man" . . . "one cannot really come to appreciate one's life": *LJL*, 69, 72, 85.

129 "The literary hack" . . . "And the sum of all this": "On the Writer's Philosophy of Life," Walker and Reesman, *No Mentor but Myself*, 7–10.

129 "Bess was several months younger than Jack": *JLT*, 101–102.

130 "Do you want to meet him?": Quoted in Boylan, *Revolutionary Lives*, 12, ASW.

130 "a pretty little ingenue": *Footloose in Arcadia*, 147.

131 "My dear Miss Strunsky": *LJL*, 133–38.

131 "incarnation of the Platonic ideal of man": Boylan, *Revolutionary Lives*, 12.

131 "It was as if I were meeting in their youth": *BJL* I, 320.

132 "I do hope we shall be friends": *LJL*, 133–38.

12: Marriage and Success

133 "As a brain merchant": *Revolution*, 303.

134 "I am writing for money . . . I shall always be its victim": *LJL*, 164–65.

134 "No man but a blockhead": Quoted in James Boswell, *Boswell's Life of Johnson*, ed. G. B. Hill, rev. L. F. Powell, vol. 3 (Oxford: Clarendon Press, 1934), 19.

134 His recorded earnings: See No. 1 MAGAZINE SALES, USU; copy EL.

135 "My father was Pennsylvania-born": *LJL*, 148–50.

135 "Dear Miss Strunsky": Ibid., 144–45.

136 "Have to get in a dig now": Ibid., 146–47.

136 "Ah! The physical basis": Ibid., 146.

136 "I see him": Anna Strunsky Walling, "Memories of Jack London," *The Masses* 9 (July 1917): 14.

137 be her literary "taskmaster": *LJL*, 156.

137 "Nobody ever 'Mr. London's' me": Ibid., 161.

137 "I am doing thus to you": Ibid., 162.

137 He was writing or seeing her: See Jacqueline Tavernier-Courbin, "Jack London and Anna Strunsky: Lovers at Cross Purposes," in Hodson and Reesman, *Jack London: One Hundred Years a Writer*, 22–23.

137 "On a certain Wednesday": Quoted in Boylan, *Revolutionary Lives*, 15–16, ASW.

139 Not recognizing the evasive intricacies: See Tavernier-Courbin, "Jack London and Anna Strunsky": "If ever a gesture was miscalculated, Anna's was . . . Jack's reaction appears to have been a measure not only of his frustrated desire for her but also of his fear of being rejected by a loved one—a fear probably resulting both from the pain of his having felt unloved by his mother and of his having been outspokenly rejected by Chaney, the man he presumed to be his father," 24–26.

139 choice would prove to be worse than foolhardy: See my review of Stasz's *Jack London's Women*, *California History* 81, no. 1 (Spring–Summer 2002): "London's impulsive, loveless marriage to Bessie was his most ill-calculated blunder, with tragic consequences for her and their two daughters, Joan and Becky . . . Moreover, the sins of the father (and mother) would be passed down to future generations," 71.

139 "You must be amused": *LJL*, 179.

139 "Jesus H. Christ" . . . "May I defer my congratulations": "Who the Hell *Is* Cloudesley Johns?" *JLJ* 1 (1994): 107. Original in HL.

139 "Why certainly you may defer": *LJL*, 180.

140–41 "Must confess you have the advantage" . . . "It will not, however, interfere much with my old life": Ibid., 178–79.

141–42 "The Klondike has waited" . . . "the Bret Harte of the frozen North": Quoted in Sherman, *JL: A Reference Guide*, 2–3.

142 "Grandma was loyal to me": Quoted in *JLT*, 225.

143 "high-up literary and philosophical society": Johnston, *Jack London: An American Radical?*, 97.

143 "a writing man primarily" . . . "With a gesture that is familiar": See my foreword in Zamen, *Standing Room Only*, xiii. Also see 193–253 for reviews of London's lectures in newspapers and periodicals.

143 "Ever bike?": *LJL*, 193–94.

143 Ida Strobridge: See *JL*, 190–91.

144–46 "Well, I'm back" . . . "on the home stretch" . . . "a failure": Ibid., 181, 183, 187, 191, 194–95, 197, 203, 240. See Reesman, *JLRL*: "[*A Daughter of the Snows*] perfectly illustrates how unchecked racialism inevitably brings about artistic failure," 67.

146 "Lord, Lord": *BJL* I, 384.

146 "love was a madness": Quoted in Boylan, *Revolutionary Lives*, 18, ASW.

146–47 "A young Russian Jewess" . . . "A white beautiful friendship": *LJL*, 214, 228–29.

13: In Key with the World

148 "Every man, at the beginning": *LJL*, 245.

148–49 "To tell you the truth" . . . "It must be great and strong": Ibid., 233–35.

149–50 was a disappointment to her father . . . "And don't be concerned about her head": *JLD*, 3–8.

150 "*Joan meditateth on the Mystery*": *JLD*, 7–9.

150 the art of photography: See Philip Adam, "A Photographer's Reflections on Jack London," in Reesman, Hodson, and Adam, *JL, Photographer*: "From 1900 to 1916 [London] made more than 12,000 photographs both on professional assignments and during personal adventures . . . To make meaningful photographs, you must do more than look: as Ruskin suggested, you must *see*. London's photographs showed me he had acquired this skill" (xiii–xiv).

151 "I understand that as soon as Jack London is elected": *The San Francisco Evening Post*, January 26, 1901, HL, and *LJL*, 241n3.

151 "is still as eager a champion": *The San Francisco Examiner*, May 19, 1901, HL.

151 "part of a great world philosophy": *LJL*, 237–38. His letter was published in *The Oakland Tribune* on February 5, 1901.

151 "Am much more finely situated": Ibid., 241.

151 "large, beautiful terrace": *JLD*, 7.

151 "The novel is off at last": *LJL*, 243.

152 A favorite rendezvous was Coppa's restaurant: Lawrence Ferlinghetti and Nancy J. Peters, *Literary San Francisco: A Pictorial History from the Beginnings to the Present Day* (San Francisco: City Lights Books and Harper and Row Publishers, 1980), 96–98.

153 brilliant tubercular cynic: Brissenden commits suicide (chapter 40, p. 343); although not tubercular, Sterling took his own life by swallowing cyanide in 1925.

153 "a prince of extremists" . . . "George was hugely entertained": Charmian Kittredge London, "George Sterling—As I Knew Him," *Overland Monthly and Out West Magazine* 85 (March 1927): 90.

153 "was a strange, fervid, almost prophetic eloquence": Joseph Noel, *Footloose in Arcadia*, 92–94.

154 "Blessed, Beloved Greek": Stanley Wertheim and Sal Noto, eds. "Dearest Greek: Jack and Charmian London's Presentation Inscriptions to George Sterling," *The Book Club of California Quarterly Newsletter* 48, no. 4 (Fall 1983): 95, 98.

154 "piano and singing": *BJL* I, 362–63.

154–55 "[W]e are both large temperamentally" . . . "I should like some time to be with you": *LJL*, 244, 248.

155 "Washoe Indians": See Wichlan, *JL: The Unpublished and Uncollected Articles*, 33–38.

155 Third National Bundes Shooting Festival: *JLR*, 215–53.

155 GIRL WHO CROSSED SWORDS: Wichlan, *JL: Unpublished*, 39–43.

155 prizefight between James J. Jeffries and Gus Ruhlin: *JLR*, 215–53.

155–56 "Despite its crudeness" . . . "There is greatness in this classic": Sherman, *JL Reference Guide*, 4–6.

156 "Am all in the chaos" . . . "To hell with them": *LJL*, 254–55, 260.

14: Anna and the *Abyss*

157 "And how have I lived": *LJL*, 279.

157 "full of worries": Ibid., 269–70.

157 "But after all, what squirming": Ibid., 270.

158 "to represent very much the best work": Ibid., 267n2.

158 "Mr. Brett took a gamble": *BJL* I, 389–90.

159 hanging of the convicted murderer Isaac Daily: See *LJL*, 281n1.

159–60 "To live is to experience sensations" . . . "It's glorious here": *LJL*, 279–81, 283, 286.

160 Charmian recollected: *BJL* I, 364–65.

160 "Every day we would walk down the path": *JLD*, 10–11.

161 " 'We shall have great joy' ": "The Golden Poppy," *Revolution*, 119–38; repr. in Noto, *JL's California: The Golden Poppy and Other Writings*, 3–13.

162 "I do not know": *LJL*, 291. Reesman commends *Children of the Frost* as London's "most compelling collection of Klondike stories," *JLSSF*, 53.

162 "Marry me, Anna": Quoted in Hal Waters, "Anna Strunsky and Jack London (Based on Exclusive Interviews in 1963 and 1964)," *American Book Collector* 17, no. 3 (November 1966): 30. Anna said she told her mother about Jack's proposal

and although Mrs. Strunsky didn't forbid her to marry him, she helped her realize how unhappy their lives would be if based upon a broken marriage and family.

163 "She said nothing of any importance": Quoted in Boylan, 24; original in the *San Francisco Chronicle*, June 30, 1904.

163 "wander off into adjacent woods": Ibid., original in HL, Franklin Walker Collection, folder HM 45261, "Notes re: Jack London's divorce from Besse [sic] London."

163–64 "I was out sailing Saturday" . . . "I find it almost impossible to believe": *LJL*, 296–98, 305–306.

164 "Of all my books on the long shelf": *BJL* I, 381.

165 "There is one beautiful sight . . . Far better to be a people of the wilderness: *The People of the Abyss*, 274–75, 288.

165 "I merely state the case as I saw it": *BJL* I, 381. See Clarice Stasz, foreword to *The People of the Abyss: With Jack London Photographs and Drawings by Gustave Doré* (Los Angeles: Joseph Simon Publisher, 1980), vii–xiii. Stasz points out that although London's book reached few readers, it inspired George Orwell's *Down and Out in Paris and London*. Also see James R. Giles, "Jack London Down and Out in England: The Relevance of the Sociological Study *The People of the Abyss* to London's Fiction," *JLN* 2 (September–December 1969): 79–83.

165 "like a torrent of tears": Quoted in Boylan, *Revolutionary Lives*, 25, ASW.

165 insulting their friendship and her love: Extrapolated from Anna's memoirs, ASW, and Jack's letter of August 25, *LJL*, 306–308. Charmian quotes only the first paragraph of his letter in which Jack talks of spending a night with "the homeless ones," *BJL* I, 380.

166 "You are one of the cruelest women" . . . "Henceforth I shall dream romances for other people": *LJL*, 306–13.

167 "Mother never stopped loving him": Anna Walling Hamburger interview, July 11, 1995. When asked, "What was the first time you heard your mother mention Jack London?" Mrs. Hamburger replied, "She spoke about him all the time, so I don't remember a first time." Copies of correspondence between Mrs. Hamburger and Russ Kingman are on file at JLFRC.

167 "Who that ever knew him can forget him": Quoted in Waters interview, 30.

167 "long-deferred vacation": *LJL*, 314.

167 On October 15 he wrote a short letter to Anna: HL.

167 "wrote the first and only love letters": *JLT*, 241.

167–68 "What an unlucky mischance!" . . . "I am deep in the mystery": *LJL*, 316, 319, 329–30.

15: The Wonderful Year

170 "There is an ecstasy": *The Call of the Wild*, 91.

170 "Writers, like other makers": Howe, "The Expertise of Great Writers," *Genius Explained*, 157–58.

171 "psychological mode" and the "visionary mode" . . . "a strange something that

derives its existence": C. G. Jung, "Psychology and Literature," *Modern Man in Search of a Soul*, trans. W. S. Dell and Carey F. Baynes, (New York: Harvest Book/ Harcourt, Brace, and World, n.d.), 156–58.

171 "archetypal images": See C. G. Jung, *Archetypes and the Collective Unconscious*, trans. R.F.C. Hull, 2nd ed. (Princeton, NJ: Princeton University Press, 1968).

171 "got away from me": Letter to Strunsky, *LJL*, 352.

171 "a purely fortuitous piece of work": *JLT*, 252.

172 "It is an animal story": *LJL*, 342–43.

172 What inspired him: See Jacqueline Tavernier-Courbin, *The Call of the Wild: A Naturalistic Romance* (New York: Twayne Publishers, 1994): "Part adventure-romance and part human allegory, the book is also a naturalistic document on Klondike life during the Gold Rush as well as a gripping tale of devolution . . . Emotionally, psychologically, mythically, and archetypally satisfying, [it] is also ethically and romantically satisfying," 21–22. Also see *The Call of the Wild by Jack London: A Casebook with Text, Background Sources, Reviews, Critical Essays, and Bibliography*, compiled with an introduction by Earl J. Wilcox (Chicago: Nelson-Hall, 1980); and *The Call of the Wild: Complete Text with Introduction, Historical Contexts, Critical Essays*, ed. Earl J. Wilcox and Elizabeth H. Wilcox, New Riverside Edition (Boston: Houghton Mifflin Company, 2004). The definitive annotated edition is *The Call of the Wild, with an Illustrated Reader's Companion*, ed. Daniel Dyer (Norman: University of Oklahoma Press, 1995).

172 he had just finished reading: Egerton R. Young's *My Dogs in the Northland* (New York: Fleming H. Revel Co., 1902).

172 "In *The Call of the Wild*": *JLT*, 252. Also see Stewart Gabel, *Jack London, a Man in Search of Meaning*, 41–50.

172 "I am on the track of a sea story": *LJL*, 337–38.

173 "By the way": Ibid., 341.

173 "Jack greeted me delightedly": Johns, *JLJ* 2 (1995), 49.

174 "I was not in a very happy state": *LJL*, 520–21.

174 "tremendous creation, Wolf Larsen": Letter to Sterling, February 18, 2005, in *A Much Misunderstood Man: Selected Letters of Ambrose Bierce*, ed. S. T. Joshi and David E. Schultz (Columbus: Ohio State University Press, 2003), 131.

175 "I believe that life is a mess": *The Sea-Wolf*, 50.

175 "You will remember": *LJL*, 520–21.

175 "martyr and gossip": Personal conversation with Becky London at the Jack London Research Center, Glen Ellen, CA, July 1983. Becky's memories of her parents were markedly different from her older sister's. See the short-lived but informative journal published by J. Michael Bates, particularly Becky's memoirs in *Jack London Echoes* 1, nos. 2, 3, 4 (April, July, October, 1981) and *Echoes* 2, nos. 1, 2 (January, July 1982). For example, she says, "Daddy never scolded or nagged, he was never mean or nasty about our mistakes. He would call them to our atten-

tion, tell us how to correct them and let us learn by experience. Twice a year there would come to our house a huge packing case addressed to Joan and me. It was not a surprise. We knew what was inside and could hardly wait for the top to be pried off so we could see inside layer after layer of books, books, books": *JL Echoes* 1, no. 3 (July, 1981): 23. Also see Stasz, *JL's Women*, 96, 148, 186–87, 244–45; and Jacqueline Tavernier-Courbin, "Bessie: The First Mrs. Jack London," *JLJ* 5 (1998): 168–218. Tavernier-Courbin's interviews correlate with my own conversations with Becky.

175 "Erstwhile worth-while fun and stunts": *JB*, 259.

176 "Lusty yachtsmen": Quoted in Stasz, *American Dreamers*, 111.

176–77 "good Inquisitionist" . . . "She had the soul of an artist": Ibid., 15–17.

179 "I began to grow pretty desirous": *LJL*, 522.

179–80 "Had you failed" . . . "We shall live life together": Ibid., 366–67.

180 "great Man-Comrade": Ibid., 370–71.

180 "And pray *who* are you": One page, August 9, 2003, AL (autograph letter unsigned), EL.

180 "If you could see me waiting": Five pp., August 14, 2003, AL, EL.

181 "You are my wife by the highest sanctions": Five pp., August 19, 2003, AL, EL.

181 "She asked me if I loved somebody else": *LJL*, 523.

182 "Just a line to let you know" . . . "it's damned hard on the woman": Ibid., 376–81.

182 "dead level of sickening brutality": Ibid., 384n2.

182 gave Gilder permission to "blue pencil": Ibid., 383.

183 "That you should be the one woman" . . . "There is frost in the winter time in Kobe": *LJL*, 389–91.

184 "At least believe this of me": Ibid., 378.

184 "He smiled carelessly": Atherton, *JLJ* 4 (1997): 166.

184 "We can both get our writing in each day": *LJL*, 394.

184–86 "writing, playing chess, arguing" . . . "They were purple passages of life": Johns, *JLJ* 3 (1996): 176–79.

16: The Wages of War

187 "I am hungry to be where you are": *LJL*, 429–30.

188 "to send each month $127.50": Ibid., 405.

189 "I knew that the mortality of war": *JLR*, 122.

189 "The situation was unique": Quoted in Herbert Croly, *Willard Straight* (New York: Macmillan Company, 1925), 126.

189 "I soon found": *JLR*, 122.

190–91 "Japanese Police 'Very sorry'" . . . "Must have given him bad dreams": *LJL*, 409–13.

192 "I want to say that Jack London": Quoted in Kingman, *Pictorial Life of Jack London*, 130–31; originally published in *The San Francisco Examiner*, June 26, 1904.

192 "Concerning Power of Attorney": Four pp., February 17, 1904, AL, EL. Fragments of this letter appear in *BJL* I, 410; *BJL* II, 3–4; and *JLR*, 12.

192–93 "saddle-sore and raw" . . . "And how under the sun am I to write": *LJL*, 414–18.

193–95 "SHIMONOSEKI" . . . "And this man [is] dispatched to Korea": *JLR*, 38–82. I am also indebted to Michael S. Sweeney's "Delays and Vexations: Jack London and the Russo-Japanese War," presented at the Annual Convention of the American Journalism Historical Association, October 16, 1997, in Mobile, Alabama; subsequently published in *Journalism and Mass Communications Quarterly* 75, no. 3 (Autumn, 1998): 548–59.

195 "the Japanese are disciplining us" . . . "eating my heart out with inactivity": *LJL*, 420–24.

196 "When I think of all those letters": Two pages, front and back, AL, EL; *LJL*, 424 (fragment).

196 "Although cheery and kindly": Frederick Palmer, *With My Own Eyes: A Personal Story of Battle Years* (Indianapolis: Bobbs-Merrill Company, 1933), 242.

196 "I was one of the lucky fourteen": *JLR*, 123.

196 "Here I am": *LJL*, 426.

197 Especially noteworthy in those pictures: See Reesman and Hodson, *JL, Photographer*, 56–114.

197 "I am clean disgusted": *LJL*, 428.

197 Two weeks later he wrote to the *Examiner*: See letter to Charmian, ibid., 430.

198 "explaining that London was a most gifted writer": Palmer, *With My Own Eyes*, 242.

198 "Article 4 of REGULATIONS": *JLR*, 25.

199 "Oh, my Darling": Three pp., ALS (signed "Mate"), EL.

17: The Long Sickness

200 "The things I had fought for": *JB*, 254.

200 "I cabled you yesterday that I was coming": June 1, 1904, three pp. ALS, EL.

200 "JACK LONDON SUED": Quoted in Waters, "Anna Strunsky and Jack London," 29.

201 "Absurd is hardly a word": Quoted in Kingman, *Pictorial Life of JL*, 138–39.

202 "As Anna told me the story": Joan London, "The London Divorce," *American Book Collector* 17, no. 3 (November 1966): 31.

203 "from drawing his money": Waters, "Anna Strunsky and JL," 29.

203 "fight it out alone": Letter from Charmian to Blanche Partington, March 8, 1907, quoted in Stasz, *American Dreamers*, 121, UC/B.

203 "I see no reason why": *LJL*, 432.

204 a "sweet-tempered baby": *JLD*, 21–22.

205 "Dear Charmian:—You know": Reprinted in Noto, *With a Heart Full of Love*, 32, USU.

205 "Coming": Quoted in Stasz, *American Dreamers*, 121.

205 "Arrived 1216": Charmian's diaries are on file in the Huntington Library. Quotations and dates referenced in the text are not repeated in the notes.

205 "Dearest—You are with me yet": AL (n.s.): copy, CCL.

205 "I've the [picture of]": August 15, ibid.

205 His datebook reveals: HL.

205–206 "Believe me" . . . "Why tie my own shoes": *BJL* II, 5–6.

206–207 "I had no understanding" . . . "For that little while, he was wholly ours": *JLD*, 25–27.

207 "I had life troubles and heart troubles": *JB*, 253–56.

207 In a letter apologizing: *LJL*, 436.

207–208 "No, dear" . . . "In many respects": Ibid., 446–47.

208 "spring" book . . . "really big play": Ibid., 448.

208 *Scorn of Women*: London's short story was published in the May 1901 *Overland* as "The Scorn of Women."

208 "In the three months since my return": *LJL*, 446–48.

208 "I would rather be heavyweight champion": *Medford Sun*, August 13, 1911; quoted in Jack London, *Stories of Boxing*, ed. James Bankes (Dubuque, IA: Wm. C. Brown Publishers, 1992), xii. Also see Charmian's unpublished introduction to "War Notes and Prizefights by Jack London": "I would rather be champion prizefighter of the world than author of the 'Great American Novel'!" (USU).

209 "sheer street-bred sensuality": Sherman, *Reference Guide*, 28, 30.

210 "Instead of the devolution": *LJL*, 454–55.

210 "I had to be absolutely satisfied": Quoted in Stasz, *American Dreamers*, 123, UC/B.

211 "a crude and incoherent novel": Sherman, *JL: A Reference Guide*, 15–16.

211 "It is pleasant to look upon Mr. London": HL.

212 "Mr. London flashed one look": Quoted in Zamen, *Standing Room Only*, 89.

212 asked President Wheeler if he should stop: *BJL* II, 21–22.

212 "Seven million revolutionists": *Revolution*, 1, 38.

213 Herman "Toddy" Albrecht: A member of the Crowd who acquired his nickname as a tribute to his expertise in mixing cocktails. Also see *LJL*, 441n1.

213 reading aloud to her "by the hour": *BJL*, II, 25–26.

214 "LONDON STARTLES STAID CLUBMEN": Zamen, *Standing Room Only*, 89.

214 "Comrade London": Johns, "Who the Hell *Is* Cloudesley Johns?" *JLJ* 5 (1998): 123.

215 "I wouldn't let my name be used": *BJL* II, 25.

215 "It was the PEOPLE": JB, 256–57.

215 "Coming tomorrow horseback": CKL diary, Tuesday, March 7, 1905.

216 "Ah! city life is the only life": *LJL*, 91.

216 "I don't seem to care for anything": *BJL* II, 31. See Labor, "Jack London's 'Planchette': The Road Not Taken," 138–46.

217 "Am going to bring the *Spray*": *LJL*, 473.

217 "I came home to bed": Ibid. His "old hurt" was a painful inflammation of hemorrhoids. Charmian tells how relieved he was to discover that the "tumor" was

nonmalignant and that he wondered how much of his "long sickness" was due to that "damned thing draining into my system": *BJL* II, 35.

18: The Valley of the Moon

218 "Part of the process of recovering": *JB*, 266.

220 The newspapers clamored for the reasons: HL.

220 "NO ADMISSION": *BJL* II, 64.

221 "They kept me poor with their bills": *Burning Daylight*, 202.

222 "It's too bad": *LJL*, 484–85.

222 "like a poker-player": *Burning Daylight*, 183–84.

222 "I am really going to throw out an anchor": *LJL*, 486.

222–23 "The place [is] a bargain" . . . "First rattle out of the box": Ibid., 489–505.

224 "promoting of an intelligent interest": See *LJL*, 531n3.

224 "Occasionally he drew a laugh": Zamen, *Standing Room Only*, 112.

225–26 "pacing the station pavement" . . . "so ugly that the children on the streets of Newton ran screaming": *BJL* II, 85–88.

226–27 "PROTEST IS MADE" . . . "One of the strongest and most trenchant addresses": Zamen, *Standing Room Only*, 114–15, 206–207.

227 Mother Jones: *BJL* II, 92–93. Mother Jones, Mary Harris Jones (1837–1930), was the popular advocate for social justice.

227 Some fifteen hundred young men: See Zamen, *Standing Room Only*, 117, 174.

228 "It astonished me considerably": "Things Alive," *Yale Monthly Magazine*, March 1906; repr. in *The Portable Jack London*, 484–85.

228 this "British-neat island paradise" . . . "ill, hollow-eyed, travel-worn": *BJL* II, 97–104.

229 "Consider the United States": *Revolution*, 16–18.

229 "The whole thing": Zamen, *Standing Room Only*, 119.

229–30 "prepared to give my hero" . . . "two young social dreamers": Upton Sinclair, *Mammonart: An Essay in Economic Interpretation* (Pasadena, CA: Upton Sinclair, 1925), 363–64; Upton Sinclair, *The Cup of Fury* (Great Neck, NY: Channel Press, 1956), 43, 50–51.

230 "The book we have been waiting for": *LJL*, 540. Source: "Jack London and 'The Jungle,'" *Wilshire's Magazine*, December 1905.

230 "Not one ignoble thought or act": introduction to *The Cry for Justice*, 5; repr. in *The Portable Jack London*, 509–10.

230 "You and I ought to have some": *LJL*, 1564.

231 "the greatest intellectual stimulus" . . . "He is rattling the dry bones": *Jack London at Yale*, ed. by the State Secretary of the Socialist Party of Connecticut (Westwood: Connecticut State Committee [1906]); (repr. Cedar Springs, MI: Wolf House Books, 1972), 11, 28.

231 "Have been miserably sick": *LJL*, 546.

231 "Jack, suddenly, with a sigh": *BJL* II, 111.

19: Catastrophe

232 "I'd rather win a water-fight": *The Cruise of the Snark*, 5 (hereafter abbreviated as *Cruise*).

232 "It was all due to Captain Joshua Slocum": Charmian London, *The Log of the Snark*, vii (hereafter abbreviated as *Log*).

232 "without power, radio, money": Walter Magnes Teller, introduction to *Sailing Alone Around the World*, by Captain Joshua Slocum (New York: Sheridan House, 1954), xvii; first published by the Century Company, 1899.

234 "Jerry-built" . . . "The first few touches were enough": *BJL* II, 126–28.

235 "Spare no money": *Cruise*, 16.

235 "You ask when you are going to see": *LJL*, 572.

235 " 'When God Laughs' ": *CSSJL* 1102–11. See Steven T. Dhondt, "Jack London's *When God Laughs*: Overman, Underdog, and Satire," *JLN* 2, no. 2 (May–August 1969): 51–57. The narrator tells about two foolish lovers who, in spite of their strong desire for consummation, "stifle it with shallow, inept logic and deny themselves its benefits . . . That is when God laughs" (53).

235–36 "make a living out of": *LJL*, 733.

236 "The First Lovers": HL.

236 "The situation of this story": *LJL*, 572.

236 "Not a tap of work did we perform": *BJL* II, 131.

237 "What I want is a description": *LJL*, 597n2.

237 "My first idea about a house" . . . "a happy house": "The House Beautiful," *Revolution*, 163–76; repr. with an introduction by James Williams, *JLJ* 3 (1996): 35–42.

237 "I think I've given the ethics": *LJL*, 597.

237 "a great happiness": *LJL*, 589.

238 "Lollypop": *Lolly* and *pop* are Charmian's words for lovemaking.

238 "Perhaps write a novel": Notes on *The Iron Heel*, HL.

239 "this summer a book": *LJL*, 558.

239 "Just Meat": This story, about two greed-maddened burglars who poison each other with strychnine after heisting a fortune in rare jewels, was praised by George Orwell as "Perhaps the best thing London ever wrote." See Orwell's introduction in *Love of Life and Other Stories* (London: Paul Elek, 1946), 11. Also see *Orwell: The Lost Writings*, ed. W. J. West (New York: Arbor House, 1985), 123–24.

239 "The shadow of the Oligarchy": HL.

239 "I'm having the time of my life": *LJL*, 605.

239 "I have now finished 32,000 words": Ibid., 611.

239 "a detriment rather than a help": Quoted in *JLT*, 310–11.

239 "It was a labor of love": Inscribed to "Dear Charley," August 8, 1916, EL.

240 "Outside the United States": Paul Siegel, "Jack London's *The Iron Heel*: Its Significance for Today," *International Socialist Review* 35, no. 7 (July–August 1974): 18. For critical analyses, see Gair, *Complicity and Resistance in Jack London's Novels*, 109–26; Watson, *The Novels of JL*, 99–122, and Johnston, *JL: An American Radical?* 119–28.

240 "From every class of society": *BJL* II, 144.

241 "returning by way of New York" . . . "Sure. Try me": *SSJL*, 3–4.

241 "All right": *LJL*, 632–34.

241 Manyoungi's replacement: Apparently unwilling to take part in what he envisioned as a long and perilous voyage, Manyoungi resorted to insolence as a means of dismissal. See *BJL* II, 154–55.

241–42 "a small satchel and a camera" . . . "And that is how I met Jack London": *SSJL*, 7–12.

243 "a series of tramp reminiscences": *LJL*, 654.

243 "In *The Road*": Ibid., 675–76.

243 "That a man of [London's] unquestionable powers": Sherman, *JL Reference Guide*, 43.

244 "Carrie and I love the simple life": Quoted in Franklin Walker, *The Seacoast of Bohemia* (San Francisco: The Book Club of California, 1996), 14 (repr. Santa Barbara, CA: Peregrine Smith, 1973).

244 "their excessive jollity": *The Valley of the Moon*, 392–93.

245 "the whole building of the boat": *LJL*, 684.

245 The anchor had been hoisted by hand: *Cruise*, 27–29.

246 "He won't get as far as Hawaii": Genthe, *As I Remember*, 75.

20: Paradise Lost

247 "Life has rotted away": *Cruise*, 170.

247–48 "At first, you fear" . . . "Will we ever reach Honolulu": *SSJL*, 51–57.

248 "I *couldn't* cry": *Log*, 20.

248 "were spanking along smartly": Charmian London, *Our Hawaii*, 6.

249 Hobron, a Honolulu "artist, merchant, good fellow": Ibid., 5.

249 "swinging in a great arc": *Cruise*, 71.

249 "very much better acquainted for the fun": *Our Hawaii*, 11.

249–50 "across a spacious, wonderful lawn . . . It was a dream-dwelling": *Cruise*, 71–72. Also see Charmian's more specific description of the Waterhouse home—including their Madonna-like hostess, Mrs. Gretchen Waterhouse, and their initial savoring of poi and other exotic victuals—in *Our Hawaii*, 12–14. The Hobron bungalow to which their host later guided them, a ten-minute walk from the Waterhouse home, was considerably smaller: three rooms plus "an ample bathroom, and windows, windows everywhere [making] perfect the indoor aspect of this arcadian acre": Ibid., 2.

250 "Every day, Jack wrote two hours": *SSJL*, 72.

250 "A long, long time ago": *LJL*, 777. The juvenile story was not reprinted for more than sixty years. See Earle Labor and King Hendricks, "London's Twice-Told Tale," *Studies in Short Fiction* 4 (Summer 1967): 334–47; repr. in Nuernberg, *Critical Response to JL*, 9–16; and *JLSSF*, 232–36.

251 "howling under the stars": *CSSJL*, 1315.

251 "a perfectly nice and affable young man": *Our Hawaii*, 49.

251 "I can't believe that Mr. London knows much": Interview with Edward B. Clark, *Everybody's Magazine, June 1907*, followed by "Nature Fakers" in the September 1907 issue. Also see *The Letters of Theodore Roosevelt*, vol. 5: *The Big Stick, 1905–1907*, ed. Elting E. Morison, et al. (Cambridge, MA: Harvard University Press, 1952): Writing to John Burroughs on March 12, 1907, Roosevelt confessed that he had no business engaging in such arguments but that he needed the diversion after a trying day with Congress, 612.

251 "Why, look here": *Our Hawaii*, 50.

251 "President Roosevelt tried and condemned me": "The Other Animals," *Revolution*, 238–39. For the president's response to London's article, which appeared in *Collier's Magazine*, September 5, 1908, and for Jack's rebuttal, see Douglas Brinkley, *The Wilderness Warrior: Theodore Roosevelt and the Crusade for America* (New York: HarperCollins Publishers, 2009), 781–83.

252 "a bearded young man . . . That's how you pay for your 'Dream Harbor' seclusion!": *Our Hawaii*, 52–58.

253 "Funny way to make a living": Ibid., 13.

253 "And straight on toward shore": "A Royal Sport," *Cruise*, 77–78.

254 "Get off that board": Ibid., 83.

254 "accomplished one successful landing": *Our Hawaii*, 74.

254–55 "How was I to stop that comber" . . . "ecstatic bliss": *Cruise*, 84–89.

256 "large swollen blotches, like hives": *Our Hawaii*, 79–80.

256 London's symptoms were diagnosed as lupus: See Charles W. Denko, PhD, MD, "Jack London: A Modern Analysis of His Mysterious Disease," *The Journal of Rheumatology* 20, no. 10 (1993): 1762–63.

256 "a couple of barrels of water": Mark Twain, *Roughing It* (New York: Oxford University Press, 1996), 526. Originally published in 1872.

256 "the operation (not an inappropriate word)": *Our Hawaii*, 81.

257 "Japanese, Chinese, Portuguese": Ibid., 90.

257 "Koolau the Leper" . . . "The House of Pride": See *JLRL*, 136–40, for comments on both stories. Reesman points out that "The House of Pride" marked a major shift in London's fiction, and it should have worried magazine editors, since it amounted to an attack upon popular American beliefs concerning family obligations, religion, race, nationalism, and imperialism, 136. Also see Berkove for parallels with Jungian psychology in "The House of Pride": "London's Developing Conceptions of Masculinity," 117–26.

257 "ship of despair": *Our Hawaii*, 117.

257 "considerable misrepresentation of the Settlement": Ibid., 103. For a history of the leper settlement, see Tayman, *The Colony*, including the Londons' visit to the island, 197–204.

257 "pit of hell": *Cruise*, 91. See also criticism of the "sensationalists," 94.

258–59 "he carries a heart as big" . . . "Can you beat it": *Our Hawaii*, 136–42. Charmian notes in her diary on July 3 that what she had witnessed gave her "bad dreams."

259 "under such circumstances, to be so light-hearted": *Cruise*, 92.

259 "Carnegie Libraries": Ibid., 111.

259 Roscoe Eames, who had failed miserably: See London's letter to Netta explaining Roscoe's multiple failures, *LJL*, 699–700.

259 "a roaring bucko of old Pacific days": Day, *Jack London and the South Seas*, 59.

260 "with neatness and dispatch": *SSJL*, 94–95.

260 "a good navigator": *LJL*, 725. Also see London's letter to Warren's mother, *LJL*, 747–48.

260 "Sandwich Islands to Tahiti": *Cruise*, 133.

261 "Our thirst grew": *SSJL*, 150–52.

261 "a sea story about a castaway sailor": London may have had this plot in mind later as one of the episodes in *The Star Rover*, ch. 19, 255–85.

261 "served up in various forms": *Log*, 60.

262 "It is nine o'clock": Ibid., 36–37. According to "No. 4 Magazine Sales," "Wrote MARTIN EDEN betwen [*sic*] July 1907 and March 1908," HL. Writing to George Brett on February 27, 1908, London said that he preferred the title of his novel "in the following order: (1) *Success*, (2) *Star-Dust*, (3) *Martin Eden*," *LJL*, 738. For representative analyses of this novel, see Watson, *The Novels of Jack London*, 123–64; and Gair, *Complicity and Resistance*, 132–49.

262 "At last we are at anchor": *SSJL*, 156–57.

262 "In the morning we awoke": *Cruise*, 157.

262 "It is a cyclorama": *Log*, 95–96.

262 "the thin line of a trail": *Cruise*, 157.

263 "We were immediately struck": *Log*, 102.

263–64 "astride ferocious little stallions" . . . "Nearby a woman panted and moaned": *Cruise*, 161–77.

264 "They do not steal, gossip": *SSJL*, 168.

264 "We hated to get up": *Log*, 156.

21: Paradise Momentarily Regained

265 "On the arrival of strangers": Quoted in *Cruise*, 198, from William Ellis, *Polynesian Researches, During a Residence of Nearly Eight Years in the Society and Sandwich Islands* (London: Fisher, Sons, and Jackson, 1837).

265 "Then I remembered": *Log*, 157.

265–66 "a tall, tawny blond man": Ibid., 177. For Darling's fascinating history, see *Cruise*, 178–87; and Day, *Jack London and the South Seas*, 106–10.

266 "long, gorilla arms": *Cruise*, 189–90.

267 "I shall only be in San Francisco": *LJL*, 728–29.

267 "good understanding" with Bessie: CKL diary, January 31, 1908: "Jack talks business with B." For different accounts of this meeting, see *JLD*, 104–9, and Tavernier-Courbin, "Bessie: The First Mrs. Jack London," 200–208.

268 "a sick miserable unhappy woman": Charmian refers to him as "Jack" rather than "Mate" in these entries.

268 "I don't know what you will think" . . . "There's no news": *LJL*, 738–42.

269 "nervously exhausted": *Log*, 181.

269 "tiny outrigger canoe": *Cruise*, 189–204.

270 William Ellis . . . "We were entertained": *Log*, 187–88.

270 "glorious raw fish": *Cruise*, 208.

270 "Tehei did the main cooking": *Log*, 188.

271 "of all hospitality": *Cruise*, 210.

271 "a jewel": CKL diary, April 16, 1908.

271 "good sailor": *Log*, 223–24.

271 'The ropes gave us much needed exercise": *SSJL*, 234.

271 "I know more about geography": *Log*, 222.

272 "with nearly as much authority": *SSJL*, 235.

272–75 "After dark several boatloads came" . . . "Such a sleep": *Log*, 227–54.

275 "nearly ten miles of toil": *SSJL*, 250.

275 "Under the wide and starry sky": *Log*, 263.

276 "a sneak of the first water" . . . "that was so satisfactory to the authorities": *LJL*, 859–61.

276–77 "The white man is a born looter": "My Hawaiian Aloha," *JLR*, 382.

22: Inferno

278 "If I were a king": *Cruise*, 282–83.

278 "We have just passed through": *Log*, 275–76.

279 "gate of heaven": CKL diary, May 15, 1908.

279–80 he stationed Wada at the bow . . . "We went back and found a big, jolly Irishman": *SSJL*, 253–56.

280–81 "Come on in" . . . "but I rule by love": *Log*, 281–85.

281–82 She concluded that Warren was crazy: Also see *Log*, 300–310, and Jack's letter to Warren's mother, *LJL*, 747–49.

282 *The Pacific Monthly* had agreed to pay: June 2, 1908, cable, HL. Also see Kingman, *A Definitive Chronology*, 90.

282 "Blight had been wiped out": *Log*, 316.

282 "When I am in my bunk": *SSJL*, 285.

282 "excessively active ulcers" . . . "the size of a silver dollar": *Cruise*, 262–63, 275–76.

283 "an animated ball of variegated colors": *SSJL*, 281–82.

283 "Hitherto I have told of the gentle": Ibid., 268.

283 "strange little men": CKL diary, June 12 and 14, 1908. For Charmian's descriptions of Melanesian fashions, see *Log*, 348–54.

283 "There is no gainsaying": *CSSJL*, 1519.

284 "I saw [them] at work": *Log*, 371–72.

285 "the slight, strong blond type": Ibid., 361.

285 "If the white man would": *CSSJL*, 1557. For trenchant commentaries on "The Inevitable White Man" and other South Seas stories, see *SSJL*, 128–40; *EL/JCR*, 88–92; *JLRL*, 142–58; and Riedl and Tietze, *Jack London's Tales of Cannibals and Headhunters*.

285 "no man can withstand": *CSSJL*, 1499–500.

286 "helped them lay out streets": *SSJL*, 304.

286 "the best treat we had": Ibid., 299.

286 "generous gallons of fresh milk": *Log*, 262.

287 "We haled forth every dispensable bottle": CKL diary, July 4, 1908. Charmian does not discuss the shooting episode in her *Log* entry for this date, simply mentioning that "today, after our noisy forenoon, we have traded peacefully on deck, the natives bringing out things they learned yesterday would tempt us," 365.

287 "in the starred darkness": *Log*, 366.

287 Most of this . . . island was terra incognita: See Russell F. Weigley, *The American Way of War: A History of United States Military Strategy and Policy* (New York: Macmillan Publishing Company, 1973): "Little was known about the terrain of the southern Solomons . . . so knowledge of landing areas had to be pieced together largely from a thirty-two-year-old Navy hydrographic chart, conversations with the Australians who had lived in the islands, and Jack London's short story 'The Red One,'" 275.

287 "Here I find myself . . . a big blond Englishman": *Log*, 368–81.

289 "Everyone was so happy": *SSJL*, 310–11.

289 "He went clear off his head": *SSJL*, 311.

289 "keeping his bowels in check": CKL diary, July 22, 1908.

290 "I was looking forward" . . . "It nearly made me sick": *SSJL*, 312–13.

290 "a gentleman's yacht" . . . "She's an embarrassing parcel": *Log*, 386–88.

291 "vegetable parasite that invades the skin": *Cruise*, 283–84.

291 "It's all I can do" . . . "insufferably hot in our bunks": *Log*, 387–88.

291 "with holes in their legs": *Cruise*, 283–84.

291 "the primeval stillness of jungle": *Log*, 390–91.

292 the image of the three of them—Charmian, Jack, and Jansen: "Wada lay at a distance, with drawn face and hopeless eyes, while Nakata rattled on affably with the blacks": Ibid., 391.

292 "a combined Fourth of July": *Cruise*, 285.

292 "a slenderly built, sandy-haired man": *Log*, 403–405.

293–94 "Bedlam reigned" . . . "leaning on their rifles and mumbling amens": *Cruise*, 286–93.

294 "I am writing on a little green-topped table": *Log*, 417–18.

295 "Almost homesick at leaving Malu": CKL diary, August 22, 1908.

295 "I *am* having a good time": *Log*, 438.

295 "'Tis the witching hour of midnight" . . . "I do not feel well any of the time": Ibid., 435–36, 456.

296 "I have just returned from a voyage": *LJL*, 754–55.

296 On November 4 he and Charmian sailed aboard the *Makambo*: Wada, "very low with fever," stayed behind; "Martin as well as Nakata took steamer for Sydney," *Log*, 482.

296 "No case like it had ever been reported": *Cruise*, 338.

296 "broke down and sobbed": Ibid., 483.

296 "miserable and weak": CKL diary, December 24, 1908. For an account of Jack's report on the Burns-Johnson fight, see Reesman, *JL's Racial Lives*, 186–89.

297 "fit out another and larger boat": *Log*, 487.

23: The Agrarian Dream and Loss of Joy

298 "I am rebuilding": *LJL*, 1601n1.

298 Solomon novel . . . *Adventure*: See Stasz, "Social Darwinism, Gender, and Humor in 'Adventure,'" Cassuto and Reesman, *Rereading JL*, 130–40, 259–61.

298 "I enjoy listening": CKL diary, April 27, 1909.

298 "the tragedy of the farmer": *LJL*, 1032.

299 not "the sort of story": Ibid., 932n2.

299 "Island McGill folk": HL.

299 He titled it "Samuel": In a 1914 letter to Professor Ethan Cross, who wanted to include this story in a textbook he was editing, London remarked, "Personally, how can you account for the averseness of the American magazine editors, regarding stories such as 'Samuel'? I have always found this so with practically all of my best stories—or what I deemed my best short stories." *LJL*, 1308–9. London's assessment of this unusual story is a valid one: see *EL/JCR*, 108–11; Reesman, *JLSSF*, 121–23; and Earle Labor, "The Archetypal Woman as 'Martyr to Truth,'" *American Literary Realism* 24, no. 2 (Winter 1992): 23–32.

299 "I took the third clean off his feet": *LJL*, 901.

299 a classic of the ring: Howard Lachtman praises "A Piece of Steak" as "one of the very greatest boxing tales in the literature of sports," *Sporting Blood*, 15.

299–300 "the most dangerous railway in the world" . . . "*Used* paper in box": CKL diary, May 21, 22, and 24, 1909.

300 "A cowardly sport": CKL diary, June 6, 1909.

300 "the essential differences between the Spanish and Anglo-American temperaments": *LJL*, 843. See Lachtman, *Sporting Blood*, 84–85, and Reesman, *JLSSF*, 110–11.

300 "to return home by way of Colón": CKL diary, June 26, 1909.

301 "I go into farming" . . . "He also kept in touch": *BJL* II, 266, 277. For a comprehensive treatment of London's agrarian dream, see Milo Shepard, *The Jack London Story and the Beauty Ranch*.

301 "Jack London was a big healthy boy": Luther Burbank, *The Harvest of Years* (Boston: Houghton Mifflin Company, 1927), 225.

302 "a tall, gangling young man": Genthe, *As I Remember*, 76.

302 He would ultimately buy another baker's dozen: See Franklin Walker, "Jack London's Use of Sinclair Lewis Plots," *Huntington Library Quarterly* 17, no. 1 (November 1973): 59–74. Also see what Lewis described as "the clash between Main Street and Beacon Street," when Jack tried reading one of Henry James's novels aloud to Sterling's guests, quoted in Mark Schorer, *Sinclair Lewis: An American Life* (New York: McGraw Hill, 1961), 164–66.

303 "is much interested in social questions": *LJL*, 873nl.

303 *Theft*, the play he wrote for her: See Clay Reynolds, introduction, *The Plays of Jack London*, 16–19: "Notwithstanding its unfortunate history, *Theft* is unquestionably the most intriguing of London's plays and stands as one of the first political plays written from an explicitly Socialist perspective, particularly by someone of London's literary stature." The play indicts the corruption in Washington politics along with the collusion between big government and big business.

303 "cut, slash, alter, do what you please with it": *LJL*, 906.

303 "Nethersole fell down": Ibid., 960–61.

304 causing McCarthy to strike the back of his head: *The San Francisco Examiner*, April 30, 1910, 7. London used this incident in the opening paragraph of his story "The Night Born," crossing out McCarthy's name and substituting "O'Brien": "O'Brien had been a clean-living young man with ideals. He neither drank, smoked, nor swore, and his had been the body of a young god. He had even carried a prayer book to the ringside," *JLCSS*, 1660. For a detailed analysis of this remarkable story, see *EL/JCR*, 111–16, 153nn12–15. Also see *JLSSF*: "The power of 'The Night-Born' is in its extraordinary amalgamation of the naturalistic and the mythic, though the weight of the story rests unmistakably in its paradisal myth of spiritual salvation," 125.

304 "I had met [London]": Emma Goldman, *Living My Life*, 2 vols. (New York: Dover Press, 1970; originally published by Alfred Knopf, 1931), I: 468–69, including Jack's reply.

305 "a good, clean, wholesome, lovable woman": CKL diary, May 1, 1910.

305 "Never did any one jump so high": *BJL* II, 184. At Goldman's request in 1911, Jack wrote an introduction to Alexander Berkman's *Prison Memoirs of an Anarchist*, pointing out Berkman's botched attempt to kill Henry Clay Frick, chairman of the Board of Carnegie Steel, as a typical example of anarchists' inefficiency. Berkman declined to publish Jack's essay. See Earle Labor and Robert C. Leitz III, "Jack London on Alexander Berkman: An Unpublished Introduction," *American Literature* 61, no. 3 (October 1989): 447–56.

305 "Jeanne d'arc of the Chicago anarchists": Paul Avrich, *The Haymarket Tragedy* (Princeton, NJ: Princeton University Press, 1984), 452.

305–306 "an ungrateful and untruthful bounder" . . . "My ideal, on the other hand": *LJL*, 869–71, 900–903n3.

306 "Do you think it would be possible": Ibid., 886nl.

309 "the vilest construction" . . . "This dive proprietor swings a string of votes": *BJL* II, 191; *CSSJL*, 1678–79. Although London fictionalized the episode in his story "The Benefit of the Doubt," the saloon fight and courtroom encounter are corroborated by Charmian and by Joseph Noel's letter to her, April 30, 1919, HL. Jack gives the story an added twist by having his protagonist get revenge when he finds the judge taking a stroll on his ranch, *CSSJL*, 1684–88. Also see newspaper reports: HL and Kingman, *Pictorial Life*, 219.

309–11 "Everybody is arriving in Reno" . . . "And where now is the champion who will make Johnson extend himself": *JLR*, 264–301. For an account of the political machinations that resulted in moving the fight from San Francisco to Reno, see Geoffrey C. Ward, *Unforgivable Blackness: The Rise and Fall of Jack Johnson* (New York: Alfred A. Knopf, 2005), 191. Also see John Dudley, *A Man's Game, Masculinity and the Anti-Aesthetics of American Literary Naturalism* (Tuscaloosa: University of Alabama Press, 2004), 47–52.

311 "Oh, the luxury of letting down" . . . "My—but I can't stand any more pain": CKL diary, June 27–30, 1910. Also see Stasz, *American Dreamers*: "Charmian herself was in danger of dying. Unaware of this fact, she insisted [Jack] go off and cover the practice camps preceding the fight," 205.

312 "It was mainly grit" . . . "I don't know just how": *BJL* II, 192–93.

312 "a short story involving how I got my black eye": *LJL*, 909.

312–13 "unfair, bullying game" . . . "like a political plot engineered by my enemies": Ibid., 916–24n2.

313 a score of stories: See *CSSJL*, 2535–42, for titles and dates of submission during this period. Ranking among his best were "War," "Told in the Drooling Ward," and "The Mexican": See *EL/JCR*, 136, 152n6, Reesman *JLSSF*, 111–18, and Don Graham, "Jack London's Tale Told by a High-Grade Feeb," *Studies in Short Fiction* 15 (Fall 1978), 429–33. In addition to his dissatisfaction with *The Abysmal Brute*, London made an abortive attempt at writing another novel based on Lewis plots: *The Assassination Bureau, Ltd.* On October 4, he wrote to Lewis, "I have 20,000 words done on the [novel], and for the first time in my life am stuck and disgusted," *LJL*, 933. The novel was completed by Robert L. Fish and published by McGraw-Hill in 1963. See Donald E. Pease, introduction to *The Assassination Bureau, Ltd.* (New York: Penguin Books, 1994), xvi–xxxii. A film version starring Oliver Reed, Diana Rigg, and Telly Savalas was released by Paramount in 1968. See Williams, *Jack London, the Movies*, 186, 228.

314 "My old, old dream come true": *BJL* II, 197. Charmian mentions their meeting several of Jack's "old cronies" during their cruise, including French Frank and Charley Le Grant.

314 "I've got five hundred dollars in the bank": Ibid., 202.

314 "a series of six stories": *LJL*, 941–42. See *JLSSF*, 36–39.

315 "Sun Tales": See *JLSSF*, 151–58. For historical background and extensive commentaries on these stories, see also Tietze and Riedl, *A Son of the Sun*.

24: Four Horses for a Chicken Thief

316 "I read in today's paper": *LJL*, 1022nn1–3.

316 "It'll be a nice winter change" . . . "One of my commissions while south": *BJL* II, 202–203.

317 According to the newspaper headlines: HL.

317 "To the dear brave comrades": *LJL*, 980–81.

318 "The Mexican": *CSSJL*, 1983–2005. See *JLSSF*, 111–13, and *JLRL*, 199–204.

318 "I have written *The Call of the Wild*": *The Marin Journal*, April 23, 1911; quoted by Howard Lachtman, "Four Horses, a Wife, and a Valet," *The Pacific Historian* 21, no. 2 (Summer 1977): 109–10.

318–19 "HUH!" . . . "Drive four horses" . . . "And it was along the Mendocino roads": "Four Horses and a Sailor," *The Human Drift*, 74, 95–96.

319 "Wonder if I'll ever be real strong again": CKL diary, July 3, 1911.

319 "Eyes swollen now": Ibid., July 17, 1911.

320 "Watching him in this phase": *BJL* II, 212.

320 WHERE IS JACK LONDON?: Lachtman, "Four Horses," 121–22.

320 "Later, go up to cottage": CKL diary, September 5, 1911.

320 "House—*Big House*": *LJL*, 1016n2. The correct date is June 22, 1911, not June 2, as noted in *LJL*.

321 "a unique building": "Jack London's Unique Country Home," *The Architect and Engineer* 25 (July 1911): 49–50. For a comprehensive history and description of this magnificent structure, see Hayes and Atkinson, *Jack London's Wolf House*.

322 Ed Morrell . . . out-of-body experiences: See Ed Morrell *The Twenty-Fifth Man: The Strange Story of Ed Morrell, the Hero of Jack London's "The Star Rover"* (Montclair, NJ: New Era Publishing Company, 1924). See also *BJL* II: "I well recall Jack, fairly frothing over the straitjacket scars Morrell had been revealing, lurching in, spilling over with emotion, to tell me what he had seen" (226). For commentaries on *The Star Rover*, see EL/JCR, 73–75, 147nn35–36, and James Williams, "Editor's Introduction: On *The Star Rover*," plus the following nine articles on this novel, *JLJ* 2 (1995): 81–155.

322 a young immigrant from Greece: Spiro Orfans would later become the recipient of London's most vitriolic racist letters: See *JLRL*, 344–45n6; and Mel Smith, "Jack London and 'Racial Mongrelism': His Dispute with Spiro Orfans," *Manuscripts* 43, no. 4 (Fall 1991): 281–91.

322–24 "Almost any passage in our companionship" . . . "naked as a billiard ball": *BJL* II, 230–39.

324 London's next two novels: *The Valley of the Moon* and *The Mutiny of the Elsinore*. The latter would be one of his most problematic and racist works. Watson calls it "the worst of London's serious novels," *NJL*, xii. Reesman suggests that the novel is "a racial burlesque," *JLRL*, 258. Also see Bert Bender, *Sea-Brothers: The Tradition of American Sea Fiction from* Moby-Dick *to the Present* (Philadelphia: University of Pennsylvania Press, 1988): "Despite the grotesque and comic allegory [this novel] is a landmark, rich with London's meaningful references to those who sailed before him," 92–93.

324 "I think it is going to be a popular story": *LJL*, 1007–8. For representative commentaries on *The Valley of the Moon*, see Watson, 187–210, and Labor and Reesman, 98–102.

325 "Among all my books": *The Hawaii Shinpo*, March 14, 1915.

325 "The Wheel": Published in *The Semi-Monthly Magazine*, December 8, 1912. See *BJL* II, 241.

325–26 "Here, remote, ecstatic" . . . "It has never mastered me": Ibid., II, 243–45.

328 "Days and weeks, nights and days": *JLD*, 172.

328 "Miss you?": *LJL*, 1098.

328 "Very tired and lazy": CKL diary, November 27, 1912.

25: Unlucky Thirteen

330 "Gone?": *JB*, 314.

330 "bad year": *BJL* II, 252–63. In her diary entry of January 1, Charmian identifies the "woman friend, an invalid" who died as "Mazie Mather."

332 American Academy of Forensic Scientists: Associated Press, "Experts Probe Jack London's 1913 House Fire," *The Philadelphia Inquirer*, May 24, 1995, B8. Also see Hayes and Atkinson, "Origin of the Wolf House Fire," *Jack London's Wolf House*, 42–45; and Kingman, *Pictorial Life*, 249. London had cut the redwood timber for rebuilding Wolf House. See *LJL*, 1359. Irving Shepard pointed out the piles of logs next to the ruin during my first visit to the ranch, in 1963.

332 "the most impressive ruin in the American West": Personal conversation with Everson during his visit to Centenary College in April 1973. Also see William Everson, "Archetype West," *Regional Perspectives*, ed. John Gordon Burke (Chicago: American Library Association, 1973), 256–59.

332 "Haven't you noticed": *BJL* II, 280.

333 "suffered hell": *LJL*, 1270.

335 "I don't think it was kleptomania" . . . *The Little Lady of the Big House*: See Stasz, *American Dreamers*, 255–62; *JL's Women*, 167–73; *EL/JCR*, 102–110; Watson, *The Novels of Jack London*, 211–34.

335 Compounding the emotional turmoil: See Stasz, "Jack London's Delayed Discovery of Fatherhood," *JLJ* 3 (1996): 146–68 (including a selection of Joan London's letters to her father, edited by Stasz).

336 "His longing for his daughters": *JLD*, 168.

336 "Mother has borne everything": Quoted in Stasz, *JL's Women*, 176.

336–37 "Dearest Joan" . . . "Yes, but, my dear daughter" . . . "Or do you want me to cease": *LJL*, 1159–60, 1215–16, 1218–19.

337 "so long as it meant seeing people": Quoted in Stasz, *JL's Women*, 179.

337–38 "No; I neither 'see' nor 'understand'" . . . "Please, Daddy, please let me feel that this is the last": *LJL*, 1221, 1257–60n2.

339 "At the present moment I am up against it": *LJL*, 1260.

339 "out of pocket about ten thousand": *BJL* II, 256. Also see *LJL*, 1265–66; 1808–9n1, and 1529n1.

339 On December 17, Jack told Noel: *LJL*, 1282.

339 "I did not have it": Ibid., 1285.

26: New York, Mexico, and Home Again

340 "I have always been a fighter": *LJL*, 1336.

341 "He swears he has absolute trump cards": Ibid., 1294.

341 "You should have seen me": *BJL* II, 286–87.

342–43 "I no longer say 'To hell with New York'" . . . "Another Scandal, Jack?": *LJL*, 1294–95.

343 "the best thing ever written on capital punishment" . . . "nothing in the world matters but love": Quoted in Boylan, *Revolutionary Lives*, 201–202, ASW.

343 "Do you know": *LJL*, 1295.

344 "Met all the performers": Ibid., 1296.

345 "All my life has been marked": Ibid., 1298–301.

345 "Even today, rereading his letter": *JLD*, 175–76.

346 "And now" . . . "I may redeem myself": *BJL* II, 289.

347 "I can't understand it" . . . "I gave him my word of honor": Ibid., 291–92. "The Good Soldier" is reprinted in *JLR*, 126–27. Also see *LJL*, 1025, 1092, 1332, 1335.

347 "Ashore all is peaceful": *JLR*, 139–40.

348 "most characteristic of the man": "Jack London: A Personal Sketch," *The Living Age*, 8th ser. 5 (January, February, March 1917): 124, 126; repr. in Tavernier-Courbin, *Critical Essays on Jack London,* 31–34.

348–49 "I want to register my protest" . . . "And as I stood in this place . . . the gentle Nazarene": *JLR*, 167–70.

349 "a brief for the oil man": Quoted in *JLT*, 353.

350 "class that foments all the trouble" . . . "Mexico must be saved from herself": *JLR*, 176–83. See *JLRL*, 275–86, for London's changed attitude toward Mexico. For additional commentaries on his complex treatment of race, see Andrew J. Furer, " 'Zone Conquerers' and 'White Devils': The Contradictions of Race in the Works of Jack London," Cassuto and Reesman, *Rereading JL*, 158–71, 261–65; and James Slagel, "Political Leprosy: Jack London the 'Kama'aina' and Koolau the Hawaiian," ibid., 172–91, 265–68.

350 "Either we believe in the brotherhood": Quoted in Johnston, *JL, An American Radical?*, 175n37.

351 "I hope for the day to come": *JLR*, 145–46.

351 "No one could be more shaken": *BJL* II, 301.

351 "I believe intensely": *LJL*, 1571–72.

352 "The Drink That Knocked Out John Barleycorn": Ibid., 1330nn2–3.

353 "If you will set out say 200 of your broad acres": Ibid., 837n1.

353 "I know of no legitimate investment that will compare": Ibid., 918–19.

353 only a couple were suitable for lumber: See Milo Shepard, *The Jack London Story and the Beauty Ranch*, 118.

353 "Dearest Sister Eliza": Noto, *With a Heart Full of Love*, 26.

27: A Sea-Change

354 "I have had": *LJL*, 1503nn1–3. Hesser, a frustrated neoplyite Writer, wrote to London, asking if he thought all her efforts were "worth the Candle."

354 "There was something inimical working in Jack's blood": *BJL* II, 307.

355 "Look at the size of my ankles": Interview with Irving Shepard, July 1972.

355 Macmillan Company alone had sold more than one million copies: Kingman, *JL Chronology*, 191.

355 "a poor fellow's plans" . . . "It is sink or swim": *LJL*, 1362, 1415.

355 *The Acorn-Planter* was to be: See Reynolds, *Plays of JL*, 23–24: "The most troubling aspect of the play is its thesis, which is uniformly London's Social Darwinian views." Also see Labor, "Jack London's Agrarian Vision," *Western American Literature* 11, no. 2 (Summer, 1976): 100–101; repr. in Berkove, *Critical Insights*, 213–15.

356 "You know what kind of a dog writer": *LJL*, 1419.

356 "I am leaving the ranch tomorrow": Ibid., 1428.

357 "kinky-haired cannibals": Foreword to *Jerry*, v.

357 "Cruelty, as a fine art": Foreword to *Michael*, vi–vii.

358 "I began studying the language": *The Mid-Pacifice Magazine* 10, no. 2 (August 1915): 117–20; repr. with an introduction by Dan Wichlan, *JLJ* 2 (1995): 4–9. Also see Valerie Noble, chapter 3, "Adventures in Friendship," *Hawaiian Prophet Alexander Hume Ford* (Smithtown, NY: Exposition Press, 1980), 70–98.

359 the group's favorite beverage: Letter addressed to "Dear Bill" from "Roy," January 13, 1944, William M. Morgan Papers, Harry Ransom Humanities Research Center, University of Texas at Austin.

359 "Literature is the last thing . . . he wants to talk about": Article by Rev. John Lydgate, *Garden Island* (newspaper), May 25, 1915. London's signature and address appears in Lydgate's guest book dated "May 13/15." For additional commentary on Jack's visit to Kauai, see Reesman, "Jack London—Kama'aina," *Call* 18 (September–December 1985): 71–76.

360 "It is so simple a remedy": Introduction to *The Cry for Justice*, 5.

360 "As I ask myself, 'Why did I like Jack London from the start?'": Alexander Hume Ford, "Jack London in Hawaii," *The Mid-Pacific Magazine* 13, no. 2 (February 1917): 119–21. Ford cited as a special example London's role in helping to organize the Pan-Pacific Union.

360 Frank Garbutt—a millionaire entrepreneur: See Williams, *JL: The Movies*, 53–65, and *LJL*, 1459–61.

360–61 "one of nature's noblemen" . . . "marshal of Tombstone": Raoul Walsh, *Each Man in His Time: The Life Story of a Director* (New York: Farrar, Straus and Giroux, 1974), dust jacket and 102. I am indebted to David Moreland for telling me about Walsh's book and to Peter Blodgett for clarifying the Earp legend. Also see Allen Barra, *Inventing Wyatt Earp: His History and Many Legends* (New York: Carroll and Graf, 1998): "For most of his lifetime Earp was something of a celebrity, though his fame was largely confined to the West," 11.

362 "a new departure": Foreword to *Hearts of Three*, v. see Williams, *JL: The Movies*, 138.

363 would be hard-pressed to escape: See Stasz, *JL's Women*, 225–26, and Kenneth Silverman, *Houdini!!! The Career of Ehrich Weiss* (New York: Harper Perennial Edition, 1997), 197–99, 229–32.

363 "I am afraid we did little but meet & observe": Letter to me from Judge Joseph M. Maltby, June 18, 1959. I thank his son Joe, my former University of Wisconsin colleague, for this contact and for permission to quote Judge Maltby's letter.

364 "Kamaaina means not exactly old-timer": "My Hawaiian Aloha," *JLR*, 401. Originally published in *The Cosmopolitan*, September, October, November 1918; repr. in Charmian London, *Our Hawaii*, rev. ed. (1922), 1–33.

364 "Hawaii and Hawaiians are a land and a people loving": *JLR*, 390–91.

364 "The news came to Honolulu": *Our Hawaii*, 289.

364 exceptionally fine stories: See *EL/JCR*, 117–29; *JLSSF*, Part 1, 158–81; James Slagel, Part 3, 245–52; and McClintock, *JL's Strong Truths*, 151–74.

364–65 "Sometimes I think I'm saturated with alcohol" . . . "The friendly physicians exhorted in vain": *BJL* II, 326–29.

365 Netta's husband, Edward Payne: Edward Biron Payne had succeeded James Howard Bridge as editor of the *Overland Monthly* in 1899 and was also co-owner of Wake Robin Lodge with Netta Eames. On December 31, 1908, Netta filed for divorce from Roscoe Eames on the grounds of desertion. Two years later she married Payne. See *LJL*, 785–86.

365 "Dear Comrades": *LJL*, 1537–38; and *BJL* II, 336: "I can still hear Jack's battletread, somewhat muffled by straw slippers, as he marched toward my door, and his peremptory voice: 'Take a letter—please!'"

366 "Some day" . . . "tell me what you think about me": *LJL*, 1538. *Jack London and His Daughters* was not published until nearly twenty years after Joan's death. See the preface by her son, Bart Abbott.

366 "a crackerjack Hawaii article": *LJL*, 1540–41.

366 "Do you remember another wonderful story": Ibid., 1542. I am indebted to Joe Johnson for "Wisdom and Illusion in 'The Hussy,'" presented at the Biennial Jack London Symposium in 2006—in which he points out the connections between this neglected story and "The Red One"—another story virtually undiscovered by London scholars until the mid-1970s. For representative commentaries on "The Red One," one of London's most haunting stories, apparently influenced by Conrad's *Heart of Darkness*, see *EL/JCR*, 117–24, 147n32, 153nn17–24; *JLSSF*, 162–70, 193–94; Lawrence I. Berkove, "The Myth of Hope in Jack London's 'The Red One,'" Cassuto and Reesman, *Rereading JL*, 204–16, 270–73; Per Serritslev Petersen, "Jack London's Medusa of Truth," *Philosophy and Literature* 26, no. 1 (2002): 54–65; repr. in Bloom, *Critical Views*, 101–13.

366 "Sometimes I wonder": *BJL* II, 334. See James I. Kirsch, "Jack London's Quest: 'The Red One,'" Nuernberg, *Critical Response to JL*: "All his life he was a seeker . . . Through most of his life he had been seeking the progress and salvation of mankind in Socialism. He was one of the great myth-makers of mankind," 215. Kirsch's essay was based upon his lecture delivered on March 11, 1955, at the Analytical Psychology Club of Los Angeles and originally published in *Psychological Perspectives* 11 (1980): 137–55. During my visit to Dr. Kirsch on August 11,

1987, I asked how he had managed to get hold of this story which had been out of print for so many years. "I read it in an edition given me by a friend in France. I was amazed by what I saw in this story," he replied. I also asked him if this may have been the first story London wrote after discovering Jung's book. "No," he answered. "Archetypal insights like those in 'The Red One' had not yet been published by Jung."

367 "I am standing on the edge of a world" . . . "As I came to look with him over that brink": *BJL* II, 322–23.

367 "loaded with leis by friends": CKL diary, July 26.

368 "It is impossible": *LJL*, 1556n1.

368 Wildwater: The old name for Graham Creek. I thank Steve Shaffer for this information.

368 "I have just reread your letters": *LJL*, 1556.

368 They would persist: See *BJL* II, 376–77.

368 "The Kanaka Surf": See *JLSSF*, 175–76.

368 "Our Jack has not come back to us": *BJL* II, 352.

368–69 "Sometimes he was very calm" . . . "on the verge of nerve-collapse": Ibid., 370–71, 377.

369 "last crisis": *JLD*, 177.

369 "With lots of love": *LJL*, 1582–83.

370 Accompanying them was Turley's young friend: I thank Bruce Knight, Becky London's grandson, for sharing a letter eighty-seven-year-old Davis wrote to Becky about this trip and for reminding me of Davis's article. See William H. L. Davis, "My 1916 Visit to Jack London," *JLN* 2, no. 2 (May–August 1969): 58–65.

370 "But don't you do this": *BJL* II, 364–65.

371 his own recipe: Jack London, "Roast Duck," *The Suffrage Cook Book*, ed. Mrs. L. O. Kleber (Pittsburgh, PA: The Equal Franchise Federation of Western Pennsylvania, 1915), 46.

371 "Oh, I love them so": *BJL* II, 372.

371 "tree of knowledge": *JLSSF*, 177.

372 "But listen, O Young Wise One": *CSSJL*, 2488–89. Also see Gabel, *JL: A Man in Search of Meaning*, 94–108.

372 his "comprehension of how to raise lower desires": *BJL* II, 354. See Jung, *Psychology of the Unconscious*, 253, London's personal copy, HL. Also see David Mike Hamilton, *"The Tools of My Trade": Annotated Books in Jack London's Library*, 175: "this is the most important book in [London's] library [with] almost three hundred annotations."

372 "a sea-change": "Nothing of him that doth fade / But doth suffer a sea-change / Into something rich and strange." From Ariel's song to Prospero in Shakespeare's *The Tempest* (act 1, scene 2). Gabel, a psychiatrist and Jungian analyst, suggests that London was also a psychological work in progress. See *JL: A Man in Search of Meaning*, 120.

28: Silver Speech, Golden Silence

373 "I would rather be ashes": Jack London, "What Life Means to Me: An Analysis of the Social Structure," quoted by Ernest J. Hopkins, *The San Francisco Bulletin*, December 2, 1916, Sec. 2, p. 1; repr. in *Jack London's Tales of Adventure*, ed. Irving Shepard, vii. In a letter to "Miss Goldstein," dated January 13, 1909 (HL), London quotes his "Credo," remarking that he said it seven years before. See Hodson, introduction to *JL: 100 Years a Writer*, 13; and *JLRL*, 350n56.

373-74 "HAWAIIAN STORIES" . . . He had not yet determined: HL. Also see *LJL*, 1588-89; *BJL* II, 366-67. London died before finishing the novel, and Charmian completed it under the title *Eyes of Asia*, which appeared in *The Cosmopolitan*, September and October 1924. A carefully edited version of London's manuscript was published by Tony Williams in *JLJ* 6 (1999): 4-92, including "*Cherry's* Conclusion?" Also see in that issue Haruo Furukawa, "*Cherry*, the Unfinished Last Novel of Jack London," 93-112; and James Williams, "Editor's Introduction," 1-3.

374 "five thousand words along": *LJL*, 1588.

374 "Come here and sit beside me": *BJL* II, 371.

374 "strange scholar man": HL, titled "Forty Horses Abreast."

375 "swinging along on *Cherry*": *LJL*, 1596.

375 "It's a pretty picayune world": *BJL* II, 375.

375 lawsuit over riparian rights: For a transcript of London's testimony in the trial, see "IN THE SUPERIOR COURT OF THE STATE OF CALIFORNIA, IN AND FOR THE COUNTY OF SONOMA. DEPARTMENT NO. 1. Before Honorable Edgar T. Zook, Judge presiding. HENRY J. CHAUVET et al, Plaintiffs, -vs- JACK LONDON et al, Defendants. No. 9913. SANTA ROSA, CAL., November 9-10, 1916." Copy EL. This 122-page document is impressive evidence of the length of time London spent in the witness chair and his presence of mind despite his weakened physical condition, revealing his thorough knowledge of both agricultural and legal matters.

376 "increasing tendency to dysentry": *BJL* II, 325-76.

376 "I'll be all right": *BJL* II, 375.

376 "My idea, would be to give my writing experiences . . . stories quite different from the ones I have written": *LJL*, 1601-2.

376 "Your letter strikes me that you are serious": *LJL*, 1513-14nn2-4.

377 London's mood . . . his closest friend, George Sterling: See Upton Sinclair's letters to Joan London, August 3 and 11, 1937: "concerning Jack's later days. The principal thing I have is the memory of George's pain, mixed with some anger. He used to tell us continually about how rude and domineering Jack had become. He could not let anyone argue with him about anything. He would pound the table and become furious" (TLS, HL). Also see Sterling's letter to "Dear Craig," *JLN* 1, no. 3 (July–December 1968): 58-59.

377 "I was on the verge of a nerve collapse . . . the real battle for Jack's life began": *BJL* II, 377.

378 "Greenlaw children's graves": Located on a small oak-shaded knoll a few hundred

yards uphill from Wolf House are two moss-covered wooden headboards marking the graves of "LITTLE DAVID . . . Died . . . 1876" and "LITTLE LILLIE . . . Died . . . 1877"—the children of pioneer settlers named Greenlaw.

378–80 "your duck was perfection . . . the real battle for Jack's life began": *BJL* II, 382–86.

380 According to the newspaper reports: "Santa Rosa, Cal. Nov. 22.—Jack London, the author, died at his Glen Ellen, Cal., ranch near here at 7:45 o'clock tonight, a victim of uremic poisoning . . . It was at first believed that the author was a victim of ptomaine poisoning, but later it developed he was suffering from a severe form of uremia."

380 "Mr. London is in a state of uraemia": "JACK LONDON DIES IN HIS 'VALLEY OF THE MOON' . . . AN EARLIER BULLETIN ISSUED BY DOCTORS": *Letters from Jack London*, photocopy, illustration 30, 246–47. This earlier bulletin was not signed by Porter.

380 The *San Francisco Chronicle* . . . the "usual remedies": November 24, 1916, copies on file JLFRC, CCL.

380–81 "Man, man, wake up!" . . . "I shall greet Death with a smile": *BJL* II, 387–88.

381 That evening . . . the following bulletin: *Letters from Jack London*, photocopy.

381 It is worth noting: For a detailed clinical account of London's medical history, see Phillips Kirk Labor, MD, "Jack London's Death: The Homicide of the Suicide Theory," *JLFQN* 23, no. 2 (April 2011): 2–7; www.jacklondons.net. Dr. Labor provides relevant information concerning the possible contributive factors not only of lupus and London's occasional use of opiates but also of his alcohol consumption and the toxic consequences of his inappropriate diet, his self-medication during the *Snark* cruise, exacerbated by his long-term dental problems and excessive use of tobacco. Also see Alfred S. Shivers, "Jack London: Not a Suicide," *The Dalhousie Review* 49, no. 1 (Spring 1969): 43–57. Neither Labor nor Shivers, a certified pharmacist, denies the possibility that London could have ingested morphine on the night before his death—although this, too, is problematic in the light of contradictory stories—however, both employ substantial medical evidence in refuting Stone's suicide claim. The numerous arguments about London's death are covered in the following: Lou Leal and Dale Walker, www.jacklondons.net/variousbiograpers; Reinhard Wissdorf, "No Suicide! Protocol of a Discussion on the Unreliability of Biographers," translated by Jack Mulder, www.jack-london.org/suicide.htm; and the 1930s interview with Tokinosuke Sekinè by Barry Stevens and Yoshimatsu Nakata, "A Hero to His Valet," 102–103. For the diagnosis of "lupus," see Denko, "Jack London," 1760–63; and Andrew S. Bomback, MD, Philip J. Klemmer, MD, "Jack London's Mysterious Malady," *The American Journal of Medicine* 120 (2007): 466–67.

381 The official death certificate: "STANDARD CERTIFICATE OF DEATH, California State Board of Health, Bureau of Vital Statistics, Local Registered No. 345, Filed Nov. 23, 1916, and Dec. l, 1916."

381 "Biographical Novel": After reviewers had discovered the numerous episodes Stone had invented and plagiarized from London's fiction, Houghton Mifflin

changed the subtitle of *Sailor on Horseback* to *A Biographical Novel by IRVING STONE*. In a letter dated August 10, 1937, Dr. Porter told Charmian that he'd just been visited the day before by "a Mr. Irving Stone" who, judging from his remarks, intended "to write a hot sensational thing, something to startle the public & sell." Copy, EL. Writing to Stone on September 2, Eliza asserted that while she'd been with Jack and the doctors all day long and through the night, "no one mentioned a thing out of the way to me [and] I still have the statement [issued by the four attending physicians to the press] and have always believed it." Copy, EL. Stone reported that Dr. Thomson told him about the calculated overdose of morphine in 1937, twenty-one years after London's death (*Sailor on Horseback*, 331). But this information conflicts not only with Thomson's earlier testimony but also with Sekinè's account. Furthermore, Stone published still another version, unwittingly contradicting himself, in *Irving Stone's Jack London: His Life, Sailor on Horseback (A Biography) and Twenty-eight Selected Jack London Stories* (Garden City, NY: Doubleday and Company, 1977), 301. See Earle Labor, "A Biographical Hydra: The Myth of Jack London's Suicide," 1–2, 6–7nn3–8; repr. at www.jack londons.net.

381 "Contrary to the assumption that Jack London committed suicide": Phillips Kirk Labor, "Jack London's Death," *JLFQN* 23, no. 2 (April 2011): 7; "The Jack London Death Controversy," www.jacklondons.net.

381 On November 23 the shock . . . around the world: See, for example, *The New York Times* website: "On This Day, November 22, 1916, Obituary . . . Birthdays, January 12, 2000."

382 "Little as he would have approved" . . . "'It was my Good-by'": *BJL* II, 391–92.

383 "Next Sunday, will you and Bess": *LJL*, 1604.

383 "Cremation is the only decent": Ibid., 1589.

383–84 "A short address" . . . "The men, uncovered, reverent": *BJL* II, 388–96. Sterling's poem was published in "George Sterling in High Tribute to Jack London," *The San Francisco Examiner*, November 27, 1916:

> *Ere the night falleth and earth's friendships end,*
> *How dear it is to have so good a friend!*
> *Be then it said of me my feet have trod*
> *As near to his as his went near to God!*

BIBLIOGRAPHY

Primary Sources

More than sixty thousand items related to Jack London (letters, notes, manuscripts, diaries, scrapbooks, business and ranch records, and more than six thousand volumes from London's personal library) are on file at the Henry E. Huntington Library. The second-largest collection of Londoniana is held by the Merrill-Cazier Library at Utah State University. Other important collections are located at the Bancroft Library, University of California at Berkeley; the University of California at Los Angeles; the University of Southern California; the Stanford University Library; the Stuart Library of Western Americana at the University of the Pacific; the Oakland Public Library; Sonoma State University; the University of Virginia; the Jack London Foundation Research Center in Sonoma, California; the Jack London State Historical Park in Glen Ellen; and the Jack London Research Center at Centenary College of Louisiana.

Books with Jack London as Author or Contributor

The Son of the Wolf. Boston: Houghton Mifflin, 1900.
The God of His Fathers. New York: Century, 1901.
Children of the Frost. New York: Century, 1902.
The Cruise of the Dazzler. New York: Century, 1902.
A Daughter of the Snows. Philadelphia: J.B. Lippincott, 1902.
The Call of the Wild. New York: Macmillan, 1903.
The Kempton-Wace Letters (with Anna Strunsky). New York: Macmillan, 1903.
The People of the Abyss. New York: Macmillan, 1903.
The Faith of Men. New York: Macmillan, 1904.
The Sea-Wolf. New York: Macmillan, 1904.
The Game. New York: Macmillan, 1905.
Tales of the Fish Patrol. New York: Macmillan, 1905.
War of the Classes. New York: Macmillan, 1905.
Moon-Face and Other Stories. New York: Macmillan, 1906.
Scorn of Women. New York: Macmillan, 1906.
White Fang. New York: Macmillan, 1906.

Before Adam. New York: Macmillan, 1907.

Love of Life and Other Stories. New York: Macmillan, 1907.

The Road. New York: Macmillan, 1907.

The Iron Heel. New York: Macmillan, 1908.

Martin Eden. New York: Macmillan, 1909.

Burning Daylight. New York: Macmillan, 1910.

Lost Face. New York: Macmillan, 1910.

Revolution and Other Essays. New York: Macmillan, 1910.

Theft: A Play in Four Acts. New York: Macmillan, 1910.

Adventure. New York: Macmillan, 1911.

The Cruise of the Snark. New York, Macmillan, 1911.

South Sea Tales. New York: Macmillan, 1911.

When God Laughs and Other Stories. New York: Macmillan, 1911.

The House of Pride and Other Tales of Hawaii. New York: Macmillan, 1912.

Smoke Bellew. New York: Century, 1912.

A Son of the Sun. Garden City, N.Y.: Doubleday, Page and Company, 1912.

The Abysmal Brute. New York: Century, 1913.

John Barleycorn. New York: Century, 1913.

The Night-Born. New York: Century, 1913.

The Valley of the Moon. New York: Macmillan, 1913.

The Mutiny of the Elsinore. New York: Macmillan, 1914.

The Strength of the Strong. New York: Macmillan, 1914.

The Scarlet Plague. New York: Macmillan, 1915.

The Star Rover. New York: Macmillan, 1915.

The Acorn-Planter: A California Forest Play. New York: Macmillan, 1916.

The Little Lady of the Big House. New York: Macmillan, 1916.

The Turtles of Tasman. New York: Macmillan, 1916.

The Human Drift. New York: Macmillan, 1917.

Jerry of the Islands. New York: Macmillan, 1917.

Michael Brother of Jerry. New York: Macmillan, 1917.

The Red One. New York: Macmillan, 1918.

On the Makaloa Mat. New York: Macmillan, 1919.

Hearts of Three. New York: Macmillan, 1920.

Dutch Courage and Other Stories. New York: Macmillan, 1922.

The Assassination Bureau, Ltd. [novel completed by Robert L. Fish]. New York: McGraw-Hill 1963

Letters from Jack London—Containing an Unpublished Correspondence Between London and Sinclair Lewis. Edited by King Hendricks and Irving Shepard. New York: Odyssey, 1965.

Jack London Reports. Edited by King Hendricks and Irving Shepard. New York: Doubleday, 1970.

Daughters of the Rich [curtain raiser written by Hilda Gilbert but published under

London's name with his permission]. Edited by James E. Sisson. Oakland, CA: Holmes Book Company, 1971.

Gold [three-act play written by Herbert Heron, based upon two London stories, "A Day's Lodging" and "The Man on the Other Bank," published under the names of Heron and London as joint authors]. Edited by James E. Sisson. Oakland, CA: Holmes Book Company, 1972.

Jack London on the Road: The Tramp Diary and Other Hobo Writings. Edited by Richard W. Etulain. Logan: Utah State University Press, 1979.

Dearest Greek: Jack and Charmian London's Presentation Inscriptions to George Sterling. Edited by Stanley Wertheim and Sal Noto. Cupertino, CA: Eureka Publications, 1983.

A Klondike Trilogy: Three Uncollected Stories. Edited by Earle Labor. Illustrated by Jack Freas. Santa Barbara, CA: Neville, 1983.

With a Heart Full of Love: Jack London's Presentation Inscriptions to the Women in His Life. Edited by Sal Noto. Berkeley, CA: Two Windows Press, 1986.

The Letters of Jack London. Edited by Earle Labor, Robert C. Leitz III, and I. Milo Shepard. 3 vols. Stanford, CA: Stanford University Press, 1988.

The Complete Short Stories of Jack London. Edited by Earle Labor, Robert C. Leitz III, and I. Milo Shepard. 3 vols. Stanford, CA: Stanford University Press, 1993.

The Complete Poetry of Jack London. Edited by Daniel J. Wichlan. New London, CT: Little Tree Publishing, 2007.

The Unpublished and Uncollected Articles and Essays. Edited by Daniel J. Wichlan. Bloomington, IN: Author House, 2007.

Parts of Books

Umbstaetter, H. D., ed. *The Red Hot Dollar and Other Stories from The Black Cat.* Introduction by Jack London. Boston: Page, 1911.

Cox, Francis A. *What Do You Know About a Horse?* Foreword by Jack London [written by Cox but published under London's name with his permission]. London: G. Bell and Sons, 1915.

Sinclair, Upton, ed. *The Cry for Justice: An Anthology of the Literature of Social Protest.* Introduction by Jack London. Philadelphia: John C. Winston, 1915.

Schwarz, Osias L. *General Types of Superior Men: A Philosophico-Psychological Study of Genius, Talent, and Philistinism in Their Bearings upon Human Society and Its Struggles for a Better Social Order.* Preface by Jack London [written by Schwarz but published under London's name with his permission]. Boston: R.G. Badger, 1916.

Noteworthy Anthologies of London's Works (arranged chronologically)

Jack London, American Rebel: A Collection of His Social Writings Together with an Extensive Study of the Man and His Times. Edited by Philip S. Foner. New York: Citadel Press, 1947.

Jack London's Tales of Adventure. Edited by Irving Shepard. Garden City, NY: Hanover House (copyright Doubleday and Company), 1956.

Stories of Hawaii. Edited by A. Grove Day. New York: Appleton-Century, 1965.

Curious Fragments: Jack London's Tales of Fantasy Fiction. Edited by Dale L. Walker. Preface by Philip José Farmer. Port Washington, NY: Kennikat Press, 1975.

No Mentor but Myself: A Collection of Articles, Essays, Reviews, and Letters, by Jack London, on Writing and Writers. Edited by Dale L. Walker. Foreword by Howard Lachtman. Port Washington, NY: Kennicat, 1979. 2nd ed. revised and expanded by Dale L. Walker and Jeanne Campbell Reesman. Stanford, CA: Stanford University Press, 1999.

Sporting Blood: Selections from Jack London's Greatest Sports Writing. Edited by Howard Lachtman. Novato, CA: Presidio Press, 1981.

London, Jack. *Novels & Stories: The Call of the Wild, White Fang, The Sea-Wolf, Short Stories*. Edited by Donald Pizer. New York: Literary Classics of the United States, 1982.

———. *Novels and Social Writings: The People of the Abyss, The Road, The Iron Heel, Martin Eden, John Barleycorn, Essays*. Edited by Donald Pizer. New York: Literary Classics of the United States, 1982.

Jack London's California: "The Golden Poppy" and Other Writings. Edited by Sal Noto. New York: Beaufort Books, 1986.

The Portable Jack London. Edited by Earle Labor. New York: Penguin Books, 1994.

The Plays of Jack London. Edited by Clay Reynolds. New York: Ironweed Press, 2000.

The Wit and Wisdom of Jack London: A Collection of Quotations from His Writing and Letters. Edited by Margie Wilson. Santa Rosa, CA: Wordworth, 2001.

Jack London's Tales of Cannibals and Headhunters: Nine South Seas Stories by America's Master of Adventure. Edited by Gary Riedl and Thomas R. Tietze. Albuquerque: University of New Mexico Press, 2006.

The Radical Jack London: Writings on War and Revolution. Edited by Jonah Raskin. Berkeley: University of California Press, 2008.

The Asian Writings of Jack London: Essays, Letters, Newspaper Dispatches, and Short Fiction by Jack London. With an introductory analysis by Daniel A. Métraux. With a Foreword by William S. Dillon. Lewiston, NY: Edwin Mellen Press, 2009.

Secondary Sources

REFERENCE GUIDES

Hartzell, David. "The World of Jack London." www.jacklondons.net.

Jack London Collection, UC Berkeley Digital Library SunSITE, http://sunsite.berkeley.edu/London.

Kingman, Russ. *Jack London: A Definitive Chronology*. Middleton, CA: David Rejl, for the Jack London Research Center, Glen Ellen, CA, 1992.

Reesman, Jeanne Campbell. *Critical Companion to Jack London: A Literary Reference to His Life and Works*. New York: Facts on File, 2011.

Sherman, Joan. *Jack London: A Reference Guide*. Boston: G.K. Hall, 1977.

Stasz, Clarice. http://london.sonoma.edu.

Walker, Dale L., and James E. Sisson III. *The Fiction of Jack London: A Chronological Bibliography*. El Paso: Texas Western Press, 1972.

Williams, James. "JL List Serv." Jack_london@lists.uchicago.edu.

———. "Jack London's Works by Dates of Composition," *American Literary Realism* 23, no. 2 (Winter 1991): 64–86.

Woodbridge, Hensley C., John London, and George H. Tweney. *Jack London: A Bibliography*. Georgetown, CA: Talisman Press, 1966. Enlarged edition. Millwood, NY: Kraus Reprint Company, 1973. (Note: An updated critical bibliography on London publications is *American Literary Scholarship: An Annual*, published by the Duke University Press, 1963–present.)

COLLECTIONS OF CRITICAL ESSAYS (ARRANGED CHRONOLOGICALLY)

Jack London: Essays in Criticism. Edited by Ray Wilson Ownbey. Santa Barbara, CA: Peregrine Smith, 1978.

Critical Essays on Jack London. Edited by Jacqueline Tavernier-Courbin. Boston: G.K. Hall, 1983.

The Critical Response to Jack London. Edited by Susan M. Nuernberg. Westport, CT: Greenwood Press, 1995.

Rereading Jack London. Edited by Leonard Cassuto and Jeanne Campbell Reesman with an afterword by Earle Labor. Stanford, CA: Stanford University Press, 1996.

Jack London: One Hundred Years a Writer. Edited by Sara S. Hodson and Jeanne Campbell Reesman. San Marino, CA: Huntington Library, 2002.

Bloom's Modern Critical Views: Jack London. Edited by Harold Bloom. New York: Infobase Learning, 2011.

Critical Insights: Jack London. Edited by Lawrence I. Berkove. Pasadena, CA: Salem Press, 2011.

BOOKS

The following list excludes many of the books and articles cited with full references in the notes, not to mention numerous other works I have consulted during the past half century:

Auerbach, Jonathan. *Male Call: Becoming Jack London*. Durham, NC: Duke University Press, 1996.

Barltrop, Robert. *Jack London, the Man, the Writer, the Rebel*. London: Pluto Press, 1976.

Berton, Pierre. *Klondike Fever: The Life and Death of the Last Great Gold Rush*. New York: Alfred A. Knopf, 1958.

Boylan, James. *Revolutionary Lives: Anna Strunsky and William English Walling*. Amherst: University of Massachusetts Press, 1998.

Bruce, Miner W. *Alaska: Its History and Resources, Gold Fields, Routes and Scenery*. Seattle: Lowman and Hanford, 1895.

Bykov, Vil. *In the Steps of Jack London*. Translated from the Russian by Julia Istomina and Charles Hofmeister. Edited by Susan Nuernberg, Earle Labor, and Hensley Woodbridge. www.jacklondons.net/writings/Bykov/titlePageCredit.html, 2004.

Day, A. Grove. *Jack London in the South Seas*. New York: South Winds Press, 1971.

———. *Mad About the Islands: Novelists of a Vanished Pacific*. Honolulu: Mutual Publishing Company, 1987.

Dyer, Daniel, *Jack London: A Biography*. New York: Scholastic Press, 1997.

Gabel, Stewart. *Jack London: A Man in Search of Meaning, A Jungian Perspective*. Bloomington, IN: Author House, 2012.

Gair, Christopher. *Complicity and Resistance in Jack London's Novels: From Naturalism to Nature*. Lewiston, NY: Edwin Mellen, 1997.

Geismar, Maxwell. *Rebels and Ancestors: The American Novel, 1890–1915*. Boston: Houghton Mifflin Company, 1953.

Gray, Charlotte. *Gold Diggers: Striking It Rich in the Klondike*. Berkeley, CA: Counterpoint, 2010.

Haley, James L. *Wolf: The Lives of Jack London*. New York: Basic Books, 2010.

Hamilton, David Mike. *"The Tools of My Trade": Annotated Books in Jack London's Library*. Seattle: University of Washington Press, 1986.

Haughey, Homer L., and Connie Kale Johnson. *Jack London Ranch Album*. Foreword by Earle Labor. Stockton, CA: Heritage Publishing Company in Cooperation with the Valley of the Moon Historical Association and the California Department of Parks and Recreation, 1985.

———. *Jack London Homes Album*. Foreword by Earle Labor. Stockton, CA: Heritage Publishing, 1987.

Hayes, Gregory W., and Matt Atkinson. Illustrations by Steven Chais. *Jack London's Wolf House*. Glen Ellen, CA: Valley of the Moon Natural History Association, 2010.

Hedrick, Joan D. *Solitary Comrade: Jack London and His Work*. Chapel Hill: University of North Carolina Press, 1982.

Johnson, Martin. *Through the South Seas with Jack London*. New York: Dodd, Mead, 1913. Reprint, Cedar Springs, MI: Wolf House Books, 1967.

Johnston, Carolyn. *Jack London—An American Radical?* Westport, CT: Greenwood Press, 1984.

Jung, C. G. *Psychology of the Unconscious: A Study of the Transformations and Symbolisms of the Libido, A Contribution to the History of the Evolution of Thought*. Authorized translation with introduction by Beatrice M. Hinkle, MD. New York: Moffat, Yard and Company, 1916. Revised edition, *Symbols of Transformation*. Collected Works, Vol. 5. Princeton, NJ: Princeton University Press, 1967.

Kershaw, Alex. *Jack London: A Life*. New York: HarperCollins Publishers, 1997.

Kingman, Russ. *A Pictorial Life of Jack London*. Foreword by Irving Stone. New York: Crown Publishers, 1979. Reprint, Middletown, CA: Rejl, 1992.

Labor, Earle. *Jack London*. New York: Twayne Publishers, 1974. Revised edition with Jeanne Campbell Reesman. New York, Twayne, 1994.

Lane, Rose Wilder. *He Was a Man*. New York: Harper and Brothers, Publishers, 1925.

Lasartemay, Eugene P., and Mary Rudge. *For Love of Jack London: His Life with Jennie Prentiss—A True Love Story*. New York: Vantage, 1991.

London, Charmian Kittredge. *The Log of the Snark*. New York: Macmillan Company, 1915.

———. *Our Hawaii*. New York: Macmillan Company, 1917. New and revised edition, 1922.

———. *The Book of Jack London*. 2 vols. New York: Century Company, 1921.

London, Joan. *Jack London and His Times: An Unconventional Biography*. New York: Doubleday, 1939. Reprinted with a new introduction by the author. Seattle: University of Washington Press, 1968.

———. *Jack London and His Daughters*. Introduction by Bart Abbott. Berkeley, CA: Heyday Books, 1990.

Lundquist, James. *Jack London: Adventures, Ideas, and Fiction*. New York: Ungar, 1987.

McClintock, James I. *White Logic: Jack London's Short Stories*. Grand Rapids, MI: Wolf House, 1975. Reprinted with a preface by Sam S. Baskett. *Jack London's Strong Truths: A Study of the Short Stories*. East Lansing: Michigan State University Press, 1997.

Noel, Joseph. *Footloose in Arcadia: A Personal Record of Jack London, George Sterling, Ambrose Bierce*. New York: Carrick and Evans, 1940.

North, Dick. *Sailor on Snowshoes: Tracking Jack London's Northern Trail*. Madeira Park, BC: Harbour Publishing, 2006.

Nuernberg, Susan M. *Letters of Russ Kingman, with Biography by Harry James Cook*. Glen Ellen, CA: David Rejl for the Jack London Research Center, 1999.

O'Connor, Richard. *Jack London, a Biography*. Boston: Little, Brown and Company, 1964.

Payne, Edward Biron. *The Soul of Jack London*. 2nd ed., Kingsport, TN: Southern Publishers, 1933.

Reesman, Jeanne Campbell. *Jack London: A Study of the Short Fiction*. New York: Twayne Publishers, 1999.

———. *Jack London's Racial Lives: A Critical Biography*. Athens: University of Georgia Press, 2009.

Reesman, Jeanne Campbell, Sara S. Hodson, and Philip Adam. *Jack London, Photographer*. Athens: University of Georgia Press, 2010.

Shepard, Milo. *The Jack London Story and the Beauty Ranch*. Introduction by Earle Labor. Interviews conducted by Caroline C. Crawford in 2000. Regional Oral History Office, the Bancroft Library. Berkeley: University of California Regents, 2001.

Sinclair, Andrew. *Jack: A Biography of Jack London*. New York: Harper and Row, Publishers, 1977.

Stasz, Clarice. *American Dreamers: Charmian and Jack London*. New York: St. Martin's Press, 1988.

———. *Jack London's Women*. Amherst: University of Massachusetts Press, 2001.

Stone, Irving. *Sailor on Horseback: The Biography of Jack London*. Cambridge, MA: 1938. Subsequent editions titled *Jack London, Sailor on Horseback: A Biographical Novel*. Reissued as *Irving Stone's Jack London, His Life, Sailor on Horseback (A Biography) and Twenty-Eight Selected Jack London Short Stories*. Garden City, NY: Doubleday and Company, 1977.

Tayman, John. *The Colony: The Harrowing True Story of the Exiles of Molokai*. New York: Scribner, 2006.

Walcutt, Charles Child. *American Literary Naturalism: A Divided Stream*. Minneapolis MN: University of Minnesota Press, 1956.

Walker, Dale L. *The Alien Worlds of Jack London*. Grand Rapids, MI: Wolf House Books, 1973.

——. *The Calamity Papers: Western Myths and Cold Cases*. New York: Forge Books, 2004.

Walker, Franklin. *The Seacoast of Bohemia: An Account of Early Carmel*. San Francisco: The Book Club of California, 1966. New and enlarged edition, Santa Barbara, CA: Peregrine Smith, 1973.

——. *Jack London and the Klondike: The Genesis of an American Writer*. San Marino, CA: Huntington Library, 1966. Reprinted with a foreword by Earle Labor, 1994.

Watson, Charles N., Jr. *The Novels of Jack London: A Reappraisal*. Madison: University of Wisconsin Press, 1983.

Williams, Tony. *Jack London, the Movies: An Historical Survey*. Middletown, CA: Rejl, 1992.

Wilson, Mike. *Jack London's Klondike Adventure: The True Story of Jack London's Personal Odyssey from San Francisco to the Arctic Circle, Across the Breadth of Alaska and Home Again*. Santa Rosa, CA: Wordsworth, 2001.

Zamen, Mark E. *Standing Room Only: Jack London's Controversial Career as a Public Speaker*. Foreword by Earle Labor. New York: Peter Lang, 1990.

ACKNOWLEDGMENTS

To adequately express my appreciation for all those who have contributed to this project would require another volume as long as this one. I can only attempt to give in these few pages a brief mention of those to whom I owe so much even while realizing that I may perforce neglect some.

In 1955, when I was an instructor at Centenary College before resuming my graduate studies, A. P. Palmer, owner of Carol's Book Shop in Shreveport, helped me assemble the core of working copies that became the foundation for my Jack London scholarship. A generation after that, Mr. Palmer's daughter, Becky, entered my life as secretary for Centenary's English Department. More than a department secretary, she has become both a friend and a research assistant who has provided invaluable professional help, especially in bringing the present biographical project to fruition.

In 1956 Rinehart and Company published a definitive edition of *Martin Eden* with introduction and notes by Sam Baskett. That edition with Baskett's essay and notes was one of the basic texts for my doctoral dissertation, and Baskett's pioneering scholarly publications on London during the 1950s became a guide for my own work. Since our first meeting at the 1962 Conference of the Michigan College English Association in Kalamazoo, Sam's friendship and scholarly integrity have continued to be an inspiration for me.

Those same words, *friendship* and *scholarly integrity*, likewise fit three of the most important figures in the Jack London "Great Awakening": King Hendricks, Hensley Woodbridge, and Earl Wilcox. Beyond his major contributions to London scholarship, Professor Hendricks gave me the opportunity to teach my first Jack London course and to work with the wealth of primary materials donated by Irving Shepard to Utah State University. Following King's death in 1970, Jeff and Jeannie Simmonds, Ann Buttars, and their colleagues in the Special Collections Department continued to give me their full support in researching the London collection at the Merrill-Cazier Library.

Hensley Woodbridge was a major force in providing access to London's work. No serious study of Jack London can ignore the importance of his contributions, particularly his monumental *Bibliography* and pace-setting *Newsletter*. He was ever the unpretentious mentor and gentle friend to all of us.

Earl Wilcox has been a leading authority on London's work, particularly on the subjects of literary naturalism and *The Call of the Wild*, for more than a generation; my heartfelt thanks to him and his wife, Bettye, for their friendship as well as for their scholarly contributions.

As owner of the Jack London Bookstore in Glen Ellen, California, and organizer of the Jack London Foundation, Russ Kingman was another major contributor to the London Renascence. His publications, most notably his *Pictorial Jack London* and *Chronology*, are basic reference tools for the London biographer. His bookstore, capably operated by his wife, Winnie, and their research center was a mecca for London scholars and fans, and a home for London's daughter Becky, during the last thirty years of the twentieth century. The Jack London Banquet that Kingman inaugurated has attracted hundreds of participants from here and abroad for the past five decades. Our indebtedness to Russ and Winnie is inestimable. Following their deaths, the important work of the Foundation, including the publication of the *Jack London Foundation Quarterly Newsletter*, has been faithfully carried on by Rudy Ciuca and Joe Lawrence. Complementing their work with the Foundation has been David Schlottman, whose publications at London Northwest, including his distribution of *The Wolf* at the annual banquets, have added a special dimension to the world of Jack London.

My indebtedness—like that of countless scholars throughout the world—to the staff at the Huntington Library is immeasurable. This magnificent research facility, including the voluminous Jack London Collection, is without parallel. The same may be said of the quality of those who oversee the priceless archives housed there. During the past half century, I have benefited from two of their grants and from their consistently excellent service, starting with director James Thorpe in the late 1960s, followed by Dan Woodward, Carey Bliss, Alan Jutzi, Virginia "Ginger" Renner, David Mike Hamilton, and, during the past two decades, by Sara S. (Sue) Hodson. I am most grateful to Sue and her husband, Peter Blodgett, for their friendship as well as their research assistance.

Speaking of Californians to whom I owe much, I should mention others who provided special encouragement for me as well as significant contributions to the world of Jack London. As the foremost London collector, Sal Noto was also a dedicated scholar and friend to whose wisdom I owe much as both collector and scholar. I also express my appreciation to his widow, Nancy: Following Sal's untimely death, she sent me the one book I needed to fill the gap in my collection of first editions: Osias L. Schwarz's *General Types of Superior Men*, with London's preface.

Howard Lachtman is a first-rate author-scholar-critic who, while producing numerous helpful reviews, essays, and book-length works on Jack London, has remained one of my most faithful pen pals for more than a generation. I tip my cap to you, Old Sport. Also to my pal Raleigh Patterson for helping me with Charmian's diaries and being a constant source of good humor and good sense. To Clarice Stasz, historian-biographer-critic, friend, and steady "keeper of the flame": Her research has provided new insights into London's many-faceted career, including his agricultural ventures, Charmian's vital influence, and the relationships between Jack and the other most important women in his life; my numerous references to her work indicate the extent of my debt. To Dan Wichlan both for his pioneering work with Jack's poetry and non-fiction and also for his faithful support. And to Steve Shaffer for his close reading of my manuscript—and to both Steve and his wife, Nancy, as well as to Brian and Kate Shepard, for graciously maintaining the London/Shepard tradition of hospitality.

Other special Californians I should mention are Palmer Andrews, Homer Haughey, Connie Johnson, Jacqueline Koenig, Ken Olivier, and Margie and Mike Wilson. Though not members of the academic community, all have been dedicated London scholars and friends to whom I owe much for their contributions to the world of Jack London and for their continued encouragement of my own work. I thank Mary Rudge for her valuable insights into Oakland's African American community and particularly into that community's influence on London. I am also obligated to the team of workers for the California State Parks who have assisted me along with thousands of other visitors to the Jack London State Historical Park. My sincere thanks to rangers Matt Atkisson and Greg Hayes, docents Lou Leal and Edith Newsome, and to curator Carol Dodge.

I thank Diane Kaplan and her colleagues at the Yale University Library for giving me access to the rich collection of Anna Strunsky Walling papers. I'm indebted to Jacqueline Tavernier-Courbin for her many contributions to London scholarship—including her insights into Jack's humor and his complex relationships to women—as well as for her friendship. Larry Berkove has been not only a major contributor to London scholarship but also a buddy whose wit and wisdom have given me many a welcome lift over the past generation. Since we met at our first NEH summer seminar, my friend Harry Cook has been a constant support of my work and Centenary's Jack London Research Center as well as the larger world of Jack London. Notable among the many others to whom I owe thanks are Donna Bartholomew, Al Brady, Ellen Brown, Andy Flink, Andrew Furer, Wilfred Guerin, Dave Hartzell, Joe Johnson, Tom McNair, Lawrence Meredith, Daniel Métraux, David Moreland, Lee Morgan, Dick North, Max Peters, Susan Nuernberg, Gary Riedl, Patty Roberts, Davide Sapienza, Dan Sawyer, Tom Tietze, Dick Weiderman, Jay Williams, Eric Miles Williamson, and Roberta Wirth. Special thanks are due Neil Johnson for his friendship and photographic virtuosity, and to Jill Riefenstahl for donating her husband Jim's valuable memorabilia to Centenary's Jack London Research Center, and to my honorary and beloved "son" Dr. Eiji Tsujii for his vision as scholar and founder of the Jack London Society of Japan and for his many contributions to Centenary's Jack London Museum.

Of all my students during the past half century, none has given me greater personal as well as professional satisfaction than Jeff Hendricks and Jeanne Campbell Reesman. Both were outstanding leaders as undergraduates, both excelled in top-flight graduate schools, and both have subsequently distinguished themselves as scholar-teachers. Jeff is an astute film critic who has also published major studies on Hemingway, Edwin Rolfe, and the Spanish Civil War. I am particularly grateful for his help in researching the London-Partington correspondence and the photographs for this book. Most personally, I appreciate him as a valued Centenary colleague, friend, and honorary member of the Labor family.

Jeanne has become coauthor of both my *Twayne's United States Author Series Jack London* and our *Handbook of Critical Approaches to Literature*, now in its sixth edition. Her Twayne volume on London's short stories is exemplary; her recent book on London's "racialism" is the definitive study of that complex issue; her work with Sue Hodson on London's photography is another pioneering achievement; and her *Critical Companion to Jack London* is an essential reference volume. As organizer and executive coordinator of the Jack London Society and the biannual symposium, along with the annual Jack London sessions for the American Literature Association, she has regularly convened a cadre of the world's top scholars to share their insights and expertise.

I am especially indebted to Jeanne and others who have read the manuscript and provided sound counsel for this biography during the several stages of its composition: Daniel Dyer, David Havird, and Marinelle Ringer. To Dale L. Walker—editor, creative writer, and veteran London scholar for so willingly sharing his expertise in the making of this book. To Don Kummings—poet, scholar, teacher—for continually reinforcing my morale not only throughout the course of this biographical project but also throughout the past five decades of our friendship. And to Per Serritslev Petersen, who has carefully critiqued my manuscript and, most remarkably, after retiring as chair of the English Department at the University of Aarhus, volunteered to teach my courses for a semester so that I could devote my full energies to this biography.

"Aloha!" to the Kaua'i Historical Society: President John Lydgate, grandson of the Reverend John Lydgate, who served as host to London when Jack visited the island in 1915; Mary A. Requilman, managing director of the Society and Archives; and Chris Cook, author, historian, and master of the surfboard—all of whom showed Gayle and me the unique significance of *Aloha* when they welcomed us to the "Garden Island" in 1999. Moreover, Chris was instrumental in helping to bring the Jack London Society to Kaua'i for our Sixth Biannual Symposium in 2002.

My debt to the National Endowment for the Humanities is immense—for the substantial grant provided for this project as well as for previous awards given in support of the Stanford editions of London's letters and short stories and for the four Summer Seminars for Teachers I directed. (Special thanks to Michael Hall for first encouraging me to apply for the London seminar.)

My colleagues at Centenary College have also supported my London studies through sabbatical leaves, research grants, and an endowed professorship. My thanks to the Faculty Personnel Committee and to presidents Kenneth Schwab and David Rowe. I am grateful to president emeritus Donald A. Webb for securing my election to the George A. Wilson Chair of American Literature, for his work in establishing Centenary's Jack London Museum and Research Center, and—most of all—for our enduring friendship over the past four decades.

I want to express my appreciation to the five editors at Farrar, Straus and Giroux responsible for the successful publication of this biography: John Glusman, who persuaded me to undertake this project two decades ago; Gena Hamshaw, who subsequently provided her steady encouragement and editorial wisdom; Jesse Coleman, who capably succeeded Gena; Jenna Dolan, who copyedited my manuscript with consummate expertise; and Miranda Popkey, who has guided this project through production with exceptional grace and dedication.

My greatest debt is owed the two families to whom I dedicate this book: the Shepards and the Labors. Irving and Mildred Shepard opened their home and their hearts to my family forty-seven years ago, and Irving conveyed upon me the honor of collaborating with him in providing an accurate portrayal of Jack London. Although our work together was cut short by his death in 1975, his son Milo welcomed me into this mutual enterprise. More than a fellow scholar, he became a big brother to me and beloved "Uncle Milo" to my five children. This biographical project would never have been pursued without his friendship and steadfast support.

Finally, the Labor Gang: They have opened our home and their hearts to Jack London during the past six decades. My children, Royce, Kirk, Kyle, Isabel, and Andrea, have provided faithful support for all my London projects, as have their spouses, Rhonda, Penny, Helen, and Jimmy—and likewise my grandsons, Erik, Christian, and Harrison. I am most deeply indebted to my wife, Gayle, who—in the words Jack himself might have used—"has travailed sore with me in the making of this book" as both expert reader and devoted soul mate. I have surely been blessed beyond all measure with the loving devotion of this family.

INDEX